# The Child is Father of the Man

BY THE SAME AUTHOR

*The Earth's Changing Surface* 1975
(with Michael Bradshaw and Anthony Gelsthorpe)

*The Iranians: How They Live and Work* 1977

*Learning Makes Sense* 1994

# The Child is Father of the Man:
## How Humans Learn and Why

### JOHN ABBOTT

© The 21st Century Learning Initiative 1999
Published by The 21st Century Learning Initiative, Business Centre
West, Avenue One, Letchworth, Hertfordshire SG6 2HB, UK

More information about The 21st Century Learning Initiative is at:
**www.21learn.org**
email: info@21learn.org

First published 1999

The moral right of the author has been asserted

Typeset by Paul Fisher, Bath
Printed and bound in Great Britain by The Bath Press, Bath

ISBN 0 9537168 0 5

*My heart leaps up when I behold*
  *A rainbow in the sky:*
*So was it when my life began;*
*So is it now I am a man;*
*So be it when I shall grow old,*
  *Or let me die!*

*The Child is father of the Man;*
*And I could wish my days to be*
*Bound each to each by natural piety.*


William Wordsworth, 1770-1850

# Contents

Dedication & Acknowledgements

Chapter 1                                                    1
**Bound Each to Each**

Chapter 2                                                    21
**The Child Becomes a Young Man**

Chapter 3                                                    47
**Becoming a Teacher**

Chapter 4                                                    81
**Becoming a Deputy Head**

Chapter 5                                                    113
**Becoming a Head Master and a Father**

Chapter 6                                                    133
**"Why don't your lot tell my lot what's going on and
   what's needed?"**

Chapter 7                                                    155
**"Education for What?"**

Chapter 8                                                    177
**Education 2000**

Chapter 9                                                    201
**Becoming a National Issue**

Chapter 10                                                    225
**Opting Out or Opting In?**

Chapter 11                                                    255
**I Can is More Important Than IQ**

Chapter 12                                                    275
**Playing the Game**

Chapter 13                                                    291
**Becoming an Internationalist**

Chapter 14                                                    311
**The Newsworthy Brain**

Chapter 15                                                    333
**The 21st Century Learning Initiative**

Chapter 16                                                    359
**What Kind of Education for What Kind of World?**
     **Do we want our children to grow up as battery hens or**
     **free range chickens?**

Postscript                                                    374
**by Peter Abbott**

Bibliography                                                  383

# Acknowledgements

*Dedicated to all those who believe that
we have not simply inherited this world
from our parents, but have been loaned
it by our children.*

This book has been written about, and with the support of, many people. My thanks, with my love, go first to my wife Anne and to our three sons, Peter, David and Tom.

In the experiences which led me to so much of what I write about, my grateful thanks go to my one-time colleagues in the Schools' Hebridean Society; to my ex-colleagues at Manchester Grammar School; to the members of the various Iran expeditions of the 1970s; to the good people of Shrah and Portumna in County Galway; to the staff and pupils of Alleyne's School, Stevenage when I was head master; and to all those who laboured in the nine projects of Education 2000.

Education 2000 was sponsored by more than 300 companies and private donors; much of this story is due to their generosity, particularly to British Airways who made it possible for me to travel so widely. I'm especially grateful to Christopher Wysock Wright for his tenacity, to Brian Corby for his enthusiasm and to David Peake as my current chairman for his wisdom and commitment. To Tom Griffin, one of the first sponsors of the Trust, and a man whose resolute determination to ensure that all these ideas impact on the body politic, I owe an incalculable debt.

Without the tireless, dogged determination of Terence Ryan, the young man who entered this story in a dacha somewhere just outside Warsaw, this book could never have been written. If more of the so called Generation X had his vision and energy, this would soon become a more exciting and more humane world. Of an older age, but with his eyes still burning bright, is Ray Dalton of Cambridge whose wisdom and humanity have kept me true to my beliefs. The meticulous attention to detail of Mary Robinson in the preparation of several drafts of this text has been invaluable, as was the help at an earlier stage of Ted Marchese, Doreen Smith, Ingrid Stimpson and Rothschild Natural Resources in Washington, DC. I'm much indebted too to my editor Paul Fisher for his guidance in how to curtail my verbosity and to keep a big story to its essential message. I must thank, too, the 60 members of the 21st Century Learning Initiative who came from 14 countries to attend the six conferences at Wingspread. Additionally, the company, real and virtual, of many learned scholars and their writings, as well as the perceptive comments and questions of audiences in many lands who have heard me lecture, have all helped to deepen the ideas that I have described.

Finally, right back where all this began, my loving thanks to my mother and father, and their parents, who started me off on asking just why it was that we humans do as we do, and think as we think.

My hope is that this book will strengthen the resolve of a younger generation to sort out many of the muddles that my generation has created, or seen fit to ignore.

John Abbott
Reston, Virginia
March 1999

# 1

# Bound Each to Each

"How do little children learn to talk, Dad?" asked eight year-old Tom. I'd started to compose a reply when he continued: "That's an easy question but I bet you'll give me a long complicated answer."

Tom is now a young man and the long answer I didn't give him when he was still a boy is here in this book. It is the autobiography of a teacher who started his career as a geography master at a grammar school in Manchester and who is finishing it as a self-appointed educational entrepreneur based in Washington, DC. The book is about a search to understand how humans learn and the conclusion it moves towards is that learning is not about schools, but about all of life. It draws on personal experience and on an emerging academic consensus about the biological nature of learning. These ideas have been synthesised by the 21st Century Learning Initiative and, as president of this august body, I have played host to researchers who have convinced me that much schooling depends on outdated assumptions. The brain does not necessarily handle information in the ways teachers teach, especially when they - we - are compelled to follow educational strategies that fail to go with the grain of the brain. We're putting children with biologically shaped brains into machine-shaped curricula based on a machine model of the brain. Our brains are not computers; our schools are not biologically compatible.

I'll start my story in the middle, just after my appointment in 1975 as head teacher of a school for a thousand 11 to 18 year-old boys. During my time as a deputy head I'd helped set up a course in household maintenance. The boys liked the combination of classroom-based instruction and hard physical work. They liked the satisfaction of seeing courses of bricks which they had laid looking attractive, as well as standing up. They enjoyed learning tricks of the trade from plumbers and electricians and, significantly, several served apprenticeships after leaving school. I often envied them the half day each week they spent talking and joking with each other as they worked but I was much preoccupied with administering a large and complex organisation. The school was under constant pressure from the local education authority to reduce expenditure, and I was far from satisfied with the quality of service that was being provided.

One day some of the older pupils asked why the household maintenance course was only available to the non-academic classes. "We'd like to be able to do it as well," one of them said. "No way will any of us become professional brick-layers or carpenters, but judging by the amount of time our Dads spend doing DIY around the house - and how useless they are sometimes - these are skills we'd like to have as well."

"I'd like to know I could build my own house one day as well as become a lawyer," said another. "I could get a good house for less money. I wouldn't have to work so hard at my law practice and I reckon I could get a better quality product. That's what my Dad keeps saying should happen and I think he's right."

These were young men after my own heart. We sat down in the study and talked it through. This, surely, was what a full education ought to be able to deal with and a thought struck me. Instead of paying outside contractors and cleaners, why could we not employ several part-time craftsmen to work with groups of volunteers and train pupils in such basic skills as decorating, minor carpentry work, glazing and basic horticulture? The boys were enthusiastic and so was the master in charge of household maintenance. But other staff were largely disinterested for this was a fringe activity of little gravitas. I pushed ahead and, by analysing recent contracts, was able to provide figures to support my claim that this would be economically and educationally attractive to the school, as well as financially attractive to the local education authority.

I presented the idea to the school governors and found them totally unresponsive. Such thinking was beyond their experience, and they looked at me almost in disbelief. "I'm confused, headmaster," said one of the governors. "You're good at teaching scholarship classes. The examination results are reasonably good and this is an unnecessary distraction, surely? It's not what schools should be about."

"I agree," said another. "The boys should be concentrating on stretching their minds. Neither the teachers' union nor the local government employees union would like it either."

"Nor would the education authority approve. They couldn't effectively monitor the quality of the work."

"I think this is a quite preposterous suggestion, head master. It would make us the laughing stock of all good schools and would show that we had completely lost our way."

The chairman quickly moved to other business. The opportunity was lost to do something truly innovative. Lost because most people could not see beyond their own limited worlds and their long, and largely fictitious, academic noses. Lost because their way of thinking about education was strictly that of a pre-eminent concern for intellectual skills. The task of reshaping just one school's approach to preparing youngsters for the twenty-first century was totally beyond them.

There are several other morals to draw from this story. It shows the limitations of a head teacher's power in the face of a stolid attachment to academic specialisation. It also revealed me as the insider, the radical who knew when to keep his head down; this was one of those times when I was intimidated by authority and didn't argue enough. Yes, a lack of nerve led to failure but, then, I agree with Samuel Smiles who said, "it is a mistake to suppose [we] succeed through success; we much oftener succeed through failure ... Precept, study, advice, and example could never have taught so well as failure has done." The household maintenance idea - obvious as it seemed to me and the boys and several of the teachers - had to wait until a decade later when linked ideas of work experience gained some currency.

There are other ideas which nobody - not even a bunch of examination-obsessed school governors - could disagree with. Children are born inquisitive. True, and true again that their questioning can drive us to distraction as they strive to make their own particular sense of the world around them. On a good day, they listen carefully enough to what we say, but only on their own terms; they reinterpret what we say in terms of their own experience, their own interests and their patterns of inherited predispositions. These predispositions vary enormously; one child in a family seems to think like a poet, another like a mechanic. There are things here that scientists are now in a position to begin to understand far better, and the implications of these findings reflect what good teachers have known since long before Socrates - that learning is not simply the flip side of teaching.

Children seem eternally new, yet in them we constantly relive aspects of our own youth, including our own attempts to make sense of the world around us. Children are our future, our guardians in our old age; our hands help them into life and we hope theirs will ease our passage out. It is the rhythm of the ages. Yet that essential rhythm seems threatened. So fast is the pace of change that conventional arrangements to help children learn how to flex their intellectual muscles are increasingly inadequate. Children will go into a world we are not competent even to predict, a world that poses problems and opportunities we can't yet envision. They are, nevertheless, *our* children; their needs and predispositions, their values, hopes and fears are those which we have given them through the ever-changing mixture of our biologically evolved nature and our culturally defined nurture. We have to prepare them to be good enough to be worthy guardians of what we are proud to call civilisation. As the African proverb has it: "We have not inherited this world from our parents, we have been loaned it by our children."

Education, so politicians in many lands are quick to claim, is at the top of the political agenda - the number one item. Yet, for most people, education is a strangely boring topic. Like religion, people sense it's important, but prefer to leave it to others to practice or think about. Search a bookstore and you are most likely to find the education section in an out-of-the-way corner and most of the books will be about specialised topics of little general interest. Few education books make it to the front of the store, and even fewer are promoted as best sellers.

This is strange for there is more material now about the nature of human learning and its importance to individuals, to society and to the economy at large than at any previous time. It is found in books all over the store: in neurology and cognitive science; in physics, biology and evolutionary psychology; in economic and political theory; in business studies and systems thinking; in information and communications technology; in cultural anthropology; and even in archaeology. It is certainly there also in the speculative work of philosophers, theologians and futurologists. In fact there is so much about the nature and importance of learning that it is impossible to keep up with all the ideas. While it is learning which will drive our future economies, the education section remains dusty and remote and to search here for a clue as to why education is now the number one item is to become even more confused.

What is happening? Is it that education, as previously understood to mean schools, is being side-lined and for some reason is unable to keep up with these new discoveries? Has education ceased to be about learning? Why is it that teachers world-wide seem depressed, fed up, disillusioned and unsure of themselves? Is school dead?

My generation was - in materialistic terms - far from wealthy. We had few toys (and most of those we did have were home-made) and there was no television, no music centre, no refrigerator. My parents didn't have a car until I was 16. Yet I never once felt deprived for I grew up in Britain just after World War II when children - all children it seemed - were cherished by a community which, having seen the horrors of war, saw in us its best hope for the future. My contemporaries and I had the love and care and, in particular, the time to help us grow into inquisitive, self-reliant and responsible young people.

Today, too many youngsters live lives largely disconnected even from their own parents, yet able from the age of three or four to programme a VCR. Embryonic couch potatoes, we fear, but we seem to have no solution to their inertia. Other youngsters, quicker to recognise the significance of getting qualifications, embark on a race to accumulate more and more apparently valuable pieces of paper, at an ever earlier age. Governments aid and abet this, pushing the acquisition of qualifications based on an old-fashioned form of assessment, with an almost religious zeal. These are children who, if we are not careful, will come to appreciate - in the words of Oscar Wilde - "the price of everything and the value of nothing."

Politicians urge us all forward. The words may differ, but the sentiment is always the same. "What you earn depends on what you learn," said President Clinton. It sounds persuasive but questions have to be asked about where all this leads. "Education for what?" is a question on many people's lips. Material aspirations may well fuel the economy, but the economy's continuing success depends on insatiable demands, real or created. Yet as individuals, so with society, we are coming to suspect that, in many areas, enough is already enough. Are we not now so busy working that we have little time for living, and aren't we too stressed out even to relax? Aren't we too busy to give our children the time they need in those early, critical, years when their brains are so malleable and impressionable? Aren't we too busy, when they are adolescent, to respond with patience to their violent mood changes?

I entitled a recent speech *Who Needs One more CD*? It obviously made its point well, for afterwards one of the audience, a father, said he'd been fooling himself into thinking he'd have to earn more money to buy his children more presents to make up for the lack of time spent with them. "What's good for the economy isn't the same as what's good for my family," he said.

The more I have found out about the nature of human learning, and the more I understand about the brain itself, the more I have come to respect the significance both of our inherited natures and of the influence of nurture. In the short term, culture can change us most. Our culture, our self-designed way of life can come to expect things of us, however, which are so out of sympathy with our inherited predispositions, that we drive ourselves mad. We have to think most seriously about what that father said if we are to avoid big trouble. Further, we have to find answers that would satisfy the ancient Navajo Indians' testing question of an innovation: "Will this improve the quality of life of our people seven generations on from now?"

\*       \*       \*

It was September 1996 and hurricane Fran was about to strike the coast of Virginia. To a family who, until nine months before, had lived in the equitable temperate climate of southern England, the heat and humidity of a Virginian summer had been quite a challenge. Now, it seemed, our experience was to be broadened still further. In England, as the saying goes, "hurricanes hardly happen!" The weather got progressively stormier that evening and by early morning the winds were vicious. Trees were beginning to fall. In the centre of Washington the sky became the colour of a dirty mudflow, and street lights came on at mid-day. For the first time I understood the meaning of torrential. This was rain of a kind I had never imagined. Lightning accompanied rolls of thunder. Buildings shook. Having spent much time on small boats off the west coast of Scotland I shuddered at the thought of what it would have been like on a small boat out at sea. Then, quite suddenly, it was all over; by mid-afternoon the skies had cleared, the wind had blown itself away, and people were quick to clear the streets of debris and get back to business as usual.

I checked my e-mail, made a few last minute arrangements in my downtown Washington office, and returned home early to pack my case for what was going to be a busy week of lectures and meetings before catching the evening flight to London. Wanting to prolong the moments before driving to Dulles Airport, I went down to the dock below our house and started to bail out the dinghy, which was in danger of sinking, so much water had she taken in during the hurricane. Peter, my eldest son and now taller than I and fast approaching his eighteenth birthday, came down from the house to help me bail. We talked inconsequentially of other storms we had known and of how, as young children, he and his two brothers had been terrified by a storm in the Black Forest in Germany, yet had slept right through the Great Storm of October 1988, which had destroyed nearly a tenth of all trees in the south of England in a single night. We are a close family and Anne and I always feel that we have learnt as much from our three sons as they have learnt from us; indeed this story is much shaped by their experiences, and my understandings informed by their development.

"Dad, I need your advice. I'm changing my mind about what to study at university. Last summer I didn't like the idea of having to drop so many of the subjects I did at GCSE to specialise at A level; it seemed to leave me disconnected to so many of the things which really interest me. When we came to America in January I had to study, by Virginian law, seven subjects in high school and I suddenly realised how much I had missed out in England by having to drop English literature and history. I'm enjoying doing American history; of course the focus is different to what I did in England, but all history is about the development of ideas, and the clashes of personalities, regardless of country. I'm fascinated by it and my grades are good. Eventually I want to work at interpreting the significance of new ideas in the sciences for the well-being of people. Here's my problem. I now know that I'd rather read English at university, not one of the sciences. Science fascinates me and I'm intrigued by the ethical implications of new technologies, but I guess I'm more of a communications person, not a research scientist."

He paused, noting my pensiveness. At last, after years of dealing with these issues as effecting other people's children, the narrowness of the academic tradition of the English sixth form was hitting me, through my own son's experiences, as we sat on a tiny dock beside a lake in far off Virginia. Personally, I say, because as a one-time English head master and sixth form tutor, I had gone through this self-imposed agony of early specialisation with other people's sons so many times before. English education is predicated on specialisation, and A levels are, in the much quoted phrase, the gold standard. Kenneth Baker as minister of education had come close to changing this with the Higginson report ten years earlier, but Margaret Thatcher had intervened to prevent this when it was suggested that it would lose her the support of the middle classes, and their commitment to the public school sixth form.

"There's something else, Dad," Peter continued. "Several of my teachers here think I ought to apply to Princeton, Harvard or the University of Virginia. Now I know you and Mum never thought that our coming with you for two years while you worked in Washington would result in me wanting to go to an American university. But well, this could be a fascinating experience. What should I do; a first degree in the UK and then go on for further study in the US, or should it be the other way around?"

He looked at me with those open, trusting eyes that fathers tend to associate with the enthusiastic confidence of nine and ten year-olds before the struggles of adolescence dent the camaraderie. Now he was almost a man, but all those years of family togetherness and open honest talk were paying off. I didn't know the answer to his question, and he knew it. Neither did I know whether a Cambridge admissions tutor, used as they are to young people following clearly defined routes through the system, could deal with a boy who, perhaps modelling himself more after my own habit of creating my own pathways more than I had realised, genuinely thought for himself.

"We could wait until you get back from England in ten days time, but we'd have to act pretty quickly after that to meet the deadlines," said Peter.

I saw some space, and took it. "That's just what we'll do, and while I'm away you must think carefully about just what it is you want to do."

Peter called my bluff. "Yes, Dad. I've done that already. Now it's up to you and Mum. We'll all be involved in this. I might stay in America when you all go back to England. That has to be thought about."

We went back to the house, I in a more reflective mood than usual. I collected my case and set off for the airport. Next morning I would be resuming my self-appointed role of being something of an educational entrepreneur, trying to develop and promote critical ideas about learning within mainstream education. As such, I had my own golden rule, "he who advocates radical ideas should always wear a dark suit." Revolutionaries are much more disconcerting when they come from within the establishment.

*         *         *

The British Airways 747 climbed quickly to avoid turbulence over New York and then, with a strong following wind, headed out over the Atlantic. I'm not one of those seasoned travellers who takes a glass of fruit juice, puts on their eye shades, ignores the offer of drinks, and has a full seven hours of sleep. I'm slightly envious of them, yet I enjoy the opportunities to sort out my thoughts. Even in the middle of the night, at 35,000 feet, I hope I'll never lose my sense of wonder at the technological achievement of flying, and the amazing opportunities it has opened up - opportunities which we take for granted and which my own father, born the day before World War I started, hardly knew about.

I looked down on a moonlit Atlantic which seemed endless and thought of my seventeenth century forebears from Devon, and from East Anglia where I had lived for many years. They came in tiny boats, far too small to have been seen from this high up, and in amazing numbers. In 1639 one immigrant ship out of London bound for Boston sighted no less than 13 other ships in the course of its three month voyage across the Atlantic. Those sailors knew their ships and, with the technology of their day, understood the ways of the sea. Of the 198 ships that sailed to New England between 1629 and 1640, the years of political turmoil preceding the English Civil War, 197 got through - only one was lost. Not so fortunate however were the more recent convoys of 1940 and 1941. The Atlantic is a cruel sea, a place where people have dreamed powerful dreams which have shaped our destinies, and a place where some disappear without a trace. Technology has brought us a long way since the voyage of the *Susan Constant*, the *Dove* and the *Mayflower*, and at no period more rapidly than the last couple of decades. That sparked another thought and one I could use to introduce the speech I was to give to a conference of some 200 business leaders and senior academics the following evening.

*         *         *

The audience settled into their seats in the university auditorium, and the chairman extended a short welcome. I got up to speak and looked around the hall at my audience, several of whom gave me warm smiles. This was going to be a good group to talk to. "Let me tell you a story," I began, my voice feeling out the acoustics of the room and my eyes sizing up those listeners in any audience whose reactions would condition the mood of the group. "During the Second World War, the US government was impressed by the performance of the ocean liners *Queen Mary* and the *Queen Elizabeth*, which transported thousands of troops so fast that the German U-boats were not able to catch them. Once the war was over, the US government subsidised the building of a passenger ship - the *SS United States* - that could go faster and, in time of military need, carry even more troops than its British counterparts. The *SS United States* entered commercial service in the mid-fifties. At a speed of 40 knots, she cut the travel time from New York to England to just under 84 hours. I sailed on her once, and she was a lovely ship. Three years into her life, the S.S. United States started to lose money and she recorded a loss for every year thereafter. In fact, less than ten years later she was taken out of service and hauled off to a Turkish port where she lay rusting for a quarter century. Why the demise of this grand ship? Because the De Havilland Brothers had built a commercial jet aircraft, the Comet, and British Overseas Airways Corporation had started flying passengers across the Atlantic. The jet aeroplane cut the travel time by 90 per cent to a mere eight hours, and the days of the great trans-Atlantic liner were over. There was nothing wrong with the design of the S.S. United States. But she was overtaken by a totally new form of travel. That new technology opened up countless new opportunities.

"This, of course, is what I want to talk about with regard to our schools. In the past they got us to where we needed to go, but I hope to show that the current structure of education and its relationship to family, community and technology are now impeding our children's chances to deal successfully with the problems and opportunities of the twenty-first century. I attend many conferences concerned with the need to reform educational systems and wherever it is in the world people list the problems as:

* Classroom discipline has broken down; children are out of control.
* We have to find better ways of motivating children, they're just not interested.
* We need better teachers with more qualifications.
* We need a more detailed curriculum ...
     ... no we don't, we need a broader curriculum.
* We must stretch the gifted child more ...
     ... no, we must stimulate the average child more.
* We need smaller classes, and more equipment.
* The parents are irresponsible.
* ... And so on and so on.

"People say they need more money yet they show little confidence that this will be forthcoming. We in the United Kingdom are not alone in fearing that we will have to get better results with fewer resources. All of us have to think in new ways about this. Basically, we just have to think smarter. Thinking smarter means seeing these issues from a totally different perspective. Critically this new perspective has to be one of learning, not schooling. Listening to all these conversations I find it difficult to recognise which country I am in. The so-called crisis in schools is certainly not limited to any particular country and the educational deficiencies people worry about are much the same in New York, Tokyo, Toronto, Warsaw, Sydney or London. I think what we are all worried about is something much bigger than what happens to children during the 20 per cent of their waking hours spent in the classroom between the ages of five and 18. It is about how humans develop and learn, and how they create particular kinds of environments around them. It's about all of our futures.

"Our schools are a product of the last 200 years. They remain locked into a paper-and-pencil technology, technology that shapes the whole learning experience. A lecture can be given only as fast as students can write it down and you cannot give them more homework than they will have time to write out. Likewise, learning does not takes place in uniform, clearly delineated stages. The curriculum consists of self-contained bits, and students are taught what you think they ought to be taught. Schools move everybody off to the next level at the end of the year, with the exception of two or three students who must stay behind and are left scarred by the experience. This system has functioned well enough for some 150 years, just so long as we had the sort of society where a few per cent of the population needed to be creative and the rest needed to be good only at conformity. And it worked according to the technology. But if you fell by the wayside, chances are that the great liner swept past you, and it was not worthwhile turning back to pick you up.

"But think about how you yourself learn and about your most powerful learning experience. What was it that changed you and the way you thought? For me, this was not at the conventional public school where I was educated but through a man who used to come to our home on Friday evenings and do odd jobs for my parents. "Old Mr McFadgen" had served an apprenticeship as a carpenter in the Royal Navy in the 1890s, but by the time he was done with it, the Navy did not need carpenters any more. So, though he had hands like a surgeon, he spent his entire naval career shovelling coal into the boilers of battleships. The one thing that kept him sane was that, in his free time, he would go up into the shadow of the gun turrets with a little bit of wood and a chisel and whittle away to his heart's content. He taught himself to become a brilliant carver. On those Friday evenings, after he had polished the silverware and the brass, he would show me little wooden figureheads he had made. I longed to carve such beautiful things for myself. He looked at me one evening and said, "If you want to learn how to carve, you first have to learn how to sharpen a chisel." So I said, "Yes, please." And for several weeks, he taught me how to sharpen a chisel, which is not actually a easy task. When I had mastered that he pulled out some strange bits of wood with the most awfully contorted grain. He said, "You'll never learn to carve unless you know how to work the grain of the wood." And so for weeks I did nothing but work the grain of the wood. Then the great day finally came. He said, "I think you're ready to start carving now." And he let me go. By the time I was 13, I was quite a good wood carver, and then I went off to boarding school, a public school.

"My biggest challenge in school was Latin. In those days you couldn't go to

Oxford or Cambridge unless you passed a Latin exam, and I failed it three times. Worse, my Latin teacher was even more bored with Latin than I was. I had six weeks to go until I could take the exam one last time; if I did not pass, I could not get to Oxford. At about the same time, the school carpenter came up to me and said, "John, I have to congratulate you. You've been chosen to represent the United Kingdom as a schoolboy wood carver at an international exhibition." My morale soared - and then it crashed, because wood carving, unlike debating or rugby, was not a recognised activity at the school. I found myself wondering why it was that I could be one of the best young wood carvers in the country but still flunk Latin. Quickly I realised I could not pass Latin because I was not in charge, and I was wasting my time with somebody who did not even believe in it. To this day I do not know how I did it, but I actually went to my Latin teacher that afternoon and said, "Look, as I have to pass Latin in six weeks, I'm not coming to any more of your lessons. I'm going to teach myself." For six weeks, nobody knew what to do with me. The other students looked at me through the windows of the library, where I spent every minute of the day. I was sweating my backside off. And, of course, I passed Latin - though I have to admit I forgot most of it within six months. But I still woodcarve.

"I have been a teacher all my life and when I started, it was with great enthusiasm. But I hit a technological barrier right at the beginning. I was teaching geography, in particular geomorphology - how mountains are built. At the time - the autumn of 1965 - a lot of fresh material had come out about plate tectonics, and I bored my classes silly with the diagrams I put onto the blackboard. For six weeks they took notes and I thought I had done my job well. Just before Christmas that year, the BBC came out with a two-hour documentary film entitled *The Restless Earth*. In two brilliant hours, it covered ten times the material that I had. So I went to see the senior geography teacher and asked if we could buy a copy of the film. He said there was no way, that it was far too expensive. I replied that between us we had five classes and that with the film, one of us could work with all of them. We could show the film and stop it as many times as we wanted to. One of us could go do some other work, and the children would learn much more. He looked at me as if I were mad and left me in no doubt that the school would find my ideas equally crazy.

"Much more recently - about three or four years ago - we had just put in a CD-ROM system at home. David, my middle son, who was ten at the time, was exploring the *Encarta* encyclopaedia CD and called me down to the study one evening. "Daddy," he said, "there's something here you ought to see." There were three video clips of 90 seconds each explaining how mountains are made. There again was everything that I had done in six weeks as a new teacher. Given his level of enthusiasm, my ten-year-old could nearly have mastered the subject by himself that evening.

"Back in 1978 I helped install what became Britain's first computerised classroom. I defined this as having a computer for every child, and insisted the computers should be used for any subject other than computer studies. Nobody had the first clue what I was talking about. Why did I do it? I wanted to see what would happen if children had the ability to word-process their essays. Almost 20 years ago, I started seeing children who got so carried away with their writing that they would say to the teacher, "Please, can't we stay here? I know the bell's rung, but can't we get this job finished?" One teacher came up to me with a complaint: "A child has just come to me with the first draft of an essay. He wants me to comment on it so that he can go back and redraft it before handing it in for marking. Which do I mark, the one he did by himself, or the one he cheated with by first asking my advice?" Even though that was almost two decades ago, we still think like that teacher. We have not come to terms with this revolution. Why? Because deep down we still do not understand how learning takes place.

"I was trained as a teacher with a basic philosophy about learning that we human beings had some form of inherited intelligence, but otherwise the brain was an absolute blank slate. The brain did not start with any particular set of predispositions. What mattered was what we put into it. This view has been overturned in the last decade thanks to Positron Emission Tomography and Computerised Axial Tomography scans and functional Magnetic Resonance Imaging which allow us to see the brain at work. You can ask a musician to listen to fine music and see a whole array of interactions taking place both in the specialised area of the brain for music and in the area that we know to be the seat of emotional understanding. Something interesting happens if you annoy and upset the musician whose head is in the scanner. Play Prokofiev at half speed and he is insulted and gets cross. The scanner reveals that much of the brain starts to close down. Carry the experiment a bit further and challenge the musician's know-how. "Now look," you say, "you can't even understand what's going on in Prokofiev when it's at half speed. You are useless." When you look again at the scan, you will see that brain activity has dropped off. Much of the area that was being used before - when the music was played properly - will have switched off.

"Evolutionary psychology, another new discipline, has also shed light on questions of learning and has begun to show us how our brains have grown and changed over the last few thousand years. To give you an example: several years ago some archaeologists were digging in France and uncovered a Stone Age encampment. With carbon dating, they established that the site was some 30,000 years old. They pulled out many artefacts, one of which was a flat bone, the shoulder blade of an ox, covered with hieroglyphics. For days the archaeologists could not figure out these scribblings. Then late one clear night, one of them looked up at the sky and realised what was on the bone: an ancestor of ours was so interested in the changing phases of the moon that he had started to record them. The bone was nothing other than the Stone Age equivalent of the back of an envelope, and each night this observer had jotted down a bit more.

"Over the next ten and a half weeks, the scientists compared this ancient astronomical notebook to the moon in the sky - and it was right, night after night after night. Thirty thousand years ago is roughly 1,500 generations ago, and even then, one of our early ancestors was intelligent and inquisitive enough to gain some genuine knowledge of the moon. This Stone Age astronomer teaches an important lesson that we tend to forget. Learning is a consequence of thinking. Stick with that. If you are interested enough in something to think about it, then you are bound to learn. Whoever that man - or woman - was, seated by his fire night after night, I like to think that he was always surrounded by two or three children. That would make him the archetypal teacher of all time, because - and this is the point I want to emphasise - learning and schooling are not synonymous. We do an awful lot of learning without being told to learn. And often the most powerful learning we do is that which builds on some innate desire, on our burning interest to make more sense out of something that matters to us. The critical thing is the quest that we feel ourselves to be on.

"The human brain has grown far faster than the rest of our body. In fact, every other mammal is born with its brain 98 per cent formed. A human being is born with its brain only 40 per cent formed. If a woman carried a child until its brain reached full size, pregnancy would last for 27 months. Human evolution is on a collision course because the brain has grown so large so quickly that it cannot get down the birth canal. Therefore there is a compromise: to enable us to survive, evolution has fitted us with incredible predispositions to learn things in the first three years of life that other mammals acquire before they are even born.

"One of these has to do with social skills. Have you ever watched children in a playground or around the house? They are great collaborators. They form teams and are good at getting together to solve problems. Why do we have this predisposition? Because long ago, during human prehistory, if children below the age of five or six had not known how to collaborate, they would not have survived. But again, as with our language abilities, nature is incredibly economical. If we do not develop the collaborative skills of children when they are very young, their brains develop in a different way. That is why employers have such trouble teaching teamwork and cooperation to workers in their early twenties. Worse still, if children do not learn to collaborate in these socially constructive ways, those same neural networks can be rewired to respond with aggression or violence, which is what we are seeing in cities like Chicago and Liverpool. Predispositions meant for our survival get reversed.

"In short, during the early years of life, there are powerful innate tendencies that we must learn to develop in keeping with the grain of the brain. Much the same is true of adolescence, a period that Americans and British have considered a problem since we coined the word teenager in the early fifties. We must remember, however, that every stage in our biological development serves a purpose. Adolescence is a period of enormous physical energy, risk-taking and emotional development. It is a time when young people learn their place in the world. Those of you who are employers know that survival doesn't only depend on what you have learned by the time you leave school. Knowledge is changing rapidly and what counts is your ability to use your brain. When I learned to carve wood, I developed an attitude toward learning that I was able to transfer to my Latin studies. There was nothing about the way in which I was taught Latin, however, that helped me to learn other things. Am I making my point? The future is not about what you know, but about knowing how to learn.

"It seems to me that something has gone terribly wrong with us if, at the end of the twentieth century, we still have people who have not been taught how to learn, and who will live in a world which is going to call for the highest possible level of continuous problem-solving, creativity and collaborative activity.

"Our current approach is upside down. The largest class sizes in Western schools are in the first year of education, at the age of five or six. The smallest class sizes are in the last year of high school, in preparation for those few students who will go on to university. In other words, we go about teaching with seeming indifference to the new understanding of the human brain and what it has to say about the basic assumptions of learning. We are rather like the people who said the future was going to be with the *SS United States* not with the airliner. When children are aged seven and under and look so small and innocent - we tend to think that school is just baby-sitting. In fact, this is the time when children need the greatest help extending their natural capabilities. It is precisely this period in their lives when we need the smallest class sizes and the greatest amount of interactivity. The point is not to fill them up with information but rather to encourage that attitude, which is there already among young children, of wanting to take responsibility for their own learning. Remember what that wood carver did for me? First he encouraged me to see how brilliant I would be if I could produce a fine carving. He gave me an ambition. Then he made clear that before I could even start toward that goal I would have to master the first sub-skill - sharpening the chisel - and then the next - handling the grain. As I went on, he supported me in other ways. But never again did he tell me how to sharpen a chisel. Never again did he tell me how to handle the grain of wood.

"My point is that it is not just smaller class sizes we need during elementary education but a whole new approach to the way we handle children. We need to move away from the idea that we cosset children as they get older. If we are going to give them small classes when they are young, then they should go into progressively larger classes as they get older, classes in which they are held ever more accountable for those skills which they learned when they were young. As a high school principal I argued for more teachers than the elementary school. Now one of the reasons I gave for this was to make up for what the elementary schools had not done earlier. But I was still wrong: the real work should be there at the beginning.

"There is another problem too, because the current system is not only upside-down, but also inside-out. As a headmaster, I argued that the greatest skill a child could learn was homework. I must confess my tongue was always in my cheek when I said this, because I also knew that homework was cost-free when it came to the school budget. All it took was a pencil, a textbook and a corner of the kitchen table. About four years ago, however, I was jolted by one of my sons who declared to me that homework was unfair because he and some of his friends were sure to get all the best marks. Why was this unfair? "Because," he said, "we're from the families that have computers with CD-ROM and the Internet at home. All the kids use the technology in school, but when some of them go home, they have to go back to using pencil and paper." He was right, of course: because of the computer, the quality of his homework was far higher. Here we see the challenge we have to take up. Until now, every Western education system has held that tax monies should go into what happens in the classroom. The premise is that the classroom is the only place where valid learning takes place. But I would tell you, speaking now as the father of three sons in an American high school, that many children from their school - a good one in Fairfax County, Virginia - actually believe that their work starts at three o'clock in the afternoon. That is when they all get together in groups to work on projects. That is when they go onto the Internet. And this work is not under the direction of the teachers. However good the schools are in Fairfax County, they have not kept up with the technology, and their curricula are not keeping up with the children. The children are finding a way of their own and I think the same thing is happening in many other countries, including England.

"At the heart of what I am saying is a new understanding about learning, a recognition that the human brain is like the rest of the human body. It needs to be handled as we parents handle our children. We try to give them the support when they are young so that eventually, when the day comes that they walk out, we know that we have given them the skills to deal with situations that we have never envisaged ourselves. As parents we wean them, yet our present educational system, I am afraid, does the opposite. It is still geared to the idea that there is a fixed point for most everyone to reach by the age of 18 and that reaching this point will stand them in good stead.

"The last thought I want to leave with you comes from Charles Handy who has applied the Catholic doctrine of subsidiarity to education. For those of you who are not familiar with it, subsidiarity says that it is wrong for a superior body to make a decision on behalf of an inferior body which is qualified to make that decision for itself. When applied to schooling, subsidiarity reflects the intentions of teachers who want to give children the capability to stand on their own feet. For this commitment to stick, we must progressively hold each child itself accountable for doing just that and, if we did things this way, the change would be dramatic. It would be the children who would be exhausted at the end of the term, not the teachers. Now go back to my opening story. They are still building great liners, even bigger than the *SS United States*. But their job is not to get anywhere in particular. They cruise around the Caribbean. Their task is to provide entertainment, to fill in time - not to get anywhere in particular."

*         *         *

It was almost exactly two years to the day since I had started to write this book and I was correcting what I hoped would be its final draft. Across the square, 36 floors below my hotel bedroom window, young Canadians were pirouetting on the skating rink, and the chimes of Toronto's City Hall clock tolled off the quarter hours. On my table were the slides which I had used three weeks earlier when addressing the 600 delegates to the premier education conference always held in the north of England early in January. I had just reorganised them as shortly I would be going down to the main ballroom of the hotel to address the 300 delegates to the annual conference of the Ontario Public School Boards Association. This was the third provincial follow-up to what I had said to senior educationalists from across Canada when they had met in Quebec, just below the old castle, the previous July.

I'd just finished writing up my notes from the previous evening's discussion with Paul Cappon, the director general of the Council of education ministers in Canada. Paul had been talking about the Canadians' plan to use the new story as set out by the Initiative's recently published Policy Paper to stimulate a structured series of discussions across Canada to awaken people to the need for radical new thinking. As we sipped our coffee Paul broached another topic. "Canada is to host the Commonwealth education ministers conference in Halifax, Nova Scotia in September 2000. I would like to invite you to address that conference. It is just such ideas as these which many of the smaller countries of the Commonwealth desperately need. It's an ideal forum for you to develop the thinking."

As I rechecked the text of the middle chapters of this book, those dealing with how I, with merely the authority of a man who had recently resigned the headship of a secondary school out of sheer frustration, seemed to be challenging the entire educational establishment of the UK, I realised just what an amazing story this had become, especially over the past couple of years. Two things had, as it were, exploded. Firstly the amount of research that was becoming available seemed to be expanding exponentially, and secondly public interest in what I was able to say about the strategic, resource and policy implications of all this was growing by the day. Thankfully I have a strong constitution for I was coming to use aircraft with the frequency that, as a child, I had used local buses.

Let me explain because you, the reader, need to know something more about the destination of this story before you join me in understanding how it all started. Writing this book has had to be a spare time occupation as my family and I had moved to America in December 1995 for a particular purpose. Six months previously the trustees of Education 2000, an English charitable foundation of which I had been director for ten years, decided I should set up a transnational team to consolidate recent research findings on how humans learn. Eventually some 60 researchers, practitioners and policy makers from 14 different countries were to be involved in six conferences at Wingspread, a Frank Lloyd Wright mansion owned by the Johnson Foundation on the shores of Lake Michigan in Wisconsin. The 21st Century Learning Initiative emerged and a Washington office gave us access to recent publications on human learning, a vast array of ideas that challenged our ability to see the whole picture. Yet it was this full picture that we sought if educational practice was to be transformed by ideas as radical as those which moved transatlantic travel from ocean-going liners to jets.

In 1943, the quantum theorist Erwin Schroedinger wrote: "We have inherited from our forefathers the keen longing for unified, all-embracing knowledge ... But the spread, both in width and depth, of the multifarious branches of knowledge ... confronts us with a queer dilemma ... It has become next to impossible for a single mind to fully command more than a small portion of it. I can see no other escape from this dilemma (lest our true aim be lost for ever) than that some of us should embark on a synthesis of facts and theories, albeit with a second-hand and incomplete knowledge of some of them - at the risk of making fools of ourselves."

Academics don't often risk making fools of themselves. Synthesis is not for them. So in the half century that followed Schroedinger's plea, the situation has become even more difficult. Intellectual thought has become more specialised and academia more concerned to find out why subjects differ than where they overlap. It is far easier to set up a research program to investigate further a tiny aspect of an already highly specific topic, than it is to assemble the expertise necessary to tease out the strategic and resource implications of what has already been discovered. There are few people good at doing this, for all of us have made progress through our careers by being specialists in individual subjects. We are just not good at understanding other perspectives.

This is particularly true of the emerging interest in the biology of the brain. At a time when it is becoming increasingly obvious that learning is moderated through a series of biological processes in the brain, fewer than five per cent of educational administrators have any professional expertise in biology. To a profession well versed in the concerns of philosophy, and to an extent psychology, the application of evolutionary principles to the brain is profoundly unsettling.

"I can't move from the scale of the synapse to what I must do on Monday morning," teachers will say, with the implied suggestion that they won't do anything. The job of the Initiative is to make it easier for practitioners and policy makers to make connections between scientific understandings at the micro-level in order to influence macro-level policy decisions. That, in turn, will make schooling compatible with young people's different aptitudes, interests and experiences. The Initiative's aim is to revitalise a system whose sheer alienating boredom must always be buttressed with extrinsic rewards (marks, grades, prizes, scholarships) to keep people going in things that don't interest them. The purpose of education has become a private good where individual advancement, formalities and credentials have become more important than the social benefits of education as a public good. We want a world where learning is a means to develop responsible and productive citizens, a liberal ideal which has become blurred by a prescriptiveness which traps us all. As both a teacher and father I have said, rather pathetically: "All this may not make much sense to you, but like it or not that is what will get you through the exam."

However things are changing rapidly. There is a new economic reality which paints a different picture even to that of just ten years ago. The changes are dramatic; suddenly there is a premium on people who know how to use their brains in an inclusive way. Problem-solving, creativity, adaptability, team-building, group intelligence, networked intelligence, the kinds of things early twentieth century advocates of the scientific management of work had tried to smash out of workers, are now what give businesses a competitive advantage.

Right here, we were to understand, was the reason for the much quoted crisis in schools. Here was the point where an old system collided head-on with a set of totally different priorities. Schools as the public understood them were finely attuned to a predictable world. That world has now gone, irretrievably. What needs to emerge is something very different. By a glorious coincidence it is much more to do with what the human brain delights in; namely dealing creatively with an ever-changing set of circumstances that demands that it remains continuously interactive with its environment. Bob Sylwester of the University of Oregon urges: "Get rid of that damn machine model of the brain. It's wrong. The brain is a biological system, not a machine. Currently we are putting children with biologically shaped brains into machine oriented schools. The two just don't mix. We bog the school down in a curriculum that is not biologically feasible."

My diary - which has formed the basis of this autobiography-cum-account of emerging educational theory - reveals an itinerary my preacher father would have found incredible. So persuasive are the conclusions from all this that the writing of this book has been interrupted scores of times by the need to fly off and make yet another presentation to still more groups of concerned citizens (not just educationalists) desperately looking for leadership as they struggle to escape the dying clutches of an old system. These presentations - in Norway, Sweden, Estonia; in Ireland and Portugal; in Puerto Rico, Colombia and in locations right across Canada; in numerous parts of England and right across the United States; in Japan, Indonesia and in Southern Africa - and the questions such people raised and the discussions that inevitably followed, have in their turn shaped this story. At the time of writing I'm looking forward to addressing Mikhail Gorbachev's State of the World Forum in San Francisco.

Despite a timetable bound together by airline schedules, my career has gone full circle and is ending much as it began. I am still the teacher, still the man to be relied on in front of a restless crowd by going from the particular to the general, from anecdote to theory, from the personal to the political. My father's recognition of the approach would have been balanced by amazement at the scale of fund raising and the generosity of an American conference circuit which has made my form of preaching possible. And - given the conservatism of parents considering their children's prospects - he'd have worried about my shift from salaried security to the uncertainties of self-employment. I'd have told him this shift has loomed large in my mind, larger than it would to many, especially those younger than myself for whom the notion of a job for life is as alien as, say, military conscription. Times change and careers change with them, a commonplace observation whose force, nonetheless, is being ignored by the politicians who drive education back into what they imagine are traditional values.

All this travelling has convinced me of what I always knew: most teachers are essentially good people. Teaching, to give this book's epigraph a new twist, has always contained the seeds of a "natural piety". You may, in all probability, smile at the notion and, if so, I'd insist that the vast majority of teachers begin their working life as idealists. Age brings disillusion but the disillusion of today's teachers is far greater than when I started in the profession. What excites me now are ideas to fuel the idealism which ought to pass from teachers to pupils, ideas flowing from new learning theory and how this can prepare young people for contemporary life.

When my father died young in 1960, he knew nothing of the information economy, still less its non-hierarchical working practices where individual contributions tend to matter more than in the old mechanistic ways of wealth creation. However, the consensus in favour of economic progress is matched by a lack of consensus about the purposes of education in a paradox which has us enjoying more and more things while seeming to know less and less about how to treat our children. My father, an idealist, would have appreciated that something should - and must - be done and I'd have enjoyed convincing him how new understandings of learning can inform new approaches to schooling.

People tell me that I too am an idealist and I'm flattered they recognise something I know exists in my temperament, experience and genes. I recognise too a double-edged compliment when I hear one because idealistic is often a synonym for naivete. If this book does its job, it will show I'm not naïve and, far more importantly, show there is nothing naïve about the kind of educational transformation I'm advocating. Indeed, to cling to the old ways and fall back into the clutches of a dying system is moral and practical stupidity.

How these ideas have become clearer, and their implications more obvious, emerges as this story unfolds.

# 2
# The Child Becomes a Young Man

We all have a story to tell, though for most of the time we are too busy or too preoccupied to delve into our memories to figure out just what this story might be. Living in the present is challenge enough. Yet it is these stories, consciously perceived or not, that condition the way we are. This is what learning is all about. Learning enables us to draw upon past experience to understand and evaluate the present so that we can be more confident about the way we think and act in the future. It's about thinking our way into new knowledge. In short, it's about being more in charge of ourselves and, therefore, more useful to others as well.

I spend much of my time thinking about possible opportunities for young people's futures and have probably spent more time than most looking back to see why it is that I think as I do. "It's all very well for you," some people say to me in consequence. "You can have these radical ideas simply because you grew up and thrived in the system. Now you're seeking to destroy the very arrangements that enabled you to be successful." I have to answer this charge immediately. My so-called success has been largely, I have now come to understand, despite of, not because of, the system. School, classrooms and teachers have been important, but they have rarely been the most important factors in how I have discovered myself and learnt how to be useful. That's the essential message of this book. Learning and schooling are not necessarily the same thing and we fail our children abysmally if we assume that schools can do everything. This observation is borne out in *The Mind, the Brain and Complex Adaptive Systems*, a collection of essays published by the prestigious Santa Fe Institute in 1995. The author who, clarifies the mismatch between emerging learning theory and current educational practice, wrote: "The method people naturally employ to acquire knowledge is largely unsupported by traditional classroom practice. The human mind is better equipped to gather information about the world by operating within it than by reading about it, hearing lectures on it, or studying abstract models of it." Here is a universal truth exemplified by my own life experiences.

\*       \*       \*

My mother came from an archetypal English middle class home, complete with tennis court, small rose garden, maid, gardener, a new car each year and chapel every Sunday morning. Her sense of comfortable destiny was reinforced by a boarding school where she learned a verse of scripture every day, and studied history from Arthur Mee's *Our Island Story*. My father was the son of a proud, self-willed farmer whose family had farmed in the Ax Valley between Axminster and the cliffs facing Lyme Bay for centuries. Having initially wanted to be an engineer, he changed his mind just before leaving school and decided instead to train as an Anglican priest. He was the first on either side of the two families to go to university and his father never understood him nor, I think, forgave him. From my mother's family I have inherited the family Bible complete with all the legitimate births back to 1778, showing links to the Dare family and possibly, given the West Country connection, with that Eleanor Dare who was the first English settler to give birth to a child in the ill-fated Roanoke colony of 1587, and naming the child, accordingly, Virginia. From my father's mother I inherited the story that we are one of the contenders of an unresolved nineteenth century law suit challenging our claim to be the direct descendants of Sir Francis Drake. This, if it were ever to be proved in our favour (an impossibly long set of odds), should mean that we would now be receiving the annual interest on the ill-gotten wealth resulting from the "singeing of the King of Spain's beard" in Cadiz harbour in 1587. From my earliest days I knew the family had a history. My younger brother and sister and I knew where we had come from.

My parents, happily married when they were 22 and 24 respectively, belonged to different English middle-class traditions. My maternal grandparents' home always smelled of wax polish, fresh air and roses; theirs was a fine nineteen-thirties home complete with a well-equipped bathroom, separate toilets and wash basins in all the bedrooms. My paternal grandparents lived in a respectable small Victorian house - small, but one of the largest in Axmouth village. Although it had been modernised to include a bathroom, my grandfather persisted in shaving at the kitchen sink and using the outside toilet. What was good enough for his father was good enough for him. He knew about grafting roses better than anyone in all the parishes round about. "To grow a good rose you must graft a domesticated rose on to the roots of an old briar. That way you get both vigour and beauty." It was my first lesson in evolutionary principles, though evolution as a human process would have been an anathema to the Biblical world-view of all four of my grandparents. Both my grandfathers took pride from work well done. One relished the prospects of the future, while the other was the authentic, stubborn, unchanging yeoman of old England who was mystified and more than slightly intimidated by the other.

I now realise that I had a blissful childhood. Born just before the start of the Second World War, one of my earliest memories was of bewilderment at my parents' distress when I cut down their flowering tomato plants in the spring of 1943 as a little thank offering for my mother. In ration-conscious Britain fresh tomatoes were a much anticipated treat. I never knew hunger, though I was never allowed to leave anything on my plate and we were too young to know of the U-boat attacks on Allied shipping which, in 1940-41, almost led to national starvation. I can just remember seeing the Allied shipping gathering in Lyme Bay just before the Normandy landings, and hearing the thud of a stick of bombs aimed at a railway bridge not a hundred yards from our home. Later on I recall making a cut-out model of a triumphal victory arch, complete with King and Queen riding though in an open carriage, issued to commemorate VE-Day (Victory in Europe). Just how old I was when I first heard about Auschwitz I can't remember.

A few months after the war ended we moved to Portsmouth, the home of the British Navy, where my father was to become vicar of a large Victorian church in what had been in earlier years the fashionable naval officers' part of the town. The sound of the bombs had gone by the time we arrived, but the devastation was all around us. For 300 and more yards, over an arc of a 180 degrees from my new bedroom window, not a house or a shop remained and war's aftermath cast a grey, cold spell over the city. However, it was a great place for a young child to grow up, for after the horror of the War there was a mood of optimism; things had to be getting better. We were, everyone kept reminding each other, the victors. Adults might have gone through all forms of horror which we could but dimly comprehend, but as children we were the country's future, and we were to be cherished. We may have had little money, but then there was little in the shops to buy. We did, however, have the love of our parents and the affection of an older generation who had already seen too many children they had known perish in war. The future was a delicate plant which they understood had to be nourished.

Displaced persons were everywhere. A Polish count eked out a living by mending clocks. People of many languages worked together to rebuild an almost flattened city. Junk shops, still to be dignified with the title of antique, were full of remnants rescued from the fires of the blitz and still with a faint smell of smoke. All this influenced me deeply. Maybe war would break out again, maybe I too would become a refugee. If that were the case I would need to be strong, I told myself, and be able to look after myself. I was preoccupied, as a child of seven or eight, with the need to know about survival - cooking, living rough, building huts from old timber, finding my way - and being strong enough to carry a rucksack. This was compounded by the repeated advice of my paternal grandfather to always make sure I had a good pair of boots. My background persuaded me that to survive I needed to be quick on the uptake and that if there was something I didn't know, then I had better find it out. Not everybody in those immediate post-war years could cope. Walking one day with my schoolmates along the beach we saw a half-crazed woman trying to drown herself. The teacher raced into the water, struggled with her, and eventually got her onto the beach. She was hysterical. Later I heard the story. Her husband had gone down with his ship in the Atlantic. For six years she had struggled to keep herself going before loneliness finally overcame her; she wanted nothing other than to drown and be alongside her dead husband.

Nevertheless, people kept on saying, this was the land of the victor. It did not always feel like it, particularly during the winter of 1947 when savagely cold weather and a series of industrial disputes almost brought Britain to its knees. As a youngster I understood what the Cold War might be all about. I knew the warships, every one by sight, as they passed the old Sally Port from which Nelson had joined his ship after bidding farewell to his beloved Lady Hamilton and setting out for Trafalgar 140 years earlier, and then to the Inner Harbour. Not just the Royal Navy, either, but American ships as well - the *USS Missouri* and *USS Mississippi* nudged dockyard space with *HMS Vanguard*, as well as the pride of the post-war Navy, the aircraft carrier *HMS Eagle*. Around them were fussy little destroyers and corvettes. I studied the atlas to see where they had come from and where they would go next. I plagued my father to contact the chaplains of visiting ships to ask if I could explore their ships from boiler room to bridge. And frequently I did. I was furious, as only an eight year-old can be, when it was decided that *HMS Indefatigable*, a wooden warship dating from the 1770s, was deemed beyond repair. In the strange way of the Navy she was therefore towed out to sea, to Spit Head just off the Isle of Wight, and with the Royal Ensign flying at her stern, her bottom was blown out with dynamite so that she sank quickly. To my young mind this was amazing sacrilege. It still is. I wonder if marine archaeologists will ever try to recover her?

Adults had time for children in ways that now seem extraordinary. Children were safe in a community that still respected the significance of the individual. My parents never seemed to worry when I set off for long walks by myself to explore the genteel sea front, the bustle of the dockyard, the fascination of the building sites, or the historic area of Old Portsmouth or Portsea where Charles Dickens wrote many of his novels. Always there were people to talk to. Few people had petrol coupons, and those who did would stop their cars for anyone stranded after the last bus had gone. The camaraderie engendered by the war lasted for a fair while and it was great. By the age of 15 I was hitch-hiking some 50 or 60 miles a day; by 16 I headed to Scotland, 400 miles away, by myself. I met endless people and learned to talk with anyone, about anything. It was the best form of schooling I ever had.

I was no more than eight or nine when I started to question why it was that different kinds of people attended different services at my father's church. The Sunday morning service was full of Royal Navy officers, professional people, and their families. The evening service was altogether different and attended by craftsmen from the dockyards who loved to sing rousing hymns and hear short sermons. Their enthusiasm for singing, "Now the day is over, night is drawing near," or "Eternal father, strong to save, whose arm doth bind the restless waves," carried a sadness and a nostalgia that I noticed but did not fully understand. Both kinds of people were good to me. As the vicarage family we were somehow detached from the social stratification of English society. I was able to move across classes with impunity: my father did and therefore so could I. I learnt a most important lesson. If you don't classify yourself, then other people will find it more difficult to pigeon-hole you. Don't conform to other people's expectations of you, just be yourself.

I didn't understand the finer points of the theology behind my father's easy conversational sermons, but I did learn, and regard this as being of very great significance, how to daydream. For 15 or 20 minutes every Sunday I was silent, but very constructively thinking things through for myself. It was only years later that I read this by TE Lawrence: "All men dream dreams, but not equally. Those that dream in the dusty recesses of the night awaken to find that their dreams were but vanity. But beware of the dreamers of the day for they live to make their dreams reality." I remained indebted to many preachers - my father included - who gave me the freedom to think my own thoughts, and to keep other people from interrupting me.

My father was also brilliant with his hands, and a master of improvisation who never threw anything away. "You never know when it may come in useful," he'd say and needless waste, of any kind, still appals me. He made my electric train set, and would spend hours helping me make things from old scraps of wood. To me it was fun. To him it was, at least partially, economic necessity. The church, once proud and well financed, was struggling. It had been the very first public building in the city to be wired for electricity, and its worn out electric cabling encased in wooden sheathing was a fire hazard. The whole thing had to be replaced and there was nothing like enough money. So he, and three volunteers, replaced the entire electric system, working in the evenings for several years, which was an enormous task in a large building seating 1,500 people. Late of an evening, trying to be helpful, I would offer to hold the trailing light to help my father see what he was doing. I tried to concentrate in a variety of uncomfortable positions, but easily lost concentration. "You'll never hold the light correctly unless you try and understand what I'm trying to do," my father would say by way of explanation, "You've got to learn to think like me. Then you'll come to anticipate what I'll do next."

I noted that his helpers were always men from the evening congregation. I don't think that he ever talked to the admirals, captains and the like about what he was doing, but I suspect that it was their money that paid for the materials. This class-segregated society recognised its essential interdependence. Torpedoes had recognised no difference between officers and sailors. All classes had been, literally, in the same boat together. They still remembered this. I learnt to think like that too. Community was something I naturally understood.

*         *         *

There was something else I learnt and didn't recognise until years later. Since the Norman conquest, England has been divided into parishes and in my boyhood there were some 15,000 of these, nearly every one with a resident vicar or rector. Several hundred parishes made up a bishopric (a diocese). As a young boy I met the bishop and was enormously impressed - from this distance I'm not sure if it was because he had once been a trans-Antarctic explorer, or whether it was because he knew the royal family (and later went on to become the Queen's dean at Windsor Castle). So I felt my parish mattered as it was all part of the great scheme of things and I was only a single person removed from talking to the King. In my father's tradition everyone who lived in the parish of St Jude's was his spiritual responsibility, be they Anglican or of another faith, or no faith at all. He was at their call any hour of the day or night. A dying sailor, a distraught child, an abused woman, all knew - from a tradition still alive after centuries - that the first place of refuge was the vicarage. I used to be embarrassed that my father almost always wore his clerical collar, even on holiday. "It's in case there's anyone in need as I walk down the street or wherever," he explained. "If they see the collar they'll know I'm a priest." They did, and they would stop him at any time.

Had I known it, I was living at the transition point from the ages old form of parochial social support, to the new era of the Welfare State designed by Lord Beveridge during the latter days of the war and introduced by Clement Attlee and the newly elected Labour government. Henceforth no one would starve, go without medical treatment, or fail to go to school - by direct provision of the government. It was humane legislation, and was the ultimate product of Christian socialism but, like so many other changes, it had an array of unintended consequences. That most feared was the possibility it would reduce the individual's responsibility for their own wellbeing. My understanding is that, initially, it did not. Previous generations were imbued with a sense of providing for themselves, or within the family. To me free medical care was a right, as it still is, to be used responsibly. However, as the

Welfare State developed, I have no doubt that its existence reduced the individual's sense of self-reliance and the wish to find alternative arrangements.

From my father I also learnt the concept of vocation: a career to which you were divinely called, even though the pay might not reflect value. "You shouldn't worry if we can't afford to do things that your friends do - though I would love you to do them - it's because I'm doing the Lord's work. The work is its own reward." Never mind that it didn't pay the bills. Years later I knew that my career had also to be something of a calling. Though I was not as dedicated as my father (I was too concerned with paying the bills), the concept of vocation has been central to my way of life. Like my father, I have always been trustful that, "as thy days, so shall thy strength be".

Years later, in 1996, my father's wisdom was quantified by a report issued by the American Institutes of Health which observes "that higher intrinsic motivation is linked to higher school achievement and psychological adjustment in children, adolescents, and college students." My father understood clearly that the key to people learning and feeling successful is an intrinsic desire to make sense of something. It is an insight most school systems don't seem to appreciate.

I garnered a small mathematical strength from my formal education before the age of 13. Each morning started with a mental arithmetic test and only the answer could be written down. This, for what it's worth, means I can still calculate the cost of our purchases at the supermarket checkout and generally think numbers in ways that my own sons, having gone through a much more rigorous instruction, just cannot do. Spelling tests were conducted in the same way, but my results were nothing like as good because it was pure memorisation stuff with nothing to calculate, or make my own. Written assignments were given spasmodically, but teachers seemed to lack any sense of urgency in marking them, and I remember to this day my annoyance (I could not have been more than 11 years of age) when I realised that I had filled up an entire exercise book with exercises and answers to exercises, and not a single teacher's correction was to be seen.

Writing now from a modern perspective, in a society that seems to have gone marks crazy, it is salutary to remember that in England as recently as 1953, when the School Certificate was replaced by the Ordinary Level of the GCE, it was calculated that there were only 16,500 16 year-olds still in school (most left at 14 or 15) who could ever take such an exam. A third of those left school after the calculation had been made, but without taking the exam; a third got less than five subjects, and only a third - 5,500 - got five subjects and above, a figure now regarded as being the minimum for further study. In England in 1998 over 300,000 young people got more than five such subjects. When elder citizens question the quality of education today it is worth asking them if they were one of the 5,500 who would have qualified for university in their day. Chances are they were not.

Most of my preparatory school experience was of little long-lasting significance, but in one way harmed me greatly. As the son of a clergyman, I tended always to do what was expected of me, and my headmaster exacerbated the situation. Himself the son of missionaries in Borneo, parents whom he had seen only every third or fourth year when they came home on furlough, he delighted in passing down to me the misery he had experienced, I suspect, in his own youth. In public he never gave me a chance. It was always, "Abbott, you of all people should know to tell the truth/work hard/not run in the corridor/volunteer for extra duties." In this respect I was just too well brought up and for too many years, I remained deferential to my superiors and later felt rotten for not challenging them when I knew they were wrong. The tension is still with me. My personal, informal experience led me to believe that I could speak to anyone I wanted to and I was, in a curious way, outside and unconstrained by social subtleties. My life has been a strange mixture of responses to these contradictory tugs.

We had splendid family holidays. They lasted the whole of August, cost very little and certainly figured in no statistical returns on tourism. My father simply agreed to exchange his statutory duties in his church for a month with a colleague in another part of the country. We went to live in his house, and his family came to live in ours. It was, however, more than just experiencing what other people's homes were like (what books they read, what paintings they thought worth putting on their walls, what gadgets they might have in their kitchens), it was experiencing, with all of the alert senses of youth, what it was like to live in other communities where we were immediately known.

Staying one year in a country rectory deep in the English Fens, they still tolled the knell whenever someone died. Two people died that August. One was old and the bell, rung once every minute for each year of the man's life, seemed to go on all afternoon. Reassuringly life, it seemed, would go on forever. But the other bell stopped after only nine minutes. I was terrified. Just around the corner someone, younger than I, had been alive only yesterday, and now was dead. Around that same corner, too, was the rather crumbling cottage where Oliver Cromwell had stayed for a whole month while training his New Model Army 300 years before, at the time when so many yeomen farmers from round about this and other parishes had set off in the Great Migration of the 1630s for Massachusetts. Cromwell would have heard that same tenor bell, a bell inscribed with the words, "I to the church the living call, and to the grave do summon all."

By the age of 13 I was fast discovering who I was, and knew enough about the world to believe I could make my way in it. I was purposeful, and life had meaning. I was alert to everything going on around me. The world excited me. In no sense was I intimidated. I could, and did, go wherever I liked. Everything seemed to be connected to everything. Not many boys could, I think, have ever gained more from his family and his community, nor emerge with more of a feel for the interdependency of all people. The widow of the one-time hydrographer royal, who had once charted the China Seas, gave me her husband's meticulously made drawing set. From Old McFadgen I inherited carving tools, and from Mrs Purse - the wife of an aged missionary from China - I learned to paint and to draw. Yes, I knew that children mattered. One day it would be my generation's world. We would have to know what to do with it. That's what grown ups were for - to help us be grown ups ourselves one day.

\*           \*           \*

Like so many of my kind and age I was sent off to public school, that great invention of the Victorian era and which was, I was told, about growing up and was to be real education. There was an underlying assumption in such schools that we were all going to be leaders within a narrow range of the professions. Many would go into the Services (the Army and Navy, but certainly not the Air Force which was reserved, it seemed, for grammar school boys), the overseas Civil Service, the church, or the law. If anyone was thinking of an academic career then it would have been nothing other than that of a professor. No mention was ever made of industry or commerce, and certainly not of becoming a school teacher.

In all these attitudes the school I attended was a product of an earlier age. With the development of the great industrial cities of England in the nineteenth century, the church authorities had seen the need to plant new churches. In such rough and tumble places, far removed from the traditional market towns of old England, each with their sixteenth century grammar schools of a kind known to Shakespeare, it would not have been in keeping with the dignity of the established church for the sons of clergy to attend schools alongside factory workers. What such young men needed, it was argued, was a boarding school especially designed to toughen them, and create muscular young Christian gentlemen. So St John's School, Leatherhead, grew up in the mid-nineteenth century in a range of buildings grouped around a central quadrangle like an Oxbridge college. Special scholarships made it possible for the sons of the poorest clergy from the industrial parts of the country, and from the overseas' mission fields, to have an education almost on a par with the older, elite, public schools such as Christ's Hospital, St Paul's, or Eton.

It was, of course, boys only. Too many of my friends had attended boys - only boarding preparatory schools since the age of five or six. Some, it seemed, hardly knew their parents. "Quae Sursum Sunt Quaerite" was the school's motto inscribed over one of the entrances, "Seek those things which are above," and directly above, due to some perversity on the part of some long forgotten Victorian architect, were the bathrooms of the school maids. For some reason known only to the late nineteenth century psychologists, it was thought to quieten an adolescent's sexual fantasies if everybody was forced to swim naked in the school's swimming pool. Only those competing in team activities against other schools were allowed to wear swimming costumes. Neither parents nor sisters were allowed inside the building. Talk about sex was continuous, but never publicly acknowledged.

After the shock of being plunged into an atmosphere that knew no privacy, I found the easygoing academic regime undemanding and unchallenging. "Taking the piss" out of anyone who tried to be serious was a favourite activity. "Don't be yourself - just conform" was the code of the young adolescent. For several years I drifted. I stayed in the bottom class for five terms. Had I known it, the school and the whole public school system with it, was going through its own trauma of uncertainty. In the post-war years Britain was fast losing its Empire and its world role, and the conventional reasons for an officer class was becoming unclear. At the end of my first year I was awarded the school prize for carpentry. I was thrilled; so were my parents. The prizes were to be given away by Admiral of the Fleet, Sir Philip Vian, the sailor who had taken his ship up a Norwegian fjord and cut out a German battleship far larger than itself. It was an epic naval achievement and the admiral was a national hero. My prize was the last to be given out. I shook hands and received my book. "So, you do carpentry, do you? Can't knock a nail in straight myself." I walked back to my seat bemused. Why should such a great man be so dismissive of what I saw as a real skill? "Maybe he was just tired, not really thoughtless," my father explained to me afterwards.

Truth was, I now see, neither the admiral nor the head master had any clear understanding of the kind of world we would be going into. Like the country as a whole, which had lost an empire, the school did not seem to understand the world beyond its gates. As a headmaster myself years later I knew I would have to do better than that.

So unsure was England in the 1950s about its New World role that we were not expected to admire Rudyard Kipling. But I did and no poem meant more to me than his much parodied *If*.

If you can talk with crowds and keep your virtue,
Or walk with kings - nor lose the common touch,
If neither foes nor loving friends can hurt you,
If all men count with you, but none too much;
If you can fill the unforgiving minute
With sixty seconds' worth of distance run,
Yours is the earth, and everything that's in it
And - which is more - you'll be a Man, my son.

Many years later I discovered that Kipling had written that poem to describe the life of George Washington and the sentiment took on a whole new field of meaning to me, as I thought of the long, often inglorious, struggle for American independence and the internal divisions within the embryonic united colonies that Washington seemed to carry almost alone on his shoulders until Cornwallis came to meet him at Yorktown.

My main pleasure was the company of an ever growing circle of friends, many of whom are still with me. In a school which valued prowess on the playing fields above all else, my ability to make things, to organise people and generally get things done, gave me eventually a status which was slightly surprising, and compensated for my weak eyesight and ungainly physique. I became a senior prefect, and a member of the elite Gourmand Club and a regular lunch partner for Field Marshal Viscount Lord Montgomery, victor of El Alamein, and now chairman of governors of the school, on which he lavished all the attention he had earlier expended on his military campaigns.

Despite Montgomery's assurance to each of us that the best thing we could do after leaving school was to undertake, joyfully and purposefully, our National Service (two years conscription was still compulsory in the UK 13 years after the end of the War), virtually every one of us was determined to go to university and thereby defer military service by at least three years, in the hope that by then it would have ceased to exist. Despite my desire to travel and my sense of social responsibility, I had no wish to risk my life for two years in Kenya where the British Army was defending our declining colonial interest by fighting the Mau Mau. I went to the first university that offered me a place without thinking too carefully about what this might involve. Coming from a school with strong church connections, it was assumed that St John's College, Durham, a theological college which was starting to offer full degree courses would suit me well. It did not. I was bored intellectually and spiritually almost suffocated by the cosy, conventional aspirations of a way of life that I had, all unwittingly, grown away from.

One very practical thing remained from my life at school as I started at university. On the last night of the school play several of us, having indulged in far too much cheap sherry underneath the stage on the last night of the production, pledged to each other that we would spend the subsequent summer, the first after leaving school, living as an expedition on an uninhabited island. It could have been simply a passing dream, something forgotten as the hangover wore off, but it stuck for the whole of that year in which we scattered to different universities across the country. I gradually assumed the role of leader.

To each of us in different ways it was a powerful dream, an opportunity to break out and do something that really interested us. We selected the island of Rhum on the West coast of Scotland, north of the Ardnamurchan peninsula, and south of Skye, one of the largest, yet least inhabited, of the Inner Hebrides. It is an island of some 60 square miles with several mountains over 2,500 feet high, and is home to several thousand red deer. It had a tiny human population of 16 people. In reality we knew very little about the Hebrides, or its flora or fauna, or about our own self-defined research topic (parasites on red deer), or about surviving as a group of ten highly argumentative individuals living under primitive conditions in tents which only just survived several strong gales. When the fishing boat landed us on the beach with all our supplies for four weeks we had no real idea of what we were in for. When the boat came back a month later I knew I had changed. I knew I needed the stimulation of people who weren't afraid to be inquisitive, who were prepared to be moved by beauty, and were prepared to share their ideas. This was more intellectually and physically challenging than anything I had experienced at school. I knew I needed a way of life not confined within a single discipline for I was almost as much an historian as I was an embryonic geographer. I would have loved also to have been an artist, and I was ashamed at my lack of knowledge of science. Running through all that, I knew I had to be useful; life just to please myself would be empty. The influence of my father's vocationalism ran strongly within me. At the age of 20 I had got to be less deferential, and make up my mind for myself. These thoughts were to be the dreams of the day, not of the dusty recesses of the night. A few days later I wrote a deferential letter to the principal of the college requesting a year's leave of absence to work things out. He replied saying he could not understand my motives and suggested that if I did not return forthwith he would refer my case to the military authorities, and no doubt I would then enjoy my two years of military adventure.

So I resigned from St John's and began a desperate search for another university. In the meantime, so as not to be a cost to my parents, I took a 12 month post as an unqualified teacher in a small preparatory school, Lawrence House in Lytham St Anne's, teaching English and history to boys between the ages of 9 and 13, for which I received £105 per term together with my food and lodging. With rumours of the imminent ending of National Service, universities were under considerable pressure from a greatly enhanced cohort of potential students for the following year. My case looked hopeless. It was hard to express in a simple statement on an application form why it was that, if one university had not suited me, I should find another one more congenial. Was anybody prepared to take me seriously?

A friend from the Rhum expedition had gone across the sea to Trinity College, Dublin, the university founded by Queen Elizabeth I to support the Protestant cause amongst her Irish subjects. He reported favourably on his experiences, and suggested the university was looking to increase its numbers. That weekend, using my first month's pay cheque from the school, I flew to Ireland. I was enchanted by Dublin, and by Trinity College in particular. With buildings dating from the early seventeenth century, Trinity sits in the very centre of Dublin, just down College Green from the Castle, the ultimate symbol of British rule that had ended with the Treaty of 1921. All around the university in various stages of decay, and occasional prosperity, were the Georgian streets and squares of a city that had, until the 1830s, been the second largest in the British Empire. Beyond Dublin were the Wicklow Mountains and then, beyond the Pale, was the Ireland of the Celt.

The student body as I saw it that weekend was like nothing I had experienced before. It was slightly older than its counterpart in England (few were under 20 years of age), and was extremely diverse. About a third came from beyond the British Isles - Americans with Irish connections, children of diplomats who had travelled the world, and people from the international business community. In the past few years there had been a significant increase in the number of English and Northern Irish students, reflecting the lessening tension then being experienced with the IRA. A third were Irish, many of whom came from the small and declining Anglo-Irish Protestant community (many of whom still lived in castles and stately homes of an earlier era, but could no longer afford the staff to keep them in the style they had long since lost), while a few were Catholics who were more influenced by Trinity's social status than by the annual encyclical of the Catholic Archbishop of Dublin stating that attendance at such a university was a mortal sin. It was indeed a heady mix.

Later that day I sought out the most senior member of staff I could find - it was late on a Saturday - and only the junior dean was in residence. The JD grilled me on my reasons for looking for a change in university, pressed my interest in history (his own subject), expressed a range of interesting perspectives on Anglo-Irish relations ... and then said I could have a place to read general studies in the following academic year. We shook hands and he clapped me on the shoulder and wished me well. I went out into the gathering darkness of a Dublin evening and had my first pint of Guinness in a real Irish pub, The Old Stand, little believing my good fortune.

Paper work, however, was a different matter. For weeks I searched the post for the promised letter of confirmation. The newspapers were full of the imminent end of conscription. My birth month, it appeared, would be the last to be called up. Still nothing came from Dublin and the tension made it hard to concentrate on learning how to teach. One morning I received a brown envelope from the Ministry of Defence telling me to report for my two-year period of conscription in three weeks time. Later that same day, by the very next post, I had a further letter from the Ministry cancelling the notice "for at least the foreseeable future". Three days later I had confirmation of the offer from Dublin. For the second time I had taken control of my destiny. Now it was up to me.

*                    *                    *

My family moved from Portsmouth to a parish in Essex, about 35 miles from London, and a place we had spent two very happy holidays. For several hundred years it had been one of the best endowed rectories in England and included a six acre garden, a lake complete with island, a bridge, a mulberry tree, a decaying tennis court and a walled kitchen garden with paths bordered by miniature boxwood hedges. It was an enormous, timeless, gracious place. In mid-summer it was quite glorious but, with a salary now only half of what it had been 50 years before, and costs having risen tenfold, winter was a totally different experience. My parents could afford to keep a fire in only one of the 14 fireplaces and stretched their resources to carpet and curtain the main rooms. We loved it. My father, then in his mid-40s and still very much a countryman at heart, relished his new life as a country priest. He talked the language both of the farmers and of the expanding professional classes who were buying country cottages, and commuting to London throughout the week.

Easter was fast approaching and I was basking in a confidence that had arrived with my letter of confirmation from Dublin. I was preparing to go to Scotland three days later to make arrangements to take some of the pupils on a summer camp when I was called out of class to take a call on the staff room telephone. It was our family doctor. "I don't want to alarm you, but your father has had an attack of jaundice and I think it would help your mother if you came home for a few days to be with her." I returned home the next morning, thinking only of the rearrangements I would have to make for Scotland, and was shocked to see how ill my father was. Later that afternoon he was taken into hospital hardly conscious and next morning the hospital said they thought he had a terminal cancer. Instantaneously we saw his life collapse and all our individual aspirations paled into insignificance. I was terrified. Four days later, shortly after eight o'clock in the morning on Easter Day, my mother shook me by the shoulder to wake me up. I was conscious of bright sun coming through the window. "The hospital has just phoned, Daddy died 20 minutes ago. We had better go and wake Michael and Susan and tell them."

My mother was 43, my brother 17 and my sister 14. I was 20 and juggling my university and life options. The pastoral arrangements of the Church of England were archaic, and spoke of a different age. We had just three months in which to vacate the vast, glorious rectory in which all our savings had gone for the carpets and curtains. Where we went was our own responsibility. A supplementary shock was to discover that my father's pension was worth exactly £60 a year.

I was stunned, but never once did I think someone else would sort this out for me. I was indebted to the little traumas earlier in my life and was immensely grateful for the simple, uncomplicated faith that I had caught from my father. The hardest moment was two days later when I went to see my grandfather - my father's father - and sit with him while all the grief of losing his only son, who he had never really understood, came to the surface.

No child ever forgets even the tiniest detail of a parent's funeral and I guess it is an event we each fear from our earliest childhood days of consciousness. It was not until that day that I realised just how special my father was to other people, nor did I really understand until then just what that precious, if subsequently overused, word "community" can really mean. It was not just we, the family, who were stunned, it was the village, and people from neighbouring villages and towns who were grieving as well. Realising that I was sharing my grief, I felt more able to cope.

The whole village seemed to be lining the road to the twelfth century Norman church for the funeral, and the local policemen saluted the coffin as it went into the sanctuary. Every seat in the church was taken, and visitors from far and wide lined the churchyard path. The bishop conducted the service which was as much about the parish reaching out to support us, as it was about celebrating my father's life.

"Do you realise," said one farmer, "your father died just as priests in their parishes all over the country were celebrating the first mass of Easter? God surely has a purpose for your father far greater than we can ever understand. How it all works out just beats me. I am not really a religious person, but surely He has a purpose for you too."

Later a man I did not recognise came up to me. He was both the undertaker and a local builder, as had been his father and his father before that. "Your father was a special man. He helped many people. If you need any help, please ask me. I expect you'll have to move out of the big house, and maybe you'll have to do up a smaller place for your mum. You're a strong young man, and probably as good with your hands as was your Dad. If you need any advice, at any time, on doing up an old place, just let me know. I'll show you how to do it." Old Mr Roast was to make as much of a difference on my life, as Old McFadgen's wood carving lessons had done a dozen years before.

Several weeks later he helped us find a row of three old cottages on the corner of a field, three or four miles away from the rectory. They were dilapidated and the local farmer, who was about to pull them down, was prepared to sell them to us for a reasonable price. Each had two rooms downstairs, and two upstairs. Mr Roast prodded around. He tapped the plaster, stuck his penknife into the windowsills and doorframes, climbed up the chimney stack and found a way into a hidden attic. "Buy it," he said, "it's much older than the farmer thinks. You'll be able to get a grant to put in water and electricity. You'll have to work hard; it'll hurt your back, and strengthen your muscles." So, for the long summer holiday before starting at Trinity, I became an apprentice builder. Mr Roast was as good as his word. Twice a week he came out to inspect and advise on my progress. Never once did he charge me, neither would he accept even the smallest present. "You're the one at the moment who needs the help," was all he said. Initially it was depressing work; the first stage in renovating an old property only serves to make a derelict house look even worse than before and he made me pay attention to the foundation, the damp course, the roof and the rainwater gullies. "Stop the moisture coming up, and the rain water coming down," he advised.

My confidence grew. I am not sure the rest of the family understood why. All that effort to so little apparent effect. But I was learning my task, and I was starting to think as Mr Roast thought and as my father would have thought. Often I would stop and amongst the dust and rubble and think of my father pondering what he would have told me to do. Often it was as if he were with me, smiling at my efforts to teach myself. I started on the internal work, and began to join some of the smaller rooms together. As I knocked off the plaster (a terrible job) I uncovered numerous heavy oak studs, four inches by seven inches, on the verticals, and with heavier transverse beams. It took me ages to get the first one out, and as I did so a simple pewter spoon fell out of the daub (the clay and plaster filling between the beams). I picked it up and looked at it thoughtfully. This was no eighteenth century farm cottage, as the farmer had suggested, but rather, given one of the window frames I had uncovered earlier that day, it was a relatively early Tudor building - certainly of a period before glass was used in windows. It was no less than 400 years old, and possibly more. The spoon was probably the same age. Mr Roast and I examined the roofline more carefully. There, at either end of the Southwest/Northeast alignment ridge to the main roof, were two oak in-filled hips masking air-vents about 12 inches high and two feet wide at the base.

"What's that for?" I asked. Mr Roast looked at me, surprised I thought at my lack of knowledge.

"Did you ever see drawings of old Saxon halls in your history books back when you were at school? In the years before they understood how to build proper chimneys they built their roofs like this so that the wind would blow in on one side, and expel the smoke on the other. I am not saying this house is Saxon, but this part of the building is certainly very early Tudor, if not older." Shortly after this we called in the county historians. For the better part of a day they crawled all over the building measuring, photographing, and sampling. Their conclusions? The end section, the oldest part, was possibly the missing manor house of the village recorded in the *Domesday Book* of 1084. I was amazed. This house that I was bringing back to life had been around through all those centuries of history that I had studied in school. Who knew what human drama and tragedy had been enacted in these little rooms?

As I worked, and my muscles ached, I had increasing admiration for those craftsmen who had first put all this together. I would have loved to have known more. All I could do was respect them for the quality of their workmanship, hidden for so long but having stood up to the test of every storm in maybe 900 years. Would that my skills were as good.

After three months of back-breaking work two thirds of the house was ready to move into. There had been insufficient time to put in the bathroom and the toilet, but there was now electricity, running water and the most primitive of drainage systems. For three months the rest of the family would have to use a chemical toilet, and go to friends in the village for baths, but I had to leave for Dublin the following weekend to begin my new life. Over the Christmas holidays I could learn to build a bathroom and plumb that up - no sweat. I now knew what I was doing.

The move from the rectory to our new house was traumatic, but less so I think for myself than for my mother, brother and sister. I was leaving a house that we all loved, but I was welcoming everyone into a new home that I and the unknown craftsmen of all those centuries before had prepared for them. Now I could enjoy getting back to the life of being a student. It was only years later that I realised just what had happened in those months. I had passed from a boy to a man, yes, but it was more than that. I had taken control of my own life because I had learnt how to make sense of things around me. I knew how to think beyond the normal parameters. I was able to find unusual solutions and I believed that I was part of something bigger than myself. It was several months later that my grief finally surfaced. I was walking by myself one Sunday afternoon in Phoenix Park in Dublin, and I passed the zoo. I stopped to look through the railings and, amongst the crowds, I saw a father with his young son walk by, talking excitedly. I froze and remembered the day, eleven years before when my father had walked me through that zoo as well, and we too had talked and talked. Then I started to cry and all the tears I had held back for months while taking the strain for the family broke out. For a couple of hours I felt awful but then a strange peace came over me. Becoming tough had not destroyed my deeper emotions.

*      *      *

I had changed more than I could at the time have comprehended as a result of that year out. It was not just the sudden death of my father and the need to create a new family home from scratch, that had done this. It had been the experience of earning my own living at that small preparatory school, and discovering that I actually enjoyed teaching, and seemed to have an easy empathy with young children. Putting the two together gave me a maturity, and a sense of direction, that before I had obviously lacked.

Within three weeks of returning from the Rhum expedition, I was doing my first weekend duty at school, and found myself for hours on end patrolling the corridors of the school, and talking with small groups of youngsters. Conversation came easily. "What did you do during the summer holidays?" I would ask and they recounted visiting grandparents, going to the south of France, or touring museums. "It was sort of fun," they would say, "but often it got boring. We'd have liked to have done something really exciting."

I told them what I had just done on Rhum. I described ordering all the food, supplies and the equipment; sailing off on the fishing boat to Shahman Inisr; of the stags baying to each other from the hill tops; of climbing Hallival, and Askival, and of learning about the Vikings who had built their duns on the rocky promontories. The boys' eyes sparkled. It was only a small school, and quickly the headmaster recognised that I had a way of talking with the boys that he felt he ought to encourage. "Why don't you collect all your slides together and give a lecture to the senior boys next Saturday evening?" he suggested.

I did. Several of the fathers came to listen as well, and I must have spun a good yarn because two of the fathers - men who had been together as boys years before in the same school - stayed behind and suggested that perhaps, as I was there for the year, I should be asked to take as many of the boys as wanted to go, and camp on one of the smaller Hebridean Islands for two weeks during the next summer holiday. We started to plan and it was to visit the island of Raasay for which I had been intending to make the preliminary visit the week my father died.

I found huge satisfaction in my first year of teaching. It was helped by my being only a few years older than the oldest children themselves, but it was much more than that. While I had found the dogma of a Christian upbringing difficult to understand and accept, I had, nevertheless, a strong sense of my personal relationship with a God who I had experienced, but could never adequately explain. Intangible as that relationship was, it was the beginning of a framing principle that was to guide my life. "Love the Lord thy God, and thy neighbour as thyself." Searching to understand God, and my relationship to Him, and the universe around me, whilst also helping my neighbour, seemed to me to be a pretty good formula for an interesting life; a mixture of the inwardly reflective, with the pragmatics of daily life.

That year I learnt two other lessons. It was the advice of a visiting headmaster at that prep school's speech day. "Whatever career you decide to follow, make sure you have at least two hobbies which capture your imagination. Stick with them. Whatever happens to your career, whether it goes well or badly, so sink yourself in your interests that they tide you over life's inevitable upsets. Take these hobbies seriously, love them and indulge them. It is these interests that will largely make you who you will become."

It made a lot of sense. I had sort of known this already but his advice legitimated the enthusiasm I had already for wood work and for travelling. That headmaster was right. A lifetime of following such interests has indeed made me who I am every bit as much as my formal qualifications and the progression marked out on my CV.

That second lesson came from a precocious, but totally spontaneous and enthusiastic 11-year old, Timothy who put this into its proper perspective for me, late on a wet, cold Friday afternoon. It was the last lesson of the day, and I had already exhausted my creativity in several earlier lessons. I was tiring, and the class was already well in advance of its schedule. "Let's have a debate, sir," said one. "Let's talk about space travel," said another. Seeing an easy way of getting through the last lesson of the day, I agreed. It could be fun. All kinds of issues that lively 11 year-olds can envisage started to emerge. Would it ever be possible to go faster than the speed of light, and if so, might we find a way of going back into time? What was beyond the last star? What sort of energy source could sustain such long-term travel? Then someone posed a more difficult question. "What would people look like on another planet?" Most of the boys looked perplexed, except for Timothy who had already contributed more to the discussion than the others. Only his hand shot up into the air. In his excitement to answer the question he could hardly keep still. "Sir, sir, I know, sir." The mood of the class was turning against him. I tried to find someone else to speculate on an answer. None came. Slightly reluctant I turned back to Timothy. "It's easy sir, it's easy. They'd look like us." The other boys groaned; Timothy had overplayed his hand. Timothy looked perplexed and obviously hurt. He needed a little help. Gently I asked him to explain. He brightened up. "Well, sir, it's easy because, in *Genesis*, it says that God made man in his own image so, if we all look like God, so would everybody else living on the other planets look like God." At a level of profound truth, that boy said more to me about the sanctity of human life than anything I had heard in the theological college, or from a pulpit. To me my neighbour, for all his faults, smells and prejudices, had to be seen as another son of God.

\*               \*               \*

That summer term, three months after my father had died and just before I started to work on converting the old cottages for my mother, I took 35 of these boys to the Island of Raasay, midway between Skye and the Applecross peninsula. For ten days we camped below the old castle of Brochel, sitting atop an old volcanic plug of pre-Cambrian times. It was uninhabited by then, but still - with only a little imagination - alive with the dramas that had been played out there when the Redcoats, in the months that had followed Culloden in 1745, had pulled down much of the castle and had fired all the houses. Alive too with memories of the clearances in the nineteenth century, and the more recent activities of submarines - some, it was suggested, being Russian - lying in a deep ocean trench but a mile off shore.

A month later while I was busy uncovering the oak beams in the cottages, I received a letter from the father of one of the boys, a doctor living in Preston. It was a nice letter, a letter of gratitude for the experience his son had had on Raasay. "It's not just our son who wants to come with you on a real expedition. I have spoken to the parents of six of the others, and they would like their sons to come as well. Perhaps in two years' time, when they will be 15, would be better than next year. If you do decide to go ahead with this, do count on us to help you get this organised. Kind regards, and many thanks ..." I kept the letter, resolving at least to keep in touch from university with as many of the boys as I could, as we each started on our separate careers. Thoughts about an expedition would have to wait until later.

\*               \*               \*

In my ignorance of the Irish education system I had enrolled to study a joint course comprising three humanities subjects, English, geography and history rather than in a single honours course. Towards the end of my first term we all had to write a graduation essay. I remember the topic well, but I am still not sure of the answer I should have given. The title was this: "The roots of civilisation are 12 inches deep - discuss." With my confidence of being an apprentice builder as well as a student who had made it to university after a somewhat unusual set of circumstances, I wrote, I think, an inspired essay.

The university obviously approved and shortly after this, the geography and history departments both invited me to transfer to single-subject honour courses. I had, however, no difficulty in declining and, in doing so, made the third significant decision of my short career. I wanted a broad perspective on life and on how people came to be as they are. Three subjects were hardly enough – I would have been delighted to have added a science as well because the search for connections interested me far more than the quest for analysis and specialisation. So began a fascinating four year degree course, to which later was added a fifth year that enabled me to do research.

I rowed for the University Junior Eight at regattas throughout the South of Ireland. I played squash, joined the debating society and enjoyed arguments at all hours. President De Valera, the scourge of the English in the twenties and thirties, still attended teas at College Races in June, and English and American politicians accepted our invitations to address meetings, and then slip off to the Curragh for the races, or to some churchyard to trace their ancestors. Trinity was conditioned by the assumptions of a leisured, property-owning class. It was a place for people to grow up and academic efforts were only part of the mix. There should be plenty of time to follow one's own interests, and to understand the perspectives of others. In a way in which was already becoming rare in the rest of Britain, Trinity – and probably St Andrew's – were still about a broad, general education, and about a quality of life that helped give its students a breadth of interest in civilisation and world affairs. The students were members of a fine, well-established university in the very heart of a small, independent country which was fast coming to accept its world role. We felt that we would, one day, matter.

After my first year I returned to Scotland and, with a map, and a rucksack and a MacBraynes' timetable for the ferries and began to search for a suitable location for the expedition I was thinking of setting up the following year when those boys would be 15.

The Island of Mull would be a good place, I thought, in which to immerse active and impressionable youngsters in the mid-twentieth century. To the west of Ulva, linked by a short bridge, "a bridge over the Atlantic ocean" as one of the few remaining crofters referred to it, was the much smaller island of Gometra, which also possessed a well sheltered harbour, overlooked by the ruins of a viking fort. I found a perfect campsite, and a landowner intrigued by the possibility that her islands were a place to be explored. Above the proposed site were two very shapely hills, one of which was called Sgur nan Ogg; the Gaelic meant nothing to me. The crofter smiled. "In the English that means the paps of the young girl. Your boys will like it here."

They did. Two years after the scout camp on Raasay, six of us, all still university students, founded the School's Hebridean Society. At the time it was little more than a legal device to authenticate our existence as an organisation and to get insurance for our proposed expedition, but the organisation was to last for 27 years. The 30 youngsters who went to Gometra in 1962 were the first of more than 4,000 who, over subsequent years, were to travel to some of the most remote corners of the Hebridean islands, experience a variety of weather and other conditions and all come back deeply influenced by living amid such beauty, and having battled the wind and tide around some of the most tortuous coastline in Europe.

Studying in Dublin, it was not immediately obvious to me how I was to raise the number of youngsters from the half dozen I knew of to the 30 that we needed for an expedition. One of the fathers suggested that I should visit his son's public school one Saturday evening and talk to all the 15 year-olds about what I was proposing. Knowing the head master well, the father organised this at short notice, and soon after that I flew out of Dublin one Saturday morning to London. I was met by a chauffeur driven car, dined well by the headmaster and then ushered into a lecture hall to be faced with more than a hundred sceptical 15 year-olds. Suddenly the second year undergraduate had to become a salesman. I did well, but had to limit the response from that school to the first five boys who were able to get their parent's signature on to a hastily devised application form. To my delight I was paid the same lecture fee that would have gone to a visiting professor, admiral, or politician and the head said he'd arrange for presentations in other schools. He was as good as his word, and by Christmas we had all the youngsters we needed. And, for the first time since my father died, I had a growing bank balance which meant I was no longer preoccupied with the fear of becoming penniless. I was learning about marketing, and how to tell a good story in public. None of this was on the university curriculum, of course, but it was easily accepted that this was what an energetic student would do and my geography lecturer became one of our four patrons.

The Gometra expedition was a success. I was able to find another eight university students, each of whom had some skill or interest that would be immediately useful to the youngsters, and who were willing to spend the better part of three weeks, voluntarily, on such an expedition. "We're not teachers," I emphasised, time and time again, "and they're not pupils. We're all individuals some of whom have skills and interests that others would like to copy." I quoted loosely from Winnie-the-Pooh: "an expedition is a long line of everybody ... we are all off to discover ... whatever it is that we are going to discover ... I am not sure really. At any rate, I'll carry the food."

That summer we climbed mountains and made maps. We went fishing, and caught very little. We were joined for a few days by Launcelot Fleming, then Bishop of Norwich, and the one-time geologist for the British Trans-Antarctic

Expedition who had so impressed me ten years before when, as a little boy in Portsmouth, I learnt that he actually talked to the King and stayed at Sandringham. He had helped found Voluntary Service Overseas and, with Prince Philip, had been active in setting up the Outward Bound Movement. Each night we gathered around our tables made from driftwood rescued from the beaches. Sometimes we sang a hymn, sometimes someone told a story, or said a prayer, but mostly we just talked as only young people revelling in their youth, physical fitness and confidence in the future, know how to do. "We must do this again, and again," nearly everyone said as they consciously found interests and enthusiasms they had never known before.

The following year we thought we could split our team and organise two parallel expeditions for different age groups. The year after that we had four expeditions and at that level we stabilised. For a voluntary organisation, operated by university students in their spare time, it was a formidable activity, involving about 150 people each year. Any larger and it would have become formalised and lose, we feared, its spontaneous, uninhibited character.

In my third year at Trinity I submitted a paper about Gometra as a microcosm of the way social and economic factors had played out in a small region of the Hebrides. The Irish University's Geographical Congress awarded me first prize and my confidence grew. I was already more than an academic; I was a competent public speaker and while I was very interested in my topic I was able to describe this with a level of professional detachment. There were other things that interested me more than simply geography and I did not feel that my future career rode simply on academic success alone. I was far more interested in the excuse which expeditions gave me to create exciting opportunities for youngsters to learn more about themselves and the world around them. I'm sure now that my success was as much to do with my ability to speak as it was to describe the ideas. I was learning fast. Shortly after this I was elected chairman of the Geographical Society and organised a number of field trips to interesting places around Ireland. Academic life was - or certainly seems so now in retrospect - extraordinarily gentle and only moderately demanding. If there was an early morning rush to find the best seat in the Reading Room, it was every bit as much on the part of the glamorous to be seen, as it was on the part of the rest of us to get the best seats to observe the various comings and goings. In that strange half-light before the so-called sexual revolution of the late sixties the Reading Room was - and was accepted to be so - a veritable human cattle market.

There were, probably, more memorable lectures then when lecturers didn't have to justify their productivity. Donald O'Sullivan, who lectured in a supplementary course on early twentieth century history, stood out as a man who had lived what he was teaching. As a young British Naval officer he had been on the bridge with Admiral Jellicoe at the Battle of Jutland, the last massed Naval engagement. In 1918 he had joined the British Foreign Office but, as an Irish resident, he had transferred to the embryonic Irish Foreign Service in 1922. He had served in Washington and was in Berlin when Hitler came to power. He was an observer at Bretton Woods, and had been at the San Francisco Conference in 1944. He had spent much time in central Europe, and had known the Czech foreign minister, Jan Masaryk, in the months before he had been driven to commit suicide when the Communists took control in 1948. Quietly, and without any self-importance, he told history from the perspective of an observer who was also a participant. In his declining years it was as if he felt an obligation to share with us experiences which, without him, we would never really have considered. He was, to me, a superb storyteller, a polished craftsman of the finest kind.

President Kennedy visited Dublin in October 1963. The university, which would never have acknowledged his ancestors when they fled the country in the 1860s, presented him with an honorary degree. Just under a month later in the same room and at the same time of day, I was to introduce the leader of the recent British Antarctic expedition to the university's Geographical Society. Moments before this was due to start, news came through of Kennedy's assassination. It fell to me to make the announcement and - hardly knowing what to say - I grasped the same lectern that Kennedy had grasped less than four weeks before. I felt part of history and at that moment our nationalities did not count. The following morning Donald O'Sullivan came in to the lecture room and, as usual, walked apparently confidently to the lecture desk. He looked up at us, his confidence suddenly failing him. "Please join me in standing to honour the life of Jack Kennedy..." As we rose in silence his voice trailed off. He was silently crying. I doubt if there was a dry eye left in the room. "It is better if we go now," he said, "out of respect to Jack Kennedy anything I might say now would not be good enough. Today's lecture is cancelled, I will find another time to talk with you." He was, I remember thinking at the time, crying not only for Kennedy but for all those other needless deaths he had witnessed. A civilised society, he helped me see that morning, ignores its history at its peril.

The geography department started to pressurise me. Surely, they said, it would be in my interest to undertake research for a master's degree? If I would do this, I could study virtually any subject I wanted. "What about," I suggested with tongue in cheek, "the social and economic development of the north end of the island of Mull from 1789 to the present day?" To my amazement they agreed. "You could do that by spending the vacations working on the island of Mull, and the term time studying in the university library." A nightly sailing from Dublin to Glasgow, and a twice-weekly sailing from there to Tobermory would make the travel arrangements quite feasible, I thought. But I was not quite persuaded. As attractive as all that might sound, to produce a thesis about an island very much on the far edge of importance, which might indeed never even be read, did not truly excite me. I procrastinated, not sure of the direction to take.

So I decided instead to investigate the university's department of education. This was a dreary place, I quickly discovered and concluded that it could hold no possible excitement. My interest in feeding young people's confidence by giving them real challenges and opportunities seemed a thousand miles away from the room in which I met with the professor one grey February afternoon. I could not get out quickly enough. "Stop," exclaimed Professor Crawford, "It's impatient people like you that education needs. We have a pretty rotten system for most young people, and someone is going to have to do something about it. Educationalists alone will never do it. I know that. It will need people who understand life, as well as schools. Don't just study education, do that research degree as well. I think I could get the university's approval for you to be registered for both courses concurrently. Education lectures take place in the afternoon, only during term time. You would need to do two days a week of teaching practice. You're strong. Spend the vacations on your favourite island, and the term times here in Dublin. Split the term between two days in school, and three days in the library, and then do the six hours of lectures." I was taken aback. Who said academics were not flexible?

My last year at university was indeed busy. The education side was easy - too easy. The departmental staff were happy to assume that intelligence was an innate, and largely unchangeable, commodity. What mattered for a teacher was to find out as early as possible what was the real potential of each pupil, and then provide each with an appropriate education - technical studies for some, academic studies for others. Learning was not an awesome potential, it was in fact all treated in a highly mechanical manner. These were the days when behaviourism was in the ascendant - what pupils knew was the result of what they were taught. We had extensive lectures on Pavlov's dogs. I found the whole course clashed with my own experience, and what I was already learning from young people, yet no one seemed deeply concerned. Once we passed our exams we would teach as we wished.

The research was too open-ended to be manageable, and the environment on Mull too seductive to give the work the serious attention it needed. Mull is a beautiful but strange island. Saint Columba would have seen Ben More from his cloistered cell on Iona every morning as he arose early 1,400 years ago, just as I did from Gometra. The Vikings knew the island well, as did the Celts before them. But the stuffing had been knocked out of Mull in the nineteenth century when the lairds, forsaking their obligations to their people, sold off the land to sheep breeders. Later the island was divided into five or six large holdings on which mid-Victorian entrepreneurs built extraordinary country homes and castles. After the Second World War these estates, too, were broken down into sub-units of little more than two to three thousand acres, leaving these much reduced holdings to attract military men seeking to eke out their pensions in what was to become an ever increasing form of genteel poverty. They were to get ever more intolerant of each other. Mull was to become known as "that mess of colonels".

This was not the place in which to put down my roots. I had had enough of looking backwards. I was still fascinated by people and ideas. I wanted to be learning with, and from, young people. I did not yet see myself as a lifelong teacher. But it was time to move on. I felt strong enough now to be really useful.

# 3
# Becoming a Teacher

My friends thought my studying both for a higher degree in education and for a masters degree in geography was a compromise, something to do with my not being able to make up my mind about what career I would eventually follow. Was I going to be a teacher or some kind of entrepreneur? In fact, my dual stranded post-graduate studies set a pattern that I've stuck with ever since and I realised I had to have an interesting, absorbing life of my own beyond schools if I were ever to be any good as a teacher. After all, most young people would make their future lives far removed from schools and I would need to live in that world as well.

To earn some extra money at the beginning and end of each of the university terms I worked as a temporary supply teacher (the lowest possible post in the educational hierarchy), substituting for teachers who were ill or just tired out. It was at Rainsford secondary modern school near our home in Essex, the school serving the bottom 60 or 70 per cent of the ability range. Teachers were unsure what to do with the pupils who mostly left school with precious few qualifications, a rudimentary education and little belief in their ability to shape their futures. Several weeks after President Kennedy's death, I was back in that school the Friday before the end of the Christmas term. "We're short staffed," Mr Middleton, the deputy head, explained. "I'll have to ask you to take over two classes of 15 year-olds for the afternoon. Do anything you like to keep them quiet. If it gets too difficult for you to handle, I'll take over midway".

I went into the oversized class unprepared, hoping for some form of inspiration to get me started. One boy had with him an abbreviated version of *The Colditz Story*, an account of how prisoners of war escaped from a German prison camp. Noting my interest the boy opened up a bit and asked, "Why did there have to be a war in 1939?" It was a red herring, a conversation starter that the class hoped would get me talking, and take any pressure off them to do anything serious that afternoon. I saw that I could use this. Improvising as only a young active mind reasonably used to children can, I got them to note a number of dates, and events, and then got each to recall as many family experiences as they could to fill in the human detail behind those events. Quickly I gained their interest; they were able to talk in class about things they heard their parents talking about at home, and they were consciously making connections between what had previously been disconnected ideas.

I divided the blackboard into six columns, one for each year of the war. In white we listed events as the boys could remember them: Dunkirk, U-boats in the Atlantic, the Blitz, Normandy, the Russian Campaign, El Alamein. In red we listed personal events: "Mum was evacuated from London to Scotland", "Dad was called up and sent to India ("Please, sir, why did he go to India if we were fighting the Germans?"), "My aunt met a GI and afterwards went to live in Alabama," and so on. Most of them did the homework I set, once they found that their own stories, their experiences, and the experience of their families, were being taken seriously. They had responded with a maturity that left other teachers incredulous.

In 1997 I thought back to this lesson when I heard a neuroscientist tell an education conference that, "the brain has evolved over the millennia to be a multi-faceted, multi-tasked organism predisposed to thinking about new data and ideas from various perspectives. The brain works in terms of wholes and parts simultaneously. The glory of human learning is that it is essentially a complex, messy, non-linear process." Yes, those boys learning about World War II and their families was evidence of how learning takes place with myriad personal connections.

By treating the pupils as intelligent, inquisitive and essentially good people, I had invited them to learn, and they had responded enthusiastically. Years later, during the Falkland War, a railway porter at King's Cross Station came up to me. "I know you, don't I? You're the man who got us all to think about the Second World War, aren't you? You got us to think about why people go to war. That must have been at least 20 years ago but I've been thinking a lot about that with the newspapers full of our army going down to the Falklands. It seems to me as if it's all a load of hype, and out-of-date pride being hurt." That meeting was a rare treat and I've been lucky in having several such conversations years, sometimes many years, after an event with a group of children that obviously had been a turning point for them. "Most teachers," said Richard Livingstone, the president of Corpus Christi College, Oxford, in 1940, "don't live to see the full fruits of their teaching. An oak tree is a long time in growing."

*          *          *

In the Spring term a friend showed me an advertisement for a geography teacher needed at the Manchester Grammar School. At first I did not even give it a second thought. I still was not sure that I wanted to become a professional teacher and, having grown up in the south of England, and now living in the fading glory of Georgian Dublin, Manchester was the grim Cottonopolis - the world capital of the cotton trade. To an ex-public schoolboy, well-versed in liberal traditions of a previous age, I believed the highly selective grammar schools (Manchester Grammar School took the top half of the top one per cent of the assumed intelligence range) had pupils who were too clever by half. It stood at the pinnacle of a meritocracy and, as such, threatened many comfortable upper-middle-class academics. Anyway, the advertisement had one sentence that held my attention: "Plenty of opportunity for an appropriate candidate to develop overseas field work".

"I'll bet you a couple of pints of Guinness you won't dare apply," the friend taunted, sensing my indecision.

"Done," I replied and posted my letter of application that evening.

True to form it was raining when I arrived in Manchester. The school buildings were well maintained but strictly functional. Long corridors served identical classrooms, with padlocked coat lockers on each corner. It seemed cold, mechanical, clinical and far removed from the culture of Dublin. I was intimidated and ill at ease. Then the secretary assigned two sixth form students to show me around for half an hour. They were pleasantly self-assured young men who parried my questions about their school with further questions of their own about university life in Dublin, and about an article they had recently read about the Hebridean expeditions I had led. Slowly both the school buildings, and the framework of the school's curriculum, so meticulously set out in all the documents sent to me in advance, seemed far more meaningful and attractive. "Hope you decide to come," was their parting comment as they delivered me to the interview.

I was shown into a large, oak-panelled room typical of the 1930s style. There were three people there. Peter Mason, the High Master, a man in his mid-fifties with a shock of silver hair, whose considerable height did not disguise a certain deep-seated insecurity, rose to greet me. "I'm a classicist," he explained shortly, "so I've asked the head of geography to ask the technical questions. But first I must tell you that I know one of your referees very well. He speaks extremely highly of you." (That must be Launcelot Fleming, I thought to myself, the Bishop of Portsmouth.) "He says you are good with boys, and want to turn the world upside down. Could you survive in a grammar school?"

There was something in the way he had asked that question that instantly told me more about him than he might have realised. He was not personally satisfied, it appeared, as High Master of the most famous selective grammar school in Britain. The way he had spoken about my referee, about himself as being a classicist and not understanding geography (still not regarded as a real discipline), and his emphasis on the word grammar, alerted me instantly to his own sense of social failure at not having secured earlier the headship of a more conventional, upper-class, public school.

"Mr Mason is mad keen on general studies," the boys had said. "We all have to spend a fifth of our time studying a variety of topics which cross subject boundaries. We're not examined in them, so we don't take general studies as seriously as our other work. This is unfortunate, it really is, because general studies can be interesting, often more interesting than our specialised subjects." I found Peter Mason easy to talk with. Broadly based in his interests, the minutiae of a large modern institution did not greatly excite him. Eventually the head of geography interrupted in a tone of voice which registered an unease which, if I was not careful, would quickly lose me his possible support. In somewhat staccato tones he asked about the textbooks I preferred using. I could not reply with the same enthusiasm I had shown in talking about general studies. I was not winning his support, that was clear. So I pressed a question of my own about overseas fieldwork.

"Where were you expecting to go?" asked Peter Mason quickly, re-entering the conversation.

"Somewhere very different to anything we could experience in the UK certainly. Somewhere we could collect materials and information that we could use in our ordinary lessons to make the subject come alive."

The head of geography looked troubled; "Isn't that too ambitious for somebody just out of university?"

That was meant to slow me down. Was it assumed that only older people could be ambitious? Maybe I ought to withdraw from the interview; if this was the way things were to be done this would be no place for me. Peter Mason looked up and, without conversing with his staff, said, "How would you like a job here?" It was so direct, so unlike what I had expected, that again I parried.

"Well, I like the students I've met. I appreciate the emphasis on general studies, and provided I can organise overseas field work, then, yes, I'm interested".

"Good. Why don't you think of an expedition to Turkey? It's very different to Manchester certainly, and to the Hebrides which you obviously know well, and I don't know of any other schools that go that far. Harrow School goes to Iceland, but Turkey - somewhere around Mount Ararat perhaps - well, that would be very different".

I smiled. I had no idea that an interview could go like this. "Good," said Peter Mason, "That's a firm offer from me. Can I assume you'll accept?" I nodded, staggered at the pace at which my future was taking shape. "We'll write to you within a couple of days," said the third man, the senior master, Roger Stone, who in subsequent years showed me how to work with and understand other teachers. "If you could give us your formal acceptance directly after that, we'll draw up the contract".

We all shook hands. Back in Dublin my friends were incredulous. That was not the way they expected things to happen. Nor were they at all sure that a grammar school (despite the world wide reputation of MGS) was actually a socially acceptable job - to those of a conservative temperament such a school was a threat to the established order. "Darling," my mother said on the phone when I told her my news, "that's a grammar school. We had all expected that if you were going to become a teacher, it would have been at a public school." The mother of another student said: "Surely, John, that's not where the important people go, is it?"

*      *      *

"Not where the important people go."

To understand the tensions within English education, a brief excursion into history is essential. Until well into the nineteenth century most English people had less than two years formal education. Virtually all of the old market towns had small grammar schools, which served the needs of the merchant classes, and the minor gentry. Nineteenth century industrialisation changed all this. New sprawling industrial cities transformed much English countryside and as the rich grew richer, life in many of the cities became nasty and brutish. Wishing to withdraw their sons (daughters were not then matters of much concern) to more refined places of learning, the Victorians created the independent public schools which were fee-paying boarding schools, sometimes based on old well-established grammar schools. It created a kind of privileged education previously only available for the sons of the aristocracy at schools such as Eton, Winchester or Westminster. Most of these were in the wealthier south of England.

The pattern in the north was somewhat different. With fewer pretensions than their southern equivalents, the new northern gentry were more interested in extending the influence of the existing grammar schools, and establishing new ones, if necessary, so that their sons' education would not be too far removed from the mills that they themselves owned and managed. The Board of Education, looking always for cheap alternatives to starting new schools, encouraged this through a direct grant to meet a significant proportion of the costs of such schools. As a result Manchester Grammar School, originally founded in 1553, expanded rapidly in the late nineteenth century along with many other grammar schools in the Midlands and the industrial north.

In the early twentieth century, with a growing awareness of the significance of education, county grammar schools were built mainly in the more affluent new residential areas where it was assumed the more able youngsters were to be found. Later money was provided to extend the old elementary schools to cater for all other pupils up to the age of 12, then 14 and later 15. Such schools tended to be in the poorer, working class districts. Intelligence, it was comfortably assumed, was inherited; the children of the poorer classes were not thought to represent a good investment.

The 1944 Education Act strengthened and extended the network of local schools in ways which will become clearer later in this story. It also made such education free. The Act, however, did not replace the old direct grant grammar schools, nor did it touch the independent public schools, which remained funded entirely privately. Both kinds of schools selected their pupils on the basis of entrance examinations which were often more rigorous for the grammar schools than for the independent public schools, there being more talent in the country at large than there were parents who could afford boarding school fees.

By the late fifties grammar schools often set a higher academic standard than many of the public schools and the older direct grant schools were some of the most academically successful of all schools. Receiving their direct grant, and being able to charge additional modest fees they were seen to give excellent value to those who qualified for admission. MGS drew its pupils from the whole of Manchester and beyond, regardless of the fact that many of its pupils would have passed several county grammar schools everyday on their way to school. MGS creamed from a population of 1,500,000 regardless of parental income and its examination results were often as good as those of Eton or Winchester - pure talent some said, versus inherited privilege. As these direct grant schools were open to bright pupils regardless of parental status, the aspiring middle classes spurned them in favour of fee-paying schools where their sons would gain social privilege. These were the places where the important people went. In practice English education has operated in a form of free market (for those with the money) long before political theoreticians thought of promoting this as a guiding principle in the late nineteen-eighties in the United Kingdom and the nineties in the United States.

In later life, public school types often derided the direct grant grammar school, and characterised them as being places which concentrated excessively on academic affairs and teaching for the test - hence the feeling that their pupils were too clever by half. Public schools, on the other hand, prided themselves as being about something more broadly based, namely the education of the whole man. Meanwhile, further down the social pecking order, the county grammar school envied the direct grant school its ability to charge fees, as well as receiving a government grant, and in consequence its ability to attract the brightest pupils. Education as a form of social sorting is deeply ingrained in the English tradition.

MGS in 1965 was thriving amidst all this muddle. It had the best of all possible worlds and, though it could not have been a more exciting place in which to start teaching, it was clearly becoming an anachronism whose privileged existence was no longer justified by the needs of the time. Held very much on a pedestal for its academic achievements, it did not have many friends amongst other schools who saw their own opportunities limited by its very success.

*        *        *

By now I was sure that I wanted to teach, but I was not at all sure that I wanted to live the life of a teacher. Youngsters fascinated me; school routines bored me. The head of geography, my immediate superior, found me hard to deal with. He was a good man and loved forms, regular marks and grades, requests for stationery in triplicate, and arrangements for field trips made weeks in advance. He took his pastoral responsibility for me and another teacher most seriously and I should have been far more grateful; "Stay in your first job for two or three years," he'd say. "Move to a good job in another kind of school for the next five years. Then you'll be ready to apply for a head of department's job. Five or so years later you should look for a similar post in a prestigious school. Stay there long enough to show that you are good and then, in your late forties, you could be considered for a deputy headship of a relatively good school. After that it's up to chance." He was describing his own progress and I tried hard not to make my disagreement painful to him. He meant very well, yet I thought he was well and truly stuck. So did the youngsters who were intolerant of such routines, however well meant they were. Just obeying the rules takes you only so far.

It was obvious from the start that I did not conform to people's normal expectations of a teacher. I valued intuition higher than logic and intrinsic motivation more than any form of extrinsic reward. I enjoyed the rigors of particular disciplines but looked for linkages between subjects. Geography was the best subject for me to teach, as it was essentially about synthesis, peoples, policies and the environment. Yet I often thought my own discipline could well have been history or art or biology. These were conflicts which Donald O'Sullivan at Trinity had understood. All this would have been simple common sense to Old MacFadgen and Mr Roast. Already it troubled me that teaching was so heavily tied to formal instruction. Was it inevitable that classroom teaching eventually tired people out, and slowly throttled that spontaneity which, as I had seen so clearly on expeditions, was what warmed the interest of young learners when first they met the lively mind of an older expert? Most young teachers seemed to be lively and enthusiastic but the older teachers became, the more dependent they seemed to be on textbooks as a substitute for first hand experiences. Talking about what the textbook said in the lesson, they relied on pupils to paraphrase whole sections of this for their homework. Classroom activity quickly became repetitious. I feared ever becoming like that. Such fear was so strong that I nearly never became a teacher.

Unknowingly I was following principles that had been written about by the Russian psychologist, Vygotsky, who formalised what craftsmen had known for millennia. First a learner needs a sense of the significance of the work to be undertaken rather like the worker in a stone quarry who said his work was building a cathedral rather than merely squaring pieces of rock. Too many lessons in traditional classrooms focused on, say, sheep farming in Australia, rather than finding out what Australia, or sheep farming, meant to the individual learner. Successful teaching strategies require immediate recognition of the significance of a sub-task to the finished product, hence the rock that might become a cathedral. Teachers often have a touching, and misplaced, faith that six, eight or ten disconnected experiences add up in the child's mind to a form of reality transferred from teacher to pupil. That simply does not happen. Vygotsky also defined the kind of support I used to receive from Mr Roast as a form of cognitive scaffolding. Every learner needs just such sufficient outside support as he learns a new skill, to prevent him from making a mistake, but once that new skill is learnt then that support is withdrawn. It is no longer needed. If left in place for too long it removes from the learner the need to become self-supporting. Vygotsky called the third stage fading; the progressive testing of the learner's ability to perform at the new, higher, level. The fourth component Vygotsky identified was that of continuous dialogue; constant chatter between the apprentices, and between apprentice and craftsman about specifics, and about the relational, the unquantifiable, the intuitive. Vygotsky defined what craftsmen have always known; expertise can never be fully defined through instruction; much of it is intuitive. I could never have learnt to restore an old building from a text book, no matter how big and thorough it was, as well as I was able to learn by talking with Mr Roast. Measurements alone are not enough, you need to step back and size it all up. You need, as any sculptor knows, to be able to walk around and look at it from all angles. Mr Roast probably didn't even realise that he knew more than he could ever have written down.

I wanted my pupils to know how to walk around a problem and my best lessons were when I knew my material both from inside-out and round-about - and I was in a good mood. That was vital because teaching is a conscious act which you have to enjoy if it's to be of lasting value. My worst lessons were when I was unsure of the approach I should use and so wrote up copious notes in advance as a way of preparing myself. Then I got tongue-tied and the pupils quickly saw that this was not what actually mattered to me. Good pupils intuitively respect competent teachers in the same way that they see through those who appear weak and uncertain.

Years later I received a postcard from an ex-pupil by then living in Australia; "I thought you ought to know that I've lived here for three years and I've hardly ever seen a sheep. I don't think I've ever eaten mutton. And no one has even mentioned the Snowy Mountain hydroelectric scheme. So much for our geography textbook. But I did enjoy your lessons."

*     *     *

I started at Manchester Grammar School with an enormous advantage. The children were bright and well motivated, and knew they were expected to succeed. They were socially assured. "I'm Gareth," said the blonde-headed 12 year-old as I walked into my first class on the first day of term, "my friends call me Egg; actually I'm E G Jones." He grinned and pointed to the class who had been in the school for a whole year longer than me. They believed themselves to be, and looked, most superior. "We're Form 2A".

A week or so before the end of that first term we were studying maps of Manchester. Someone commented on what a very obvious feature the Manchester Ship Canal was when seen from the air. Most children had not flown at that stage, and they were intrigued. I remembered an advertisement I had seen in the Evening News, put in by a small airline, offering short, charter flights to make use of their spare capacity during the winter season. "What would your parents think if we tried to charter a plane for half an hour and flew over Manchester and possibly went as far north as the Lake District? We could then see all this for ourselves." There was a productive uproar and we organised a Christmas treat which, given the economies of the time, cost no more than a weekend in a modest hotel.

It was I who learned the biggest lesson. There were three Jewish boys in the class, boys from relatively comfortable homes. They spotted quicker than I that a couple of boys could not ask their parents to pay even that amount of money. On their own initiative the three of them organised the sale of lemonade at the classroom door after school most mornings, until they raised enough money to cover the cost of the other two. That class started to bond together and this bond has lasted now for thirty years and more.

Teaching the scholarship class, third year sixth formers, hoping to carry off the ultimate accolade of selective English secondary education, and win a scholarship to Oxford or Cambridge, was a lesson for me. "I'm Chris Whittaker," said a young man nearly my own height, as he shambled comfortably into the classroom minutes after I thought the lesson should have started. "You must be John Abbott. The others are just coming over from the common room. Sorry I'm late. I've just been practising my French horn for the concert on Friday." I did not know quite how to respond because, to him, this seemed not an excuse but a simple explanation. Unlike me he was not at a loss for words. "Was Trinity Dublin a good place to study geography? I'm trying for St Catherine's, Cambridge but, to tell you the truth, what interests me most is the opportunity to further my skill as a French horn player."

Another five students ambled in, smiled pleasantly, shook hands and one of them produced an old scholarship paper with questions of the kind that had so floored me at university. The kind that says, "The roots of civilisation are twelve inches deep. Discuss," and asked if we could indeed discuss this. "Yes," I said, putting aside the notes I had so carefully laboured on the night before, "let's do just that."

Several weeks later we were working on a more practical question about collecting data from fieldwork and using this as a contribution to theoretical study. "We didn't have much field work last year. Perhaps we could all go up to Hadrian's Wall for a weekend next month - we could fit a lot into both a Saturday and a Sunday. After all it's less than 100 miles away." With little fuss we went and one of the students negotiated the loan of tents from a local Scout troop, another found a farmer with a field in which we could camp, and another organised the bus. So they learned about organisation as well as about the geology of the Whin Sill, that volcanic intrusion that shapes the topography of the Scottish borderlands, and whose military significance the Roman Emperor Hadrian had exploited so effectively 1,600 years before. Several pupils from a more junior class volunteered to fill up the spare spaces on the bus and keep the costs down. Of all the ludicrous things I have ever done, we took two large blackboards and easels, together with lots of coloured chalk and dusters and carried them for nearly ten miles each day along the remnants of Hadrian's Wall. The younger pupils were fascinated by the technical knowledge of the older pupils and in each of the subsequent years, as they got older themselves, insisted that other trips should be organised, and that they too should have a mixture of age groups. Although it was time- consuming for me, it was not particularly hard work and it was extraordinary to see what good teachers the older pupils became, and how involved and questioning were the younger ones. Vygotsky would have approved, so would Mr Roast and Donald O'Sullivan.

I enjoyed that first year of teaching enormously. But I had time for nothing else; teaching can, all too easily, swamp the teacher. Preparation was relatively straightforward and holding people's attention was not difficult. It was the endless marking of essays written by young enthusiasts that was such a challenge. Here I set myself a punishing schedule, one I never kept up with.

Being interested in English I wanted my pupils to write clearly and imaginatively. I marked, or tried to mark, essays both for their English as well as for their geography. It was an impossible task, one that left me feeling inadequate, and the pupils frustrated, and many a meaningful learning experience lost.

*          *          *

Peter Mason held to the promise made at my interview and had me organise an expedition to eastern Turkey. Travelling on the route of the old Orient Express from Paris to Istanbul, the nine of us - seven 17 year-olds and two teachers - then boarded a bus for the three day drive through Anatolia, along the Black Sea coast as far as Trebizond and climbed over badly maintained roads to the ancient city of Erzerum, scene of quite vicious fighting in the first World War. There we were delayed for nearly a week whilst the Turkish authorities deliberated about the wisdom of allowing us to study in an area which, until very recently, had been closed to all foreigners. Eventually we were allowed to proceed 200 miles to the south west to the small town of Bulanick, midway between Lake Van and Mount Ararat, whose snow capped peak was reputed to hold the remains of Noah's Ark. This was an ancient landscape, a landscape where biblical allegories had an immediate echo and where our senses were flooded with questions. Bulanick looked, and smelt, like nothing the boys of Manchester had ever experienced. All the buildings, except that housing the military governor, were single storey mud-brick constructions with flat roofs and antique roller blinds which - incongruously - bore the imprint, Made in Derby, England. The streets were unsurfaced and bullock carts outnumbered old cars and lorries by at least five to one. We found the town unbearably hot and dusty and its strangeness intimidating. A legless beggar boy of 12 or 13 shuffled through the gutters with an old wooden chair seat strapped to his backside, shoes on his hands and with a small bucket hanging by a string around his neck in which villagers would throw the occasional coin or piece of bread.

We unpacked our belongings in the two-roomed schoolhouse provided for our use for the next six weeks. Out of nowhere it seemed, a blue UNICEF jeep was put at our disposal and Taziz, a young geologist from Ankara, joined us as guide and interpreter. Conventional text books about landforms in semi-arid climates, which in Manchester had seemed so informative and authoritative, here seemed shallow and superficial as we started to explore the local topography. Wide valleys, cut into the enormous lava flows that had poured out of Mount Ararat, and other volcanoes, many millions of years before, were of a shape and profile more akin to Nevada and Arizona than anything any of us had seen in Europe. There was a profusion of ruined castles, derelict caravanserai (the camel-age equivalent of a large motel) and roofless stone churches.

We travelled great distances in the early parts of each day, before the sun rose high. We mapped the valleys and hillsides, studied the crops and, as best we could, questioned the farmers about agricultural practices. Taziz was a good interpreter but, we quickly realised, there were topics about which he would not talk, nor even answer our questions - nothing about who owned the land, or what had happened in the recent past, or what were people's hopes for the future. He was in a difficult position, and our very freedom of speech compounded his own vulnerability. As a westernised Turk he knew how dangerous it was to allow political discussion to be vented in such a volatile area and a local farmer became greatly agitated at Taziz as he very obviously side-stepped political questions.

"What are they trying to say?" asked the mild-mannered and rational English schoolboys. "Why won't Taziz tell us? What's all the fuss about?"

"It is better not to talk about these things," replied Taziz curtly, and obviously embarrassed. "These are unpleasant matters, and there is nothing you can do about them. Go and study something else."

"But we could write about all this in our weekly newspaper article for the *Manchester Evening Post*. It would make a fantastic story. It could be published within ten days and everybody - well at least people in Manchester - would know what the problem is. Then somebody, maybe the Ambassador in London, will have to do something about it."

Taziz blanched at this naïvety. "Stop them," he said to me in the greatest agitation. "They just don't understand. This is not their land. No one knows whose land it is. That's the problem. Too many people have already been killed. It's impossible to trace land titles any more. Look at the children as they play in the streets. Haven't you noticed, they're not all dark skinned and black haired like I am? Some of them look almost like you English, they have blonde hair and blue eyes. Once, not long ago, there were many more such Caucasian people here. Whole villages populated by Armenian people." He paused and looked away. He was much moved, and I thought his lip trembled. "It is not good to talk about such matters; too much blood has flowed already." It was only after we got home that we learned of the genocide in 1920 and 1921, when the Armenian settlements in this part of Turkey had been virtually exterminated, one of the most horrific events of its time but something which had not figured in any history curriculum I had ever studied.

The students and I were learning fast. They wrote that week for the Manchester Evening News not about racial issues, but about the treatment of animals, a subject far more likely to incite an English audience. It had happened like this. Late one evening, shouts and cries from further down the street, and the yapping of a dog in obvious pain, led us to explore. A stray bitch dog on heat had come into the village, and was exciting the local dogs. The young men saw in this some sport for the last hours of the day, and started throwing rocks at the bitch. They cornered her and quickly started to compete with each other to see who could hit her the hardest and who could break the most of her bones. It was absolutely sickening. One of the English boys was so incensed that he went to find a local gendarme, hoping that he would at least shoot the creature and put it out of its agony. Initially the gendarme did not know what was agitating Steve. When he saw what was happening, he laughed and, putting down his gun, started to throw rocks himself. It was a full hour before the dog was dead.

Long before the article ever reached England, an earthquake centred about 30 miles east of Bulanick devastated the area, causing upwards of 35,000 deaths and providing the British media with endless opportunities to speculate on our own assumed, horrible, deaths. Although no seismological tests accurately predicted this forthcoming event, many of the villages around us had started taking preventative measures the previous evening. "Why?" asked the boys when it was suggested that we should get out of the schoolhouse forthwith and sleep outdoors in the streets with the locals around blazing fire. "What's the matter?"

"The people in the villages way up in the mountains say that the wolves have left their caves, and for the past three days have just been wandering around the mountainside. They're too frightened to return to the caves. Those wolves know something is wrong. It's possible they can sense that the earth's starting to shake so if that's the case we'll shortly have a *deprem* (earthquake). If we do, it's not safe to be in a house. When houses fall down you're more likely to be killed through suffocating from the dust than you are from falling down a crack in the ground." Forewarned, we too slept in the open. We could hear the wolves calling to each other on the mountainside. They knew something we did not; moreover, they knew what to do about it.

We were travelling in two jeeps when the first shock hit our area. We did not understand what it was for at least 20 seconds. It felt as if we were driving through quicksand, or like being in a small boat in a very heavy swell. The driver knew immediately, and so did the people in the first village we entered, where at least two people had been killed when the house front under which they had been resting fell on top of them. We hastened back to our own village, reaching there two hours later. Everyone was in the streets, talking and arguing. The governor, a young military officer, who felt himself a cut above this kind of job, was glad to have our company. "That was the first shock. There will probably be more. I have just heard that the town of Malazgirt, 30 miles away beyond that mountain range, a town of 6,000 people, has been badly damaged. The army will probably try to get to it from Erzurum but it is likely that all the roads in that direction are blocked. Many people are dying. I advise you to move all your belongings into the schoolyard. Do not go indoors under any circumstances. Always walk in the middle of the street so that anything falling from the houses does not hit you."

We needed no second bidding. There were a number of lesser shocks and each time a cry of "deprem" went up from all around us. People fled from buildings like rabbits bolting from a hole. Loud wailing told of where a family had found the body of a loved one. Later we turned on the World Service of the BBC. The earthquake was already headline news and there was speculation that up to a 100,000 people might be dead or missing. Then they mentioned we were known to be in the middle of the area and that no one had news of us. The inference was all too obvious; it was thought we too had been buried alive. We were horrified at the agony which our parents and loved ones were going through. Every telephone line had been severed. There was no radio link. We, and thousands of others, were stuck. Believing in fate, and the ultimate authority of Allah, most people sat down and wept. We, the product of a Western work ethic, and a Christian tradition of self-help, felt compelled to do something, whatever that might be.

We approached the governor. "Please, if you would loan us two jeeps and provide us with us as many spades as possible, we could then drive to Malazgirt and start digging some of these people out." Initially he was helpful and agreed, but then to our amazement he reversed his decision. "No," he said apologetically, embarrassed about what he was going to say to us, "you can't do that. The people believe that this earthquake is the work of Allah. He has pre-ordained that these people should die." The boys could not believe this and started to argue. The governor blushed for he was deeply embarrassed. He took me to one side, out of hearing of the people, and said, "tell your students that we don't all feel like this. I for one don't believe in fate. Most of us are just hoping that, if there is another earthquake and it hits this area, then you and your students will be around and be able to dig us out. Maybe that is why Allah pre-ordained that you should come to this area, at this time." Our accumulated sense of theology was becoming deeply confused.

It was a full five days before we knew that our families understood that we were safe. Two of the expeditioners set off on a bullock cart with all our available money, in the direction of Erzurum. After three days travelling along badly fractured roads the bullock cart reached a point where cars could be driven safely, and had eventually reached Erzurum the following day. They sent a telegram to England. Every radio in the village, it seemed, was tuned into the news bulletins to see when information might be broadcast. For once the BBC, in its haste to announce our safety, made an interesting blunder in its initial statement. "This is the BBC World Service. The Foreign Office has just announced that the nine members of the Manchester Grammar School expedition, believed lost in the Turkey earthquake, are alive again ..." Our relief - and that of our families -- was immense. So too was the interest of the sponsoring newspapers with such a story to tell. The excitement at hearing the name of their town mentioned on the BBC that afternoon, gave the villagers momentary relief in the grim business of recovering their neighbours still buried, but dying fast, in the shattered town thirty miles away.

Ten days later we were preparing to leave and feeling somewhat nostalgic. We had experienced more than we could ever have anticipated. I had enough anecdotes and case studies on which to build numerous subsequent lessons. We had made many good friends. When we arrived six weeks before we had been nervous about the local customs. On one of our first evenings, as we sat in the village square, one of the boys had, unguardedly, commented to the chief of police (a relatively young man who spoke some English) that "it must be strange to live in a town of this kind where there are no girls to talk to", *purdah* being strictly enforced. To the boy's amazement, and my horror, the chief of police put his arm around the boy's shoulders and said affectionately, "It does not matter; we have each other." Not sure quite what was implied, we all moved very rapidly back to the schoolhouse, with the police and some others in pursuit. Subsequently I was assured they wanted nothing other than English conversation, but at the time it was disconcerting. The police returned minutes later, with guitars, and for the next hour or so they serenaded us. Cultures, we were coming to understand, comprise many layers.

Recalling this episode on the night before we left, the governor, at a meal given in our honour in the town square, remarked that soon the expedition would be back in Istanbul. He turned to me. "In Istanbul there are plenty of women. How many do you want?" he asked teasingly. I had to make a response in Turkish and my Turkish was still not good. I thought that, in saying "you" he had said it in the plural implying all the members of the expedition. I got up and tried to pass this off light-heartedly, using the best Turkish that I could manage. I held up my fingers and, counting one off at a time said, *Bir, iki, üc, dört, ves, alti, yedi* ... (One, two, three, four, five, six, seven). A look of profound admiration spread across the police chief's face as he jumped to his feet, "You, Mr John, you Mr Quick-Quick, yes." Hilarity swept through the assembled group. My confusion was complete. The editor of the Manchester Evening News censored the boys' writing up of that story, but it circulated through the prefects' common room within minutes of the first day of term.

\*　　　\*　　　\*

Returning to a new school year in Manchester, geography teaching had a new immediacy, and I had a renewed sense of the inter-connectivity of issues where my subject readily gave way to religious studies, to sociology, to history and cultural anthropology. Nearly every youngster enjoyed trying to keep up with my enthusiasm, but a few were confused. "I like geography but I don't like history. I'm lost. I'm not sure what we're doing any longer," said one youngster. The head of department was more specific. "Are you sure you'll cover the formal syllabus in time if you carry on talking with your pupils like this?" he said. I heard the caution but I was not worried. I saw what they were doing with their homework and it was causing me a lot of extra work as I struggled to mark ever more substantial essays and projects. I was more concerned when some staff started to complain, "Richard/John/Chris/Jeff... still hasn't given me his work from last week. He says your projects take up all his time."

The parents of the boys who had been on the Turkey expedition saw things differently.

"You can't believe how our son has changed," said one of them. "He's much more of a man now. He thinks more carefully. It's hard to put it into words, but he's sort of become his own person."

*          *          *

That, had I been asked to put my philosophy of education into words at that stage of my career, was a pretty close description of what I was trying to do; helping youngsters to become themselves. Mostly teaching was enjoyable, nearly always challenging and frequently fun. Each class had a textbook whose chapters concluded with essay-type questions. Such textbooks were bland, but well meaning, and gave youngsters the confidence to respond to an avuncular question as to which part of England made jam and why, or where shoes or gloves were made, or ships or railway engines. The questions went further with the older age groups to give geographic reasons for why the diamond industry was in Antwerp, or why the Dutch had decided to reclaim the polders. ("Sir, do you know what Churchill said when the Dutch government asked if they should flood the polders before the German army invaded them? 'Hold your water until the Jerries arrive.'" Schoolboy sniggers all around.) The course books were the jumping off point for imaginative teaching and I pitied the youngster whose teacher held too closely to the text.

Geography, from the perspective of students below the sixth form, was a politically neutral study of contemporary peoples, mainly removed from the passions and conflicts recorded in history classes. Here the English academic played very safe because modern history ended in 1918 leaving an extraordinary no-man's land of the next 50 years. Consequently no one asked questions about the ethnic mix of Yugoslavia, the fate of the Pontic Christians or the Armenians or the Cossacks in the Crimea, and no one had any reason to know even of their existence. Engaging in genuinely modern history was why I had met with such success several years previously when I had filled up the whole of an afternoon getting those boys in the secondary modern school to create the history of the Second World War out of their own family stories. That was what youngsters wanted to know about.

Yet, to a young teacher like me, someone fascinated by the land-forming processes of geomorphology with mountains being squeezed up and other land masses being sucked down, geography was a fascinating topic. The search for evidence of the last Ice Age with its various advances and retreats, each marked with terminal moraines, drumlins and hanging valleys, was the perfect excuse to get out into the countryside and get youngsters to open their eyes to what was around them. It called for powers of imagination as well as synthesis. To think of the mountains of the Lake District under 3,000 feet of ice as the reason why a granite boulder was sitting atop a ridge of old red sandstone in the middle of Cheshire was, to young rationalist minds, almost as much an act of faith as were my attempts to teach religious knowledge.

Both subjects led to extraordinary open, virtually unanswerable questions. "Why do both the Island of Staffa and the Giants Causeway in Ulster look as if they've been chiselled by a Michaelangelo with a predisposition for hexagonal stone organ pipes?" Faith was challenged in the fraught six weeks when one of the boys in my class withered away with a rampant form of leukaemia. Being an absolute coward and hardly knowing how to take myself to visit the boy in his home, I delayed two days too long in taking him a present from the class. He died in his bath the day before his thirteenth birthday. "Why, sir, did a just God let Andrew die like that?" I couldn't answer the question, but weeks later, Andrew's parents came and talked to the class. Their simple faith and their courage in describing Andrew's last days were impressive beyond description.

Geography was, for me, essentially about people. Landscape and climate were fascinating, but both needed people to make them interesting. No place in the world, I thought at the time - and still secretly do now - could compare with the British Isles with its evidence of such multi-layering of human activity. Geography in the 1960s was just starting to take itself seriously. It was beginning to formulate practical applications for theories of hinterland and central business districts, and was even daring to move into the study of such mildly contentious subjects as the European Iron and Steel Community (the precursor to the European Union). Little of this was as yet in the textbooks, so teachers like me delighted in making up our own theoretical models with which we thought youngsters could make sense of phenomena around them. A model I used was the growth of fishing ports. Given an imaginary coastline of large and small bays, with the occasional broad estuary and rocky headland, and backed by a variety of land forms ranging from moorland to open farmland with fast and slow-moving rivers, around which of these bays would human settlements have first grown up? How would this have changed as boats got larger, roads improved and canals and railways were built? Map after theoretical map covered the blackboard as the class calculated why tiny bays that were once thriving fishing communities when boats were small, fell into decay as boats got larger and one harbour found the capital to build a massive harbour breakwater, and so take all the trade to itself. Later they linked this to the opening up of new markets as technology made it possible to bring frozen lamb from New Zealand, and chilled bananas from Africa and South America. Pupils turned in the most complex and thoughtful scenarios of possible developments and marking these took hours and hours. Yet I was never in any doubt but that they had learned all this most thoroughly. A teacher's life, I quickly discovered, could expand to fill every moment of the day, and at a time when syllabuses were still relatively broad, the only limitations to what could be covered in such lessons were our imaginations.

*          *          *

Meeting one of the boys from my class in that year after the Turkish expedition on a train some 25 years later, he asked me what I was currently doing. I cast around in my mind and mentioned a few of the ideas set out in the first chapter of this book. He grinned broadly over his now confident 40 year-old face. "You haven't changed, have you! That's exactly what you were doing with our form all those years ago. You really kept us on our toes, didn't you, and got us to think things out for ourselves! Most of us enjoyed it hugely ... but then you shrewdly got us to do all the routine work for ourselves. It certainly worked - didn't our class get the best results of any class in the school at the end of that year?" I nodded. That was right. I well remember the afternoon when the High Master had actually come into the classroom to tell them how well they had done. I had known that "their doing well" was because our lively discussions in the classroom, and the excitement they could feel for the subject, gave them such a sense of direction that their entire lives were far more meaningful.

*          *          *

The Turkish expedition was an extreme version of what MGS had been doing for many years - extending boys' experiences in ways that went far beyond the conventional curriculum, and beyond the classroom. For a week at Whitsun, as the older boys prepared for public examinations, the younger boys went off to one or other of the two large camps, one at Borrowdale in the Lake District, and the other at a small country estate, Nash Court, in Shropshire. Each attracted upwards of 150 pupils. Teachers organised the catering, and did all the cooking, assisted by relays of boys peeling potatoes and doing the washing up. Games of football were organised; each tent contributed an item towards a concert organised on the last night; new games were continuously being invented.

Find the Teacher was one such game. It was very simple to organise, cost nothing, but suggests now a leisurely age long gone by. Each of the 15 teachers, having laid their plans over previous days, went down to the local town of Tenbury Wells, one hour before the boys left the camp. We each had to disguise ourselves as a local inhabitant and go about our apparent daily tasks. If a pupil thought he had recognised one of us he had to ask the rather banal question, "Are you the goose that laid the golden egg?" Not the easiest question for an adolescent to ask if not too sure of himself. Teachers had to reply, "Yes, but only if it's got a lion on it" - and then give their name. The winning boy was the one who had found the most teachers. The disguises were a delight. One unassuming chemistry teacher made himself look even more insignificant by donning a white overall and putting on a white slouch cap and spent the entire afternoon stacking shelves in a supermarket. Another, a man of dark and forbidding countenance, collected a set of old man's country clothes from a second-hand shop, and then went to the river with a fishing rod. Knowing nothing about fishing he did not know how to keep his line taut in the water so, being a resourceful physicist, he tied a brick to the end. His line stayed in the water, but the water was so clear that everybody could see what he had done. His disguise was quickly blown. So too was the man who, scorning any disguise other than dark glasses (the eyes are indeed a mirror of the soul) wore his running kit and, for two hours, ran around the streets of that little town as if he were in training for an Olympic marathon. Few boys could get close enough to question him, but he quickly assumed the guise of a modern version of the *Pied Piper of Hamelin* with such an entourage.

A more sober disguise was that of the teacher who borrowed the verger's cloak and spent the afternoon brushing the paths in the churchyard. The most sedentary of all was the school chaplain who came to an arrangement with the local antique shop that he would sit, cross-legged, on top of a table near the back of the shop, wearing a kimono. From a distance he looked a near perfect replica of a Buddha, so perfect that no boy thought to come into the shop. After an hour or so the owner decided to slip out for ten minutes to make a delivery, and asked Buddha to keep an eye on the shop.

A few minutes later a shifty looking individual in an old raincoat shuffled in, looked around carefully to ensure that the owner had not returned, and started to push some of the more expensive items into his expansive pockets. "Put those back," said the voice of Buddha. The thief froze. He looked around to find the source of the voice. He saw no one. "Put them back," repeated Buddha. Again the thief looked around the shop. His gaze rested on the Buddha, and then, to his consternation, Buddha winked. With a gasp the thief, doubting his own sanity but not stopping to enquire further, tore off the overcoat and dropped it, and all the items he was in the process of stealing, on the floor and fled from the shop. As for me, I had to disguise both my height and my prematurely balding head. I borrowed a second-hand car and parked it in the car park for the afternoon. For two hours I sat, window open, with a jaunty broad checked cap, slouched forward over my eyes, slowly scanning that day's copy of the *Racing Times*, ostentatiously marking up my bets, and pulling on a large, evil-smelling cigar. To complete my disreputable image I had, sitting in the back seat, a senior English teacher with a fulsome blonde wig and wearing a dress so inflated in the bust as to suggest that I had picked up the most extrovert of the town's women of the street. Several boys called my bluff, but none realised that the woman behind me was their English teacher. I felt my reputation sink rapidly or was I wrong? Did it not, perhaps, go up?

A long story of an almost irrelevant activity which I tell for a reason. If teachers are not also people that youngsters find interesting, and if these youngsters are not surrounded by other adults who, in a variety of ordinary and natural ways, show that they have time for them, then the life of each young person suffers accordingly. And so, too, does the life of the community. There is much, much more to education than book learning, and it is enormously sad now to realise that an event of the kind I have just described seems an account of days long since past. If we are to do right by the present and future generations such activities must be re-established. This is the stuff that gives humour and purpose to our lives, and it is certainly the material of which life-shaping memories are made.

*         *         *

Manchester Grammar School was the most selective of all grammar schools in England. Yet its curriculum was, by today's standards, gentle and uncomplicated. There were only six lessons a day, given the need for youngsters to travel great distances to school, so we worked a six-day cycle. For the first two years every student followed a reasonably broad curriculum, but early specialisation limited this for some who did an additional language or an additional science in the second year. Specialisation started for everyone with the third year, as students embarked on the two year O Level course, a year earlier than pupils in almost every other school. Six subjects were normally studied, though a few studied seven subjects, but never more. "Too much O Level work kills off enquiry and rigorous thought," went the argument. "It's better to do a few subjects well, than to get pupils to memorise vast bodies of facts. Besides which, there is more to growing up than just studying for exams." Despite its reputation for academic excellence, the school believed that, yet now 30 years later it sounds almost too good to be true. Virtually every teacher was involved in some form of extra-curricular activity and it was an unwritten assumption that every teacher would use their own particular interests, passions - for some even obsessions - to spark the interest of youngsters beyond the classroom. We did all this voluntarily. We were never paid, not even for giving up the entire summer holidays, or most weekends during the summer term, for fieldwork. Enthusiasm kept too many of us as bachelors and strained too many marriages.

Completing their O levels by the age of 15, every student had then to narrow their study down to three subjects for the A level examinations taken at 17. The English system had been terribly specialised for a long time and MGS provided a major correction in general studies, so strongly endorsed by Peter Mason as high master and spoken of highly by the students I had met at my interview. Every student had to take two or three general studies courses (each with a classroom commitment of one and a half hours a week) throughout his time in the sixth form. While the school year book listed all the numerous combinations of A level courses that a sixth form of over 600 students could justify, its true glory was the listing of those courses that teachers volunteered to teach because the subject interested them. This was almost a reincarnation of a medieval university. The courses were not examined directly, but such was the quality of the offerings that there was no difficulty in ensuring students' attention. Courses included subjects such as Eastern mystical thought, the art of Ancient Greece; contemporary design; the politics of the Welfare State; strategic thinking in the North African campaign; an amateur's guide to the law; industrial archaeology; landscape and culture; the music of Africa. The list was apparently endless, and frequently changing. At different stages I ran courses in the Celtic world; the politics of the Middle East; the IRA, and even organisation administration and efficiency. "I like to be well organised," I used to explain, "so that I have the space to be spontaneous whenever the opportunity arises." Indirectly, of course, such courses contributed greatly to the students' ability to handle scholarship papers and to prepare for the Third Year Sixth, where they were coached for the Oxford and Cambridge Scholarship Examination in November, exams in which MGS, Winchester and Eton jostled with each other every year for the maximum number of scholarships.

MGS was a splendid place to start a teaching career. The staff was so busy that we gave little thought to the influence on the education system of the country as a whole, though we were rightly proud of general studies and surprised that other schools did not seek to emulate us more closely. It was several years before I realised the true cost that the MGS entry examination placed on the primary schools of Manchester, whose individual reputations rested on getting just a few of the highly coveted places that MGS standards specified. Neither did I start to question, until several years later, why it was that many pupils, having got such good results in the scholarship exams at the age of 18, failed to get particularly good degrees or were never anything like as successful in their subsequent careers as many had anticipated. MGS was a hothouse; it brought children on very quickly. The staff greatly enjoyed doing this, and the students responded warmly but, and it has to be a most significant but, it was at the cost of giving them continuous support and direction. We were not as good as we liked to think at giving them the ability to stand on their own feet.

\*       \*       \*

The Turkey expedition gave birth to other expeditions over the next nine years. British Petroleum, the modern successor to the old Anglo-Persian Oil Company, still exercised a strong proprietorial interest in the Middle East. Shortly after returning from Turkey, I was invited to meet with them and the Iranian ambassador to London to discuss a possible expedition to the Zagros Mountains to the north of the Persian Gulf.

"We would like to welcome some of your students to my land," said the ambassador. "We are an old and proud kingdom seeking to combine the best of the old, with the most outstanding concepts for the future. Your young men would learn a lot with us."

The man from BP said: "We could offer to provide all the on-the-spot resources you might need such as: jeeps, lorries, tents, marquees, cooking equipment, drivers, servants, and we would negotiate with the local officials for an armed guard." I obviously looked taken aback. "It's more to protect you at night time from the wolves and the like, but there were still a few bandits in that area several years ago," he added reassuringly.

"Yes," said the ambassador, "the local tribes in the Zagros were so unappreciative of the Shah's wish to provide them with new amenities that we had eventually to enforce the acceptance of these with some limited military action." I shuddered, and hoped that my expression did not become too hostile.

"You'll be quite safe if you're sensible," said an older man who had just joined us. "I have lived in those mountains for the better part of 30 years. I did all the original geological survey work on which the current maps were based, and which paved the way for much of the current ideas about plate tectonics which you've probably been studying in your school." Norman Falcon, who had recently retired as chief geologist for British Petroleum, was to be a special asset as we prepared the boys for life in remote territory.

Ensuring that we got the right team of 15 boys had to be done carefully, and the selection had to be eminently fair. Interest in participation was, of course, enormous. Selection was not made easier by my insistence that we needed students from a variety of disciplines, not just geographers. The majority of the money was raised through commercial sponsorship. We declined, however, the offer made by a national newspaper to give us nearly all the money we needed in exchange for their having sole rights to the full story of any survivor should the majority of the expedition be killed in an accident. I avoided carefully making any reference of that proposal to the parents!

The journey out to Iran by train took just over a week, with a 36-hour stop-over in Moscow. As we would find ourselves in restricted territory once we left Moscow for the east, Intourist insisted we were accompanied at all times by a guide. Tasha turned out to be the most stunningly beautiful guide the Secret Police could ever find, leaving the boys on edge for three long days and nights. We then drove by bus from the Caspian shore right across the central desert by way of fabled Isfahan and its great bazaar, past the ruins of Persepolis to Shiraz, world famous since the days of the early caliphs for its roses, its sweet white wine and its poetry. Then we collected our three Land Rovers, and two five-ton Bedford trucks, and set out on the arduous two-days' drive high into the Zagros mountains. To the students, who had never seen more than an English Pennine, these mountains were awesome, with mountain tracks clinging precariously to the edge of near precipices. I, for one, was quite terrified.

The nomads, who we were later to get to know so well, were on the move. Mainly of the Bakhtiari tribe, they lived in large tents made of coarse black wool, or beaten felts, and moved in extended family units using horses and camels for their essential provisions. "These are the people the Shah's air force bombed three summers back," explained our guide. "The Shah thought they presented a challenge to the stability of the country. The nomads ignored the air force; the people just kept on going, and the bombs had little effect on them. Eventually the Shah just had to give in."

We prepared to sleep rough that night, close to the tents of a Bakhtiari chieftain. I was asked to take a meal with the chieftain - the khan - as the sun went down. Three students came with me. What, on the outside, had looked little more than a moth-eaten, ill-constructed shelter, was furnished with hand-knotted silk carpets, and cushions made out of stuffed, embroidered, saddle packs. Not saddle packs like those in the American west. Heavy copper and bronze drinking cups, full of crystal-clear water, were passed around. Candlelight flickered on the steel shafts of great studded swords. Dishes of *dough*, pronounced "doog" (a yoghurt dish with cucumber and garlic), of fresh fruit, of various oils and herbs and of rice, were placed in front of us as we sat cross-legged, shoeless, on the carpets. Each of us was given large plates of unleavened bread which we placed in our laps, and out of great dishes of stewed meats, each with an enticing array of spices, generous portions were heaped into the middle of our bread plates. Fresh salad was available in profusion. We were waited on by the women of the family, who were heavily veiled and totally silent. The khan and his sons, little older than members of the expedition, sat watching but not eating. This was hospitality of an earlier era, the courtesies showing an ageless self-assurance of a people bred to a life which was hard but lived in regular and predictable rhythms.

Mehrypur, our oil company expedition manager, was uncomfortable. He was a partly westernised Iranian but, given his heavy dark physical features, he was probably of Kurdish origin. Proud of his western attitudes developed over 30 years serving English geologists, he was intimidated by the natural grace of his own people here in the mountains, whose traditions he would have liked to dismiss for being primitive. Each despised the other. The students noticed Mehrypur's unease and were fascinated. His discomfort increased when the khan requested him to translate an incident of some five years previously when some American agricultural advisers had visited his tribe. As Mehrypur translated, the khan passed the bubbling hookah to one of his sons. He spoke slowly, carefully weighing his words. He was not used to speaking through an interpreter, yet his natural courtesy favoured a slow, deliberate way of talking, and this in no way limited his effectiveness.

"Some wise men had come to observe our tribe from America," he recalled, "and we were told that they were extremely knowledgeable about sheep and goats. But I saw that they did not have the hands of farmers. They travelled with us as we moved into the higher mountains as spring gave way to summer, and the new grass started to grow. They were polite men, but I do not think they were happy. They did not know how to put up tents, nor did they like our food. They told me that they had found a way of impregnating ewes, which was more efficient than leaving this to the rams. This seemed to us most unnatural, but then the wise men said that by using this method they could be sure that almost every ewe would have twins, rather than single births. 'The size of your flock would quickly double, and then you would be rich,' the wise men had said. We were confused. If we had any more sheep the grass could not sustain this, and we could not live as we did. The wise men had then become very talkative and argumentative. They told me that, with this new knowledge, we should realise that to be nomads migrating through the mountains in search of grass was stupid. We were a backward people, they said. We should stay on the flat ground below the mountains, and find ways of bringing water from the hills to the fields, in which we should grow grass. We should exchange tents for houses - just like the people who live in the towns. We were amazed at these suggestions. They obviously did not understand who we were. My people may not be rich, like the Americans, but we are a contented people who live well with the land."

He paused, and let his words sink in. His sons passed the hookah back, and the khan took several deep inhalations. No one spoke. I had never seen such rapt attention on the faces of the English students, who were listening to a real story told by people who felt deeply about their way of life. Here were issues of a profound kind set out in a way that no textbook could emulate.

"Later those wise men went back to Tehran," continued the khan. "We think they spoke to the Shah, for the next winter many soldiers came to the mountains and built small castles to prevent us migrating to the summer pastures. But we knew those mountain passes better than they did. Overnight we just walked around those castles and by the morning they did not know where we were. The same thing happened the next night, and the next. Some of our people were killed by soldiers, and then we were attacked by bombs from planes. Again my people scattered. Some were killed, but most survived; no bomb can destroy a whole mountainside. For a whole year this went on, but eventually the soldiers decided to leave us alone. We are almost happy again now, but in every large village there is a castle, and some soldiers. You will see these for yourselves. The soldiers are a sorry people. All they want is to be back in the town. Our way of life means nothing to them, nor theirs to us. We each wish to be allowed to live in our own ways. The Shah now builds roads into the mountains for the soldiers to come and go more easily into our lands. These roads cross and recross our ancient paths. Sometimes lorries driving too fast kill many of our sheep as they cross these roads. Our fathers, and their fathers before them, and theirs before them, lived from day to day contentedly leaving the future in the hands of Allah. *Inshallah.* May Allah be praised."

"Now I do not know what will happen, and what you," he turned and looked closely, not in a hostile way but questioningly at the three members of the expedition, "will think about us primitive people. Will they say that we all have to be the same, and all obey every rule of every institution of a great Shah from far away? Or will they say that we ought to be allowed to be ourselves? Will they think the world is the better for being made up of diverse peoples or not? What will they think when they have got to know my people better?"

Outside the tents we retraced our steps across the valley to our little encampment, and the sound of English voices. "I need a strong drink," said

Mehrypur, mixing a lethal, and most appetising concoction, of vodka, fresh limes and a bottle of Seven Up. "These are ignorant people who give the Shah much trouble. They behave as if they own the place (he had picked up English idiom well from many years of working with English geologists) yet they are backward, and don't understand the value of progress."

"But if they did," said 17 year-old Richard, a quietly spoken boy from a south Manchester suburb, "would anyone actually live here anymore?"

"Probably not," replied Jack in the broad accent of Tomyfield Market in Oldham - or was it Bolton, I never could tell the difference - "and that would be sad. This looks a fascinating, beautiful place. But you'd have to be tough to live here. That mountain we're heading for, Kuh-i-Dinar, is over 14,000 feet high. The guards say there are wolves up there. Those fires you see flickering on the hillside, each one of those is a hunter's camp or a shepherd keeping his sheep in a fold. I envy them their freedom."

Throughout five such expeditions over the next seven years there were large numbers of moments like that. Moments to treasure; atmospheres that seemed as old as time; moments rich in the all too obvious clash of cultures and values. Moments in which young, intelligent but surprisingly naïve 17 year-olds became young men whose parents were proud to meet them six weeks later. And years later I understood well what the anthropologist Jared Diamond meant when he wrote about his time living in New Guinea. "The people there impressed me as being on the average more intelligent, more alert, more expressive, and more interested in things and people around them than the average American or European," Diamond continued. "At some tasks that one might reasonably suppose to reflect aspects of brain function, such as the ability to form a mental map of unfamiliar surroundings, they appear considerably more adept than Westerners."

*         *         *

In one village we were offered a cool, strong, tasty *dough* served with unleavened bread. We sat down and talked for several hours with the local khan. "We are deeply honoured to have you and these fine young men visit us. But we are confused. How is it that such young men are not at home helping their parents with their work? Surely they are needed to help their fathers, and surely they should be learning from them what it means to become a man?" He looked at his own sons, Manesh and Ardavan, not with any deep emotion, but rather as a businessman looking at his most treasured investment. "If my sons did not work with me, if we did not discuss things together, how could I be sure that I was passing on to them the wisdom of my father, and his father, and his father before him, and all the knowledge that I myself built up in my lifetime?"

I tried to explain the Western model of schooling, deeply immersed as it is in a way of living which these people could not comprehend. I was not successful.

"You know," said one of the boys quietly later on that evening, "I'd have just loved to have had that kind of relationship with my father." There were tears forming in his eyes as he continued. "I feel I hardly know my Dad. He works hard to support my sister and me but we hardly ever talk, he's always too tired. Once I've finished my schoolwork I've got free time and I miss the chance of being able to be useful to him. Manesh and Ardavan have got a reason for being around. They might be young but somehow they seem important. In a sense I'm just a cost to my parents. I don't think they get very much back from me. It's all wrong, I feel I'm sort of disconnected".

*  *  *

Returning one evening from a particularly difficult assignment some distance away from base we were overtaken by darkness long before we reached the top of the intervening mountain range, and stopped the jeep to allow the engine to cool. We were tired and pensive. As the sound of the cooling engine faded away I became aware of someone playing a one-stringed zither in an encampment somewhere across the valley; a strangely timeless instrument, it seemed, but with a haunting tune that was foreign yet curiously natural. It was as if I had never heard it before, yet recognised its beat from instincts I did not really understand. The extraordinary sense of timelessness increased as I smelt the bitter aromatic smell of a camel dung fire fed by dry crackling brushwood. As my eyes became accustomed to the dark I saw first one, then two and then many other flickering fires high up on the hill slopes far away in front of me where latter-day Davids had rounded up their sheep and lit their fires at the entrances to their primitive sheep folds. The stars shone bright. I would not have been surprised to see Abraham or Moses walk up beside me. The Garden of Eden was only some three hundred miles away. Nothing, it seemed, had changed in thousands of years.

Almost inevitably Mehrypur did not like it. He could not stand the silence any longer. He flicked a switch in the jeep, and suddenly Western music delivered from New York via a Tehran radio station drowned out all our thoughts. In Mehrypur, within a single generation, was the result of the ultimate culture conflict.

"I'll never ever forget this evening," said Jella, a Dutch student who had been studying in Manchester for two years, and whose normally cool and detached self was so appealing to the girls back in England, "it's magical and mysterious. It's spiritual too. Out here I can more easily understand timelessness, and transience. My Dad's talked to me of feeling like this when he was out in the

East Indies. The experience is both exciting and daunting all at the same time, isn't it? You can't help thinking about all those other people who have thought the same kinds of thoughts as us. I'm beginning to wonder where I'll fit into this world."

These, and many other instances like them, became the real stories around which my future classroom lessons were to be based, and they became the moments that were powerful turning points in the lives of the numerous students who came with me to the East, and the even larger numbers who tramped the mountains, valleys and beaches of the Hebrides, or the hills of northern England. It was my own living and learning that kept me teaching and it was the western education system's failure to respond to the idealism of adolescence that first really alerted me to the incredible waste of human talent that this seems to have accepted as in some measure inevitable.

Like Jella, the Dutch boy, all my life I had been trying to find out how I, too, would fit in to whatever might be "the scheme of things". To be so near to the Garden of Eden, on a night where eternity seemed to stand still, prompted questions about ultimate issues that none of us could ignore.

I was brought up in an apparently timeless English tradition that believed its spiritual well-being was dependent on an ever more forceful repetition of doctrine and dogma that owed its origins more to the seventeenth century than it did to the mid-twentieth century. I was the generation waiting for John Robinson, the Bishop of the small diocese of Woolwich, to publish *Honest to God* in 1963. I was waiting, and waiting anxiously, because I just did not know how to fulfil my obligation towards teaching religious education in the sixth form. I was confused by the new insights I was gaining but could not fit together. My experience in Turkey, Iran and in the outer islands of Scotland and the west of Ireland had exacerbated the situation. Here I had met people who did not believe the same dogma I had been brought up with, but I could not believe that they were all eternally damned because they were not conforming Christians. I was moved, by forces which I did not understand, by living in these wild places in the Middle East, and on the windswept islands of the west of Scotland and elsewhere, yet I knew, too, that for spirituality to be meaningful it had also to be thoughtful and coherent. I was, therefore, most struck by the words of Robinson's preface: "I suspect that we stand on the brink of a period in which it is going to become increasingly difficult to know what the true defence of Christian truth requires. There are always those (and doubtless rightly they will be in the majority) who see the best, and indeed the only, defence of doctrine to lie in the firm reiteration, in fresh and intelligent contemporary language, of the 'Faith once delivered to the Saints' ... (That was the position that I had come from). Yet, at the same time, I believe we are being called, over the years ahead, to far more than a restating of traditional orthodoxy in modern terms. Indeed, if our defence of the Saints is limited to this, we shall find in all likelihood that we have lost out to all but a tiny religious remnant. A much more radical recasting, I would judge, is demanded, in the process of which the most fundamental categories of our theology - of God, of the supernatural, and of religion itself - must go into the melting pot."

While Robinson was writing for my generation, his open-minded search for the reality of God working through natural laws was highly appealing to inquisitive teenage minds. His insight was to understand that the old categories were fast losing their meaning, particularly the idea of a God out there, who stands outside time and space, but who acts, some would say interferes, within both. He knew that the sixties generation could not be won back by a stronger, clearer, more up-to-date presentation of the Christian faith, specifically one that owed much of its teachings to interpretations from the Victorian era. Robinson glimpsed the reality that, somehow, as this century wore on, the world and how it understood itself, was changing. He was looking not for a God who was out there, apathetic in the old sense of the word in that nothing could touch or change him, but for a God who was immersed in the most profound experiences and longings at the depth of each of our beings. Robinson argued for a form of religionless Christianity, organised not to defend the interests of religion against the inroads of the state, but to equip Christians, by the quality and power of its community life, to enter with their secret discipline into all the exhilarating and dangerous secular strivings of our time, there to follow and find the workings of God. Christianity was more about how spiritual truths could be lived out in the future than it was to do with the transference of apparently eternal truths from one generation to the next.

I was living with sharp young minds that were eager to explore underneath established tradition, yet I was also living close to the visual demonstration of Biblical times that permeated the mountains of Iran and Turkey, and the interpretations of this through both the Catholic tradition of Ireland and the ultra-free Presbyterian tradition in the Outer Hebrides. All this meant that I became more committed spiritually, and less religiously, than my earlier upbringing would have suggested. My early years of teaching religious knowledge were, in best Robinson style, more to do with working out the concepts of the God within - the 11 year-old Timothy's, "If we look like God, then everybody else looks like God too" - than it was to a particular orthodoxy. Even so, I have found it easy to revert to the rich language of the Anglican church when all other words have failed me.

*        *        *

I was midway through my third year of teaching, and just starting to question the cost to my social life of such a wholehearted commitment to teaching, when the High Master called me to his study. "The school governors think it's time for the school to undertake a major building program," he said. The staff need better accommodation, so does the sixth form. We need better laboratories, certainly a better library. The governors have decided that we should ask the old boys, as well as local industry and commerce, to donate half a million pounds. I'm told it's quite possible to raise that sort of money if the appeal is well organised and the people presenting it know what they're talking about. I've suggested to the governors that you're the person for the job. It will probably take 18 months. I would like you to give up teaching at the end of this term, and then organise an appeal amongst the 10,000 old boys for whom we have addresses. You will have to go and see many of them, and get them to set up meetings that you and I will then go and address."

My mind was thrown into turmoil. "What about the expedition going to Iran in six months time? We've already selected the boys and many of the arrangements have already been made."

"That's all right. Count that as your holiday time. It's partly because you do interesting things like that that you're a good person to do this work. It means you have plenty of interesting things to talk about." Thanks very much, I thought, not quite sure if I had been offended or not.

"The important thing is that you very obviously believe in what it is that we're doing." That stopped me in my tracks. Did I really, deeply, believe in it all that much, or was I just enjoying it? I fumbled for the right words, and in so doing missed my opportunity. "We will, of course, keep your post open until you return. Incidentally, the governors accept that you are right at the bottom of the salary scale, and probably haven't got all the smart clothes you'll need for this, so we'll give you a clothing allowance of £2 a month ... that will cover the cost of a new suit spread over the 18 month period."

I never doubted that I could do such a job, but was I prepared to give up, for 18 months, the day-to-day thrill of working with bright young minds? Collecting money to put up a set of buildings, however grand, seemed pretty ordinary in comparison. I felt my spontaneity evaporating as I went back into the classroom. I needed time to think about this. I could not face talking to the 30 keen 13 year-olds sitting in rows in front of me. "Get out your text books, turn to page 39, and do exercise three," I said. The class looked up surprised. This wasn't how I normally behaved. Their faces begged a question and mine gave no sign of being expansive. Slowly they pulled out their books and started to write. I went to the back of the class and looked out of the window at the playing fields and the distant science laboratories. Was this going to be just about raising money, or might it open up other opportunities? Amongst the

10,000 old boys I would have to talk with, there must be some interesting people, people who had, in years gone by, sat in these very desks. Some were now sitting in the House of Commons, others were research scientists, some were journalists, others playwrights. I looked at the bowed heads and the busy hands writing, and wondered what they would be doing in 20 or 30 years time. Suddenly I saw an opportunity, to discover for myself what might be the connection between what happens to children when they are very young, and what happens to them in school, and what happens later in life. This could be extremely interesting. The bell sounded. "Let me have your books," I said in an unmistakably cheerful voice, "I'll get them back to you tomorrow."

"What's happened, sir?" said the last boy to leave the room. "You were in a bad mood when you came in, but now you seem more cheerful."

"You'll know soon enough," I said conspiratorially.

\*             \*             \*

And so began an extraordinary 18 months. With five days training from a firm of fund-raisers I was on my own, equipped with a tiny office behind the science labs, a secretary who minded me like a mother, and a list of last known addresses of the 10,000 potential contacts. I was joined by a young assistant, Howard Davies, who had just finished his third year scholarship work and who, by the time this book was written, had progressed from being director of the Audit Commission, director of the Confederation of British Industry to being deputy director of the Bank of England. As students world wide rose in rebellion against conventional authority in 1968 - as the barriers went up in the Sorbonne, and thousands of Americans marched against the war in Vietnam - I, a student of three years before, set out to collect money for bricks and mortar from intelligent men who had long ago come to realise that the most important aspects of education were nothing whatsoever to do with bricks and mortar. I was caught in a dilemma that I only dimly understood.

For several months I toured the country and met numerous people. Some were good talkers, others were taciturn. Many were busy, too busy to have had the time to read the literature that I had sent them beforehand. "When you first meet a client, get them to talk about their memories of the old school," was the advice the fund-raiser had given me. They were too thoughtful to fall for such an obvious dodge. "Tell me about yourself," they would say instead. "Why are you a teacher and what's it like nowadays in the classrooms of the old school?"

I was sociable and found it relatively easy to plant the essence of what I had to say amidst a description of what life as a teacher - at least for me - was about. Quickly, however, I had to balance what I said. My form of education had little to do with the bricks and mortar for which I was supposed to be collecting money. I found it fascinating to meet relatively successful people, years after they had gone through the best of the much vaunted grammar school system. They were, it seemed, overwhelmingly good, clever people; they held reasonable jobs, but I noticed rarely did they hold the very top jobs. Very few were in business, or any form of commercial activity. They had, essentially, worked the system; they knew what other people expected of them, but few had gone outside the narrow bounds of the career that earlier they had set out upon. They let me take their money, but they virtually wrote the first draft of the speech I was to deliver in so many different forms 20 or more years later. "We have been so well educated," they would say, "that by-and-large we are conformist. Few of us are good at doing unusual, enterprising things. We are good at analysing what other people are doing, but we are essentially careful people and we are not good risk-takers. We are good analysts, good observers, but many of us find it difficult to be leaders. At school we were never encouraged to be this. We were so busy working that the only adult role models we had were those of teachers - from them we learnt to be careful and conformist and methodical. The country needs more than that now."

One of them went much further, "I wish I were more like my younger brother. He failed to get into MGS and was so fed up with school that he left at the age of 17 and started his own business. He's done very well. He retired early several years ago and now lives in a fine house in the Algarve. He's worth a fortune after selling his company. I'm fearful that my professional pension won't be sufficient to keep me in even moderate style once I retire. If you want to be useful in education, don't stay in either the grammar school system, or the independent system. Go and make a success of the newly emerging comprehensive schools; that's where the future of the country is waiting to be made. Redefine what is meant by education ... make it possible for people to become themselves ... and find ways of being useful."

It was the first of two messages I was to bring back from being an educational salesman. The other came from America when I visited a small high school in Connecticut. Used as I was to the formal discipline and carefully regulated pattern of instruction found in English schools, I was amazed at the easy discipline, yet evident intellectual rigour, of a school that was superbly equipped, and staffed by hard-working and dedicated members of staff. I sat in on several classes. The teachers were well prepared and imaginative. What surprised me was the liveliness of the class, the rapid give and take of the questions, and the respect - real respect - shown by the teachers for each and every student. I was intrigued. The difference between the American children and English pupils I knew, even at MGS, seemed stark. Fortunately my guide, a professor of education from one of the East Coast universities, knew the

English system well from the days in which he had completed a PhD. at Oxford. "I guess you should understand that we Americans still think of our young people as potential frontiersmen. One day they'll have to sharpen their axes and cut their way through some form of concrete jungle - just what the challenge will be we don't know but, undoubtedly, the one thing they'll need is confidence in themselves. We want to build up that confidence - so we give our children their head. If I understand you Brits, you have a clear expectation of what you want your children to be. It's defined in very academic terms. You try very hard to get children to conform to your preconceived expectations. All too often you try to squeeze square pegs into round holes. I guess in the process you break the confidence of many youngsters and mould them into something they are not. We won't do that. These people are going to have to cut their way through that concrete jungle at some time in their lives. They'll need to know how to sharpen their axes wisely. We prize self-esteem very highly."

This reinforced the more general message I had been hearing from the alumni. Redefine what is meant by education. Make it possible for more people to become truly themselves. Don't push youngsters into too clearly defined slots. Let them be part of shaping their own future. Develop a form of education that doesn't waste so much talent. Go and make a success of the newly emerging comprehensive schools. That's where the future lies. These views were the beginnings of my move away from the conventional career path that lay before me.

While many of my colleagues were moving to jobs in well-known public schools, I decided to move into the state system. My reason was simple: I was more interested in teaching young people whose parents could not afford private school fees than I was in teaching youngsters who were already privileged.

# 4

# Becoming a Deputy Head

"Wanted," said the advert in the *Times Educational Supplement*. "A second deputy head, to assume responsibility for the development of the curriculum of this sixteenth century grammar school now being reorganised into a five form entry all-ability school for boys aged eleven to eighteen, as part of the Hertfordshire Plan. Apply: Headmaster, Alleyne's School, High Street, Stevenage (re-advertisement)."

Stevenage? A sleepy market town - little more than a village if I remembered it correctly - on the Great North Road and a place I had hitchhiked through in earlier years as I went up to Scotland. Yes, of course. That was the place where I was mocked by some boys in navy uniform who obviously felt that hitchhikers were below their own adolescent self-importance. An old grammar school being reorganised? I'd better be careful with this one for I knew that many forced reorganisations of old grammar schools had met with vicious reactions from staff and parents. I wonder if this is one of them. Maybe that's why it's being re-advertised? But it's about curriculum reorganisation; that's what I want. It's near London, and that would be good. Ah, I nearly forgot. Stevenage, once the site of a Roman villa, was the first of the post-war new towns, designed to take the population pressure off London. It wouldn't look much like a village any longer, I thought, and I nearly gave it a miss. But there was nothing else attractive that week and, as it was getting very close to the end of the job-changing season, I sent off an application. I might only have been out of university for seven years, but this was a job I thought I could do.

Late on a Thursday afternoon I got a message to phone the headmaster of Alleyne's School. "I'm interested in your application to be my deputy," said an obviously polished - was it contrived? - Oxbridge voice. "I've spoken with your referees. They speak well of you. Are you interested in coming to a small, provincial town, struggling to maintain academic standards?" A strange question, I thought. "I could be," I replied, trying not to sound indecisive. "Good," he replied. "I'll be interviewing next Wednesday. Get down here on Tuesday afternoon and we can then have an informal talk together."

I made good time on the journey and the English countryside got progressively greener the further south I went. Spring had come late that year, but in Hertfordshire the trees were already in full bloom, and the great rolling downlands shimmered with the bright green of the young corn. Stevenage looked just as I had remembered it - straight off a picture post-card. Then, as I neared the end of the High Street, it all changed. The road broadened, the trees stopped, and before me was a medley of concrete and glass buildings and I drove round numerous roundabouts with signs to Zone 6, or Zone 8, or Recreation Area, or Industrial Zone. I turned round, and as I drove back into the High Street a notice proclaimed The Old Town. It was like going through a border post between two countries.

I was still a little early and I went into the local garage and asked the mechanic to check my oil. As he bent over the engine I explained that I was thinking of moving to the area. "What are the secondary schools like?" I asked. He looked up sharply. "Huh," he snorted, "not as good as they used to be. It's all this b----y reorganisation. No one knows what's happening any longer."

"What about Alleyne's? Wasn't that the old grammar school?" I asked.

"It was; but not any longer. Anyone can go there. It used to be good, and clever children went on to university. Now the kids are cheeky and scruffy." He spat on his hands and rubbed them on his sleeves.

"Did you go there yourself?" I asked innocently.

"Good Lord, no," he said scorning my simplicity. "I wasn't clever enough for that by half. I went to the secondary modern and left at 15. I know my place. I'm no good at learning. Now even that school is saying it's the same as the grammar school. B----y nonsense. Kids need to know their place, and stick there."

Little did he realise how accurately he had described English attitudes towards learning, and English assumptions about themselves. This little exchange shows how the English are hung up on how true education is about the intellect, rather than about making a living. A definition of education of this kind has divided England on social grounds every bit as obvious to those who can read the signs, as have racial issues wrecked the social cohesion of the United States. England is concerned with the maintenance of the social status quo in ways that most Americans cannot understand.

*     *     *

I parked the car in the school drive. "Can you tell me where I find the school secretary, please?" I asked a passing boy. He waved in the direction of two doors. Should I knock or just walk in? I compromised. I knocked and walked in, and hit my head on a low door beam. I almost blacked out. I certainly saw stars. The room was dark, and at the far end, behind a large desk, sat a crow-like figure of a man with heavy rimmed glasses. "I'm sorry," I said, "I was looking for the headmaster's secretary." He appeared to scowl. "Through that door over there," he pointed and, as I turned to go he called sharply after me.

"Who are you?" I turned back. "John Abbott," I said, rubbing my badly hurting head.

"My dear man, I am so sorry. I was not expecting you through that door. I'm Burridge. I've been looking forward to meeting you. Sit down. Sit down. We must talk. There are things I must tell you before you meet the staff and governors."

Sitting down I felt better. My head stopped spinning and I looked round a fine room, with plenty of heavy oak beams and small windows. "Fascinating, isn't it?" said the headmaster. "Built in 1558 as a classroom for 12 boys, each of whom had to bring a log of wood to school every day throughout the year to keep the room heated during winter time."

"This place is a mess," he continued. "The town, the school, and the whole education authority. The staff needs shaking up. The whole place is soft to the core. Far too full of social care and concern, full of unrealistic expectations about the working classes, and nothing like concerned enough about academic rigour. I need a deputy who understands academic concerns and someone who is essentially a good communicator. I need to have the parents on my side if I'm ever to get the staff to work harder. So, one of your jobs would be to become an exceptionally good sixth form tutor - to set the academic pace. Another would be to develop the parents' association, and another would be to develop the curriculum."

I winced at the width of his expectations of his new deputy. "I'd need help in understanding a curriculum appropriate for a comprehensive school," I said. "It's not what I'm used to."

"Whatever you do, don't use that term - comprehensive school - again. We were a grammar school, we have now to be an all-ability school. I want this school run as if it were still a grammar school. I came from a quite ordinary background," he continued, almost reflectively. "I did well at grammar school, and again at university. There's nothing wrong with everybody pursuing a highly academic curriculum. Some will do it easily; others will have to work very hard. Others will just have to have their diet watered down, and some will fail. That's life. If the staff will support me we could get as good results with our best boys as any public school. That's what we should be aiming for - then we'll be even better than the old grammar school. We must put all our best resources into our brightest pupils."

At last I had a chance to make a point. "But what of those from restricted backgrounds, and what of those who have genuine learning difficulties? The ones I'm told the authority is now insisting that you take?"

He scowled for I was obviously picking on a weak point. "Damned socialism. Egalitarianism. You'll have to find some kind of solution. Give them plenty of rugby and athletics if necessary. Give them lots of extra English and mathematics. Keep a strict discipline; I've told the governors that I insist on the right to use the cane for ill discipline. However, discipline won't be your responsibility. I have another deputy for that, and he's in charge of staff discipline as well. I don't imagine you two would get on very well." He looked over his heavy-rimmed glasses and smiled. "I believe in constructive tension. It's good for everyone, and I'll watch with interest." He again smiled, this time demonically. "I'll expect one of you to be the officer and the other to be the NCO. You'll have to work out between you which is which."

If the borderline between the two warring cultures was at the bottom of the High Street, the self-appointed control room for old England was right in the middle of Alleyne's. Was he talking to all the other candidates like this, I wondered? What were they like? What experience did they have? Before I could ask any question, however, he was called away - with bad grace - to attend a meeting of the other headteachers of the town - a meeting that had been waiting a full 20 minutes for him to arrive before it could start. "Damned waste of time. I ought to be allowed to get on with what I'm good at," he snarled. "Take a look around, but if any staff speak to you, keep your own judgement. Meet me at the school house at six-thirty and I'll introduce you to the other candidates - to the opposition."

It was late afternoon. Most of the pupils had gone home, though there was an impressive number still playing cricket, while the orchestra was rehearsing in the main hall, and the art department looked active. There were extensive grounds and some fine trees, but the majority of the buildings dated from the 1950s and I remembered that for 400 of its 430 years of history the school had indeed been small, with an annual entry of only 20 or 30 pupils. Mainly these had been the sons of local tradesmen, some had been the sons of farmers and had needed stables for their horses while they were in class. For a few years, after the building of the railways in the 1840s, some came from even further afield, and slept in a dormitory from Monday to Friday. The school's connection with its distant past was tenuous; a board in the dining room listed all the head teachers going back to 1558, but the school was largely a recent creation much influenced by nineteenth century assumptions about public schools. Even the school song, "in 1558, 'ere Beth to the throne ascended/ what can I do, said his reverence true/ when my time on earth is ended?" dated from the 1950s.

Walking around the school I was not short of company. Staff seemed to appear from every corner. "Oh, hello," they would say casually. "Are you a candidate for the deputy's post?" They told a different story to the head, a confused, uncertain story, a story with more questions than answers and full of English ambivalence. Many of them had been in the school for 20 years and more, during which time pupil numbers had more than doubled. As a grammar school it had admitted only the top 25 per cent of the ability range. Most of the teachers could well handle the traditional curriculum the head so favoured. Situated nicely in the old part of the town, Alleyne's had benefited enormously by being able to draw the best of the talent from the developing New Town, without losing its old town ambience and without concerning itself as to what happened to the majority of pupils who were rejected at the age of 11.

"What happened to all those other pupils?" I asked.

"Oh, they went to the newly built secondary modern schools between the ages of 11 and 15, and most of them then went into local industry. Sometimes those schools recognised that a few of their pupils should have come to us. A small number of them did transfer but they seemed ill at ease and never did well," said an older member of staff with a degree of complacency that I found frightening.

"It was basically an unfair system," said a much younger woman teacher. "Many of these children could have passed the entrance exam if they'd been at a better primary school. But even that's not the main point. Children learn - and excel - in different ways. Each child needs taxing, needs encouragement to work hard. But to say that you split them on academic criteria at the age of 11 is to divide society in ways which effectively destroy the confidence of many people forever." Several of the others agreed with her. "The challenge Alleyne's has to take on is both academic and social," said one. "This is becoming an incredibly class conscious town. However painful it's going to be we've just got to find a curriculum that respects the different traditions from which these children come, and raises the whole community's expectations. Only then will we be able to extend the abilities of the individual child."

"That's all very well," said an older man. "I read English at Oxford. I've taught English scholarship work in the sixth form for 25 years. I'm good at it. I don't even know how to talk to these people, I have to admit."

"What sort of help did you get from the education authority when the school started to change?" I asked. People laughed. "Help? It was the blind leading the blind. The advisers were all like us, totally unsure. If you asked each of them to say what their subject needs were in the curriculum, you'd find that the sum of all their requirements would mean doubling the length of the school day!"

"That's not absolutely true," said the younger woman, "The help is there, just waiting for us. The people who understand this are the primary school teachers. There are some good teachers here in Stevenage and to them it's how they can help every child to learn that gives them their excitement. It's almost as if primary schools teach pupils and secondary schools teach subjects."

"Are you suggesting that after three years at Oxford, and all those years teaching English literature at scholarship level, I should now go and learn from primary teachers? That's ridiculous," responded the older man sharply. "I couldn't do that. Maybe the head's right after all. We should stick to what we're good at. The children should change, not us."

When I sat down to write this section of the book in late 1998 the absurdity of such attitudes struck me once again. We know from the evolutionary sciences that every child is born with a powerful toolkit of predispositions that go a long way in explaining how they learn and make sense of the world. This is what Howard Gardner means when he writes about multiple intelligence. Education has to be careful to devise learning environments that take such predisposition beyond what comes naturally, but the evidence is striking - in doing this we must go with the grain of the brain. The most forceful description of why education must be about helping children master their own learning strategies came from the cognitive neuroscientist Michael Gazzaniga in 1997 when he wrote, "life is about discovering what is already built into our brains. All the ways that human societies try to change minds and to change how humans truly interact with the environment are doomed to fail. Indeed, societies fail when they preach at their populations. They tend to succeed when they allow each individual to discover what millions of years of evolution have already bestowed upon mind and body." The English have never been happy with such a conclusion, be it in 1972 or 1999. Such a conclusion, they think, is too open, too unquantifiable and too threatening to the social status quo; yet by ignoring this we lose those very human qualities on which a society is dependent for its continuous evolution and development.

*          *          *

Over sherry that evening I met the other deputy. Trevor was tall, like me, and he was obviously incredibly efficient. He was never separated from his notepad, and knew lots about me - and presumably about the other candidates as well. He even knew (goodness knows how) that I had quizzed the garage attendant, and he gave me the cynical low-down on the teachers I had met. In many ways he was the antithesis of the head but in their clinical, detached assessments of their colleagues, they were like blood brothers. It did not feel comfortable.

"Let me tell you about tomorrow's interviewing panel," said the head. He was drinking gin while we had been offered only sherry, and was amazingly indiscreet.

"Firstly, the chairman of governors. By anyone's standards he's a remarkable man, but he doesn't look it or sound it. He left school at 14, and if I understand it correctly went both into the railways and the Labour party. He knows how to keep the trains running on time (ha ha) and is the politician largely responsible for Stevenage becoming the first of the post-war New Towns. He's just become the first Labour member to become chairman of the county council; that's quite an achievement. His son went to Alleyne's when it was a grammar school, got a scholarship to Cambridge, and then joined the Ministry of Overseas Development. Philip Ireton agrees with me and Harold Wilson [then prime minister] when he says comprehensive schools are effectively grammar schools for everyone. The deputy chairman is an ex-public schoolboy, and never forgets it. He's also chairman of the bench of magistrates, and a bachelor. He has pretensions and I have to admit that I don't see eye to eye with him." That, I was quickly to understand, was a classic understatement.

"Then there's Johnny Pryor who was once chairman. So were his father and grandfather before him. He's an old Etonian, who owns a lot of land and has a big estate just outside Stevenage. He says exactly what he thinks, and does exactly what he likes. The people of Stevenage love him – he's a sort of Christian Socialist who donates to all kinds of good causes, opens his land up to endless Boy Scout groups, but loves to dress up and go to Henley and Wimbledon." He took a deep pull of his drink and, I thought, shuddered. Johnny Pryor, it seemed, might eat him for breakfast.

"Then there's the statutory New Town councillor, Tony Wiltshire. He's shrewd, I suppose, but often seems slow on the uptake. His personal crusade is to limit how many times I physically chastise pupils. You'll be amazed. I now have to fill in a punishment book after each chastisement and produce it at every governor's meeting. It's the first, and sometimes the only, thing he looks at. Look out for the sly questioning from the divisional education officer – David Little. He'll be representing the county education officer. He has far more influence than he should. He's a one-time teacher who, I suspect, couldn't stand the strain of teaching, and is now an administrator.

"So, gentlemen, these are the main people you will have to convince. And of course me. Then whoever is appointed will have to be able to work with each of us, and with Mr Fox over there." Fox's smile put us all on edge. Was all this so farcical that I ought to get out right now, or was this the kind of chaos within which I could thrive?

One candidate withdrew that night, another the following morning.

At the interviewing panel I immediately established a working relationship with Philip Ireton who, I was later to discover, was one of the most fascinating, tough, kind and imaginative men I had ever met. Johnny Pryor was quite outrageous in his views, but immensely supportive of the people he liked. Tony Wiltshire was, as a quarryman once said to me in Ireland about a lump of granite, "solid, right through to the Maker's name" and I sympathised with his wish to rid the school of the use of the cane. David Little, far from being the failed teacher turned administrator, was the highly articulate voice of the thoughtful educationalist trying to come to terms with a collapsing public morality. Geoffrey Powell-Davis was ponderous, personally lonely, and publicly arrogant - sometimes great fun, but all too prone to let his pretensions undermine his judgement. In understanding how to get my way past him, I learnt innumerable lessons that have subsequently served me well.

Although it was Burridge who confirmed my appointment later that afternoon I knew, intuitively if not fully consciously, that neither he nor Trevor Fox could ever be the people that I could work with for long. Deep down I think we all knew that we were just not interested in the same things. They might have been more sure of what they thought the school was all about, but I thought I knew much more about what children needed.

*         *         *

Four months later, I moved from Manchester to Stevenage, from being an assistant teacher of geography to being a deputy headmaster. I was young; I'd left university only seven years before, and two of these years had been spent largely promoting a highly selective grammar school. True, I had fitted in a number of other interesting activities, but I felt myself desperately under-qualified to take responsibility for shaping the curriculum for nearly 1,000 pupils in the formative years of 11 to 18. How was it possible that I came to be in this position? By what set of historic quirks was I now answerable to such an extraordinary governing body? What did they think I should be doing? What did the parents think? Even more to the point, what did the pupils think I might be able to do to help meet their needs? (That is, the tiny minority who might even have thought that this was a valid question.)

Stevenage was a microcosm of English educational thought. A school for young boys existed long before the Reformation, maintained by the church, and offering an education designed for a tiny elite of students. Between four and seven miles away in each direction similar schools had existed, each being within reasonable walking distance of healthy youngsters able to walk through forests and around fields. Following the dissolution of the monasteries in the 1530s and 1540s, a number of wealthy merchants and clerics built and endowed their own schools.

Thomas Alleyne, one-time vicar of Stevenage, did just that in 1558. He built the school and provided land to yield an income for the teacher. Many similar small town grammar schools were to be found across the country, teaching the rudiments of Latin and Greek. Shakespeare attended one such school, as did Thomas Paine and George Washington's ancestors in Northamptonshire, but the majority of young people had had no such opportunity. They had either learnt from their parents, or the apprentice master, or were left entirely to their own devices. This was the model of schooling that early settlers had taken to Boston, and it led to the creation of the Boston Latin School.

Stevenage was far closer to London than Manchester, but in its educational provision it remained strictly provincial. No wealthy textile merchants had existed to provide capital for the school system in the nineteenth century. Formal education was for the rising intelligentsia only, and of little concern to the majority. The Education Act of 1870 legislated for all children in England to attend school up to the age of 12. Its concerns were as much custodial as they were educational, utilitarian and highly pragmatic. Schools were more concerned to keep children off the streets, now that they could no longer go into the factories, than they were to provide a program of study that would lead to the all-round development of the young person. Eventually elementary schools were built, either by voluntary organisations or by the local authority, or a combination of both.

Stevenage had an elementary school in the late 1890s, and Philip Ireton had been one of its earlier pupils. Bright children could stay at such schools until they were 14, and could later transfer to technical schools, or carry out further study on a part-time basis as they worked. Many did this through the Worker's Education Association; frequently they did well, and often became leaders in the trades unions, and many of them went on to shape the post-war welfare state. Many others were content to leave at the earliest opportunity - from the outset school had been to them an alien world, and learning a strange mystery. The garage mechanic was such a man; they invested men who went to the grammar school with a strange mystique.

Stevenage was the epitome of the working-class dream that inspired the welfare state during the early years of the Second World War. It was specifically the creation of Philip Ireton. He quickly recognised the significance of its location immediately to the north of where the railway line from Scotland to London split. As a locally elected member of the Urban District Council in the mid-1930s he started lobbying for Stevenage to become a government sponsored new town which would give tolerable living conditions to the over-spill population of London. Increased impetus to his cause was provided by the destruction of housing during the London blitz, and by 1946 the new Labour government - of which Philip hoped one day to become a member - announced Stevenage as the first of the post-war new towns. Stevenage was to grow from 5,000 to 80,000 over the next 30 years. Not everyone was as delighted as he, though fortunes were made in the property boom, not least by the farming community whose sons had, for generations, attended Alleyne's.

\*          \*          \*

Two years before the decision to build Stevenage, the Education Act of 1944 (an integral part of the welfare state as devised by Lord Beveridge) established a tripartite form of secondary education. Elementary education would be provided on a common basis for every child up to the age of 11, at which point a decision would be made on the basis of an intelligence test to allocate the brightest pupils to a grammar school. The slightly less gifted would be sent to a technical grammar school, and the rest, about 60 per cent of the total, would go to a secondary modern school. While the proportion varied from place to place 25 per cent normally went to the grammar school. If you were in any sense a promising youngster, you left your local community by the age of 11. Only those with limited potential were thought to be worth educating around their own homes. Educational practice did immense damage to the sense of local community. Children were forced to become rootless. This was to be the pattern of education adopted across the whole of Stevenage; and indeed Stevenage with its massive building program was to be a national model for the future. This was where it was all to happen. Stevenage was to be a social laboratory for post-war England.

Educational thinking was led by an amazing bureaucratic confidence in the concept that intelligence was a fixed commodity, and that so clear were the manifestations of this that scientifically designed tests given at the age of 11 could reduce such intelligence to a meaningful quotient. With such a quotient, child could be compared to child, and a hierarchy of provision established. It was, in fact, a great conspiracy. Even while the bureaucracy to support all this was being set up, initial research was finding that the results gained by an individual child could vary significantly if taken twice within a single month. This could result in a child, on a good day, qualifying for a place in the bottom class of a grammar school, but on a bad day being assigned not to a technical school but to the top form of a secondary modern, and vice versa. Yet, once having been set up, this form of selection was remarkably resistant to change. Numbers, it was thought, have an authenticity that imprecise words and sentences lack. A single number, be it 140 or 95, came to describe what a child was. Its long-term implications were devastating to individuals.

It took 20 years for this set of false assumptions to be both challenged and changed. The 11 plus exam became a much-dreaded event on the road to adulthood. The middle classes were the first to fear it. While the test gave a cultural bias towards them, bad performance on the day split many a family in ways which, emotions put aside, individual parents knew was not right. They also knew that the criteria used in the exam were strictly limited and not fully embracing of whatever it was that actually comprised intelligence. Intuitively they also knew that many children develop later, if given half a chance. They knew that a hard and fast rejection at 11 had devastating results on youngsters that would remain with them for a lifetime. Even today you can go into a room full of people aged 50 and over; probe gently and you will quickly sense the deep feeling of failure that memories of this exam still conjure up. Of all my governing body it was Johnny Pryor, the old Etonian, who most understood this. "People are more complex than a simple number - it's just a balmy idea."

\* \* \*

A new secondary modern was built in the Old Town, with its front entrance facing the back entrance to the grammar school. Even the gift of a Henry Moore statue could never rid that school of a public assumption that it took those pupils rejected by the grammar school. Alleyne's meanwhile thrived. Not only did it get significantly more money per pupil than did the secondary moderns, it was now able to pick the best 120 pupils each year from a town of approaching 80,000 people, rather than the 30 pupils a year it had previously taken from a town of a mere 5,000 citizens.

Alleyne's had a specific vision; an academic education for the academically able youngsters whose early career expectations were to go on to university, and subsequently join the professions. The qualification you left school with largely determined where you went to university, and your university qualifications put you on the appropriate rung of a ladder within a single career path. Education was about getting paper qualifications. It came from assiduously following the lessons given by the teachers, and it largely ceased when university was over. By that time you knew it all.

It had been an easy system for the headmaster of the day to administer, but it was so comfortable that the staff, in a gentle and kindly way, started to acknowledge its limitations. They recognised that the exams measured what pupils had learnt in class-based subjects. Yet they knew in their hearts that education was much more than that. Education had to be about values, about judgements, about diverse interests, about critical thinking, and about taking responsibility. These things were not easily taught, and they certainly could not be examined and reported on a logarithmic scale. So a relaxed and caring staff ran an extensive array of extra-curricular activities - classroom teaching was not overtly demanding and many of them had energies for post-four o'clock activities. Pupils were responsive and enthusiastic. Games of all sorts, clubs, societies, drama, debating, social services groups and the like, flourished. It was a version of what happened at Manchester Grammar but inevitably limited by the smallness of the school, and the more limited expectations of a still largely rural, working-class community with a reasonable scattering of professional people and some old, landed money.

"Jonathan has three good A level grades in maths, physics and chemistry," my predecessor would write on a university admission form, "but what is really noticeable about Jonathan is...." Several pages of careful analysis of the broad and well-conceived education beyond the classroom would then follow. The English liked this. They didn't fully understand what those A level grades actually meant, but they did understand a youngster of good social standing who held his bat straight, or played at scrum half. It was a very English compromise. Those things which seemed to be most valued were those which were done by teachers in a voluntary capacity. Education was essentially a gentleman's activity.

It was what I had grown up with and is what many parents tend to remember. It was, however, very expensive, elitist, and essentially unfair. Those teachers were relaxed because there was enough money for Alleyne's to have small classes, and for each teacher to have adequate free periods for preparation and marking. The money for this came, indirectly, from the fact that the other schools - the secondary modern schools catering for three-quarters of the population - had far larger classes and fewer teachers who, in turn, had less time to do their preparation.

What mattered, the English thought, was the proper education of the able, not of those who might be slower learners. It was a system, however, which produced far too many young men and women who would later look back, as an earlier generation had told me about MGS, and say that they were just too well cosseted - too comfortable - within a path set for them by the teacher. They knew little about taking responsibility for themselves or of asking questions that might rock the establishment. There was little or no room in their lives for an old McFadgen, no room during term time (and frequently none in the holidays either) just to be themselves. The school became their all-embracing community, and without it many of them were lost. Years later they would flock back for old boys' dinners, cricket matches, or rugby festivals, and seek to recreate that camaraderie they had not been able to find elsewhere in their lives. Their old boys' ties acted as lifejackets, not first-class tickets to an uncertain destination.

*          *          *

Initially it had been the teachers who had welcomed the 1944 Education Act, but they were amongst the first to recognise its flaw - the inadequate understanding of intelligence. Not only did they see their own children inappropriately allocated to the wrong secondary schools, they saw also the children of other parents misplaced on a frighteningly large scale. They became angry and through all forms of associations lobbied to have the system changed. What they had in mind was very roughly comparable to the community high school as best understood in America at that time: a school serving all the children of the community, and by its size and diversity, able to provide any course, to any level of previous experience, and in any combination. Frequently they called this (in a nice piece of jargon) a bilateral school - a school combining a grammar, technical grammar, and secondary modern school curriculum, under one roof, or at least on one campus.

The theoreticians got it wrong for two reasons. First, they ignored the child's need to be able to relate to something of manageable size, something which in a human way belonged to them. The significance of group size has not been lost on those of us living in the late twentieth century. We need to remember that we are who we are because of evolution and, up until recently, humans have lived and worked in relatively small groups. Businesses, especially those which breed creativity, are increasingly understanding this and limiting work teams to no more than 12 or 15 people. Even today in the most primitive tribes in the Brazilian rain forest if the group gets beyond 12 or 14 fighting men (with women, children and dependent relatives, the entire group numbers 50 or 60 people), it either divides of its own peaceful volition or splits through bloody rivalry. Ask yourself why so many adults have as their best friends throughout life those they played team sports with or played with in a band?

The second reason theoreticians got it wrong is that they did not understand quickly enough the stresses that would be created by this English form of desegregation, the mixing of children from different social backgrounds. Some parents, while delighted that the academic curriculum of the grammar school was still readily identifiable, wanted the school to reflect their own cultural expectations - school uniforms, neat hairstyles, prefects, public award systems, collegiate assemblies, and the use of the Queen's English. Other parents, either of a liberal or an egalitarian persuasion, saw uniforms as an anathema and hairstyles as being largely irrelevant. They wanted forms of discipline that would represent agreed and acceptable norms and award systems that would truly reflect multiple forms of achievement. Such conflicts devastated a sense of genuine community. They put school and parents into frequent conflict, and even more frequently led to that awful phenomenon of English secondary education - the badly tied tie, the dirty blazer with the badge half torn off, the loosely tucked in shirt, the scruffy trousers, and the implied message "I don't belong to this." It was schooling on an inhuman scale. It was the school as factory, which led to children seeing themselves as products of the system, not people who in any sense felt themselves to be in charge of their own futures. The more it failed the greater the incentive for more well-to-do parents to send their children to private schools.

*       *       *

Much of the pressure to scrap the 11 plus came from the new thinking in primary schools. The immediate impact of the 1944 Education Act had been to put a straight jacket on primary school practice, forcing those schools progressively to teach for the test. Primary teachers disliked this intensely, seeing as they did every day, young children whose own home and community culture was at variance with book learning and standardised testing for all which were of an exclusively pencil and paper kind. These children were not unintelligent, such teachers argued, it was that they had different kinds of values, and different forms of potential expertise that had to be assessed in an altogether different way. Put them through the wrong hurdles, at the wrong time, and they would come to lose faith in themselves - in ways similar to my own experience in Latin years before.

In the years after the Second World War most professions remained virtually closed to women. The one exception was teaching, particularly of elementary pupils; the grip of subject-specific skills in secondary schools still favoured male graduates. So, for a generation and more, bright, determined and thoughtful young women entered the primary sector. Many were mothers as well, and learning to balance the demands of a profession with the needs of the home, few sought promotion to high administrative posts. They wanted to teach, and they wanted to teach pupils not subjects. They stayed long enough to learn exactly how to do this.

In 1965, 21 years after the Education Act of 1944, and the year I joined MGS, a Labour Government issued Circular 10/65, requiring all local authorities to prepare plans to reorganise their secondary education along non-selective lines. The terminology was important. Many a Labour politician was pledged to support grammar schools; after all, it was in their classrooms that the young aspiring politicians had learnt the skills that, years later, helped them to power. The prime minister, Harold Wilson, was pledged to maintain an essentially academic grammar school tradition within comprehensive schools, thereby compromising any profound thinking about the nature of learning in secondary schools. "Grammar school education for everyone," was the formula.

Educationalists were not so simplistic. Many feared the implications of applying a strictly academic education, led by a heavy dependence on external examinations, on all pupils. The best of the primary teachers, and many old time secondary modern teachers, feared this most of all. They wanted a complete reassessment of the nature of secondary education with a focus on the skills of learning and the recognition that pupils could excel in a variety of ways. They wanted to go beyond reassessing the content of single subjects, to a reinvention of the curriculum. They were to be bitterly disappointed. Comprehensive reorganisation was to be an administrative task - one undoubtedly of great complexity, but lacking any profound questioning as to what exactly learning in secondary schools was to be all about. At that critical, once-in-a-lifetime, moment educationalists and politicians stepped back from the fundamental question that they could not adequately answer. "Education for what?" The failure to have a clear goal behind which the country could be united and which would survive the rise and fall of politically expedient objectives, is the fundamental flaw in the English education system. "Learning to succeed" means little if you do not define first what success means.

*        *        *

Hertfordshire, unlike other shire counties which were more conservative and traditional, started to devise plans for reorganisation. By 1968 plans were complete. They called for a complete reorganisation of the county's 120 or so secondary schools - grammar, technical grammar and secondary modern (of which the latter outnumbered the grammar schools at least four to one) - into what they called the "11 to 18 all-ability school". The term comprehensive was studiously avoided as being too egalitarian. Taking the most optimistic of all population projections, it was expected that there would be sufficient pupils for each school to have five forms of intake each year (five times 30 pupils would equal an intake of 150). It was also assumed, with a confidence bordering on the whimsical, that so good would be the quality of primary education that this entry would be statistically skewed towards the higher abilities, so that at least half of each year group would eventually remain in school beyond the age of 16, and so create sixth forms of at least 120 in each school (MGS had had over 600; Alleyne's as a grammar school in previous years, had just over 100).

It was an ambitious plan. Every community in a county of over 1,250,000 people was, in effect, to have a grammar school with an extended tail which would, somehow, incorporate everybody. In the late sixties, with the political will to develop primary education further and an expectation that Hertfordshire as a wealthy county with the support of a strong government at Westminster would continue to raise taxes for education at levels considerably above the national average, it seemed to many an optimistic vision well worth gambling on.

Amongst the enthusiastic optimists there were others who realised that this was pushing optimism to its limits, and that any reduction in funding would immediately make the entire system nonviable. A few, just a few, kept on asking what education in a post modern world would be all about. Without a community-wide understanding every school would be left to define its own mission - a mission for the school in isolation, not for the school as part of the greater community. Each school presented its own version of revealed wisdom. The age of the individual was created almost by omission.

*          *          *

In Stevenage the majority voice was that of the New Town and the secondary modern schools. It was a strictly egalitarian voice. Alleyne's felt vulnerable, its former privileged position under public scrutiny. Of course it had done well in the past, with the cream of the pupils, small class sizes, and the best capitation allowance. How would Alleyne's cope with disruptive pupils, rootless recent arrivals from the East End of London, whose home culture did not understand academic expectations? The one-time secondary moderns contemplated a richer diet made up of their fair share of the academically able, and a reduction in number of those for whom nobody, it seemed, had an answer. Being a relatively compact town with a good internal transport system, parents were given a choice of schools they wanted their child to attend, and asked to nominate three alternatives. "Grammar schools for all," they clamoured. "Now our sons can get into Alleyne's without even taking an exam."

*          *          *

With local variations, these were the scenarios that were played out across England in the seventies and early eighties. A partially thought-through educational theory compromised with the historic and social priorities in numerous communities in ways that led to confusion, dismay and the loss of much untapped potential. And so in Stevenage, as elsewhere, parental and other expectations hit the logistic and political buffers.

"What would your parents say if I told them of the language you used to your history teacher?" I tried remonstrating in my naive, selective grammar school style, as I sought to help an older teacher restore some sense of self-esteem after a disastrous session with a truculent 13 year-old boy. The boy looked puzzled. "They'd say he was a b----y old fool," was his only comment. It was all "give, give, give," said the hard-pressed teachers. "These parents take everything and give nothing back. Look at this note I got from a mother this morning after I tried to enforce school uniform yesterday."

> "Darren has advised me that you have criticised the shoes he was wearing for school. Unfortunately, being the size he is, I can't afford to buy him shoes for school and for social occasions, therefore I buy shoes that will suffice for both....He will be returning to school next term in these same shoes, but when they wear out I will try and buy shoes that suit both yourself and Darren."

"I had a similar problem yesterday as well," said a chemistry teacher. "There's one boy in my class who's as idle as hell. His class work's awful and his test results appalling. Yet he turns in homework that is technically good, but very obviously not done by him. So in yesterday's lesson I challenged him to explain who helped him. He said it was his Dad who did most of his homework, so I told him to work hard enough to do it by himself so that his Dad wouldn't have to help him so much. Look at the letter I got."

"Jimmy has produced for the second time your request concerning the drawings on page 26 - lesson 6, reference his homework. Without prejudice I take your point concerning your statement. However there can be nothing more destroying to a boy's confidence than disbelief by his seniors. Therefore, in view of your statement perhaps you will consider restoring the confidence he used to have in your teaching."

\*       \*       \*

My appointment as second deputy head was two years into this period of a transition which, as far as teachers were concerned, had seen the progressive dilution of the entry. It was also a time at which the numbers of teachers had to be reduced to bring Alleyne's into line with staffing in the other schools so the teachers rightly felt confused and under-valued. Appointed headmaster in 1970, John Burridge did his utmost to strengthen the grammar school tradition. Dismissing the management of school as "mere logistics", he had appointed as his first deputy, the year before I arrived, a logistics specialist in Trevor Fox. While the head dreamed dreams of a bygone academic Utopia, Trevor cajoled the demoralised staff with his conviction that everything of value could be reduced to a set of prescriptive instructions. It had been a chance quirk of the new staffing formula that, while the school was having to achieve more and more through a better use of existing staffing, a mysterious statistical point had been reached whereby the school administration could be increased. That's why a second deputy was to be appointed. Desperate to find some workable accommodation between his own idiosyncratic style, and the rigorous administrative direction of Trevor Fox, Burridge was looking - I later discovered - for a good public relations man who would look somewhat like himself, but do the thinking about the broader curriculum that he was totally unwilling to do for himself. Probably there was no other school in the country which would have appointed me at that stage, yet I believe I was, for reasons that Mr Burridge himself did not understand, the right person to be appointed. Time was to prove my case, but time was also to prove that the unanswered questions of the late 1960s were to make the very school that I was to labour so hard to create, nonviable within a further decade.

For the next two years I found it prudent to stay in the background. There were great tensions swirling around which most people thought related to the struggle between head and first deputy, but in reality they were actually the tensions between an old world of simple academic expectations and a new world of utilitarian qualifications for a contemporary society. I could not see it as simple as that at that stage, because I was too deeply involved in day-to-day affairs. Without realising exactly what was going on I spent an invaluable two years learning to bridge these two worlds. It was a traumatic experience I would not have survived if I had not had a personal world of my own, far removed from the struggles of contemporary schooling, and the expectations of a New Town, a world where ordinary people mattered, and the voices of children unconstrained by the classroom, could be heard.

*       *       *

A 16-hour journey separated Stevenage, with its interminable struggles and confusions, from the ageless charm of the tiny hamlet of Shrah on the shores of Lough Derg in County Galway, in the far west of Ireland. A hamlet so small as only to figure on maps of the smallest possible scale. "Go as far as Power's Cross, on the Ennis Road," locals would say, "turn left, and just keep on going for three miles. You're bound to get there. There's nowhere else."

Before I'd left Manchester, I'd teamed up with three friends from Trinity to buy a small farmhouse with an acre of land and some foreshore. We had shared the expense, so my investment was limited to £200. The house, with three rooms downstairs, the largest of which was dominated by an open fireplace, complete with a chain to hang the pot over the peat fire, had two bedrooms. It was in a bad state of repair, but the roof was strong enough, and all the other jobs were, I reckoned, within my capability to handle, always, I trusted, with the help of some friends.  Shrah was to become the other side of my life, the antidote to all the pressures of life as a comprehensive school headmaster.

There was some confusion the day we finally agreed to buy the farmhouse from the shifty farmer who had recently inherited the farmhouse from his bachelor uncle. No one knew exactly where the boundary of our land lay. The local factor (realtor), and I agreed to meet with the nephew and finally sort out where the four corners of our property should lie. The nephew was accompanied by a son of his old age, a boy I thought to be about twelve. We had agreed one corner of the property and marked it with a large stone and were arguing as to whether the next corner would place a fine sycamore tree within our property or not, when I noticed the nephew apparently scratching his back vigorously. It was a strange form of scratching. I was suspicious and looked around. His son was way back at the first stone, pushing it far back from the position we had earlier agreed; the scratching was the nephew's signalling of the new unagreed position. "Come now, Michael," exclaimed the factor, John Taylor, "that's the oldest trick in the book. You're not thinking, are you, the English would fall for that? Were you never in England yourself?"

"I was that," Michael Clark replied sheepishly. "I worked on the London buses for 12 years."

"Well you ought to know you can't fool a man like me in such a manner," I said, responding to the light-hearted banter set by the factor, which was the only alternative to my being very cross. "Because I had already counted the number of paces from the house to the corner stone - it should be 56."

I made the journey to Shrah several days after the end of each term. The respect I had earned when buying the house increased when the local people saw I was a worker as well as a talker. One of the first tasks - I had still been in Manchester at that time - had been to lay on a water supply to the house, which meant replacing an open concrete tank that collected rain water from the roof. "I've got a fine spring on my land 600 yards away from your house, and about the same distance from mine," said Martin Flanagan, a neighbouring farmer. "I'd like to put in a pressure pump to lift the water from down there up to my house. Trouble is, my cash flow at the moment is not too good. But, tell you what - if we split the price of the pump between us, and you pay for the blocks to build the shed to house it, my son and I will build it and you can have all the water you want for free, forever."

That sounded a good deal to me. We walked back towards our house, looking at the land where we would have to lay a one and a half-inch pipe. It would mean crossing three other fields, two of which belonged to other farmers. I anticipated a problem with way-leave. "Not at all," the inventive Martin retorted. "Offer to put a cattle trough into each field and they'd be delighted, as they could then keep the cattle in those fields even in dry weather."

"What about crossing the road?" I asked, looking at the ten-foot wide hard-core track that led between the farms.

"Just warn the others down the road that you're going to close it for four or five hours, and then dig the trench extra deep under the road, put plenty of sand all around the pipe to protect it, and then back-fill it and level it off. If we can get Mick Carey's nephew's digger, we could have the whole trench dug, pipe laid, and back-filled within a couple of days."

I tried grasping at reality. "What about getting some kind of approval; after all, the road belongs to..." I thought hard trying to solve the problem in the logical, bureaucratic way of a deputy head teacher. "Well, I suppose it belongs to the county council?"

"And why would you be wanting to tell them? They'll never know what it is that you'd be doing in any case and, sure, they'd not know how to stop you anyway."

Ten days later we did just that. Four boys from Manchester, and one of their girlfriends, were touring Ireland at the time, and had recently arrived at Shrah. They were so captivated by the atmosphere that they had shown no signs of wanting to move on. They joined in and, over a glorious sunny weekend, we dug the trench, closed the road, laid the pipe and back filled the trench so that we reopened the road in just over a day. "I'll borrow the bike and cycle down to the other farmers and tell them it's now open again," said Pauline, a bright-eyed, dark-haired girl from Manchester, whose normally pale face was already filling out with colour from such an outdoor life. It wasn't just me who didn't want to go back to Stevenage or Manchester. And it wasn't simply the fresh air, or the sense of space and colour, or lack of phone or television, that made Shrah so attractive. It was the people, and the very special sense of community, that made the most powerful impact on one's emotions. This was community at its best; community vested in a sense of place and a feeling of common destiny.

Our nearest neighbours, two fields away, were the Lyons. Seamus, the youngest of seven children, had recently taken over the running of the 40-acre family farm from his father, Gus. Seamus had married an orphan girl, Bridie, who had been brought up in Portumna by an uncle. They were now starting a family of their own and by then already had a son aged seven, Brian, who was a skilled assistant to his father in the milking parlour. Gus himself had inherited the farm from his father who had bought it in the depression of the 1880s from "an Englishman, Foster, who was a planter like yourself." As he said that a look of horror had crossed his face, "How stupid of me. I didn't mean that, you know. I meant to say that he was an Englishman like yourself. I meant no insult. You know you're very welcome here. You're one of us. You're not a planter." Planter is the term used both in Ireland and in the early American colonies to describe a farmer, or small businessman from England, who had literally been transplanted to the new country in a government-sponsored land settlement. Being planted in this way, the indigenous population had been displaced and to be called a planter could, indeed, be seen as a term of abuse. But nothing could have been further from Gus' mind.

Gus retired many years ago yet every day he still walks the field, replaces a fallen stone from a wall, cuts down some newly emerging thistle, watches the young calves, and is always ready to help. The nightly news bulletins on television make him as informed about world events as anyone on the Washington, DC Metro reading the Post on their way to work. He married Mary 40 years before I met them and their children have long since scattered - to New Zealand, Australia, Canada, America, England and even to far off Dublin. Gus is now 95 and Mary 93; her eyes still sparkle when, sitting by the fire, he gently takes her hand and squeezes it. To be with them is to engage in constant, probing dialogue; everything to people living as near to the every day concerns of existence is of significance. In an intuitive way, they know that everything is connected, and that nothing is too insignificant for serious consideration. Without escaping to the reality of Shrah I could not have survived the first few terms in Stevenage which were in retrospect, a world turned upside down.

Within communities such as this there are few divisions by age alone; everyone is valued according to their contribution. Children especially are cherished, and within the west of Ireland, in what has been an outward migration for centuries, the years of childhood are especially concerned with ensuring that, wherever they might go later, they will not forget the traditions from which they came. It is, of course, a subject on which outsiders are prone to sentimentalise and not appreciate the flip side; community can be hard on someone trying to be different.

"Irish country life certainly has its difficulties," observed Brother Patrick, headmaster of a Catholic boys' school in nearby County Tipperary. "These youngsters come from such closed, self-contained - often loving, but not always - communities, that when they go off by themselves to the big cities - Dublin, Galway, Limerick, London, Liverpool or New York - they easily get confused and lost. Much of their confidence is - in the jargon you understand - context specific; what we are not very good at doing is preparing youngsters from the rural community to scale up their confidence progressively, so that, being comfortable in a town like Portumna with a thousand people, they don't leap to a city of a million without first finding their place somewhere in the middle."

His thinking interested me, especially as I saw such problems daily in Stevenage, where so many of the families that had moved in when the New Town was built were first generation Irish, whose men folk were more able to dig trenches and mix cement on building sites than hold down a steady job in a factory. "It's all to do with the different cultures," I said, tentatively. "Yes, what exactly do you have in mind?" said Brother Patrick inviting me to open up.

"Well, there's the well-argued case that England and America are both dominated by the Protestant work ethic - it's right to work hard, and you're entitled to get your just rewards. The Bible story successful English people love to hear is the Parable of the Talents." Brother Patrick grinned. "But you Catholics are different," I continued, "and Irish Catholics are different to other Catholics." I knew I would have to tread carefully here. "Catholics, it seems to me, are conditioned to be ready to hear what the priest tells them. Here in Ireland this seems especially true, but there is an Irish twist to all this. You are more mystical, more poetic, more otherworldly than European or American Catholics. It's as if you haven't quite got rid of the idea of the little people at the bottom of the garden; your Celtic past permeates its every corner. When people from this background find themselves living in an apartment building mid-way between a factory and a noisy road, they crack up."

He nodded, conceding the point. I continued, "Yet the most useful, suggestive, philosophic guide that I've had in recent years, at least as far as education goes, comes from the Catholic doctrine of subsidiarity." A troubled look started to spread over Brother Patrick's face. "Let me just finish," I said. "If I understand this doctrine correctly, it states that it is wrong for a superior body to make decisions on behalf of an inferior body which it is perfectly able to decide for itself. That seems to be the heart of the issue for all forms of teaching, secular or religious. I don't think we're very good at it. In fact many of our activities contradict this. Especially in schools, where we seem to be far more concerned with teacher authority, rather than pupil autonomy. In fact we are far more interested in teaching than we are in learning..."

Brother Patrick quickly got up, "I think we need a drink if we're going to make sense of something as profound as this." He reached for the monastic supply of whisky and hitched up his cassock more comfortably over his knees. "Are these the kinds of issues that you discuss with your colleagues back in England?"

"No way, I'm afraid. The conversation there is all about how many pupils make up a viable class; how many options can you put on at one time; is it fair that one school should have more pupils than another; or what to do about declining grants for the purchase of books. Really boring stuff."

"That's a real pity, because I'm afraid that is largely the case in many schools in Ireland as well. Now about the doctrine of subsidiarity. Firstly I don't think the Holy Father ever intended this to apply to teaching, but it's an interesting point that you raise..."

Shrah was, in a phrase I used often at the time, "a real place with real ordinary people". It helped to hold me true to my beliefs in people, that each and every one of them mattered and that every person had a right to be different. It helped maintain my sense of balance between the excitement of the new and the opportunity of the moment, and my equally deep-seated love of quietly going about the ordinary affairs of life at an even and equitable pace.

I needed Shrah to give me the opportunity to stop and stare. This was important to me. Time for reflection was something I had gained during chapel services and was where I got so many of my ideas. The hobo poet WM Davies summed it up in his lines; "What is life if full of care/We have no time to stop and stare." Staring, for me, has always been a prelude to doing.

I had no opportunity to do much staring in my first hectic, and very unpleasant, two years as deputy head in Stevenage. The tensions between a headmaster who refused to compromise with the changing nature of the school around him and a common room of teachers who were fast losing faith in themselves to cope, were quite enormous. They were given a daily sharpness by the constant reminder from Trevor, good staff officer that he was, that none of us was meeting the schedule he saw as being necessary to support the expectations of the head. People who lose faith in themselves become fearful, and suspicious. An increasing number of teachers took sick leave. Then one member of staff, who it had been obvious for several weeks was being held up as soft and inefficient, had a car crash; within the day, long before anyone could have spoken to the man as he recovered in hospital, the rumour mongers were at work. "He was so on edge, so worried at the innuendoes that he was no longer up to the mark that it had got on his mind. He was no longer fit to drive. The crash and his broken legs are the head's fault."

"John, you must do something," members of the parents' association would tell me. "Everything seems to be going wrong. The pupils are getting restless, they sense that the staff are unhappy, and are not being creative in their work; they're always preoccupied. There is a whole new generation of children working it's way up through the school who are beginning to feel alienated; everything about the way the school is organised tells them that they are second best; that the school does not welcome them. This is a powder keg, and it gets more lethal with the passing of every term."

After five terms Trevor could stand it no longer, and left for another job in South America. The governors insisted that the headmaster appoint an internal candidate to replace him, a man whom he himself had rejected on two previous occasions. During the summer term the pressure on me became almost impossible. I was virtually the only member of staff the headmaster would speak to, and mine were the ears that everyone else wished to bend. But the headmaster was not for turning for, in truth, he could not. He had no empathy with Stevenage, nor with a school which was now, most obviously, not a grammar school anymore. I sensed a personal disaster building up, yet was powerless to do anything about it.

Midway through that awful term, however, there was a week of pure bliss. Earlier in the year I had agreed to take a class of 14 year-old boys away for the Whitsun break so that we could walk along the English-Scottish border. Thirty of us started at Gretna Green on the Solway Firth, and gave ourselves seven days to walk the 110 miles across the ridge of the Pennines to the Island of Lindisfarne near where Northumberland meets the Scottish border. It is splendidly remote and beautiful country with the massive bulk of the Cheviot hills dominating almost every perspective. With the south west wind behind us and the open expanse of sky above, the boys literally romped their way up hill and down dale. Skylarks seemed to greet us with their shrill calls as we breasted every slope. It was good to be alive and young. For a few days it was like being back in Manchester; I could associate freely with the boys and we could share those open, inquisitive, fascinating questions that so excite teenagers. However the spell was inevitably shattered on the last day as we walked across the causeway to the ruined monastic island of Lindisfarne. One boy picked up some flat stones and skimmed a couple of them across the water. I stopped to watch and for a few moments we became separated from the others. The boy, emboldened by the camaraderie of the week, seized the moment. "What's going to happen to the headmaster? My parents think the school is falling to pieces, and you'll have to do something about it."

It was my turn to try skimming a stone across the water – something I was not good at doing – as I played for time. The boy looked hard at me, expecting an honest answer. "I just don't know," I said, both honestly and pathetically. "I just don't know." I didn't know. Nor, it seemed, did anyone else. For the rest of the term the head was hardly to be seen, and he paid me the grudging compliment of leaving me to preside over the meetings, functions and occasions that were his prerogative. We exchanged a few words, yet decision after decision was delayed. I felt I was being set up; I was the person everyone now looked to for a decision, but I was powerless.

*         *         *

Whilst Shrah in the west of Ireland was becoming my home, I still retained strong connections with Iran. In 1974, five years before the revolution led by Ayatollah Khomeni was to end the Shah's reign, and most of what he stood for, Iran was very much the focus for many of the world's most energetic entrepreneurs. Maybe, I thought, I ought still to be part of that scene. Maybe my sense of vocation for teaching was untenable. Perhaps I ought simply to go and make some money.

A year before, I had agreed to become guardian to the two sons of Iraj Bahraman, now farmandar (governor general) of Hamadan, one of the oldest provinces in Iran, who wanted them educated at Millfield, a leading English public school. Every two or three weeks for the past year I had had lengthy conversations with their father by phone, and he was anxious to link his own future with things European, and saw me as one of his main conduits. With his encouragement plans were afoot for a major expedition of sixth formers and university undergraduates from the United Kingdom to go to the hill villages south of Hamadan, in the summer of 1975, and work with a comparable team of Iranian students. I was to lead the expedition under the auspices of the recently formed Young Explorers' Trust at the Royal Geographical Society in London. There was much work to do in setting all this up, and Iraj suggested that I spend several weeks with him in Iran.

I flew to Iran after a stopover in Jordan where Amman Airport was in a state of red alert against the possibility of an Israeli attack. Quickly the tensions of that comprehensive school several thousand miles away started to shrink to their proper proportions as armed soldiers escorted us singly to the toilet in another building.

Iraj met me in Tehran wearing his impeccable dark suit, straight from a Paris fashion house. When I had first met him he was governor of the minor province of Semnan, but Iraj knew where real power lay and how important it was to be part of it. Quickly he had risen to become farmandar of Hamadan province, and then he had caught the eye of the prime minister, Hoveyda, and moved to Tehran to be his special adviser. Although a further five years were to elapse before the Shah was driven out, Iranian society was already starting to split at the seams. Fortunes were being made daily by those merchants who could get their goods out of the docks down on the Persian Gulf, which were virtually choked by the volume of imports coming in from all over the world. So great had been the boom in oil prices that Iran had money, it seemed, for absolutely everything. All the latest TV sets, dishwashers, and refrigerators could be purchased in the bazaar, but so weak was the public utility infrastructure that electricity was only intermittently available.

Standing with Iraj were his two sons, Ardi and Anoush, whom I had last seen some weeks before at their boarding school in England. They had accompanied me and the boys from Alleyne's as we had walked the Scottish border lands and got on extraordinarily well with boys whose social background was a world apart from life here in Tehran. Yet their interest and enthusiasm were almost identical. "How's Jeff getting on with his football?" asked Ardi; "Are the girls starting to take notice of Gareth's crew cut, and don't they think it's stupid?" grinned Anoush. "Will Manchester United lose again this year?" The questions seemed so ordinary, yet the surroundings totally extraordinary. Iraj beamed delightedly. "Come on," he said, "there is much to do. This is the land of opportunity."

To be governor of Hamadan had not been enough to contain Iraj's ambition and he had returned to Tehran three months before, rather hurriedly it seemed, to the prime minister's office. Tehran was the place to be, Hoveyda the man to know. If there had been other reasons for his speedy withdrawal from Hamadan, he did not mind. Money was to be made quickly, and friends in the West cultivated. I was to be feted over the next few weeks.

"Soon I hope to buy an apartment in London so that Pary can visit the children whenever she likes; she misses them a lot now that they're growing up. Maybe I'll get an apartment in New York as well." He was expansive, highly hospitable and very obviously living on the edge. Iran was changing at break-neck speed, people were getting hurt, and he wanted his well-prepared bolthole - preferably more than one. We drank our brandies in the Intercontinental hotel later that evening. "I've got a couple of little projects I'd like your help with," said Iraj. "This clingfoil material I have seen being used to wrap up food. We don't have it in our own country, and it would be immensely useful to every housewife. It's an oil by-product. Do you know how I could get the patent and how much the machinery would cost to manufacture this? I would like to become the supplier across the Arab world."

My mind was still befuddled with issues of curriculum balance and the logistics of the school timetable. "I've got two other ideas," he said at lunch several days later. "One for you and one for me."

By this time I was more alert and more ready for any possible action. "The idea I would like to follow through," said Iraj, "is the cement business. Iran is having a property boom at the moment, and according to my calculations there is just no way in which we will ever be able to make enough cement from our present plants. We are spending fortunes buying cement in from other countries. We need more cement plants here, in Iran. The prime minister will let me have an exclusive right in certain parts of the country if I can quickly identify a foreign country who will provide a total turn-key operation; if they will design it, import the materials, build it, train the staff, and then sell it to us as an on-going operation."

I tried to keep up with the basic conversation but with limited success. I knew little about cement making, still less about the cement-making machinery.

"Now, here is the opportunity for you. Many of my friends are also sending their children to English, French or American boarding schools. The children like it, but they then want to go on to foreign universities and then get jobs in Europe or America. The Shah," he looked around the room, and then followed up, rather obviously, "long live the White Revolution. The Shah thinks that by doing this we are wasting our resources. These young people, our very best, are being lost to Iran. The Shah wants an English-type boarding school built here in Iran so that our children will stay with us until they are 18. Then, maybe - Inshallah - they may remain more idealistically attached to our country. I have a site in mind for you. It is a beautiful place between the mountains and the Caspian Sea. It is where the Quashar Shahs had a palace 60 or more years ago near Banda Pahlavi, where the old Russian princes also had their summer houses. Mr Hoveyda is very interested and I know has started to talk to your ambassador. Next Friday, when you come back from Hamadan, I will take you to see the land, then you must go and talk to your ambassador. I will help you to be the man who makes this work."

I spoke carefully. "That could be very exciting. But an English public school is the product of an English culture. It's about a particular set of values and an accepted way of doing things. Even now it is about creating Christian gentlemen, strong people who are able to do many things, but who are united by a common view of life and an agreed set of values. At its simplest these schools are about responsibilities, as well as rights. These things are more important to us than the examination results. Your children, and other children from Iran, are able to gain much from this because they are being absorbed within the dominant culture of the other children in the schools they are attending. I'm not sure that it would work standing in isolation from either England, or France or America, even from mainstream thinking in Iran." I looked back at him and smiled. "Which is a pity, isn't it, because the site you're talking about is immensely beautiful."

"Ah, but our culture is changing very rapidly," he replied, "just you look around you over the next few weeks and you will see for yourself." I did indeed looked around, but what I saw with my Western eyes was not what Iraj wanted me to see.

\*　　　　\*　　　　\*

Hamadan is the capital of the oldest province in Iran, a land whose mountain peaks are over 13,000 feet and whose population includes many nomads. Around Hamadan itself many factories had been built, and it was rapidly coming to resemble a new town on the edge of the Arizona, Utah or New Mexico deserts. It was easy to see how a clingfoil factory or a new cement making plant would fit in. But there was not the same exuberance in the provinces as there had been in Tehran, nor the same faith that material goods were an unmitigated benefit. I went into the covered bazaar, and down the street of the carpet makers. Would modern Iran be anything like the old Persia, I wondered, if all these beautiful carpets - each the product of thousands of hours of tedious knot tying - were replaced by factory-made clones of their favourite patterns?

I met the teachers at the local university who would come to work with our students the next year. They were a curious, and confusing, group. Book-learned, rather than practical, they were nevertheless a generation away from being a practical people, who made a living by doing, not talking. They were careful in their speech, always fearful of the ubiquitous presence of the SAVAK, the secret police. "We have been well enough educated," they said, "to want to have more control over our own destiny. It is not right that some people are making such enormous profits and investing their money outside Iran. Everyone has to think far harder about what kind of country we want to build, here, in modern Iran. We are Muslim people. We have the teaching of the Koran to guide us. We have to come to terms with what that teaching means now, in the present age." I kept quiet. I felt it prudent not to mention my friendship with Iraj who, I suspected, might have been run out of this place for being too much of a modern liability. I thought more about our last conversation, and its significance to British culture. How were we, sophisticated England, to combine truths from the past, with the opportunities and constraints of the technological age?

I talked at length with three members of the Literacy Corps, intelligent and articulate young men of 19 or 20, who had graduated from a Tehran High School 18 months previously and were teaching villagers to read and write as an alternative to doing service in the military. They knew the villagers well, and obviously respected them deeply, yet they were also the products of a Western education system that practised objectivity, analysis and detached experimentation. They, too, were confused.

"We've learnt so much since we've been out here in these mountain villages," these young men said, "we wish our teachers from high school could have had the same experience. They simply don't know what it is that makes our people tick. They're sort of disembodied. To these villagers the mullah is more important than the Shah." Worried lest their candour were misplaced, they looked around furtively for the possibility of an eavesdropper. Fortunately there was none. "Don't worry," I said, "I will keep your comments very much to myself." I did, and I thought deeply about what they had said. The clashes of the future, it seemed to me, might well be more between rival cultures, than between nation states. Technological and economic change were forces that could be either benign or destructive, or even both at the same time, I wrote in my book, The Iranians; how they live and work, which was published early in 1977 and which was promptly banned by the SAVAK.

Iraj was on splendid form when we returned to Tehran. His business deals were obviously thriving and we went out to yet another dinner party. One of the other guests was an English man whom I knew was married with several young children. That evening he was accompanied by a young and beautiful Iranian woman, whose physical relationship to him was so flagrant that I had to conclude that she had been purchased for the evening. To my confusion I found myself sitting next to her at dinner. My normal style is to enquire what my table partner does for a living. Shortly she turned to me, inviting dinner table conversation. In some confusion I picked up a wine bottle and offered to pour her a glass. Her face darkened and her eyes raged. "Surely you must know that I am a Musselman. You should know that I am forbidden to drink. Why do you try to tempt me?" My confusion was absolute. I saw her as a prostitute, albeit a very beautiful one, but she saw herself as an official concubine, sold to one man for a 24-hour contract as demanding, for those 24 hours, as any marriage contract. Such relationships were legitimised by the power of the

Koran. To me, alcohol was an accepted drug which wise people knew how to handle; to her it was a temptation prohibited by all the authority of the Holy Book which she obviously valued so much. Cultural clashes are something we all need to understand far better in the inter-dependent world into which we are moving.

The next morning we set out on the five-hour drive to the site of the possible English-style boarding school. It was absolutely stunning, but it was a world removed from the surroundings of any school I could comprehend. "We would knock down those old palace walls," said Iraj, "and start all over again. We would make it very modern. We would need a helicopter landing site."

I winced. "Surely," I said, "when you visited all those English public schools with me you thought it was the old walls that gave the schools their gravitas, their authenticity. Wasn't that one of the things which you envied?"

Iraj was silent, and turned away. I left him with his confusion. A country has to have some connection with its past, some accommodation with its earlier history. We'd been staying at his parents' house and the next day he was confused again as we came to leave. He embraced his father and his mother, and we did the same - we had come to grow fond of them. Then his mother said something to Iraj that I did not understand. Beneath his dark skin he coloured badly; he was deeply embarrassed. A moment later his mother reappeared, holding the family Koran. She nodded to Iraj who, meekly as a child, knelt down and allowed his mother to place the Koran on his head whilst she said a short prayer. Then he got up. Deferentially, and rather unsure of herself, she looked at me wonderingly, and I too knelt down. Deftly she placed the Koran on my head and, with all the calm assurance that comes with age and deep faith, said a prayer over me and then over my two friends. At that moment that Iranian grandmother could have been the Catholic Mary Lyons saying the rosary in her kitchen back in the hamlet of Shrah in the far West of Ireland.

We got back into the Range Rover (a successful English export) and set off up through the mountains. Iraj eventually broke a long silence. "That was an ancient Persian custom. It does not mean anything." I knew he lied to himself, and I knew then that his country was in for a terrible culture struggle. How terrible neither he nor I had any comprehension; neither did the whole apparatus of the CIA, nor the British Intelligence Service. We did not think that the Ayatollah Khomeini mattered. More importantly we totally misunderstood the nature of how people learn new ideas. We were to forget that it was the learning that children did at their mother's knee which shapes the nature of adult assumptions, far more than political or economic assertions later in life.

Back in Tehran I had a highly matter-of-fact conversation with Sir Tony Parsons, the British ambassador, and two of his staff about what might be involved in setting up a school. He had a well-prepared brief from the British Council representative, and a strong endorsement from his trade attaché; this would be good for British invisible trade, and a demonstration of Britain's desire to be an honest dealer with the Shah's government. I was nothing like so sure.

I was asked to write a paper for the embassy, but to Iraj's disappointment nothing more was heard of the project. I suspect the embassy officially recommended the project, but I doubt that the Shah trusted the idea. He was rapidly growing suspicious of his own people. What he desperately needed, and had needed for years, were honest people who could help frame a vision for his country that was respectful both of its ancient traditions, as well as its new aspirations. Just as much as the Western countries in 1999 are failing to ask the critical question, "Education for what?" so Iran in the mid-seventies was caught in the same dilemma. To put an English-type boarding school into the palace on the Caspian would, if it had started to do its job even half well, have exacerbated the situation. "To be a good teacher," I had been told by Roger Stone at MGS at the end of my first year of teaching, "you have to be prepared to live dangerously. Good teaching helps pupils ask questions many people prefer not to have asked." The issue goes back to Socrates and I am sure far beyond. A good liberal education and autocracy are ill-suited bedfellows.

Iraj was despondent. I was missing what he saw as being my big opportunity, and he knew how miserable I was in Stevenage. This should have been a way out, he thought, and it was something he had created for me. I should have been grateful. Then it all changed with a single telegram. "Head master resigned. Governors offer you post of acting head. Confirm acceptance immediately." The telegram reached me via the prime minister's office in Tehran. The cryptic language was amusingly designed more, I thought, for the satisfaction of an authority officer in Hertfordshire than any political sensitivity I could think of. Who, in money-conscious Tehran, could possibly have been interested in the affairs of far-off Stevenage, and a temporary acting headship worth all of £4,400 a year?

Iraj organised a celebratory dinner at the Tehran Hilton, while I managed to negotiate a cheap flight back to London two days later by flying Aeroflot through Moscow. Iraj could not understand the need to economise. "Charge a first class fare to your employers. They need you. Make them pay." Culture clash again. It was a good dinner, but I was thinking about curriculum issues, and the clash of cultures, not just between East and West, but between grammar school and secondary modern traditions, between education for a competitive advantage and an education for a collaborative life-style. I was thinking about my father in the pulpit, and my father in the workshop. I was thinking also about the humanity of old Mr Roast and, most of all, I was thinking of the spontaneity of young minds. "It's easy, sir", that 11 year-old had said 15 years before, "if we look like God, then everybody else will look like God as well." Everybody matters. That was what comprehensive schools had to demonstrate.

Iraj insisted that we went to a party afterwards. Some minor members of the royal family were present. Several people were openly preparing and smoking the very drug which two days before a drug dealer in the bazaar had been shot by a firing squad for selling. It was good to be going back to England, and to issues which I now felt were within my power to deal with.

# 5

# Becoming a Head Master and a Father

Alone, I walked into the head master's study. Truly it was a splendid, if starkly simple, room. Built with no pretensions in 1558 when the old charity school of the thirteenth century had fallen into disrepair, it was strictly functional. Heavy oak beams framed the corners, the walls and the heavy roof trusses. All had been exposed in a restoration of some 30 years before and clean white plaster had replaced the old wattle and daub. Two cross-bracing elbows gave stability to the central cross member supporting the queen post - the piece of timber that joins it to the pitch of the roof. Heavy wrought-iron hooks were still inserted into these timbers to hold lanterns which, in generations long past, had provided light on dark winter afternoons. The room was almost bare. The books had gone, as had the pictures and the furniture bar the formidable desk and an even larger oak refectory table. I might only be acting head but I was going to have to stamp the room with my own identity, if I was not to look like a purely transitory functionary. I looked again at the table. Swept up into one mighty heap were all the papers that had been accumulating on Mr Burridge's desk throughout that long summer term. In them were the minutiae which had driven him out of office and I dreaded the problems they contained.

I shuddered, and walked back into the brighter light of the school drive. Four youngsters, carrying their rugby boots, came towards me. I could not escape. "Hello," I said.

"Hello, sir," A silence, then one, bolder and more confident than the others, asked "Are you the new head? That's what my parents told me last night. They think that's good; so do I. At least you smile when you talk to us."

I grinned, non-committal. Surely there had to be some form of formal induction into my new position? To have walked out at the end of the previous term not sure if I even wanted to come back, and then to walk back in again six weeks later in total command, seemed utterly unreal.

I had dinner with Philip Ireton. Not for nothing had he survived the politics of the New Town for 30 years and risen to be the first Labour chairman of the county council in what was a staunchly Conservative area of Britain. We talked for hours. He was reassuring on all matters of detail and procedures and had produced a statement informing the staff that, until a permanent appointment to the headship could be made at some indeterminate time, I was acting head master. All powers were vested in me. He suggested I read similar words to the assembly on the first day of term, and then incorporate it in a letter to all parents to go out that afternoon.

I talked of my concern for the curriculum and what we thought children should experience but found Philip, like so many of his generation, strangely ambivalent and unreflective in his thinking. "Alleyne's was a great grammar school," he said, "I admired it enormously. It did well by my own boy, who went on to Cambridge and is now in the Ministry of Overseas Development." (I couldn't help thinking of the young, articulate trade attaché at the embassy in Tehran with whom I had been dealing the week before - somebody who knew the logical explanation for everything, but lacking any form of imagination or intuition to help him see the whole picture). "My boy had more opportunities than I did. Comprehensive schools - remember that Hertfordshire doesn't like that term - are an even better idea. They'll give grammar school opportunities to everyone. Just how they'll do this you'll have to work out. The boys ought to be grateful for the opportunities they have."

In my heart I knew it was not like that because nobody is ever really grateful for something they don't understand. I wondered, too, whether Philip himself would have done anything like as well if he had been forced to stay in school until he was 18. He was a University of Life man who was so driven by his own sense of direction that he had patience only to listen to those things that interested him directly. Later that evening I started to unpack. I had brought back a Turkoman rug from the bazaar in Tehran, intending it to go on the floor of my apartment. I looked at it carefully and thought of the open space above the fireplace in my new study. What better way of establishing my presence than to have this rug hanging there? I gave it but a minute's thought before returning to school and hanging it from a beam. I felt far better. This was my place, and I had a real job to do. "This looks like the inside of a nomad's tent," my secretary said the following day. I grinned. That rug was to hang there for 11 years.

*         *         *

England had rejected the 11 plus examination, and the theory of intelligence testing on which it had been based, because of the inequalities in the testing procedures and the gut feeling that many children were late starters. While primary school teachers were becoming increasingly interested in how children learn, virtually all secondary school teachers were concerned to teach the content of the disciplines. A few secondary teachers hated this distinction and they, every bit as much as their primary colleagues, sought to educate what they called the whole child. The youngest and best of them devoted hours to extra curricular activity, but by definition this was indeed extra. The curriculum - the lessons set out on the timetable - was defined strictly in terms of subjects and just how many lessons of each, just what kind of exposure young people should have to various forms of knowing at different ages, was fiercely argued through year after year. In terms of easy accountability, examinations could be set for subjects with clearly defined boundaries and where work was done on an individual basis. It was this clear definition of task, and the emphasis on individual attainment, which gave secondary teachers their well-defined authority, and left them generally indifferent to what happened in the primary schools, where teachers sought to encourage children to think widely and to act collaboratively. So, for the staff of Alleyne's as in other secondary schools, the curriculum was the balance which was to be set between the different subjects. The timetable in any one year was the uneasy truce in a trial of strength between departmental interests and could be viewed as a battlefield of heavily fortified positions, of lost ground, of shattered hopes and an uneasy lull in hostilities while pupils were regrouped for the next campaign.

"Where you fitted in too easily became where you stayed," observed the primary school teachers. This was the nub of the problem. Should children be encouraged to raise their expectations by associating with other children who were already well-motivated, or should they be kept with other slower moving pupils for fear of holding back the more gifted, and themselves getting confused? Discussion was loaded with phrases such as "the gifted", "the most able", "the least able", or "the unexaminable". Teachers might justify their roles on the basis of being able to develop a youngster's capability through hard work, yet they behaved as if intelligence was a fixed commodity, modifiable only around the edges. So Alleyne's was desperately seeking a structure to accommodate the right pupils, in the right place, at the right time with the best teachers, teaching the appropriate subject.

"You've got it all wrong," said some of the youngest staff from the ex-secondary modern schools. "You should hardly ever teach to the whole class at the same time. What's needed is more collaborative project work. In that way the brighter pupil, by helping his less able friend, improves his own understanding of the subject by having to explain it, and the slower pupil catches up with the rest of the class because of so much individual attention."

The two kinds of teachers glared at each other across the staff room. They epitomised the two traditions about which there was to be so much argument for years: whole class teaching or mixed ability learning. In 1997, David Blunkett, the new Labour secretary for education, said in his first white paper, "Mixed ability...requires excellent teaching and in some schools has worked well. But in too many cases it has failed both to stretch the brightest and to respond to the needs of those who have fallen behind." In one respect Blunkett was right. Mixed ability classes are hard work to organise and manage; they need good teachers, but can certainly be good for both the intellectual and social needs of all children. Whole class teaching is easier, but only if the range of pupils (however defined) is not too great. Grammar school teachers thought that a seven or eight per cent ability range was the maximum. When they attempted to handle a class with a 15 to 20 per cent ability range in this way they did indeed lose pupils at both top and bottom ends. Sometimes they panicked and tried setting up project-type mixed ability programmes. Mostly these failed, as they had no clear understanding of how to do this.

A little more theory is necessary to comprehend what was starting to happen. When learning is defined as what happens when students are taught, then it is essential to provide a teacher when a child has something to learn; that was the starting point. Where the timetable is kept simple - such as when all pupils in each year group are doing the same subject for the same number of periods each week - then staff can be used most economically. However, when some of the pupils need more, or fewer, lessons than the average, then arrangements have to be made which tie up other parts of the school's available staffing. The greater the flexibility in the timetable, the more expensive this is of teacher time.

In the old grammar school, highly successful pupils might have taken 10 or 11 subjects at the age of 16 (the old GCE O Level), while others - the kind who had gone to a secondary modern school - needed at least twice as much teaching for half that number of subjects. In Alleyne's as a comprehensive school at any point during the week some pupils might need to move through 10 subjects, each with four periods every week, while other pupils might study six subjects with six or sometimes seven lessons in the week. Fitting that together often caused gridlock and the challenge to find solutions seemed, on occasions, to provide more intellectual stimulation to teachers than thinking about the nature of what the children actually learnt.

To complicate matters further, different ability groups needed classes of different sizes. Working within a model of learning that was heavily dependent on instruction, it had long been assumed that pupils in the sixth form needed the smallest possible classes, so that the teachers could work on a tutorial basis. Classes of 15 to 18 were deemed large in the sixth form; those of seven or eight thought desirable. This was obviously expensive, but if anyone ever considered this they quickly rid themselves of any financial embarrassment by equating this as an investment in the people who would matter. Not so important, it was thought, were the needs of the 11 and 12-year olds to receive similar attention. As these classes were receiving routine instruction, and learning to do as they were told, classes of 32, 33, or even 35 were tolerated.

Those early years of secondary education were still seen as being part of the primary school sorting process; the kind of "keeping the milk simmering so that the cream will float to the surface" mentality. It was in the latter years of secondary school that the cream was further purified into specialisations.

Where a school did not have an even distribution of ability, then additional problems arose and this was a serious matter for Alleyne's in the mid-1970s. Parents working the system meant that fully two of the six forms of entry at the age of 11 remained of grammar school calibre. At the same time, the authority insisted Alleyne's had its share of pupils with remedial needs, thus necessitating a class of their own. Having a disproportionately able top in any year, and a small bottom, meant that the ability range in each of the three middle classes was as much as 20 per cent or more. "It's in these classes, head master, where we have problems. They're not particularly interested in what they're taught but are intelligent enough to be awkward."

What I faced at Alleyne's was typical in many ways of what other schools in England were facing, as they tried to come to terms with what should have been a massive philosophic rethinking of secondary education, but which had become, in reality, a matter of juggling scarce resources in ever more novel and mysterious ways. To the logistics of time-tabling was added another immutable factor. Alleyne's was a collection of separate buildings, which had grown up over the centuries, some containing one or two classrooms, others eight or ten, scattered almost randomly across the 35 acre site. Aesthetically pleasing as this might have been, it was an administrative nightmare. Team-teaching, which had been possible in many of the purpose-built secondary modern schools in New Stevenage, was impossible at Alleyne's. A five minute walk between classes on a warm summer's day was a very different experience to the same walk during a February snowstorm and the timetable could result in a child crossing and re-crossing the entire campus five or six times in a single day, almost invariably losing something en route, sometimes even themselves.

Alleyne's accepted that every teacher was a monarch in their own classroom, and teachers thought little of things beyond the four walls of their domains. In my first term I suggested that arrangements could be made for all those teaching in the first year to spend a day in one of the neighbouring primary schools, to get a better understanding of where our pupils came from. Few teachers were interested. "We just haven't got the time, head master; we're committed to being with our current classes. Surely that has to be our real priority?" Some went further and said, conspiratorially, "Actually I'm having to work the boys hard indeed to make up for what they didn't learn in primary school. So I don't think I've anything to learn from their teachers, do you? Mind you, I could teach *them* a thing or two."

I personally taught a one-third timetable, concentrated into two and a half days of the week. In the English tradition, inherited from earlier, gentler times, head teachers are expected to lead by example; administration is a lowly activity, done in one's spare time, on holidays, or at weekends.

I started a practice that I was to persist with for the next 11 years. Two or three times each term I would follow a pupil for a day, to see what the curriculum felt like to those for whom it was devised. Initially the staff had found it off-putting, which was hardly surprising. To have me, sitting all cramped up in the back row, must have looked intimidating as well as absurd. It was, needless to say, an enlightening experience. Some of the staff were quite expert, few were truly poor, but even the best of them taught as if no one else in the school was doing any teaching whatsoever. Their material either overlapped, or missed out chunks of necessary ideas. Teaching styles differed astonishingly and so did the standard of work they expected from their pupils. While most teachers were conscientious, they were so preoccupied with their subjects that they just did not see their pupils as individuals at all. In theory there were institutional safeguards for this. Form teachers met their classes for ten minutes twice a day (which worked out at an amazing 45 seconds per pupil per week... just about long enough, if you try the experiment, for both the pupil and teacher to utter about 30 words each). Year heads, in addition to an almost full teaching load, were responsible for the pastoral well-being of 150 pupils. Many of these they never spoke to from one term to the next for all their available time was taken up with problem children. The ordinary child was left to carry on being ordinary and in my enthusiasm I made myself too available to everyone. Endless proposals and suggestions came my way. "I'll come back to you on that," became my much quoted response.

I was particularly concerned about homework. The assigned tasks were those which could be easily administered, and which preferably did not involve too much additional marking. Much of this involved catching up on class-work, or reading extra books for which there was sometimes little justification. Homework was often rushed and held in low esteem by the pupils. The library was not well used, and private study periods in the sixth form were a time for mirth and play. Too often, it seemed, the pupils' every action demonstrated their belief that it was the teachers' responsibility to teach them, not their responsibility to learn. This, to me, was a perversity. "But it's natural, head master. We teachers are paid to teach; if pupils could learn by themselves, to any significant extent, then our professional skills would be called into question." This was crazy thinking in the 1970s, but it was still what most people, inside and outside of education, thought when I wrote to the British education secretary, David Blunkett, in early 1999 that researchers in the 1990s had uncovered much evidence in the cognitive sciences, and in neurobiology, evolutionary biology, evolutionary psychology, and even archaeology and anthropology which showed us in great detail how it was that humans actually learn. We could now understand why learning was much more than just the flip-side of good teaching and schooling.

\*  \*  \*

The *Pirates of Penzance* is one of the best Gilbert and Sullivan shows to put on as a school production. It necessitates a large cast, involves the school orchestra and provides plenty of opportunity for creative stage sets. My mother and stepfather came to the penultimate performance just before Christmas that term and enjoyed it enormously. Later, sitting having supper at home, the phone rang. It was Philip Ireton. "Can you come round and split a bottle of champagne with me?" he said, obviously happy. "That's a bit difficult," I replied, "I've got my mother staying with me." There was a moment's silence. "Well then, you'd better give her the good news. We've just had a governors' meeting and decided unanimously to offer you the permanent position of head master. I'll see you tomorrow morning. In the meantime, keep the news to yourself and your mother, and I'll announce it at the conclusion of tomorrow night's performance. That'll be a good time. The hall will be full of parents and teachers."

He did just that. There were loud cheers, which I took to be genuine. "Strangely enough," the head of drama said afterwards, "we've performed *Pirates* twice before, and on each of the previous occasions we also had the announcement of a new head. But that was many, many years ago...."

\*  \*  \*

Shortly after I became head, a government-appointed committee of enquiry, under the chairmanship of the historian Sir Alan (later Lord) Bullock, reported on English teaching and focused on reading, writing and speech. The Bullock Report was 600 pages long and, as I was young, hard-working, and had no wife or children with whom to share my home life, I read it from cover to cover. I was impressed by the argument which showed that children learned to develop language skills in a variety of formal and informal ways, but that they were often frustrated in school because too many teachers did not accept a responsibility to use their particular disciplines - be it history, physics or even mathematics - to extend children's appreciation of language. In many instances, "there was an enormous discrepancy between children's reading and retention ability, and the language used by both teachers in the classroom and the writing styles of text books. Rather than language acting as a connection," argued Bullock, "too often classrooms are characterised by language as a disconnection." This was what I believed as well.

Each morning as I met my senior staff before putting on my gown to preside at assembly, I tried to share my enthusiasm, gained from my reading of the night before. At first they were mildly interested, then politely tolerant, but eventually they became indifferent. "Surely, John, we should leave such things for a while yet? We've quite enormous amounts of work on our hands already, sorting out the proper relationship between departments and interpreting this for different age groups to have the time to get started on a topic as big as this. In any case, just think of Tom Smith, in the science department (they named a young and totally inflexible member of staff who lacked the confidence to look either to his left or right). Can you imagine what his reaction would be if you said he should also become a teacher of English?"

I could indeed, and that was just my concern. I had followed a pupil into a couple of that man's lessons the previous week. He was as uncompromising a young man as ever I had come across, totally committed to his subject, but nothing like as profound or knowledgeable as he liked to suggest. He covered this up moderately well, at least as far as the pupils were concerned, by dictating endless notes which they were supposed to learn parrot-fashion. And that was just where the problem lay. His notes were more appropriate to a class of first year undergraduates than they were to 14 year-olds. He used words which many pupils could not understand and even more, could not spell. His pupils were learning lessons in the management of boredom and low level survival, not science. It was such teachers as this who needed to be confronted by Alan Bullock's thinking.

Just to get people to read the report was not enough. I needed people to talk about it, argue about it, and allow themselves to be changed. The problem was that there was absolutely no tradition of serious discussion across the staff room of matters academic, as opposed to those matters of administration that they delighted in discussing at any hour. I decided to set up a day-long staff conference to consider the implications of the report. "You'd better make attendance voluntary," said the governors, "we're already asking a lot of the teachers." I scoured the school calendar, and found a Saturday early in the Spring term when there was neither a rugby match nor an athletics fixture. "Ah," said the games staff, "that's the one Saturday in the school year we keep for ourselves. It's the one Saturday we never ever come into school."

Having no funds for such activities (not even to buy copies of the report for the teachers), I then asked the parents' association if they would provide a good lunch and high tea so that the conference could go ahead in some style. On every previous occasion the association had been enthusiastic to help me in any way I had suggested. Not this time. "This is difficult, John," said the chairman, "we're in existence to help the pupils, not the staff. Directly this is for the good of the teachers, not the pupils - at least not in the short-term. Incidentally, most of the members of the association haven't even heard of this report. That's one of the reasons they don't see it as important."

I persevered and eventually some two-thirds of the staff attended the conference on a damp Saturday in late April. There was the beginning of a meaningful debate, but this was damaged several times by bitter recriminations between those subject teachers (including science) who said they were just too busy with all their subject content "to have time to correct children's appalling spelling, which was surely the responsibility of the English department?" Towards the end of the day they did, however, agree that we ought to be more careful about considering the level of English used in certain text books before they became prescribed reading for a particular class. How was this to happen? A long silence was finally broken by a young member of the biology department, someone who had recently qualified as a teacher, uniquely with training in both primary and secondary science. "I'll do that for the sciences if people would let me see the text books." There was instant relief in the room. At least they could say something had been decided, even though they did not believe it would change anything very much. Everyone went home, relieved that the pressure on them to do something different was receding.

"Don't do that too often," said an older and much experienced teacher, "you'll tire us out. We need Saturdays to recover. You know, I've seen many head teachers in my time; the ones teachers respect most are the ones that tell us what to do and then stand by us if we get it wrong." He gave me what he thought was a warm smile, but the warning was explicit nevertheless. Support the status quo. Don't ask us to depart from the tradition we understand. I was vastly disappointed. I tried to re-open the discussion with teachers the following week, but conversation quickly waned. It was back to business as usual.

Then, to my surprise, I started to get phone calls from other schools. "We hear you've already set up a staff conference on Bullock. We feel we ought to do this as well but we haven't a clue as to how to go about it. Could you come over and make an opening presentation to our staff and governors?" Soon, it seemed, I was the most popular speaker on the southern circuit. "Tell us what happened after the conference," they would ask. The blind, I thought, leading the blind.

The difficulties of organising the Bullock conference stimulated me to think further about how a pupil could use the writing of, say, a physics report to improve his written English. It also made me think more directly about the professional needs of teachers. Teaching is an emotionally draining experience; even the best teachers need not only respite but also time to reflect and develop new ideas. Just how was this to be provided started to preoccupy me and led, years later, to an important part of Education 2000.

*          *          *

Early in the summer term of 1976 I had a vacancy in French. I made the phone calls, placed the advertisements and selected five candidates. One was an Anne Brown, who had studied modern languages at Oxford and was currently doing her post-graduate course at York. Like other candidates she was nervous but responded well to questions with that firm use of the English language I still associated with girls' grammar schools. From a clergy family similar to my own, she had no difficulty in dealing with the governors' representative, who that afternoon was Johnny Pryor. Johnny always worried me. I had no idea if on any particular day he was going to be serious or flippant. He immediately took an avuncular interest in Anne, and over coffee after the first interview, started talking to her about his experience in the army in North Italy, "when I was shot up the arse by an Iti". Anne, schooled in the social graces of many a vicarage tea party - which gives one ready tolerance of everyone and a commitment to none - smiled sweetly and, by parrying his comments, offended no one.

Anne was appointed and joined the staff in August. Six weeks later, doing my social bit, I invited the new staff to dinner. As a bachelor, I was but a moderately good cook, frequently relying on wives of friends or girlfriends of ex-pupils, to act as my hostess when the need arose. A staff dinner, I thought, I could handle alone. I chose cod for the main course, which I determined to cook in milk and serve with mashed potatoes. I had no ideas of quantity, so I decided on a pound of fish per person. As I sought sufficient saucepans in which to cook all this I realised that I had over-ordered. Whether by intention or not, one of the other members of the French department had suggested to Anne that she should arrive early in case I needed help with the cooking. She gently made some suggestions. Half the cod was removed from the pans and I was sent out to get some more colourful vegetables to go with the white fish, white sauce, and white potatoes. It was a lively dinner and I was confident that I had set up some good bonding within the common room.

Just before Christmas, a dinner party to which I had been invited was cancelled at short notice. Anne was one of the other guests and we went out for a drink together. We chatted easily and I suggested dinner together the following week. Respectful of our different positions, I was at pains to talk about anything other than school. This proved immensely easy. We quickly discovered that we had many common interests and experiences. The following May we were engaged. Some people did not know how to handle this. The local paper ran a front-page story under the witty headline "Head marries French Mistress"; many of the senior boys went out of their way to congratulate me. The parents' association was enthusiastic; a married head, they thought, was almost a necessity.

The thought of marriage made me ecstatically happy. It was not that I wanted to leave the world of action and ideas that had increasingly come to dominate my first 37 years, but that I wanted to share it. Anne knew this, and was the perfect partner to balance my normal, every-day activity, and she shared my growing determination to develop education in ways that enhanced opportunities for young people.

We spent the summer holiday together in Ireland. Anne had never been to Ireland before and had no idea of the love and friendship that was to be extended to her by the many Irish families I had come to know over the years. And it was as one of their own that they welcomed her. "A man," they said, "who accepts the right of turbary to cut peats on the township bog will never be treated as a planter. His wife will be as strong as he, and will be one of us." I knew it went much deeper than just peat cutting. In the eight years that I had owned Shrah, more than a 100 pupils, or ex-pupils, had made the journey to Ireland to help rebuild the house. Many of them had endeared themselves to the local people, but now it was time for me to have children of my own. Anne, they said, looking at her with the appraising eyes of farmers versed in the realities of life, would make a splendid mother. Anne had to get used to large glasses of neat whisky served in front parlours opened up specially for us to sit in. Faded sepia photos looked down on us out of heavy oak and mahogany picture-frames and children, hoards of them on some farms, would peep around the door, delighted by Anne's obvious welcoming smile and unusual accent.

We talked for ages about our backgrounds and about our education. She, the product of a girls' grammar school in Brackley, an English market town in Northamptonshire, had grown up in a large, rambling country rectory (much praised by John Betjeman) with few outside distractions. She got straight As at A level, far, far better than I, and had immediately been offered a place at Oxford, where her elder sister was already studying. She was one of the youngest students in her year and felt much intimidated by the expectations of the college from the day she entered. She had not enjoyed Oxford very much, but had worked incredibly hard and given herself little time to relax. To this day she feels intimidated by academics. As we talked I was grateful for the broader, if more chaotic, education that I had received and was mindful of the range of ideas from history, travel, and from the sciences that had never figured in her life. In turn I became aware of my dreadful spelling, my tortuous writing style, my inability to speak foreign languages, my split infinitives and my ignorance of so much English literature, music and drama. I think we made a good pair right from the start. It certainly felt that way.

We were married in the October half-term in Anne's father's church in the parish of Culworth, three miles from Sulgrave, the family home from which George Washington's ancestors emigrated to Virginia in 1656. Anne's mother was, we knew by this time, dying of cancer, so we had a small, quiet wedding, and did not invite many of that army of people who had figured so largely in my life up to that time. One telegram, however, seemed to say it all. "From Bot's 4,000 Hebridean children...."

Our first baby was due at the end of the following September. Never had a head master walked so tall as I did that Spring term. Never, I thought, had I taken such a deep interest in the way those boys at Alleyne's were themselves growing up. I might have been young to become head master, but I was certainly moderately old to become a father for the first time. Enchantingly, the two events were happening at the same time with curriculum blueprints and guidebooks to nappy changing getting all mixed up. It was the best thing that could ever have happened to me. I was to have two separate, but totally complementary, lives - complementary lives that infuse all aspects of this story from now on.

We spent a blissful Easter in Shrah where the daffodils lent enchantment to our little acre of land. We were planning to let the house to tenants for the first time for a few weeks that summer and I discovered that the roof of the stone-built front porch was leaking so badly that there was no real alternative but to demolish and rebuild it. A three-week task, said a local builder, and quoted a figure beyond our meagre resources. "But we can't leave it like this," said Anne and I agreed. Martin Flanagan's eldest son, Oliver, who was 16 years old and immensely strong, despite his adolescent gangliness, offered to help. "We've got seven working days," I said.

"Aye," Oliver said, pensively, "I know that. There are some things we'll be needing." He knew enough to list the building materials we would need to buy from Brian Tuohy's store, seven miles away. "If I cycle up now on your bike, Brian would be able to deliver those by midday tomorrow. By that time I can have dug out the new foundations." I was stunned. Here was a young farm boy, who was not doing particularly well in school and who had thought things through even faster than I.

I've never worked physically so hard in my life. With Anne trying to keep out of the way - I suspect both of us were obeying some primeval nest-building urge - Oliver and I worked from six in the morning until 10 or 11 o'clock at night. The weather remained fair. Farmers came and leaned against the gate; they shouted encouragement and I think they were as impressed with Oliver's natural intelligence as they were with my preparations to be a family man. Oliver and I drank gallons of tea; too busy to talk, we worked as a perfect team. We were doing what extended families have done since the beginning of time. We self-organised, learned rapidly and it was as purposeful, and as happy, as any a New England barn raising. Anne put daffodils in vases in all the rooms and we finally closed the job 12 hours before going back to Stevenage.

"What are you going to do with your life, Oliver? You've a great future in front of you," I asked, thinking of other boys of that age that I had known and who had but a tiny fraction of his commitment, his physical strength and his ability to anticipate emerging problems in a visual way. "Don't know." He shrugged his strong shoulders and was silent for a long time. "Not much point in staying on at school. Might try studying for three years at college to be a pig farmer, that's if I don't get bored first. I don't much like being told what things are all about. I just like getting on and doing things. Trouble is, there's not much future in farming around here, unless you've got money to buy a farm of your own. It's farming and building that I really like doing."

I was tired, but not so tired that I did not recognise the significance of Oliver's troubled thoughts as I went back to thinking about the curriculum for boys of the same age, but living under a Hertfordshire sky.

The next weekend I was in London and, having an hour or two to spare, visited a second-hand bookshop where I found a copy of Samuel Smiles' *Self-Help*, a Victorian self-improvement manual. The language is direct and self-assured, and the tone puritanical but it is easy to see why it so inspired so many ordinary people to do things that were anything other than ordinary. "Energy," wrote Samuel Smiles, "accomplishes more than genius. Daily experience shows that it is energetic individualism which produces the most powerful effects upon the life and action of others, and really constitutes the best practical education." Oliver Flanagan, good ordinary lad that he was, would have thrived under the tutelage of Samuel Smiles far more than ever he would under a régime that thought comprehensive schools should be grammar schools for everyone.

\*          \*          \*

I was one of many who were pondering such questions at that time. Jim Callaghan had become prime minister when Harold Wilson resigned in 1976 and with Shirley Williams as his education secretary, had invited the public to explore "the secret garden of the curriculum" when he addressed a conference at Ruskin College. This inaugurated the Great Debate. "This Great Debate is a strangely arid affair," I told Shirley Williams one morning after she had addressed the school assembly (as Member of Parliament for Stevenage as well as being secretary of state for education I saw her frequently) and I knew that she agreed with me. So far the country had not got a focus on what was wrong. Robert Runcie, then Bishop of St Albans and shortly to become Archbishop of Canterbury, had a better grasp of the changes that were needed. He also visited Alleyne's twice a year "just to have informal conversations with the sixth form to hear what they're thinking," he would explain. "I need my reality check." He got it. The man who had earned his Distinguished Service Cross for exemplary duty in the last months of the war (and had been one of the first troops to enter the Belsen concentration camp) knew how to listen to youngsters and was deeply sensitive to their concerns. But he was exceptional. Mainly the Great Debate consisted of academic talking to academic. They did not know how to listen to the numerous Oliver Flanagans in each and every constituency of the country. Nor did they even think this was necessary.

By mid-summer we knew that Anne's mother's death was imminent and that it was unlikely she would live to see our baby born. In the evenings I was building a crib for PC (P for Peter, C for Catherine) and was working with yew, an unusual timber that when finished matures to a glorious plum colour and leaves a fine, hard well-defined surface. On the side of the crib Anne drew a picture of the animals' birthday party in Alison Uttley's *Little Grey Rabbit* stories with Paddington Bear at the foot of the crib and a rabbit and a hedgehog standing guard at the head. These I started to carve and it became a sort of allegory, I think, for my mother-in-law, as she lay in great pain knowing that she was unlikely to see her first grandchild, but wanting desperately to join in with our happiness. Twice a week we drove to see her. She was anxious to see how far the carving had progressed, and anxious still more to feel the ever stronger little kicks of her grandchild through the walls of her daughter's stomach. These were precious and strangely beautiful days, which meant an enormous amount to me and Anne as we consciously became more of a couple. They meant much to me as I struggled with Alleyne's, which I could not see simply as an institution but as the place where young people like Oliver and our own unborn child should be able to relish growing up. Anne's mother peacefully gave up her struggle and died seven weeks before Anne went into labour. She was buried in the churchyard at Culworth, close to the garden wall of the rectory in which Anne had grown up. We had little time to grieve, nor would she have wished us to do so.

The autumn term started with record numbers of pupils, and many staff felt a false optimism that this meant that Alleyne's could continue forever. I did not share such a faith because the numbers of pupils coming up through the primary schools would steadily fall off in two years time, a direct result of the easy availability of the contraceptive pill over the last ten years. The baby boom was over and I sensed, too, that the economic problems facing the country were steadily getting worse. Much as I knew we needed more money to carry on running the kind of school teachers wanted, I saw no chance of this being available. The public didn't think we were doing the best possible job. On the other hand they did not know what that job was. No one seemed to be thinking much beyond next year, or the year after, yet, as I thought about our unborn child, I wondered what life would be like when he or she was 20, 40 or 60.

Anne went into labour the day before the expected date, and I was excited to be with her throughout the delivery, though as the day wore on I was happy to be the father not the mother. After ten hours PC materialised. "It's a boy," I cried out excitedly. "It's Peter John," whispered Anne, tired but radiant. A vigorous sustained cry was Peter's acknowledgement of his, and our, existence. I had frequently read that the birth of a child can be - should be - the most marvellous experience a couple can ever have. Whatever you are told beforehand, nothing compares to that moment when the midwife leaves mother and father alone with the new born child you have longed and prayed for. Two have become more obviously one by the arrival of the third, and that new person will be with you for life, both learning from you, learning with you, and surely teaching you as well. Within that partnership we each, surely, change, as the postscript to this book clearly shows.

As I look back I think of how fortunate Anne and I were not to have faced the economic pressure that many young parents face today in leaving the early care of their children in the hands of day care providers. We cringe when we think about all the economic incentives for young mothers and fathers to farm out the care of their babies to others, often in settings not conducive to meeting children's irreducible needs. In 1998 the America psychologist, Stanley Greenspan, wrote that the impact of such arrangements "will be slow and insidious. People may gradually become more self-centered, and less concerned with others. Thinking may become more polarised...impulsive behavior, helplessness and depression may increase." I didn't know about research into infants and young children at the time of Peter's birth, but Anne and I knew intuitively that emotions and emotional attachments to mum and dad were critical components in the later learning of children. There are now shelf loads of books showing just what we had always thought, yet most of this flies in the face of official policy towards childcare. Early childcare is critical to economic growth, so the political argument goes, therefore it's "good". We now know how short-sighted such arguments are.

\*　　　\*　　　\*

Don't pupils learn anything in primary school which enables anyone to rank them one with another?" moaned the Alleyne's staff.

"We're bitterly opposed to ranking pupils at such an early stage," replied most of the primary teachers when I spoke with them. "Once we or you do that, the youngster will quickly start to perform at the general level expected of that group. Many children have enormous potential. Much of this only comes out after many years of schooling. Rank them too early and you'll never see that potential." I had to agree, having been one of those slow learning pupils myself.

Not getting the prognostic material before youngsters entered the school, Alleyne's went ahead with a complex scheme for the next first year intake. During the first ten weeks of the autumn term all pupils were to be taught in mixed ability classes, with pupils from the same primary school grouped together. Then, just as the new pupils were getting into their stride and finding their way around the rambling school, the English department (with the support of the other art subjects) and the maths department (with the support of science and technology) set internal tests to assess linguistic and numerical capabilities. The teachers were well meaning but the tests quickly became more concerned with measuring how much each pupil had memorised from lessons during the preceding ten weeks than they were with aptitude and a capability to think in numerical and linguistic terms. In the jargon our tests were "culturally skewed towards the values and understanding held by the teacher", and certainly favoured those pupils who thought in the most abstract terms, the ones who would eventually do well in school but not necessarily anywhere else. Children from middle class homes had an advantage. Oliver Flanagan would have done badly.

The tests gave teachers a mass of numerical results and heads of departments wrestled with their significance in an attempt to distribute pupils. As the allocations became known, teachers who had seen a particular pupil working from day-to-day recognised the inappropriateness of the assigned class set and endless conferences were arranged to resolve the differences. Ten days before Christmas the first year pupils were told: "You've got just over a week to get to know each other and your new teacher and from the beginning of next term the real work will begin."

"Can't you secondary teachers ever learn?" the primary teachers said. "All you've done is reintroduce the 11 plus six months later than previously. The tests you're administering are at least as ineffective as the old exam, maybe even worse. Don't you recognise the trauma of moving to secondary school or that you're making it harder for them by breaking up their earlier friendship groups, just as they were getting established?" I was confused, and all I knew was that we had not gone beyond an intuitive rejection of the 11 plus to think about what should replace it.

For guidance I increased the number of visits I paid to primary schools. A small proportion, mainly those found in the wealthier parts of the town, was traditional. They felt like miniature versions of the old grammar school, with their fixed desks, a formal school uniform and a carefully prescribed curriculum. "What Alleyne's is doing is right," their head teachers would say, "we can give you any amount of information on these pupils. It's a pity you can't rank them straight away according to ability rather than wasting time in the first term that they're with you." I asked about the nature of their intake, back at the age of five. "Ah," said one, "that's our secret. We're a church school. Nearly all the pupils who come here are from middle-class homes. Their parents know how to play the game and show up enough times at church when their children are young, so they can make the case that their children don't go to the nearest primary school but come to us instead. You see, we can count on parental support and we're doing what our parents understand."

In Woolenwick primary school, which was built as the New Town grew in the late 1960s and early 1970s, I saw something different. Gone were the regular classrooms with their stereotypical desks and long corridors. Instead there were bright open spaces, broad corridors, small and essentially cosy little meeting places, and lots of colourful equipment. The teachers were predominantly young and female. The noise level was higher but essentially friendly and purposeful and the pupils were not distracted by my presence. Older pupils were helping younger ones. "I appreciate your coming," said Woolenwick's young head teacher, (younger indeed than I was, and I felt young enough), "because we think you've got it wrong at Alleyne's." I sat up, reprimanded by someone whom I had expected to be deferential. "You people are so concerned with the content of your subjects that your staff just doesn't have time to think about the nature of how children come to understand their own learning. Did you see how those older children were helping the younger ones to read?" I nodded. It had been impressive. "Actually the older ones were learning as much as the younger ones. It's just that they were learning different things. Remember the old adage - 'You never learn something until you have to teach it'." I nodded. It was so true. I asked her about her intake. "We're largely a neighbourhood school. We get pupils from all kinds of backgrounds here, but many are quite restricted. We spend a lot of time helping parents to understand their particular role. It's interesting. Recently we've had several parents taking their children away from a private preparatory school several miles away, where they were paying a lot of money, and asking for them to come here instead. I wish they'd give us the money they were spending on fees." I did not want to leave. This was exciting because these children looked confident and their confidence ran deep. "I would want Peter to go to such a school," I told Anne.

Most of the primary schools did not conform to either of these two types.

Being mainly products of the industrial approach to primary school building in the 1950s, they were a curious mixture of old-fashioned classrooms, and teachers who wanted to apply new techniques, but weren't quite sure how to go about it. They were noisy places, and many of their teachers looked confused, which indeed they were. "We started teaching years ago but now times have changed. I'd like to do what they're doing in that new school up the road, but quite frankly I don't know how to manage that kind of class. Right now I think we're all making a big mistake. We're trying to extend this new form of experiential learning far too fast. It's easy for it to become trivialised into what some call discovery learning. It's much, much more than that. It needs good teachers, and it needs the support of parents."

Her comments applied equally to Alleyne's. Most of my staff yearned to stay within the old certainties as understood by the middle class-type primary school. Few had the confidence to go with Woolenwick and transform themselves into new kinds of teachers. Unless I was careful we, like so many of the other secondary schools of England, would settle for the a little bit of everything hybrid. Then the best teachers, sensing the compromise, would not have the confidence to send their own children through the system. I thought of Peter in ten or eleven years' time. Ten years was not a long time to change the system. Could I make any significant impact in that period, because I wanted him to go to a comprehensive school and I wanted any other children we might have to do the same. Why did I feel so strongly? It had been well expressed by Michael Hinton, one-time head master of both a private and a public school, when he had written: "Comprehensive schools expose children from a full range of backgrounds to a full range of challenges and opportunities...since they are hard up against the reality of our society, they cannot opt-out of its bad and ugly aspects, but they can help young people live well in the real world. They stand for the principle that children are persons...all equally, and infinitely, valuable."

There were other problems in the school. By 1978 the wider intake had reached the sixth form and, though some of them were getting good results, the proportion doing so was smaller than it should have been. "The trouble is, head master, that our A level courses are strictly academic with little direct practical application," my head of science told me. "We still behave according to the old English dictum "I am pure, you are applied but he, poor fellow, is strictly technological". This is just stupid. We need to develop our work in science in conjunction with technology. That's where the new jobs will come from."

We convened a meeting of the chief executives of the largely hi-tech companies in the town to try and win their support for an applied science course. The chief executives were not, however, impressed. "Give us a dozen or so first class scientists each year, and a score or so of competent draughtsmen, and we'll be happy. Oh, and of course, there'll always be a place for a few good humanities graduates, regardless of disciplines, in our personnel structures." They then told me that, in their view, young people ought to become specialists at the earliest opportunity and, without knowing it, echoed the Trinity College governor who said: "The job of the university is to develop specialists. We are good at that, providing, of course, that the schools do their job properly first. We would be worried if there were any move away from pursuing rigorous subject-specific skills."

Between 1945 and 1970 Trinity College, Cambridge alone won seven Nobel prizes for the sciences, in a period when Japanese universities had won just two. Yet within weeks of that statistic becoming common knowledge, the Japanese announced that two thirds of their technological products had their origins in British research and a new quip gained currency. "The British invent it; the Japanese make it; the Americans sell it." The economic benefit to the salesman was even greater than that to the manufacturer, and certainly far greater than that to the inventor. No wonder Britain had financial difficulties as a nation; we were in the wrong part of the market. Britain was paying the price for pretending it didn't know how to knock a nail in straight and English intellectual arrogance was costing the country dearly.

# 6

# Why don't your lot tell my lot what's going on and what's needed?

Speech day speakers at Alleyne's had traditionally been eminent academics or highly placed men and women from the professions. That year I had asked the Confederation of British Industry to nominate a speaker and they had suggested Sir Hector Laing, chairman of United Biscuits and a close friend of the new prime minister, Margaret Thatcher.

Sir Hector arrived by helicopter for a whirlwind tour of the school during which he asked sharp questions, and got good answers. The pupils who stood up to these questions did us proud and our visitor was obviously impressed. More impressed, however, than were many of the teachers with his speech. He spoke quickly, and compellingly, about his own experience of school and of his business life. Exam results were not the only things that mattered, he stressed several times; what counted was your ability to think for yourself, to be able to work with others, and take carefully thought-through risks. You had, he said, to know yourself, and then you would know other people and together you could solve problems that were beyond the scope of a single person.

The boys warmed to his dismissive comments about examinations, while the teachers were shaken by his failure to give a stronger endorsement to what they held to be so important. I rose to propose what would be a difficult vote of thanks but Sir Hector held the rostrum. "Just you sit down, head master, because it is I who have to thank you. I've never been in a comprehensive school before and I had no idea what good things were going on in such places." I was taken aback. Here was one of Mrs Thatcher's favourite businessmen expressing surprise over the quality of provision that I knew hundreds of schools could emulate, and some certainly surpass. I rose to my feet. "I find that hard to believe, Sir Hector. There are 4,500 state secondary schools in England, educating some 94 per cent of the country's children. This is where the future of our nation is being shaped."

"I'm sure you're right, head master," he continued, "but the truth is that I have never been invited into a state school before today. I'm impressed with what I've seen. Why don't your lot tell my lot what's going on and what's needed?"

I slept well that night, and awoke the following morning with his words still ringing in my ears: "Why don't your lot tell my lot what's going on and what's needed?"

These words were to give a new course to my career. Teachers had to stop the self-indulgence of always talking to each other. Unless we took the lead in explaining to a confused public exactly what were the issues, and what needed to happen, it should be no surprise if others made the decisions for us, acting on out-of-date assumptions and incorrect connections. From that day onwards it became my self-appointed mission to help people - often people in high office - to think about the learning needs of young people, without immediately thinking about schools, and in particular their own schooling of years gone by.

Computers played a part in this. My fascination was for technology I could touch - the Meccano form of nuts and bolts, gear wheels and drive shafts, the feel of a piece of wood and the edge of a chisel. I knew little of electronics and still less of the new language of bytes and megs, of loading and down-loading, of booting-up and systems crashing. But I also knew that the most popular of out-of-school clubs was the new computer club, and the most over-subscribed option in the fourth year was computer studies.

I started to investigate. The nature of the black box and what was in it was beyond me; what immediately attracted me was what people were starting to do by applying technology to issues that did interest me. Like word processing. As a slow writer who had always been reluctant to redraft anything, the thought that text could be modified without everything having to be re-written excited me enormously. Initially, however, I was slow off the mark. "That would be helpful for my secretary," I said, in what seemed like a well-informed tone.

Then I thought back to that conference on the Bullock report - *A Language for Life*; in this Sir Alan Bullock argued strongly for teachers to regard every piece of a child's written work as an exercise in English composition. To be fair this was what my teachers had found so unrealistic. "There's no time for that, head master, and it's not our job. We've too much content to cover in our own subjects to give us much leeway," they would often complain.

When personal computers became available, Alleyne's (with the assistance of a generous grant from the parents' association) bought three. While the technologically aware appreciated the purchase, computers were largely dismissed, by those who saw themselves as the academic lite of the school, as merely to do with vocational preparation. I took a different view. What would happen if each pupil in one class had a computer to replace the current paper and pencil technology? What would such a classroom look like? Would all the desks face the same way? Would there be a teacher's desk, or even a blackboard? How would the data from one child be separated from another, or was that a wrong question? Should, in fact, pupils be encouraged to share data and ideas? Would this give students opportunity to work at their own pace and concentrate on things that interested them? I remember smiling to myself late one afternoon when I realised I was talking more like a primary teacher. That impressed me, though I was still too proud to acknowledge this publicly.

"We need to experiment," I said. "Let's go ahead and set up such a classroom and try and work all this out for ourselves."

Most people didn't know what I was talking about and it was difficult to get relevant information on which to base my argument. "This is all unproven, head master. No one has done this before. Why don't you wait and learn how to do this from someone else?" The cost of personal computers was coming down, but the technology was still expensive and I estimated that equipping a classroom with 20 computers was likely to cost £45,000. In 1980 this was enough money to educate 60 pupils for an entire year and most people were not impressed. Many were downright sceptical, and even aggressive. "Surely you won't direct money away from your hard-pressed departments, who even now can't afford to buy all the books they need," argued many senior staff.

"Yes, it's a speculative venture but don't panic," I said, with a confidence that was only skin deep. "I'm sure we could get the money from private sources. If this is the breakthrough I think it could be, then look to the future. In the long-term I think this could really change things."

"The idea is crazy," I heard one member of staff mutter. "Technology should be kept out of school." Few people were with me, but I sensed that I was right. Just as I had gone out on a limb in setting up that Bullock conference three years previously, so again I set out to do something which most people thought was not part of my job. But I knew the two issues were linked; information technology was important if it was exploited to do what Alan Bullock had argued for - to give youngsters confidence in their ability of communicate. When I met Alan Bullock five years later, he said that, in a way, his report had been ahead of its time. Had he been writing more recently, he could well have called it *Word Processing for Everybody* instead of *A Language for Life*.

Calling on my fund-raising experience at Manchester Grammar School, I started with a number of merchant banks in London. I wrote to them explaining why this experiment could be of long-term national significance and that what was needed, first of all, was a practical demonstration of what could be achieved. Most of the replies were strangely similar. A good idea, they acknowledged, and the kind of enterprise needed within education. However they were independent corporations and we were a state school and therefore money for such a project should come from government. Their money should go to help independent schools that had no recourse to any government grants.

I was stunned at their simplicity. Didn't they realise that independent secondary schools were charging fees nearly three times higher (not counting the boarding element) than the amount of money then being allocated to educate a young person in a state comprehensive school? I wrote back to each of the merchant banks and explained that if we were to demonstrate beyond all reasonable doubt the cost-benefit of school computing, then the amount of money we might receive from the government in the future could well be larger. Alternatively we might even be able to fund this at a later stage by reallocating some of our existing funds. Whichever way, they, as employers, would get the benefit of a nation of young people who could use new technology in creative ways. I heard nothing. I had tried taking Hector Laing's advice and telling "that lot" what was needed and why, and they just didn't want to know.

After several months I received a letter from the local authority offering us £500 from a discretionary fund "as there is no money currently available for such innovations of which you speak, but we hope that this will be useful to you in demonstrating our interest in the project when you talk to private sponsors." Like hell it would be, I thought. One chink of opportunity opened up. The New Town council, more aware of the need for people in the town to learn about how to use the new technology than they were of the receding historic hostility towards Alleyne's, proposed that the computer centre should be developed as a joint school and community project. In exchange for the school providing accommodation, they could fund the purchase of the equipment, and then the community could use the computer centre five evenings a week, and during the holidays. This was a novel idea at the time, and one which the authority feared might set a precedent by encroaching on their jurisdiction and their premises. However we (plus a team of lawyers) pushed ahead and by late 1981 the Open Terminal Computer Centre was working.

It so happened that one of the first visitors was John Rae, head master of Westminster School, one of the oldest and most prestigious independent schools. He was fascinated and quickly saw its potential to open up the development of computer skills across the curriculum. "I must have something like this, only mine will need to be at least twice as large."

"Where would you get the money for that?" I asked, extrapolating a figure of nearly £100,000 for such an expanded concept.

"Oh, I don't think that would be much of a problem. I'll go to the big city institutions - the banks, the pension funds and insurance brokers - they've got the money. They'll quickly understand why all this is so important."

John Rae did just that. He went to the very institutions I had approached. They said "yes" to him, and he had no difficulty in collecting the larger sum of money. State education did indeed have a problem. I was getting even more worried. Was anybody going to join me in telling "that lot" what the problem was and how it ought to be solved? And would they listen?

*           *           *

"Why don't your lot tell my lot what's going on and what's needed?"

Hector Laing's words had been given additional meaning by the rejection of my request to the merchant banks for funds. Yet they seemed to unstintingly support the private sector, so what was going wrong? Who should I talk to, what should I say? Certainly it needed to be more than platitudes and generalisations, and more than just asking for money. I had to find a way of getting people to see beyond present arrangements and the flaccid thinking that characterised educational debate. Most practically, how could I ensure that anybody would ever take any notice?

At the governors' meeting each term I had tried to interest them in the complexities of the curriculum, but they ended up lost and confused. I had tried to share with them my conviction that the decisions made by politicians eight or ten years previously had created a school that could not deliver everything that was expected of it. This led to an inconclusive discussion where each person took up a party political position and tried to justify the compromises which political expediency, or their own indecisiveness, had forced on the schools. One thing was clear however. The governors, despite their title, did not think that, for anything of importance, they had any real responsibility. They implied that if I publicly said they supported my request to primary schools for more information, this would have political implications in their private lives that they could not accept. Governorship seemed a pretty shallow concept. "It's all a compromise between different power groups," Philip Ireton, the skilled politician had explained. "It's based on a series of checks and balances designed to keep things going ad infinitum. There is no one person, or institution, in charge. Even as chairman of the county council I have little direct influence, though I may actually have more influence than the minister himself. It is a system actually designed to stop anyone changing it. The purpose is to keep going along a course based on past good practice."

Past good practice was no longer the guide we needed and I wrote a letter to the parents entitled *Some Thoughts at the End of the Year.* "You have many reasons to be proud of your sons and what they have achieved. Several of you have written recently in most glowing terms about the debt of gratitude which your son feels for certain teachers... yet you all know from the national press of the continuing attack on schools for not delivering the right curriculum, or not demanding high enough standards. Several of you regret the passing of the grammar school, yet many of you laud the setting up of comprehensive schools ... In Stevenage the speed with which re-organisation was implemented, and the sometimes crude surgery involved, was a measure of the political will of successive governments to replace the earlier selective system ... The very broadening of opportunity which was given as a basic reason for reorganisation was made a virtual non-starter in many areas by schemes which concentrated on small or medium size comprehensives, like Alleyne's. Let me give an illustration. As a grammar school Alleyne's offered three sets of physics; now as a comprehensive school we have four sets... but for four times the ability range. Don't get me wrong. I am in favour of comprehensive education. I believe deeply in the concept of a Community School with opportunities for everyone, but we need enormous help in achieving this...."

Not a single parent commented to me on the letter but several months later I met a one-time chairman of the county council. "You write interesting letters to parents," he told me. "Several parents spoke to me about what you said in your circular letter. But you know, you and your generation have got it all wrong. You shouldn't place such an emphasis on what the state could do for education. I have brought up seven children and grandchildren, and not one of them has been a charge to the State. Each has been educated privately, and all are doing well."

This was the language of Elizabethan Poor Law - Elizabeth the First that was - at the time my study had been built more than 400 years ago. Old England was still thriving in the early 1980s and education and the welfare of the poor were all part of this muddled thinking. If those were the private thoughts of such people, perhaps spoken more willingly because he was not in the council chamber, what chance had I or anyone else to shake such prejudice? I felt a sense of moral outrage for children who did not get the chances they needed because education too easily became the carve-up of politicians who thought only in the short term. I had become a teacher to play a small part in giving young people opportunities that would, in the fullness of time, make them good parents and good citizens. I wanted opportunities for my own children too, for them to get a good education in state schools where they would learn to live with, and appreciate, all kinds of people. In exchange for my personal commitment to this I expected the maintained state schools to be fully and properly supported by the state. That, as it were, had to be the other side of the deal. It was a deal that many other teachers, with the enthusiasm of youth, had made when they decided to become teachers, rather than following more lucrative careers. We saw education as a national investment, not a social cost, and we were becoming vastly disappointed.

*         *         *

I was increasingly concerned that, difficult as it already was to provide a high quality education for a wide range of children, it was about to get even more difficult. The reason was partly biological. We, with our expectation of raising a large family, were strictly in the minority. Stevenage, which, in the early

1970s, saw 1,800 11 year-olds coming out of primary schools each year, was to see that number drop to 1,300 by 1983 and to just less than 1,000 by 1988. Such a calculation appalled me. It was difficult enough to provide satisfactory provision with an entry of 150, staffed up as six forms rather than five. Even that was not giving youngsters a fair deal. To pretend that we might eventually do this with 90 was sheer fantasy. I had already been forced to cut expenditure on books and other equipment to the point where the entire school expenditure was less than the annual salary of one teacher. Our teachers were being driven backwards into old-fashioned methods of chalk and talk instruction because there were ever fewer resources for pupils to use to learn for themselves. It wasn't just cuts to expenditure on books, either. Funds for staff training had just been reduced to less than half a day per teacher per year...some two and a half to three hours per year per person. It was getting more difficult for teachers to consider themselves learners.

Yet Alleyne's was still the most fortunate school in the town. Our numbers were still the highest, our examination results were persistently good, our curriculum perceived by the general public as being broad and challenging. "Why do you worry, head master, that the other schools will go to the wall first? This is a crazy situation, but at least Alleyne's will survive." I was unnerved by the narrow-mindedness, and by the politicians' unwillingness to look honestly into the future. The more pupils a school had, the more money it got. Each school wished to show as broad a curriculum and as full a set of A levels as they could muster. With decreasing pupil numbers some schools were bound to be losers. The local education authority seemed to be taking a callous, cowardly way out of making decisions. "Let's see which schools start to die of their own volition," it was saying, "and then, when they're already weak, we'll make sure they're not strong enough to continue the fight." It was tough, and obviously getting tougher. People were becoming depressed.

Rosemary Solbé, a biologist, and one of Alleyne's best teachers, asked to see me. "I'm sorry, John, but this has just become impossible. I enjoy my subject enormously and I'm deeply committed on broad ethical principles to opportunities for all, so I approve of the comprehensive school in theory. I've wanted to make this work. I have no real difficulties teaching the less able classes alongside scholarship work with sixth formers. But I just can't carry on working under these stressful conditions. We're just being stretched and pulled apart too much. I've just accepted a post at Haberdasher's (a leading girls' independent school). I'll have a far lighter timetable, and much smaller classes, and a larger salary. I'm sorry. I really am. I respect what you're trying to do, but we're just not winning. You can fight the system more effectively than I can. At least I hope so. Good luck, you'll need it."

I too became depressed. I felt let down and was beginning to understand the meaning of loneliness. I produced a paper for the governors setting out my fears, and put forward a proposal for reducing the number of schools so that those remaining would be viable. Already there was talk in the air about closing one or two schools. The staff of these schools, and their communities, were already mobilising to defend themselves. "It's not good enough just to close sufficient schools to defend a five form entry system", I wrote in my report, "we need to grasp this issue properly. If we believe in all-through 11 to 18 schools, with a full range of options, then each school needs at least seven forms of entry - some 210 pupils. To achieve this Stevenage will need no more than five or six schools, not 12."

There was a shuffling of papers around the table at the governors' meeting. No one knew how to come at this one and then they all started to speak at once. "Aren't you going too far? "You'll be seen as one of the hawks." "You'll find the other heads all lining up against you." "Would Alleyne's survive in its present shape as a boys only school if numbers were reduced as much as all that?"

"These views are those of the head master alone," said the deputy clerk to the governors in an aggrieved voice. "The authority thinks it is best to leave things as they are for the time being. It would not be wise for the governors, at this stage, to take any particular stance. We should see what happens of its own accord." Tensions around the table subsided. I, however, was furious. Was anybody really in charge? Was anybody prepared to stand by what they believed? Leaving a school, its pupils and teachers to die off by indifference, and through apparent lack of administrative responsibility, was cowardice. Those youngsters would not have their school days again.

                    *              *              *

The completion of the fully computerised classroom - now named Open Terminal to signify its role within Stevenage as well as within the school - gave me an opportunity to develop the idea of collaboration with two other schools. Slowly their staff overcame a reluctance to see their pupils walk onto our site and share the occasional lesson in Open Terminal. Slowly they started to welcome some of our pupils into their schools. There was a new opportunity here if we could take it.

I talked with the head of the adjacent one-time secondary modern school. "Why," I asked, "don't we think about combining some of our sixth form classes? The distance pupils would have to walk is negligible. Your biology class is over-large, my second set is too small. I'm running two physics classes which aren't very economic, nor is your single physics class either. We could do the same with some of our middle school classes as well."

He looked apprehensive for he already knew of what I had said to my governors. He was fearful, he said, of being seen by his staff as having in any sense sold out to the old rival. "Let's talk further about this, but don't let's feed people's suspicions. I think I had better come over to your place. It wouldn't look so conspicuous. If you came to us, everyone would start talking and jumping to conclusions. It would probably be safer, too, to start talking about collaboration on non-examinable subjects, rather than mainstream subjects. There would be no loss of status to any of our schools in doing that." Again I had to bite my lip.

So, for 12 months, covert conversations were held; slight adjustments were made to timetables and a few pupils crossed the line that separated the two schools. My impatience started to show. Right across the town (and to the best of my knowledge in many other towns) head teachers continued to offer a curriculum that placed impossible loads on teachers and created classes that were so small, and often with such differing ability levels, that the essential spark associated with good sixth form classes too often became a damp squib. Teachers became stressed and A level results started to drop. The same thing started happening in the middle school years. But everyone kept quiet. It seemed that the first duty of head teachers was the maintenance of their own schools, rather than the development of an education system that best suited the needs of children. No wonder the public was losing faith in a service that it sensed had become inward looking and complacent. While I sensed that many of the practices that we teachers cherished were nothing like as effective in giving young people the essential skills of learning which they needed, I still did not have the right language to persuade people that a change in teaching styles was essential.

Despite this I wrote to Donald Fisher, the chief education officer, suggesting that he ask the heads of the town to get together and start thinking in terms of what was good for all children in the town, rather than what was good for their individual schools. I was deferential, probably too much so. My early training, in retrospect, made me uneasy at mounting such a challenge. The CEO was, after all, in charge and I should leave decision making to him; that was the natural order of things. We met in his office and talked at length. He acknowledged my arguments, but appeared preoccupied with the ramifications of such thinking on the politics of the county council. "We ought to talk further about this," he said eventually. "Which other head teachers do you think should join us? Let's talk off-site, so that no one will start taking sides in advance of anything I might say." Why was everyone so nervous? What were we supposed to be afraid of? Was it our own faint-heartedness or the power we held but which no one was prepared to use?

Another head and I met with the chief in our house in Hitchin three weeks later. We talked for a couple of hours and I was content that I had said most of what was on my mind. If we heads continued to act solely in the interests of our individual schools, without using our professional expertise to find ways of improving the overall situation for everyone, we would be acting irresponsibly, I argued. What we needed was for the chief to say just that to all of us head teachers. "There's the termly meeting of all the secondary heads in Stevenage in two weeks' time," the chief said. "It's already arranged. I'll come and join in the discussion. No one will be suspicious. Then I can talk about this issue and we could start drawing up plans."

I was cautiously optimistic about that meeting. The chief spoke well - he always did - but what he said was so wrapped around with ifs and buts and 'they're your schools' and 'the authority has to be answerable to its members', that one head (who, I'm sure, was unaware of my earlier discussions with the chief) asked him outright just what it was he was talking about. The chief flushed and started again. He could not, he said, given the nature of his being answerable to the committee, require us head teachers to do something that the committee had not so far considered, but he felt personally, that we ought to be working more collaboratively. At last he had said it.

"Does that mean that I can tell my staff that I'm being told by you to be collaborative and that, in providing next year's time-table I'm being loyal to the authority first, and the school second? Without that sort of statement anything which I do looks as if it's not in the immediate interest of my school - and would not necessarily help ensure that we survive. This might well undermine my credibility in the eyes of my staff and governors." The head concerned looked at the chief carefully. Everyone did. I thought the chief looked at me, daring me to say something. The chief eventually replied, "I can't go as far as that. You can't quote me as saying that. This is not yet an authority position. It's what I think you should consider doing but it's not what I'm saying you have to do - at least not yet." I was furious. This would get us nowhere. I interrupted to say that we needed more of his support if we were to be seen as concerned for the overall system rather than just for our own schools. "Why is John asking you to produce a stick with which to beat us?" said one of the heads, irritably.

Before I could reply there was a knock at the door and a secretary asked to speak with me. "We've just had a call from your secretary. No one's been hurt, but your wife's just had a small car accident. Someone in Hitchin is taking her and your son home, but she's asked if you could get back as soon as possible." Anne, now seven months pregnant, in a car crash. The affairs of an unintelligible authority that seemed to have no heart, no confidence, or no moral authority, no spirit, or no real sense of conscience, were as of nought to me at that moment.

In later years the boys would tease Anne about her little bump at seven months. Manoeuvring out of the car park, she had inadvertently pressed the accelerator rather than the brake and had gone into the side of the next car with such force that it had been thrown against a third car. There were repair bills to pay on two of the three cars, but there were no broken bones, and no upset foetus. David, our second son, was born fit and lively ten weeks later. Peter immediately took charge of the new arrival. This was his brother and it was his self-appointed job to interpret every cry. He'd just started at play school and by special arrangement he started early each morning so he and I could go off to work together in the car. I used to linger at the play school and watch fascinated – and fascinating – children choose their toys, negotiate with each other and share their news. At the time I didn't fully appreciate the significance of the social interaction and friendship building between Peter and his young friends. In the mid-1990s I thought back to their infancy when I heard a chilling presentation by an American journalist at a Chicago conference on brain development. The Pulitzer Prize winning writer noted, "what we thought we knew about the relationship between a deprived or bad upbringing and the increased risk of criminal behaviour is now being traced to the brain's chemistry. It is the biological smoking gun of violence. We [brain researchers] are now finding the molecular answers to the things that happen in the brain that we could only grope with from psychology, psychiatry and sociology. If we don't provide young children with the supportive and nurturing environments in which they can develop their predispositions towards social, collaborative and team-building skills, young children's brains react with astounding speed and efficiency to the violent world they experience around them by rewiring trillions of brain cells that literally create the chemical pathways for aggression." It was a terrifying contrast: as my young children were learning how to collaborate, share and work in teams, other children in threatening and deprived environments were learning how to be selfish and to use their intelligence to be successful aggressors.

Peter was reading almost before we realised it. After listening to Anne or me reading *The Hungry Caterpillar*, or *The Giant Jam Sandwich*, or *Postman Pat*, or *The Little Engine that Could*, he would take the same book and read to David either from memory or with some help from the first words he could recognise. He read to himself during church services and sometimes the reality of his reading would get confused with his embryonic sense of theology. "Daddy," he announced one afternoon. "Mummy's got me a new book." He thrust *Captain Pugwash and the Ghost Ship* at me. "What's it called, Peter?" I asked. A look of concentration crossed his little face and he replied, "Captain Pugwash and the Holy Ghost."

Anne and I, like most parents around the world, were constantly amazed at the ease with which all three of our boys seemed one day to start speaking. It was after the boys had already entered secondary school that I started to understand why language acquisition happens apparently so magically. Humans are born with brains that have strong predispositions to learn language in a particular, natural way. The brain is no clean slate as regards language development, rather the analogy is closer to that of an old fashioned gramophone record needing a layer of wax removed from its surface before revealing its pre-formed structure. Subsequently, virtually every child born today has the innate capability of recognising about 100 sounds - quite enough to combine in various forms to create all the alphabets in each of the earth's 6,000 plus languages. The neurological structures that make this possible are identical to those of all races. Biology provides a kind of blueprint. The blueprint is that baby's exquisite ability to hear the difference between all sounds; then culture jumps in and provides this information, the input, language information, that the baby's brain then begins to map. New-born babies can tell the difference between 'pah' and 'bah.' By four and a half months of age, an infant understands the significance of clauses; at 10 months the ordering of noun and verb phrases fit in sentences. Below 18 months babies learn the meaning of new words at about a third of a word a day; from then onwards it speeds up to about ten words a day. By listening to the language spoken around them, kids set the rules appropriate to their own language at 18 months of age, and in many instances earlier. To release this language potential virtually all that a child needs is plenty of opportunity to hear people talking and encouragement to join in. At less than 18 months Peter had amazed us by correctly humming the tune to the World War I song *Daisy, Daisy, give me your answer do*, which he had heard his grandfather sing twice the day before.

From the earliest stages David was more careful, and neater, than Peter. While his older brother rushed from one thing to another, David would line up his toy lorries in order of diminishing size, and was fascinated by their finest detail. Unlike Peter who, by the age of two, had created his own imaginary world called Hemly-Hemly (which, whenever he was asked where it was would say, knowingly, "You go up the A421 and turn left."), David's world needed to be more real and tangible. What he liked were pictures of railway engines and models of American-style trucks.

Tom was born 21 months later. David did not accept him as easily as his older brother had accepted him and this was partly our fault for we had not prepared him for the arrival of a younger brother as well as we should. Also he was younger than Peter had been. Tom was alert from the moment he was born. He walked earlier than the others and rode a bike without stabilisers quicker than any other child at play school. His infectious laugh accompanied a quick sense of humour. But with two highly articulate elder brothers he was far lazier in his speech and always more willing to be read to, than to read for himself.

Our children possess our abilities and our faults and those of our innumerable ancestors over the last two million years of evolution. In turn our children reinforce our faults and abilities. Every generation of humanity is truly interconnected through learning. But which dominates in any one particular generation? Nature or nurture? All human development is an intricate interplay; nature and nurture don't compete, they cooperate. Learning is a delicate, but powerful dialogue between genetics and the environment: the experience of our species from aeons past interacts with the experiences we have during our lifetime. We are - as it were - at the cutting edge of evolution.

Anyway, three children below the age of four and a half gave me emotional distance from professional problems and meant that I was not interested solely in employment prospects, nor in the minutiae of changed regulations for university entry that dominated my agendas as a head master. No, I wanted to know what the world of 2050 was going to be like - that was where our little family was headed.

*          *          *

In the summer of 1981, the prime minister, Margaret Thatcher, replaced an old-style Tory as secretary of education with her trusted lieutenant, Keith Joseph. It was an unexpected move that unnerved many within the education establishment. Joseph was intellectually detached and emotionally unmoved by many of the materialistic expectations of members of his party and was determined to drive at the heart of the cultural and social assumptions that he thought weakened the English psyche. His intention was two-fold; to improve the quality of the education service for which he had a personal commitment, especially for the bottom 40 per cent, while secondly to restrain and pull back the power of local government which, with its high level of local autonomy, could undermine the monetarist policies the conservatives so avidly espoused. With education being by far the largest spender within each authority, to become secretary for education gave him direct access to local government's greatest weakness, their inability to conceptualise an education service appropriate to the needs of the twenty-first century.

Teachers and administrators were frightened by his early statements about profligate spending, especially on central services, within each authority. He called for a reduction in educational spending, and "cutting the fat from the educational bone". Teachers, and their unions, became apoplectic. Authority officers rushed to defend central expenditure as an essential component for strengthening schools. Government most certainly did not agree. Independent schools had no such central services, Keith Joseph said, and they did well on their own. "An unfair comparison," said the authorities. "Independent schools charge fees that are far higher than that which we can provide through the rates, and so the only way schools can meet all their obligations is for us to provide many services centrally. Without us the schools would have a far harder job," they said. These were the early exchanges in a bitter campaign, a campaign that is still raging 20 years later. Joseph started an argument that has subsequently been taken up in many other lands, but which has not necessarily unfolded in the way he expected. In the House of Commons, Sir William van Straubenzee, chairman of the Education Select Committee (and one of my recent visitors to Alleyne's to address the sixth form), issued a warning to the new secretary - one of his own party - that "cuts in education have not just cut through the fat, they are already into the bone." Teachers cheered him. I rushed into print, as did many others, and had my letter of 15th October, 1981 published in *The Times*. It got an acknowledgement from Joseph's office saying that he wished to respond to me personally when he had the time.

The school governors were confused, angry and feeling increasingly powerless. "Are we running this school or not?" exclaimed Johnny Pryor irritably. "Why the hell can't government keep out of this? I know Bill Straubenzee well. I'll invite him to dinner. He needs to tell this new secretary a thing or two." Old Tories were making a common cause with a middle party. Initially it seemed that this was going to be a battle for control for it was easier to argue about administrative arrangements than to argue about the curriculum. Certainly it was easier than challenging people to think about how children learn. The governors endorsed my letter. "But be careful, John. This is going to get very political. The teacher unions are on edge and are likely to go on strike. Everything you say and do - even those things you don't do - will be carefully watched." Old Stevenage knew about playing political games, but it was still ignorant of the needs of the young people it was supposed to serve.

The Open Terminal Computer Centre was inundated with visitors. "What you will need shortly," said one young engineer, "is to be linked to an electronics laboratory to give some of your youngsters the opportunity of seeing how to apply all this to control systems of various kinds. That should be the next part of the revolution." I asked for more details, which came back both as specifications for equipment and as something far more radical. "You will have to consider your timetable," I was told. "Once youngsters get started on these kinds of issues the last thing they need is for the bell to ring every 40 minutes." I asked one of the primary heads for her thoughts about how we might use this new centre. "I have a feeling that this might change the way we will have to teach in future," I said. "You see, with all these computers I don't even know if the teacher's desk should be at the back or at the front."

"Maybe it should be on the side," the primary head said. "And just maybe this is the time secondary schools will start coming to terms with the nature of how children actually learn. I agree with that engineer from industry. There is no educational reason for the bells to ring every 40 minutes."

I laughed.

"Don't mock," she replied. "I think primary schools know more about how learning takes place than the secondary sector. We know about developing skills of collaboration and problem solving, or the ability to work under pressure and to deal with uncertainty. Something goes wrong for children when they go to secondary school. They lose their sparkle, inquisitiveness, fun, responsibility. And don't tell me it's all to do with hormones and adolescence. Children I've seen in other countries are not necessarily like that. The English system knocks something vital out of them. Here's my answer to your question about how to organise the computer centre; treat it as if it were a primary school classroom. Have plenty of space for people to move around in. Have a corner for the books and where the pupils can talk with each other without upsetting other people. As for the teacher's desk - put it in one of the back corners so he can get on with his work, as well as the children."

Keith Joseph was as good as his word and wrote me a sturdy rebuttal of the points I had made. The letter had the feel of being directly from his own pen so I was flattered. I was also annoyed that he was misinterpreting what I had said, and did not seem to understand my point that schools were only part of the complex world in which children were growing up, that learning was essentially a messy process, and that to confuse learning with schooling was to trivialise each. I wrote a careful reply and three days later received a phone call from his office. "Sir Keith would like to come and discuss this with you; would the afternoon of Friday of next week suit you, probably allowing him to stay for three hours?"

"Of course, I'd be delighted. Tell him I look forward to this very much."

"Good. Oh, by the way, we've already asked your CEO if this would be in order and he's agreed."

Why had Sir Keith felt it necessary to ask the chief's approval before approaching me to talk about a letter I had written? Who's in charge? It doesn't feel as if I am, at least not with the issues that matter, the ones I want to talk to the minister about. I know the chief himself doesn't feel he's in charge and sees himself answerable to an ever-changing committee. The committee doesn't think they're in charge either. Would Keith Joseph say that he's not in charge as well? Is that why each of us feels that we are the only ones who are worried?

I would have to focus carefully if I were not to lose an important opportunity to influence his thinking. I wanted to talk about giving children the ability to be enterprising enough to handle anything the world threw at them. I wanted to talk about the need for them to understand community; to be tough yet responsible. (I'm almost talking like Samuel Smiles, I said to myself.) I wanted to talk about new technologies, and the limitations of a small school trying to create a breadth of opportunity. I needed to talk about money.

Sir Keith and I talked alone for well over an hour and then spent a further hour and a half walking around the school. He was a good listener and knew how to ask the kinds of questions that drew out my concerns about providing opportunities in the middle years of school, when numbers were small and resources limited. He had been well briefed by his department. "I'm not sure why you should be worried. My department tells me you've got good examination results, and that you've a stable staff and you know how to mobilise the power of the local community. I also know that you seem to have talked the Department of Trade into supporting you. You're obviously doing well."

I was ready for this. "If I'm doing well, it's because I'm in a fortunate position. Other schools are finding it hard to do the same thing and, if they did, the community as it's currently structured, wouldn't be able to respond. This kind of success is not replicable."

He nodded. "Yes, I understand that."

I took him to see the Open Terminal and he was better at talking with the children working at the keyboards than he had been with the teachers. Accomplished politician as he was, he was socially reserved and seemed more concerned to learn for himself than to score points. He was obviously impressed and asked for more ideas about the electronic laboratory that I thought was the next stage. "What does this technology do for children's reasoning ability? Does it make them deeper thinkers, or does it encourage them to be simplistic? I like what I see of word processing and spreadsheets, but I'm fearful if this were to degenerate into teaching machines. Will this make them more, or less, thoughtful? Will it make them creative, imaginative and enterprising?"

He seemed well satisfied and went away still firing off questions as he got into his car. The union representatives had found him approachable, polite, but largely unmoveable. What difference it would make I was not sure, but I was intrigued at the requests I got from his office over the following weeks, asking for a reference on this, or the title of some further book. He had clearly not stopped thinking about what he had seen or heard and wanted to learn.

Maybe, I thought to myself, he will find a way to fund further developments of this kind. I recalled that Bullock conference and the other experiences which had led me to believe that children, once their imaginations were fired up, were capable of so much more than we usually asked of them. What could be achieved if Keith Joseph could release sufficient funds to enable a child to access a computer whenever he had any written work to do. What would happen if every child expected to incorporate the teacher's comments on a piece of work, in a redraft - a redraft that did not have all the tedium of handwriting? It was an intoxicating dream, and I wished Joseph well in whatever scheme he might come up with.

*          *          *

Three days later Donald Fisher offered me a large cigar. I think he was unsure of my political leanings and he probed to discover what Sir Keith and I had spoken about. As one of the country's most influential CEOs, he wanted insights into a politician who was challenging the status quo. He was not comfortable with the observations I had made about the shortcomings of the small comprehensive schools, nor was he happy that I was beginning to question the basis of the statistics that were then being bantered around about per capita expenditure. Just how much money was actually being siphoned off for central services I had wanted to know, and I had never got a straight answer. As a one-time academic historian, the chief found the new technologies of information and communication disconcerting, and to the man who saw himself as the balanced academic, my obvious enthusiasm for things new was, at least partially, suspect. Keith Joseph's questions about the nature of the curriculum worried him most. In times past secretaries of state had been distant figureheads, leaving each CEO to work out structures appropriate to their own authority. If the secretary of state were to become more interventionist, then it was inevitable that authorities would see their power constrained. I got the feeling I was being warned off as I realised the agenda I was setting out for myself existed in a no-man's land owned neither by central government nor by the local authorities. An uncomfortable place to be in, with few natural allies, claimed and fought over by those who did not know how to shoot straight. This was going to be a messy, confused, and uncomfortable terrain to explore.

*          *          *

The centre of Hitchin, a town some four miles from Stevenage and to which Anne and I had moved when we married, is dominated by a fine parish church. Most of the external stonework is thirteenth century, though the short dumpy tower, topped off with a narrow lead-covered spire so typical of that part of England, was rebuilt in the fourteenth century, using bricks recovered from the foundations of old Roman buildings found elsewhere in the town. Half of the foundations are older, and are thought to go back to the reign of King Offa, just over 1,000 years ago. Recognising my interest in both history and building, the job assigned to me by the congregation was to act as the voluntary, unpaid chairman of the Fabric Committee. It was my "job" to make sure the church did not fall down when I had finished with the affairs of the school.

By the time he was five, Peter would follow me on my tours of inspection, over the roofs, and up the bell tower and down into the crypt. I relished giving Peter his first history lesson, and I enjoyed the close contact this gave me with the honest workmanship of generations past. Often I would draw analogies from this when addressing the school at morning assembly. The church had been used as a stable by Oliver Cromwell's army, but was magnificently restored by the Royalists of Hitchin following the return of Charles II in 1660. New lead was laid on the roof, with the names of the churchwardens cast into each sheet. Of such high quality was that lead that it is still in place 340 years later, and the oak beneath it totally dry. A hopper-head to collect the rainwater and funnel it into the down-pipes, last recast in 1797, cracked with the ice of a severe winter in the early nineteen eighties. It was taken down, and recast. Several weeks later, the builder went up a ladder to reset it. He pulled some new nails from his pocket, but quickly recognised that they were nothing like as good as the 18th century nails he had pulled out weeks before. He fumbled in his tool bag, found the old nails, and drove them hard back into the oak blocks- nails re-used at 200 years old.

Holding my hand after morning service one day Peter, by then nearly six years old, and with three year-old David on my other side, we walked together down the nave towards the altar after everyone had left the church. Peter was counting the large York flagstones on which we were standing. "Twenty-seven, 28, 29 ... Daddy, there are nearly 30 big stones." He looked around him. "How old's the church?"

"About a thousand years old," I said.

"But how old is that? I wonder how many people have been in and out of here!" I thought for a moment and remembered the flagstones. I did a quick calculation. "Well, you know that I was more than 30 years old when you were born. If every person was perhaps 25 years old when they had a child, there would be four generations in every 100 years." He nodded. David looked perplexed. "Can we go home?" I smiled. "In a minute."

I turned to Peter. "Let's imagine that each of these stones on the floor were one generation, one person. Now you and David stand on the first stone and look towards the back of the church. Now I'll stand on the next one, number two. I'm your father, one generation before you. If Granny or Grandpa were here they could stand on number three - they're the next generation. I knew my grandfather well; he would stand on number four, and actually I can just remember my great-grandmother and great-grandfather; they would be on the fifth stone."

"Gosh," said Peter. "That's old but there are lots of stones behind them. Who were the people who stood on them?" We did a few more calculations. "A thousand years ago the people would have stretched to the very back of the church and out the other side."

"Gosh," said Peter again, "It's very, very old, isn't it?"

Timelines can be learned in many ways. Some are so powerful they are never forgotten. We often talk like that, as a family. And we draw out linkages at every stage. When the good citizens of Hitchin finished the restoration of the church late in 1661 they put up a new sundial to tell the time of day. It is inscribed *Anno salutis 1661*, Latin for "We salute the year 1661".

*     *     *

Six weeks before Christmas the early morning news reported that government was to announce a partnership between the Department of Education and the Department of Employment. The Manpower Services Commission (MSC) would involve both new technology and vocational development skills. I was only partially interested and not much surprised to hear that the local education authorities feared the MSC might intrude on their responsibilities. I forgot about the news until a highly excited Bowen Wells phoned that afternoon. Bowen was Stevenage's MP and parliamentary secretary to the secretary of employment, Norman Tebbit. He said, "This is your idea, John, I've been tracking it for weeks. After Keith Joseph talked with you in April he got so interested in the ideas that he started talking to others. I don't think he found his own department too enthusiastic and they said they hadn't got any money. So he approached David Young, chairman of the MSC. They're old friends and quickly got a scheme together. There are to be pilot projects starting next September and Stevenage must be one of them. I'll send you a copy of the press statement and look in to see you in a couple of days."

I put down the phone, somewhat bemused. Had it really happened like that? I phoned Anne. "My luck's changed. You remember that radio report this morning about technology and vocational education or something? Well, Bowen Wells has just phoned from the House of Commons. Maybe all that fuss I was making will actually pay off." I talked on excitedly and then walked around the school for half an hour. It was a cold November afternoon and the heating system had just come on. Many of the classroom windows were getting steamed up. But not half so steamed up, I was soon to discover, as the authority officers.

Documentation for the New Technological, Vocational and Educational Initiative (NTVEI for short) contained faint echoes of my conversation with Keith Joseph. While the main points were there in the passion-free language, something more important had been lost. I had talked of the use of information technology as a resource to transform learning strategies - not as a subject but as a tool whose influence could permeate all subjects. This policy statement was a hybrid, which doffed its cap to trade and industry with the use of the words technology, employment and vocational. The interests of education took third place and by talking about an initiative, this programme could be seen as giving local authorities assurance that it was not, yet, a new policy. It was difficult to know exactly what it was all about. There was, however, the promise of a dozen community pilot projects for a scheme in the middle years of the curriculum with an overall budget of some £70 million over five years. If Stevenage were to become one of these, I thought, we as a school might eventually get £500,000. Everyone in the school could have access to a word processor. We could create a communications policy that was true to the spirit of the Bullock Report. Everyone could draft and redraft whenever necessary. No subject area would be untouched. Every child could escape from the limitations of the pencil and paper technology - something I had suffered from all my life.

I was so excited that I forgot to be cautious. I wrote an enthusiastic letter to the chief, citing my earlier conversation with Keith Joseph, which of course he knew all about, and the phone conversation of the day before, of which he knew nothing. I connected my enthusiasm for TVEI with my earlier experience of Bullock and the setting up of Open Terminal. I dared to speak of the possible opportunity of providing access to word processing for everyone, and hinted at the changes in the teaching profession that would then need to follow.

I urged him to put forward Stevenage as an ideal location for one of the pilot projects, and enthused as to what we could do with the money. My reply arrived by return of post. It was not what I had expected. The chief, and the rest of the local authority world, were highly suspicious of the NTVEI. They doubted if it was legal for the Manpower Services Commission, "that's about employment and we're about education", to be involved with children below the statutory school leaving age, and it was highly likely that they would refuse to participate. In any case, it would be up to the authority to decide whether they would support an application from Stevenage, "you're only one tenth of the county", and even if it did, "you don't speak for Stevenage." It would have to be a decision taken by the elected members after meeting with all the head teachers in the county. As to word processors across the curriculum, the chief did not think that the connection I had made with the Bullock Report was what ministers had in mind at all; they were thinking about specific vocational qualifications. Speculation was largely wasted until further details were released and I could expect to hear more later.

I felt chastised, disheartened and naïve in failing to anticipate their worries about central government using education policy to undermine the autonomy of local government. Later that afternoon, Bowen Wells arrived in my study. He was not as ebullient as I had expected. "I've just been to County Hall to suggest we apply for your NTVEI scheme to operate in Stevenage. To my surprise they were not at all enthusiastic - almost negative I would say. I thought I was bringing good news. They're certainly suspicious. I can't understand them at all."

"I know. I've just had this letter. Here's a copy."

He read it through carefully, and looked crestfallen. He had entered parliament with the Thatcher victory of 1979, and had been re-elected with a bigger majority in 1983. Essentially a businessman, and not pretending to be an intellectual, he was nevertheless interested in getting things done; and he liked children. An archetypal achiever, he could not abide procrastination and was an advocate of the kind of education I was trying to develop. We agreed that we would have to bide our time.

"Come on. Let's go and look at the computer centre, that's the real world." We walked across the drive and up the stairs of the building opposite. The room was a hive of activity. It was the bottom English set of the second year and they were using their computers to write a letter to an imaginary friend in hospital. They were deeply engaged in what they were doing. Normally inhibited by bad and slow handwriting, and all the problems of crossing out inappropriate words, here they were able to concentrate on expressing what they truly thought.

*       *       *

I built Peter and David a wooden castle for Christmas. More correctly, I suppose, I relieved my pent-up frustration by creating my own medieval fantasy world. "Couldn't you make it a bit smaller?" asked Anne. "Where's it going to go?"

She was right. It was pretty large. It had a square keep with battlements and even a medieval toilet fashioned after one I had used, years before, as a guest of Sir Charles McLean at Duart Castle on the island of Mull. It had outer ramparts and towers at each corner. It was complete, right down to the portcullis and drawbridge. True, the paint was still wet when we went to bed, but dry by the time the boys awoke at five on Christmas morning. We spent hours that Christmas afternoon crawling around the floor with miniature catapults, hurling little canvas pillows filled with rice that Anne had sewn, while more and more of the soldiers fell off the ramparts.

*                    *                    *

"How far back in the church would the castle be?" asked David all of a sudden in the middle of the Christmas morning sermon. I was confused. What did he mean? Peter interpreted. "He's talking about the stones on the floor in church, Daddy. He wants to know where the castle fits...near the front or the back?" I thought for a moment. "Just over half-way back," I said. "Gosh, the church is old," said David in amazement, catching the amused attention of the elderly couple in the pew behind.

Later, as we sang a carol, David edged to my end of the pew. He peered over the side and looked at the flagstones on the floor. Then he looked up at me and grinned, knowingly. "It's very old!"

# 7

# "Education for What?"

In mid-February, two months after the announcement in the House of Commons, the authority evidently received an invitation to submit a proposal to be considered for the New Technological, Vocational and Educational Initiative (NTVEI). I only heard of it second-hand from one of the advisors, who let slip that two other towns in the county were interested in becoming involved, and not until the authority had seen these would they know whether they would support us. My enthusiasm wavered. Was any of this going to be worthwhile?

Was this in any way connected to what I had suggested to Keith Joseph? Would this explore the use of information technology to support far higher levels of communication skills across all subjects?

The advisor passed me a sheaf of papers. "Read these and get some of the other head teachers together. Fill out the proposal form, it's quite easy. You just have to answer certain standard questions. Get it back to me by Monday at the latest. I'm the officer in charge of this project. I'll try and get the authority to back you but it may not be easy. Then we'll get it off to Sheffield and should have an answer by 23 March." He left in a great hurry. I felt confused and annoyed. I looked at the forms, designed by a civil servant in a way that could reduce the most abstract of ideas into a series of administratively convenient pigeon-holes that could later be marked with a tick or a cross. Or be thrown out altogether as just not fitting in.

I read the form again. Unless I was careful, the way I filled this in could lead to the idea being immediately rejected. Whoever had constructed this pro-forma had not anticipated the kind of radical thinking I had in mind. Radical thinking doesn't easily fit into boxes. I resented, too, the sudden incursion of authority officers who thought they had to demonstrate their personal superiority by making me feel as if I were at the bottom of the pile. Where were they, I thought to myself, when I was trying to persuade Sir Keith Joseph of the need to think about how technology could transform education?

Four of us met in my study the next morning and cast about for the right expressions to use in each section. The other heads certainly didn't share all parts of my vision, yet each saw in this a possibility that their lives over the next few years could be a little more exciting, and by linking technology to vocational training they could be seen as using children's educational experience to good purpose. It was not an unworthy goal; it was just that it didn't go anything like far enough. Like the others, I signed the proposal, but with little of the enthusiasm that I had espoused for the initiative when it was first announced.

What we wrote was good enough for the authority to endorse, but they then modified it significantly to fit into their overall framework. That, in its turn, was good enough for the MSC to include Stevenage in the fourteen projects for which it announced approval at the end of March.

My worst fears about the initiative becoming a top-down programme, largely applied from outside the school, began to materialise as the summer term opened up. Special meetings of parents and pupils approaching their fourteenth birthdays were held so that, in addition to the already complicated set of subject choices already available, thirty-two pupils could be specially selected to follow a TVEI set of subjects. They would be technologically streamed out, leaving the education of the other 120 pupils as it was before.

It seemed we were recreating the old technical grammar school in the midst of a comprehensive school. Pupils studying computer studies within the school option system had to take their turn, every other week, to have a double period in the computer centre; those studying it through TVEI, however, did it in lavishly equipped buses that visited the school every other period. Pupils studying English under the school's option scheme had no opportunity to use computers; those studying basic English for business studies did so in a room where each had an electric typewriter for every lesson. We were creating a cadre of computer specialists and I found myself having to defend the indefensible.

These were, I tried telling myself, teething problems that would be worked out. But it was hard to reassure angry teachers. "You've sold your intellectual soul for a mess of computers," one spat out contemptuously. Technology became such a dirty word that I suspected the English department no longer even included it as one that needed to be spelt properly. I had visions of the history department stopping its modern history course at about 1750 for fear of contaminating itself by talking of the first industrial revolution. I joke now, but at the time it was most uncomfortable and, had they known it, I was as worried as the most worried of the teachers. I asked myself the same old questions. How could I get people to see technology as a tool for enhanced learning across the curriculum? Who was in charge? Who was thinking about a broad balance within the curriculum? Who did I need to convince?

\*     \*     \*

Johnny Pryor sensed my despondency, "Cheer up," he said (the voice of old England always seeking to jolly things along). "You and Anne ought to come and have dinner with us. A decent claret would do you a power of good."

"It's not just me that needs cheering up, it's the whole staff," I responded.

"Tell me why?"

I complained at the muddled thinking behind TVEI. "I didn't come into teaching to preside over a system preoccupied with sorting children and then using the school as some form of narrow job training." I complained about how the Open Terminal ideals had been diluted into an ill-applied initiative dominated by bureaucrats.

To look at, Johnny was more like a farm labourer than the owner of several thousand acres of the best farmland in the county. Old string held up his trousers, his boots and leggings were caked in mud, yet he still wore with pride his Guards tie. Civil servant-type administrators awoke in him a sense of total disdain. For all his wealth, Johnny was a man of the people. Something of a rebel himself, it often seemed his estate was staffed by people who, in their younger days, had so got up against the system that, as a last resort, Johnny had been asked to help. The technicalities of my problem were largely beyond him, but he knew I needed cheering up and again he spoke of the claret as a cure for my blues.

"Sounds like everyone needs a party. Never get anywhere by being miserable. Bring everybody out to Weston Park. Let 'em bring their girlfriends, husbands, wives or whatever with 'em. Tell you what, you've got that German choir coming over for the last week of term. Bring 'em too - I promise not to prattle on about Itis or filthy Huns. We can have a jolly time, and everybody can go off for the summer holidays feeling good."

So, two days before the end of term, we did just that. The house easily absorbed a hundred or so people, and the choir sang beautifully. Long into the night staff sat curled up in deep armchairs, or perched on the steps of the great staircase as if they were students again at a college ball. Johnny kept on talking and talking and everybody felt more good-tempered on the last day of term.

Several months later Johnny died suddenly. It shook Hertfordshire, old and new, to the core. I had known he was well regarded by many and that his unostentatious patrician generosity extended widely across the county, but even I was not prepared for his funeral. It took place in the Norman church just off the estate, where his grandfather had established a family crypt in the church. Philip Ireton, still trying to manage crutches on which he was now totally dependent, was not strong enough to attend. This upset him greatly. Two great men, from very different classes of society, had each respected the other deeply. I took two senior pupils with me in his place. All those who came that day were drawn together out of deep personal respect for a man who never wanted to be taken too seriously. In fact the organist played the Eton Boating Song as the coffin was lowered into the crypt.

I had lost a real friend, and one of the few men able to help me take the long view of what the school needed. A man who, in a bumbling but essentially shrewd manner, got things into the right proportions. Without him the governors were to be ever less effective. They would, I feared, play everything by the rules.

*          *          *

That summer in Shrah Peter was old enough to fetch milk from Seamus' farm by himself each evening, and several times David went with him across a couple of the fields. We cut down the briars that grew up so quickly in the soft Irish climate, and made bonfires that crackled and spat and added a further rich glow to our tanned cheeks. Oliver Flanagan was now five years older. He had filled out a bit on the lanky youngster who had been such a tower of strength to me in the building of the porch, but he had lost much of his sparkle. On leaving school he had spent a couple of years around his father's farm doing odd jobs and then gone on to an agricultural college to study pig farming. I asked him what it was like. "Pretty boring. I'm not sure I'm interested in pigs any more."

"So what will you do?" I asked.

He shrugged. "Don't know really. I'll just see what turns up." I was sad. He was in danger of wasting himself, another human being made to feel a failure by a system that didn't match his potential.

Watching my own sons growing up, I found myself looking at other young people more from the perspective of a father, than as a teacher. I'd always known that parents were important but I was beginning to appreciate that unless children come from homes where their relatives give them the time and space to grow up within a loving and stimulating environment, then children would find school of only marginal benefit. Home and school have to be a partnership and I, a person who made my living by being a head master, was in no doubt as to which was the more important - the ultimate challenge was to be a good father.

One family, some miles down the road from Shrah, epitomised this for me. Brian Tuohy and his family were traders, not farmers. Brian had inherited from his father a general purpose store at Coose, some 15 miles further down Lough Derg. Being a good 20 miles from any other significant hardware supplier, both father and son had built up the store to sell everything from sacks of seed corn, to timber, bricks and drainage pipes; from ladies underwear to greeting cards and even coffins. As the business had grown, so more and more sheds and barns had extended the old farmyard into a veritable rabbit warren of rambling storehouses. All this Brian managed within his own head; very little was ever written down. He trained his sons well. Each of them was a walking stock list able at any moment to identify the exact part of a shelf in any of the dozen or so buildings in which the particular item could be found. "Is it a left-handed, or a right-handed bracket on that water pressure pump you bought from me last year, John?" he would enquire as I tried to describe the job I was doing.

I would look confused and blank. "Take both shanks," he would say quickly, "you can always bring back the one you don't need. Have you a yoke (an Irish term for a tool with no precise meaning) for fixing this? OK, borrow mine. Brendan!" He called his younger son over. "Go back to the end of the loft over the timber store and root out that yoke for fixing high pressure output valves. You know the one I mean - the one Mick left off a while back." It was like this all day, and every day. A man exercising his various forms of multiple intelligences. A man who intuitively appreciated the simplest biological fact about the brain - "Use it, or lose it!"

Brian's memory was encyclopaedic. So too was his imagination. Without seeing any formal plan for the numerous jobs being undertaken at any one of several hundred locations, over almost as many square miles, he could anticipate any demand. Between times he was intensely curious about things "beyond" - that is, across the Irish Sea. Late of an afternoon, with a steady stream of customers being supplied by a son or daughter or a long-standing employee, he would question me about politics, about international trade and - at least when the priest was sitting in the back parlour - about things ecclesiastical. His children were as inquisitive and had almost the same hunger for information. Often they could be seen doing their homework at a corner of the shop counter.

Only once did I ever see him flustered. It was early on a Saturday morning and Brian was in his glass-fronted office at the back of the store, almost hidden by rolls of barbed wire, incongruously juxtapositioned between stacks of wallpaper and women's dresses. He was apparently making endless phone calls - turning the hand-operated generator each time to call back to the operator. He waved to me, with a worried look on his face. "What's the matter?" I enquired, not imagining that any problem could possibly be beyond him.

"I have a terrible problem. I've got two funerals booked for 12 o'clock and only the one hearse. Both corpses are properly in their boxes but I can't get them both to the church on time." He was undoubtedly perplexed. The phone rang. "You mean you can get over here with your hearse shortly after 11 o'clock? You're a real friend! You've saved my reputation. I'll do the same for you one day!" He beamed. "There's still just time to get that load of materials ready for the German down Rosmore Pier then I'd better be changing into my black." He and his family were contented folk, living a life where virtually every change was within the capability of their flexible thinking. I could not help pondering the differences between his children's attitude and capacity, and the dejectedness that had latterly crept over Oliver Flanagan.

Several days later, back in Stevenage and the term started, I was browsing through my bookshelves waiting for a meeting to begin. I pulled my dog-eared copy of Samuel Smiles off the shelf and, the meeting being delayed a further ten minutes, started to reread one of the opening chapters. Smiles wrote: "Schools, academies and colleges give but the merest beginnings of culture in comparison with life itself. Far more influential is the life-education daily given in our homes, in the streets, behind counters, in workshops, at the loom and the plough, in counting-houses and manufactories, and in the busy haunts of men. This is that finishing instruction as members of society, which Schiller designated 'the education of the human race,' consisting in action, conduct, self-culture, self-control - all that tends to discipline a man truly, and fit him for the proper performance of the duties and business of life - a kind of education not to be learnt from books, or acquired by any amount of mere literary training."

How well that described the vitality of the Tuohy establishment; how true it was of Oliver when he and I were busy building, but how far away it was from the simulated life experience which teachers tried to give their pupils in the classrooms of Stevenage. And true, I thought, of the kind of lives lived outside of school by many of those youngsters. It worried me greatly. Stevenage, with it's well-planned estates, cycle tracks and portion-controlled gardens - not to mention portion-controlled food in its cafeterias - was an essentially lifeless place, and I felt sorry for youngsters who had never experienced the thrill of having to take responsibility for an ordinary job, well-done.

I remembered my attempt to get pupils involved in maintaining the fabric of the school. That would have been an excellent antidote to what many youngsters saw as an over-academic and largely irrelevant curriculum - it had been thrown out by men (and at that stage there was only one woman on the governing body) who were largely incapable of imaginative educational thought. I thought of the limited understandings of the employers with their expectations of highly specific but limited skills, and then I though again of that dreadful form devised by government through which we all had to crawl before we qualified to become involved in the TVEI programme. Whoever had devised that was obviously convinced that his (or her) job had been to limit radical change and to perpetuate the status quo.

I became evermore frustrated. I winced as I thought again about the dilatoriness of the country council in letting some schools fade away through falling pupil numbers, rather than anticipating the decline with any bold constructive solution. I felt furious at the way youngsters were being let down, both by "the system" but more especially by parents who, in far too many cases, just did not realise how significant they could be in their children's lives.

*        *        *

I, like many other head teachers across the country, often found it appropriate to start the first assembly of the school year by arranging for a senior pupil to read the *Parable of the Talents* in St Matthew, Chapter 25. A certain rich man, so the biblical story goes, was going off into a far land. He called for his three servants. To one he gave three pieces of gold and asked him to look after these while he was away. To the next he gave two pieces of gold, and to the third one piece. Years later he returned and asked his servants to return the gold bars - the talents. The first said that, as his master was a hard man, he knew that he would not have wished his servant to be idle, so he had used the money to make more money. In fact he had doubled it and was able to return six talents. The master was delighted. He was delighted, too, when the second man showed he had doubled his money and turned it into four talents. The third man was different. "I knew that you were a hard man, so I went out and hid your talent in the ground. See, here is what belongs to you." His master replied: "You wicked, lazy servant. You should at least have put my money on deposit with the bankers so that when I returned I would have received it back with interest." The master then took the one talent that the man had and gave it to the man who had made the most money. It is not only head teachers who have seen in that parable a justification for encouraging hard work and suggesting - in the title of a recent best seller in the United States - *God Wants You to be Rich*. On this one story so much of the Protestant work ethic of the western world has been built and justified, and so much of the natural world plundered.

As I thought through the issues that troubled me that summer, I thought that this ethic was now too simplistic for the complex world we have created around us. Some pupils the previous year had, I knew, worked very hard for examinations for which, in all honesty, they should not even have been entered. They were not successful - and were very disappointed. The jobs they had anticipated, perhaps unrealistically, just did not materialise. They saw themselves as failures. I could not teach a doctrine that implied that these people should be further penalised.

I reflected on our recent speech day. The parents' association had donated a new prize - a prize for the pupil who had been most useful to the school. A committee was established to nominate such a person and their task proved easy for one boy stood out above all others. He had never gained any academic prize in his life and barely persuaded the sixth form staff that he had sufficient ability to undertake the least demanding of the courses. But, whenever there was a difficulty, all and sundry would call for Tim. Tim would think his way through any practical problem, and he could always draw together a team of others to get things done. "Tim should have the prize," everybody said. Our formal priorities were, I thought, all screwed up; without that prize Tim would have left the school unnoticed, like so many others. Up until now he would have been ignored.

The next autumn I arranged for a different lesson to be read at the first assembly. The *Parable of the Labourers* in St Matthew Chapter 20 is nothing like as well known and it is unsettling to the Western mind. It goes like this. A certain farmer had a large vineyard in which all the grapes needed to be harvested. Early in the morning the farmer went into the market place and offered a penny to 20 men to strip the vines for the whole day. Unemployed people clamoured for the job, but most were turned away. By midday it was obvious that so good was the harvest, that 20 men alone could never complete the task by evening. So the farmer returned to the market place and offered a penny to another 20 men to work for the afternoon. Again men clamoured for the job and again most were disappointed. Late in the afternoon the farmer realised that even 40 men could not complete the task. So he opened the vineyard gates and offered all those remaining in the market place a penny if they too would go in and help finish the job. The job was eventually finished. But there was trouble. "It's not fair," said the men who had laboured all day long, "we've worked far longer but we're getting the same money as those who started after us." "I don't see your problem," the vineyard owner replied, "you have each got what you thought you were going to get and those who thought they were going to get nothing will not starve tonight. I have my vineyard harvested. It has cost me more than I had expected, but then again my harvest is bigger than I had anticipated. We should all be happy."

Within ten minutes of the reading two of my senior staff were knocking at my study door. "We must be careful. Unless we can claim that God is on the side of hard work, we won't be able to hold the curriculum together. We must believe that the harder you work, the more rewards you should get."

I was taken aback by the simplicity of that statement. "Surely you don't actually believe what you're saying, do you? I know you work very hard yourselves, but - be honest - you're getting a fraction of what men of your qualifications would get if you were working at British Aerospace. You are always reminding me of that. And remember the case of Tim last term? It was you who said it was right he should have the prize for being the most useful person in the school." But, of course, I knew they were right to be concerned and I knew that by choosing that parable I was challenging many people's reason for schooling - the gaining of economic advantage (through qualifications) by the successful.

Schools were getting bogged down with the multiplicity of trivial issues that prevented us from thinking about things that mattered. In an emerging age of technological wizardry, when it was likely that those with very particular, almost unique, skills could command enormous salaries, what was the balance that would have to be achieved between education as a benefit to the individual, and education as a good for the whole community? Was our ethic to be that of the Talents or of the Vineyard, or was there a middle ethic that we so far had not described? We, as teachers, were not asking that basic question: Education for what?

*       *       *

On holiday once again in Shrah I started to see a way forward. Two things had led me to that point. Firstly a booklet, *Shaping Tomorrow*, had just been published by a group of eminent scientists who were also practising Christians. It sought to tease out the ethical implications of new scientific understandings of the way we should live. It was boldly written: "We contend that, when we fearlessly follow the light and are true to our scientific and theological insights we embark on an intellectual endeavour that renders talk of threats to belief irrelevant. An adequate theology must explore chance and purpose, mechanisms and free will, ecstasy and suffering."

Several of us had spent several early evening sessions discussing these ideas. "My trouble is," said one of the others, "I've hardly thought about such matters since I left university more than 20 years ago. I've struggled to find time to keep up with my own special period in history, but frankly I know precious little about modern trends in science and even less about developments in philosophy and frankly I don't understand modern economic theory either. I just can't keep up with all these ideas. Keeping my school going from day to day is hard enough." There had been nods of agreement from the others. We had all felt like this, to varying degrees. We led our school assemblies regularly, using the well-tried and nicely anaesthetised words found in various anthologies of prayers and then, minutes later, had to deal with many of the sordid details of life in contemporary Britain - drugs, abuse, family break-up, physical violence, abortion, pornography. We had been too busy to work out the relationship between the two. Busy-ness all too easily became the excuse for not thinking. *Shaping Tomorrow* made us think and had concluded by saying, "So, because you are more than a number in a databank, or a statistic in official records, because you are a unique human being, made in the image of God, do what you can towards shaping the future. Don't just sit there lamenting the present situation - for God's sake, do something!"

The second immediate influence was a meeting with the head of an independent school who had visited the Open Terminal and listened to my descriptions of fragmented politics out in the state sector. "It seems to me," he had said, "you need to find a way of getting Hertfordshire on your side. If people understood these issues then they might well start making better connections. Reality might, as it were, become more real. Get everybody together and help them to realise that it's in their long-term interest to stop thinking in little, separate, pigeon-holes. Hertfordshire's not a big place - I doubt if any spot is more than three-quarters of an hour's drive from any other. You need a crusade..."getting Hertfordshire ready for the twenty-first century."

I threw more briars onto the bonfire, which crackled and blazed. "Mind you don't set the trees on fire," shouted Anne above the noise of the burning.

"We need some form of campaign. Get the whole county to pool its thinking and experience so as to build some strong examples of good practice. Get the people of Hertfordshire excited about it. Give them a recognisable picture of just what it is that they have to support. Get everyone talking together. Even get the rich commuters going into the City every morning to realise that they - because they live in Hertfordshire - have to be part of the solution. Let them realise that, if they don't join in, then frankly they become part of the *problem.*"

Anne listened patiently as I babbled on. "Sounds good," she commented, "but so ambitious. Who's going to do it all? You, and who else?"

"Well, of course, I couldn't do it on my own; but I could build up a team and I'm sure together we could find a way. It's the only thing we can do. Just to talk to the Alleyne's parents on their own gets me nowhere. They're not the cross-section of Hertfordshire society we need - it's something much bigger and more all embracing. The main problem is that personally I don't have the authority to do this. Somebody, some organisation, has to start all this off. Someone has to say 'go and produce a plan of how this might work'; then I could start putting the pieces together'."

"So does that mean going back to the authority?" asked Anne. "You know they've never given you the support you needed in the past, neither with TVEI nor with Open Terminal nor with Bullock. Why would they change their minds now?"

So I tried once again. On returning from Shrah I wrote to the Chief Education Officer suggesting that the county should attempt to mobilise all its resources - not just those of the local government, but those of private individuals and of the business community - to investigate just what it was that pupils would need of a twenty-first century curriculum and how this should form the basis of a country-wide crusade.

Officials listened to my suggestions to the extent that, nine months and many meetings later, I was granted a term's leave of absence to carry out a feasibility study into what was optimistically called "Hertfordshire 2000". My excitement in getting started was muted by the apathy of the local authority officers. "It's better if this is done on my own personal authority rather than passing it through to the committee," the chief had told me. "Officially they'll not know that this is going on. It will be time enough to tell them when you've completed your work and they know from you exactly what support they can expect to have from other people. That will be the critical bit. You finding the extra money. Just where you work from while you do this will be up to you, but obviously you can't use your school study. Your deputy will need that. The only expenses I can authorise are for travel within the county; anything other than that you'll have to fund yourself."

So - yes, I was excited, but very much on my own. Rather than setting out to plan a crusade with the full blessing of the establishment, I was - it seemed - being let out of the back gate of the castle, under cover of darkness, and being told not to return until I had slain the dragon and was carrying it back in triumph for all to see. I exchanged my study, where I had worked for 11 years, for a commodious office provided for me by the chief executive of a large insurance company. The atmosphere was altogether different to a school; there were no bells to shatter concentration every 40 minutes; the chief executive, with whom I was to work closely, made a relatively small number of important decisions each month and to prepare himself was surrounded by people who, while they worked hard, didn't look as stressed as the teachers back at Alleyne's. As I set to work on the feasibility study it became obvious that I had bitten off more than I could comfortably chew. At the very least I would need more than a single term to do this.

My opportunity came a week later. The Stevenage Chamber of Trade had invited David Young, the newly appointed chairman of the Manpower Services Commission, to address their monthly luncheon. At short notice I was invited to attend, and at even shorter notice asked to propose a vote of thanks for his speech (I think this was because there was so much competition between the industrialists of Stevenage to do this that I was the safest outsider with, apparently, no vested interest to push.).

David Young - of whom Mrs Thatcher said, "he brings me solutions while other people bring me problems" - made an up-beat speech which contained good points but was unclear about issues at the centre of my work. "Work smarter, not just harder," was his theme and I sensed that he did not understand what being smarter would entail for education.

I got up to respond. "That was a most stimulating speech. It reminds me of the two cows, quietly chewing the grass in the corner of a field, who see a bulk milk transporter go by. Painted on its side are two idyllically happy cows and the slogan 'New Homogenised, Pasteurised, Sanitised, Calcium-enriched Milk ... just right for your family's health'. One cow looks at the other and says, 'Makes you feel kind of inadequate, doesn't it?'"

The audience laughed. So did David Young and it won me the opportunity to extend my speech by three minutes to explain what I was doing. As I sat down, Young passed me his business card with a scribbled note. "If you believe what you said, come and see me in my office in London at ten o'clock next Friday."

So, within less than a fortnight of starting the study that, in terms of Hertfordshire, did not really exist, I was talking these ideas through with the man who was to become infamous for the speed at which he was able to cut through bureaucracy to get things done. "How long will it take you to get all these ideas together?" he asked after several penetrating questions. "Longer I would expect than the single term you've been allocated?"

I was not prepared for something so direct, yet I was anxious to get the programme itself started, not just the work on the feasibility study. "A couple of terms should be enough," I said. "Probably up to Christmas."

"OK. In that case, tell Hertfordshire I'll pay your salary for the second term, as I would like the MSC to be a partner. I'll provide you with travelling expenses to go anywhere in the world where you need to see a particular programme you think might be important for us. There's one condition: at the end of the study you and I will go and explain to Keith Joseph what you think needs to happen. If you accept, my people will contact Hertfordshire early next week to make the necessary arrangements."

I had stepped into dangerous political waters between central government and the local authority, but I was hopeful I could stay afloat in the turbulence. At this point the important thing was that I could plan the study over the course of a full eight months and hopefully make it really persuasive. Even this, I knew, was a short time to get everything worked out. I arranged to do my travelling - to the United States, to Scandinavia and to Scotland - in the early autumn and planned to write up the first parts of the study by September. Then, with that in hand, I would start on recruiting supporters within the county - by that time I would have something to show them. I would need a decision to get such a programme started made long before Christmas, or otherwise I would return to Alleyne's as head master the following January.

I visited America and found America's teachers reeling at a report called *Nation at Risk*, which had claimed that "if an unfriendly foreign power had attempted to impose on America the mediocre education performance that exists today, we might well have viewed it as an act of war." I met Dr Ernest Boyer of the Carnegie Foundation who spoke with clarity on the aims of secondary education and how it fits in with society as a whole. "Any report card on public education is a report card on the nation," he told me. "Schools can rise no higher than the expectations of the community which surround them. To blame schools for the rising tide of mediocrity (as the report had) is to confuse symptoms with disease". I appreciated that statement enormously. Schools did not, nor ever could, stand in isolation from the community. The two had to grow together and, if the schools needed reforming, then surely the community would have to change as well.

Boyer also gave me one excellent piece of advice. "John, when you write an important document, never publish it until you have first read it aloud to a group of critics. Get them to tell you what it sounds like. It's not so much what a report says, it's what it sounds like that matters. The two are not the same thing. Remember that."

Then I visited Pittsburgh, a city whose economy had been devastated by the collapse of the American steel industry. As fear and uncertainty had swept through the community, so too the schools had lost confidence in themselves. Yet when I arrived in the fall of 1984, a partnership between the corporate and public sectors was already beginning to transform the down-town area into a show-piece of what the future could be all about. Much of the rest of the city, however, remained in terminal decay, and those in the wealthier suburbs were protesting at the ever higher taxes needed to support an ever expanding but, as they saw it, less effective set of public services.

Amidst those services were the schools, and it was in the high schools that despair was at its greatest. In the periods of full and expanding employment that had characterised earlier generations, high school had been an easy social rite of passage before its students passed out of the school gates and straight into the steel mills across the street. Education had not demanded much of its students, and it certainly had never considered a future for its students which would be about personal creativity, enterprise and flexibility. They had come to accept the notion of the early twentieth century efficiency expert, Frederick Winslow Taylor, that free-thinking workers were not as efficient, or subsequently as productive, as workers disciplined to labour in a tightly defined system dominated by a clock. What was needed for success in the giant steel mills were workers who could conform to a scientifically prescribed form of work as mechanical as that of a machine.

This was the culture that the majority of teachers understood, but it was the antithesis of what was needed for Pittsburgh in the mid-1980s to leap into a new world far removed from the days of labour intensive steel production. Economic revival was dependent, so the leaders of corporate regeneration

argued, on rejuvenated high schools, in particular on the re-motivation of the
teaching force. Unless schools changed dramatically, they said, there would
never be sufficient young employees of a quality to sustain growth.

Richard Wallace had been appointed a year or so before as superintendent to
transform the Pittsburgh school system. I met him in the press club on the top
floor of one of Pittsburgh's newest skyscrapers. "I'm a member," he said by
way of explanation, "because this is where the power is. Pittsburgh has to start
believing in itself, yet it often wallows in self-doubt. Often that self-doubt is all
about schools. Even if they do well in many areas, it's only been their failures
that have made newspaper headlines. So, when I came here, I decided to get
myself an invitation to join this club. I come here two or three times a week. I
feed the members here with success stories. They have to face me at the bar in
the evening if they've over-dramatised our failures.  People have to learn to
believe in their schools, and I have to know how to work the media.

"There are six universities in Pittsburgh, many with powerful research
departments, but they have  virtually no contact with the schools. When I
arrived, the chancellors invited me to a dinner and asked what I wanted from
them. So I set them a challenge: find out all you can about how children learn,
and how teachers teach, and what I can use out of all that, I'll pay for.

"I knew what I was talking about. Across the most deprived part of the city,
the part which would drag Pittsburgh back down into the abyss from which it
was struggling to climb, were a dozen high schools which had to be
transformed in a very short time. It wasn't that we needed new buildings - they
were solid enough to last a thousand years - it was better teachers we needed.
There was no way we could lay off the 750 teachers and immediately employ
750 better ones from elsewhere; we had to get the existing teachers to be far,
far better - not just better, but different as well.

"So this is what we decided to do. We took one of the high schools - Schenley
- in one of the most run-down areas, and at the end of the summer term put
all the existing teachers onto special contracts, which meant they were
guaranteed full salary, and a small bonus, to become support teachers in other
parts of the city. Then we appointed a completely new set of teachers, the very
best we could find, to become the new permanent teachers at Schenley. We
then linked these new teachers with the researchers at the university and
effectively turned Schenley, over the course of just one summer vacation, into
an educational equivalent of a teaching hospital.

"When the students came back in early September they could hardly
recognise the run-down, dispirited school they had left at the end of June.
They soon noticed there were two teachers in every class; the new teacher, who
was in charge, and their old teacher, who was now obviously very much in
training. The students didn't quite understand what was going on, but their old

teachers did. This was their opportunity to learn new techniques quickly because, one or two terms later, it would be they who would each go to one of the other high schools and replace a teacher in that school for one or two terms while that teacher went to study, on the job, at Schenley. It's a rolling programme that has now been going for two years and will take at least another four years to complete. It's not perfect, and there have been problems, but it's moved the schools on far faster than we could ever have anticipated."

I'd had a fascinating three days watching the workings of a programme which, to the English, would sound positively draconian, but which actually worked. My next stop - on Dr Boyer's recommendation - was Princeton High School. Externally it reminded me of the red brick semi-collegiate architecture of the school in Surrey I had attended as a boy. Internally it was utterly different, as I found on a two-day visit which took me in, through and around just about every corner, closet and corridor of that school of some 1,800 students. I was alternatively amazed, enthralled and eventually made deeply jealous of what I was seeing. Jealous, because as a practising head running a school for students of exactly the age as these young people, I felt that our provision was desperately inadequate. It was not just the equipment that was obviously superior; it was the vitality, the inquisitiveness, the cheerful maturity of the students that was so very different to what was happening in England.

I saw large numbers of computers scattered through libraries, classrooms and corridors, most of which were in use. I saw students accessing the Reuter's Database in the main library, and others reading yesterday's *Times* from London alongside today's *Wall Street Journal*. I saw great, strapping, 18 year-old boys and girls coaching youngsters four years younger than themselves and from a variety of ethnic backgrounds. I sat in with one student while he and 17 others went through a twice-a-week counselling session with two well-qualified and experienced teachers, in how they could handle their own tutorial groups of eight 14 year-olds. These student counsellors-in-the-making were doing, with far more time at their disposal, what a good form teacher in England would have loved to have done, if they had had the time. I listened to the school orchestra practice some pieces which, to my admittedly untutored ear, sounded brilliant. "Yes, it was," said the principal later, "They're often ranked as one of the three or four most outstanding school orchestras on the East Coast."

I met Ron Horowitz, who ran the Learning in the Community programme. "It's a relatively easy programme to explain," he said. "We believe that, by the age of 16 or 17, young people should be required to organise much of their learning independent of the school or the teacher. So, in the final two years of high school, virtually every student has to have a community tutor, as well as an academic tutor. They have to demonstrate they can take their academic studies and develop these while working with a professional, well outside the school premises."

"How much time does that take?" I asked, expecting that this was a project that might last three or four weeks, or a term at the most.

"As much as two days a week for the last year of high school, and for some as many days as that in the last two years, not just in one year."

I was amazed by this level of co-operation between community and school, and asked for an example of what was involved. Ron turned to his computer and asked me to scroll through a long list and pick a name. I did. It was that of a 17 year-old girl, studying the sciences and hoping to go to an Ivy League college to study medicine. He said: "She's a trainee midwife, working in the birthing centre at the hospital with one of the professors. She does that for two days a week, helping mothers in labour. For the three days she's in school she carries a bleeper and if they're ever short-staffed in the delivery room she gets called out of school to assist. There are two rules that govern all this. They're very simple. Whatever school work she misses, she has to agree to make up in her own time. The other one is that any student behaving in a way that, in the environment in which they are working, might bring disrespect on the school, will be reprimanded in the presence of their peers."

I was amazed, and humbled. When you're in the business, you know what you're looking for and these young people were confident, in a non-aggressive fashion; they were alert, sensitive, inquisitive, enterprising and fun. Not just the bright few - these attitudes ran throughout the entire school. A school peopled, if you like, by youngsters whom one would be proud to call your own - people to whom you would willingly trust the future. I spent the evening of my second day with the head teacher, John Sekala. "How has all this happened?" I asked incredulously, "I don't see how you get a school to function like this." His story went back several years to a time when sectional interest dissipated any coherent educational policy in the town. Teachers had one set of objectives, parents another; academics at the university suggested other priorities yet could not agree amongst themselves what these might involve. Some types of employers wanted one set of skills, while others argued for something else. The town decided to write a mission statement for education - not just within the school, but across the entire community. It took two years. People argued their own position rigorously; sometimes debate became heated and acrimonious. But they got their statement which read:

> This community believes in Functional Literacy for all; that is, the ability to feel comfortable amidst all the change and confusion of a fast-moving, technological society. That comfort comes with knowing that you have learned-how-to-learn and feel confident

in your ability to face the future. This depends on developing to the full the ability to think, to communicate, to collaborate, and to make decisions.

"Everything done in this school," said the principal, "from the plan for a particular lesson, through to the school rules, is designed to develop these abilities in each child. Our teachers understand that, first and foremost, they're educators; they're seeking to build up the confidence of young people so that they can become free-standing. They teach these skills within and across particular subjects because the skills we're seeking to develop have universal application; the subjects are inter-dependent."

John Sekala drew attention to three critical factors.

"First of all, the process of building a mission statement is still with us - that first two-year period got us to think, talk and work together. It means no one in the town any longer expects the school to do everything; we - that is, the town - understood that the work in the school is complemented by what children experience in their lives outside of school. School and community pace each other." How I resonated with that statement.

"Secondly, the cross-disciplinary approach makes teachers far more managers of a learning process and counsellors to the students, and far less instructors within separate disciplines. The use of computers is important - one to every three students. Every essay ever written, every report ever produced, across all subjects, is done on a word processor. This approach was embedded in the process," Sekala explained. "We do this not to create fluent keyboard operators but to exploit the technology to support the learning process. Once an essay is written the teacher will comment on it, often at length. Not until the student feels the draft is the best she can produce does she ask for a mark, a mark that reflects not just the quality of the finished text, but the improvement made on her first effort. The staff don't set anything like as many essays and time is now spent developing verbal and audio skills. And, remember, these youngsters' academic results are outstanding.

"Thirdly, at the heart of our experience," continued Sekala, "is our staff development policy. Because our pupils work more independently we don't need to put them into classes so frequently. With a staff of 81 we never timetable more than 70 with about 15 per cent of our teachers on a retraining programme at any one time. Most work with a local employer, or professional group to develop new programmes. The community is our resource. We can't conceive how we could run such a school without continuous, locally devised, teacher-development. That's what gives our school its vitality. If pupils are to be continuous learners, it is essential that teachers are learners as well."

\*      \*      \*

I arrived home anticipating a further three months to tie this together before presenting the study. This was not to be, for there was a memo from the authority summoning a dozen head teachers to a two hour meeting in ten days time at which "John Abbott will present the outcome of his feasibility study". The memo noted that there would be a subsequent meeting with 20 subject advisors a few days later and that both meetings would take place in the chief's study.

A scribbled note suggested I should write up the study and provide everyone with a copy of my conclusions at least a week in advance of the meeting. I had four days and I swallowed hard trying not to feel outraged. Still, there were no procedural rules for building an inter-dependent curriculum or challenging existing structures. By listing my main ideas I set out a de facto agenda that I would have to live with for years, but not necessarily in the way I had anticipated. Forgive the officialese, but this is what I wrote:

> 1. Hertfordshire 2000 will stimulate a county-wide debate about the nature of education that will be needed for the twenty-first century. This debate must involve all sectors of the community, and must be seen from the start to deal with all aspects of young people's experiences, in school and out. In practice this debate will be broken down into small community groups, each one eventually contributing to a county-wide mission statement.

> 2. To facilitate the rapid implementation of totally new ways of doing things it will be shown how one relatively self-contained community in each of the seven parts of the county can be given "special development status" over a period of years to experiment with a totally new way of organising learning opportunities.

> 3. At the same time the authority will share this thinking with external bodies, such as the Department of Education, the examination boards, other government departments so as to ensure that each is kept closely in touch with the implications of these ideas as they begin to impact on their communities.

My fellow heads were unsure of what was expected of them by the authority. As they entered the chief's office they were reminded that this was not an official feasibility study. The chief needed to be reassured, he told the head teachers, that they would support me and have proof that other agencies would find the funds. It was a cautious meeting and I did not find it easy to be expansive. While many of the heads identified with the argument I was advancing, the thought of implementing any of it frightened them. "You can take one of three decisions," said the chief. "You can agree wholeheartedly and suggest we go ahead on the basis of what information John has already given us. Or you can reject it as just not being possible, or at least not possible at this stage. Or you can ask John for more specific recommendations, and in particular you can ask him to do more work on where the money is going to come from." It was not very subtle. The third decision, the one that plays for time and puts the onus on someone else was the one they took. The meeting, with the subject advisors, only had a minority who wanted to proceed straight away. Result: stasis.

If the authority understood the significance of these ideas, how dare they leave the implications of all this dependent on whether I could or could not raise the money? "They have this all wrong in their minds," I told Anne. "The reason they're saying there isn't any money is that they won't put this high enough on their list of priorities and fight for it with the Council. They want me to do this on my own, leaving them to carry on with their own set of priorities totally separately."

"So what will you do?"

"Just keep on trying, I suppose. I've no other option. I'm the one who believes in this. The chief says we'll have a further meeting shortly and by then I'm supposed to wave some kind of magic wand which makes it safe for people to proceed."

"You mean, you've got to find the money yourself?"

"That's what they think they mean. I can't raise the money if I'm not sure they're pledged - emotionally, logically, practically - to share the responsibility. By getting me to present to strictly academic audiences, they must have known the odds would be weighed against me. What I need is the chance to whip up outside enthusiasm among people who are not always thinking about what this will do to their precious little schools. One day, schools may even be irrelevant. But the needs of children need to become far more relevant."

"Did you say that to them?" asked Anne.

"No."

"Why not?"

I was silent for a moment. "It's difficult to explain, but I think if I'd allowed myself to be emotional they would have closed up even quicker. As individuals they're fine - but as a group, well, they kind of prevent anybody from getting into the personal realm of the emotional. As administrators they can only deal with passion by ignoring it. The emotional, the intuitive, the passionate are not allowed to figure. Maybe that's why schools often feel sterile and aimless."

\*　　　　\*　　　　\*

Next on my schedule was a visit to Sweden and the Work Orientation Programme in Örnsköldsvick which is north of Stockholm and close to the Arctic Circle. I was told it was a high-tech city - mainly high-grade steel and paper - where many of the young people had had little understanding of what their parents did at work, and consequently little clear idea of what careers they might eventually follow. Some years before, a decision had been taken that, at the age of seven, every child should spend a day shadowing his or her father at their place of work, and a day shadowing their mother at her place of work - one on one. They also spent a day following each of their best friend's parents, again one on one. So successful had they been that they increased the frequency of such shadowing to five days a year by the age of ten, ten days a year at the age of 13, and 15 days a year at the age of 16. "By the time a student reaches the age of 18 and leaves school, he or she will have had some 24 weeks of such a programme, and possibly have observed 60 or 70 different jobs," my guide said.

"That must be very good for the students," I said.

"Naturally. But think what it has done for the adult community. On average we clean our shoes 12 times more a year than we did before as we tend to get shadowed about once a month. Secondly, we get used to being asked apparently naïve questions about our work. Believe me, children have many useful insights. What is more important is that there is hardly an adult in the town who does not realise the education of young people is too important to be left to teachers to handle by themselves - every adult has to be involved and this does the community much good."

I was impressed. Here was an easily developed programme that helped to create a far better sense of community.

*       *       *

Three meetings had been set up for my return to England: the first with David Young who had left the MSC and had moved still closer to the seat of power by taking over the Enterprise Unit at the Cabinet Office in Downing Street; the second with Sir Keith Joseph at the Department of Education; and the third with the chief in Hertfordshire.

Young's attention had shifted, and I sensed he was only interested in me if my interest had shifted too. It hadn't. Keith Joseph was relaxed, appeared to have plenty of time to listen and he was intrigued by Princeton. "That's the kind of thing the Americans are so good at. They get hold of an issue, get everyone involved, build up a head of steam ... and just get on and do it."

"That's what I think we should do," I said and set out the proposal for seven pilot schools across Hertfordshire, "so that we can build a model for a new way of doing things ... something far more persuasive than a good lecture, or a carefully worded book."

"Will the authority back you?" Sir Keith asked directly.

"I'm not sure. They say their problem is shortage of money. I think it's lack of resolution," I said, picking my words carefully and hoping my comment would not be repeated outside his office.

"Well, you can tell Hertfordshire that I would be interested in how such a programme developed, as this is the kind of initiative I have provided funds for in the latest rounds of grants to the authorities. While I can't actually require your authority to spend the money on what you're doing, it would seem a great shame if they didn't use it to get your programme started. This is what I had in mind."

I met the chief and senior assistant the Friday before Christmas. I had already learnt that none of the heads or advisors had been invited and for several minutes the officers talked about the carols they had just sung at a local Christmas service. I got the message quickly that this was to be a polite termination meeting, and over lunch I was asked if I had had a good time in Sweden. I pushed the conversation around to Keith Joseph and mentioned how he'd said the grant he suggested was intended for such a programme as this. "That's not possible. We've already decided where to put that money," said the senior advisor. "You've got to find separate money. This is not one of our priorities, but that you already know."

I tried once more. "I don't understand this distinction between we and you. I thought I was setting all this up because it would benefit the children of Hertfordshire. I thought I was acting on everybody's behalf. I thought I was part of the "we" and, if you like, you were part of what I was doing." I was aware of a vein throbbing in the back of my head. They looked embarrassed, the mince pies and fresh cream sat half-eaten on their plates. "The fact is, John, this is not a very appropriate time to raise this issue with members of the council. They're worried about the budget, and worried about the apparent intentions of government to strip them of some of their roles."

There was the silence of embarrassment and I was not going to break it. Eventually the chief, looking more drawn than usual, said "We think you ought to go back to Alleyne's at the beginning of next term, and keep the idea on the back burner. We'll give the school the equivalent of an extra half teacher for the rest of the year as some recompense for the extra work you'll have to do - use such a person as and how you will."

I wondered why it was I had ever tried to get them started on the feasibility study but I expelled my doubts because I had already seen too many examples of powerful innovations in other countries that were giving children a better chance to live useful lives. By the time I reached the door out of the office I had reminded myself that I had never set all this up for the authority in the first place. I had set it up for the children - mine and Anne's - and thousands of others who deserved better than this from the adults who were supposed to be their guardians. This wasn't to be the end. After the TVEI and Open Terminal fiascos I was not going to be deterred. The more difficult this became, the more convinced I was that I hold to my convictions and find new ways of proceeding. I was finally forgetting those lessons of deference I had learned too well in my youth.

# 8
## Education 2000

Eighteen months earlier an unusual assembly of some 60 people had come together for a week at Westfield College, London to discuss changes needed over the next 20 years if young people were to be properly prepared for the challenges of the twenty-first century. It was a diverse group: academics mingled with industrialists; city bankers with entrepreneurs; media-folk with housewives and students. They divided themselves into groups and discussed weighty topics such as *Society in AD 2000, Lifelong Education*, and the *Challenge of Change.* Each group produced a statement, and by the week's end had the text assembled for a book entitled *A Consultative Document on Hypotheses for Education in AD 2000.* It is a potpourri of a book, where the text is as verbose as the title but what it lacked in coherence it more than made up for in urgency. It eschewed taking up any party political stance, for the delegates were divided by political and personal perspectives. What emerged was a powerfully expressed non-political consensus of disquiet with every aspect of the status quo, as well as a genuflexion towards the altar of new technology. It attempted to set out a broad, national agenda for action and reform. The book did its job well because it annoyed many sections of the educational establishment. Its appeal was, however, strictly limited and, though prophetic, would not capture anyone's emotional heart. You read it, appreciated its message but, not knowing what to do about it, you put it down, and got on with what you were doing beforehand. No one knew where to start.

I heard about this conference several months after it met and was told it had been set up by a businessman and an academic, the one a reactionary posing as a radical, and the other a radical posing as a reactionary. I first met Bryan Thwaites, the academic and a mathematician by profession, who had been stung by criticism of the book and was unsure of how to proceed. "What we need is someone like you to convene four study groups to collect further information," he said. "We need to provide a greater in-depth coverage of these ideas. Then we'll need further conferences."

He was obviously disappointed in my lack of enthusiasm; the writing of more reports, or the organisation of more conferences, was not for me and I tried instead to interest him in my idea to develop such concepts in a real community, over a lengthy period of time, probably within Hertfordshire. He was partially interested. "That sounds highly risky to me. Too many intangibles to deal with. Practical concerns could quickly distort the intellectual issues that have to be addressed," the academic in him worried. "Come to think of it, you ought to talk to my co-chairman, Christopher Wysock Wright."

*          *          *

It was with difficulty that I went back to headmastering in January 1985. That people genuinely seemed glad to see me back made me feel even worse, but I felt my ideas were about to be squeezed back into the narrow parameters I had been so relieved to escape nine months earlier. A set of parameters that I knew, with ever greater confidence, were at least partially responsible for creating the problems we were trying to solve. The proliferation of diktats from beyond the school had grown unbelievably and so too had the complexity of the curriculum. At long last people were coming to understand what the fall in pupil numbers would mean. My fellow head teachers were becoming ever more rattled and confused.

I had been back at Alleyne's for ten days when Sidney Melman, chairman of the Letchworth Garden City Corporation, asked to visit me at school, accompanied by his chief executive. Letchworth was the world's first garden city, created at the turn of the century by a Quaker architect, Ebenezer Howard. Very much a planned community, Letchworth had grown up in the years before World War I around broad, tree-lined avenues, and substantial Tudor-style houses, each in good-sized gardens. Industrial, domestic and commercial properties were nicely intermingled. It was a town of sturdy, owner-occupiers, with a fierce pride in their individuality. It was also inclined to be complacent and self-satisfied, but the harsh epithet of outsiders that "it's full of open-sandaled do-gooders talking about their souls and their poetry", was unfair.

The corporation had been invested with the right to the ground rents on the majority of the properties, which it had then to use to improve the general quality of life of the entire town. As a non-statutory public body the Letchworth Corporation was unique in Britain. With a reputation for paternalism its directors could largely set policy for themselves, untroubled by the concerns of national and local politics. It lived with these, of course, but was separate from them. It was in no way responsible for the schools, the roads, or the drains, yet, in a good year, it could accumulate a million pounds or more of profits on its commercial dealings, and then offer grants wherever it thought these would benefit the town. Recently they had built a splendidly equipped sports centre and given it to the town. They could, I knew, make grants to the schools, and the Hertfordshire authority would find it hard to refuse them.

"Let's get straight to the point," said Sidney Melman, a dapper 60 year-old of impeccable charm who, as a younger man, had been a Socialist before making a career in banking. He had been the corporation's chairman for the past two years. "We've heard a lot of people talking about your ideas. Bringing schools and community together for the best interest of children excites us greatly. Your talk of investment in technology also appeals to us. Could we perhaps persuade you to consider making Letchworth the first of the test communities that you're talking about? Time and again people say that they're afraid to change because they don't know how to learn new skills. That's just what you're talking about, isn't it? How to learn. Changing what happens in schools must be the key to later economic prosperity and social creativity".

I nodded vigorously, thinking of the conversation in Pittsburgh three months earlier. Here was a deal, just five miles from Stevenage, which I could never have anticipated. I listened to offers of grants to the schools (four secondary and two boarding) to get them started with technology and a suite of offices from which to administer the programme for however long might be necessary. "The chief executive and I have thought a little further," Sidney continued, "Dealing with the authority is not easy. We know this only too well and we could offer help in ways that might encourage them to assist in your efforts. Our help would stretch over many years. You need time to think this over, but before we go we'd like to arrange a meeting with a London businessman called Christopher Wysock Wright." I remembered he was co-chairman of the Westfield conference with Bryan Thwaites. Things were falling into place.

After that discussion in the school's study, Anne and I had driven around Letchworth several times. We had walked through the shopping centre and visited the new sports complex, and attended one of the churches. The previous evening I had spent several hours with one of the head teachers and, with as much confidence as I could share, had taken him into my emerging thoughts. A wise man, he cautioned that at the earliest possible stage I should share such confidences with the other head teachers and, for good measure, invite the heads of the two independent schools to join us as well. "We've never, ever, thought of doing anything like this before. As soon as you sniff the possibility of this becoming a reality let's all talk together."

Five days after meeting Sidney Melman I met Christopher Wysock-Wright in his office in Grosvenor Place, directly facing the back gardens of Buckingham Palace. A secretary ushered me into a heavily panelled room on the first floor where I looked out of the big bay window at the trees in the Palace garden; I noted a heavy decanter of whisky on the oak refectory table and I smelt the aroma of good cigars. Armchairs were deep and very comfortable. This was a room, I sensed, where business deals were done.

"Hi, I'm Chris, Bryan's told me about you. So has Sidney Melman. Sit down.

Heather," he yelled through the door, "Divert the phones for the next half hour will you, I don't want to be disturbed. And bring a couple of glasses of the Chardonnay."

A man of my own age, with bright staring eyes and a ruddy complexion, he sank into the chair opposite and adjusted his socks. "Education 2000 is a great idea," he said, "But I rather gather from Bryan that you wouldn't be too interested in convening more talk shops. Can't say I blame you. Damned good report that came out of that conference, but some of the folk just talked for the sake of talking. Bryan and I have known each other well for years. He's got more faith in the education system reforming itself from within than ever I have. It seems to me it needs a good shake-up. Sidney tells me you're a bit of a shaker yourself. Here, have one of these glasses and tell me more about where you're coming from."

This was a man who could easily intimidate, but who would, I sensed, respect the person who spoke what he thought. So I said what I thought. He made notes and occasionally interrupted with questions that were, in turn, flippant and profound. He was a successful head-hunter at one of London's largest executive search organisations and knew how to sum people up quickly. That's what he was doing with me. Summing me up. I was a stranger to his world, so all I could do was tell him about things as I saw them.

He apparently liked it enough, especially the story about Hector Laing and "Why don't you lot tell my lot what it's all about." He let rip his fury at tedious academics on the one side, lily-livered businessmen on the other, and none of them was up to the challenges they should be exploiting. All was not well in the state of England, expounded the head-hunter, and at its heart was an out-of-date education system. We understood each other.

The surroundings were strikingly traditional, but here was a man fired by radical discontent. I had met my partner. He would not, however, be an easy compatriot, for he said the first thing that came into his head, and had the disconcerting habit of changing the agenda every few minutes. Better out on the hustings, I thought, than negotiating around a table; he was, nevertheless, extraordinarily well-connected. Making connections was his business.

The vision had first to be shared, but in sharing it I had to be careful not to upset the authority. Despite all their pleas to the contrary, they did not want their head teachers to become too innovative; that was obviously threatening. They were nervous enough about me in particular, and what they sensed was the increasingly hostile attitude of central government in general, to be ready for knee-jerk reactions to what could be seen as a town starting to take its destiny into its own hands. Whatever the strength of Sidney and his team and his contacts, I could not afford any unnecessary antagonism. I knew that in the end politics would play the determining factor for success or failure.

Of first importance was opening up the discussion with the head teachers. If Education 2000 were not a vision they wished to make their own, then all this would be still-born. At a time of increasing teacher disaffection, and with talk of industrial action over salaries, a careful approach to the unions would also be necessary if an initiative that was to be supported by industry and commerce were not to be seen as some form of under-cover action by government. I needed friends within the authority to help shape the strategy for change, and I needed friends within central government as well to help protect us. Had I known it, I would also need friends within Education 2000 for I should not have assumed that because Christopher was enthusiastic, other future trustees would follow suit. Many of these trustees were educationalists, members of the establishment first and foremost, and radicals only if it fitted within their own expectations.

While I was trying to develop a coalition for change, I had a school to run and a nervous staff to lead.

*     *     *

I was certainly nervous before meeting with the Letchworth head teachers. They'd already read the feasibility study written three months earlier and quickly saw the authority's unwillingness to do anything with such ideas as being to Letchworth's ultimate advantage. Now, with the support of the corporation and the recruitment of me to their team, they could have all this to themselves.

"I feel good," said Peter Jackson of Highfield, the longest serving of the heads, a man who always wore a rose in his buttonhole. "It was for this view of education - this view of the sort of people teachers need to be - that I first came into teaching 35 years ago. Let's go for it. But tell me - a delicate question - how real is the support this man Wysock Wright can deliver? If we're going to put our careers on the line, can we trust him? Will he, and Education 2000, stick with us?"

This was a moment of truth and I replied, "Bryan Thwaites most of you know of through his work in setting up the Schools' Maths Project. I've met him once. He's articulate, knowledgeable, and used to getting his own way. Wysock Wright I've heard about from several sources, and I've now met with him twice. He's a most determined individual and has a lot of contacts. I suspect he's pretty impetuous too."

"What kind of contacts?" inquired Colin Reid, head of the independent St Christopher School, and a man more used than most to sizing up whether people had the financial resources they claimed.

"Commercial, manufacturing and banking," I replied. "He makes it his business to recommend suitable candidates as chief executives to main boards of companies. That kind of thing. Those people he doesn't know he phones straight through to and invites them to lunch. They usually come."

\*          \*          \*

I was anxious to know how best to reopen this with the local education authority. If the moment had not been right only six weeks before when I was told to go back to being a head master, how could I now present this as a possible successful modification of the earlier plan? I decided to approach Ian Leydon, the chief advisor, who had been head of a school not unlike mine and who was on record as encouraging heads to be more imaginative. He knew how impatient I had become and how disappointed I had been with the decision to put the project on the back burner. He also knew the chief's strengths and weaknesses, and more than anyone else understood the reality of educational politics at the council chamber level.

I explained what was beginning to come together and, good ex-head teacher that he was, he questioned me about the attitude of the Letchworth heads. I told him that they wanted to be enthusiastic but were nervous about the possible reactions of the authority, and needed to know more about the financial resources of the Education 2000 Trust.

"This is certainly an exciting idea but it's radical," he told me. "All authorities are becoming unsure of their relationships with central government, and they are pretty well convinced that government is determined to limit their powers. Parliament's already reduced the authority's financial autonomy and what you're proposing could be seen as a further attack from below - an attempt to create a strong feeling of ownership within a single town would threaten their power-base. The chief will have to show the members of the council that Education 2000 is not some form of under-cover operation mounted by influential sponsors acting with government to squeeze the authority from both sides. After all, John, you do talk directly to the minister, and the Education 2000 trustees look suspiciously like government supporters."

That upset me. "No, calm down," Ian urged. "You don't have to justify yourself to me. I know what you're about, but just think, for a moment, of possible alternative interpretations. If you want to win this one, we're all going to have to think carefully about every move. I'll talk to the chief when the moment's right."

Donald Fisher positively beamed when, two days later, I was shown into his office. "I owe you a good dinner. Ian's told me of the possibility of linking together Letchworth Corporation and Education 2000. It sounds very promising, but you'll have quite a job holding the two in hand, and preventing them from running in separate directions."

"Yes, I know. But there'll have to be at least one other major partner and that has to be the authority. We would have to ensure that Education 2000 didn't become another bolt-on initiative foisted onto the schools from outside. This has to be about challenging the very way schools are organised, so that we can create better opportunities for all young people to learn how to learn".

Suddenly the atmosphere became less congenial. "You must be careful with language like that. It sounds too revolutionary. Each of us has to work with what we've already got. After all, many of us personally owe our own success to the systems you seem to be criticising."

I moved more carefully. "You remember what I told the officers about the school in Princeton, New Jersey, the one with all those computers?" He nodded. It had been a good story and not easily forgotten. "Well, we're already beginning to feel the implications of that in Alleyne's. Children are starting to discuss first drafts of their essays with teachers, before handing in their finished texts. Teachers just don't know how to deal with that - which draft do they mark? It's almost as if the answer to the Bullock Report is now emerging out of the new technologies. There's another example," I said, probably following up slightly too quickly. "The business of children understanding the world of work better. That story from Sweden of children as young as seven shadowing their parents at work, and gradually increasing such work orientation until each child does as much as three weeks of this each year, that is really impressive."

"Well, that's something we're starting to do already," said the chief's assistant. "Don't underestimate the influence of the authority's career service. By providing five days for every child at the age of 15, at least we're doing something. And we're doing this all centrally so we're achieving considerable economies of scale."

"I'm not sure that, by achieving economies of scale, we're not also in danger of losing touch with the enormous amount of local goodwill towards becoming involved with young people. The public want to be involved not because they're offered the chance of becoming small cogs in a big, efficient authority structure, but because they want to be part of a local solution to a problem they have themselves defined," I said. "It's all to do with an emerging desire to rebuild local community - a sort of local feel-good factor."

I had blundered again and gone too fast. Being convinced that most, if not all, communities have within themselves enormous powers of creativity and leadership, I was not being sensitive enough to the bureaucrats' conviction that, unless they told people what to do, nothing would happen. Nor was I being sensitive enough to the chief's own responsibility. He was, after all, being paid far more than I was to make the present system work. What I was setting out challenged much of the structure that he worked through day after day and he looked less happy than he had at the start of the meeting.

He eventually agreed however to a tripartite meeting between the Letchworth Corporation, the Education 2000 trustees and the local authority. There were nine of us. Sidney Melman came with his chief executive and the corporation's secretary. The chief was accompanied by Iris Tarry, chairman of the committee to whom he was most deferential, and by his assistant (to whom he was to delegate day-to-day responsibilities for the initiative). Bryan Thwaites and Christopher Wysock Wright represented Education 2000.

The Letchworth people were totally open, almost unsophisticated. "This will be very good for the town," they said. "These are our children, and we're very concerned that what happens to them, both in schools and in the community, should be the most stimulating and creative we can find. So Education 2000 seems to us to be a very good idea. We'll be happy to support this."

"Well, thank you, chairman," responded the chief. "On behalf of the authority I must say you are making a most generous offer to our schools here in your town. I think Mrs Tarry would like to explain what the education committee is already doing to prepare for the twenty-first century."

Listening to Iris Tarry it would have been easy to think that all was well with the curriculum of the schools and the intellectual leadership of the authority. All, that is, with the exception of money. Of that there was just not enough. If Education 2000 could provide the authority with more money, then the trust would be very welcome. Sidney Melman had not anticipated quite such a blunt approach. He had been most courteous in his welcome, and had refrained from making his own personal criticism of the school system, which he frequently articulated, using Charles Handy's words as quoted in the feasibility study: a system designed at other times, for other purposes.

He looked a question at Chris and Bryan. Both were caught off their guard. Not for the first time I had to leap in and, unprepared, try to save the situation. "The trustees are very interested in working with an authority in a single easily identifiable community. One which is committed to bringing some coherence to what often feels like a flood of disconnected initiatives and programmes designed largely from outside. Many of these programmes are good in themselves, but they're not properly understood. Their potential is often dissipated through lack of support from teachers who have no time to learn how to implement them." I then picked my words very carefully. "This is particularly the case with computers and new technology and with relationships across the community, especially those with the primary schools. I think the trustees of Education 2000 see any money they might contribute as being used to show how things could be done in a different way -

how new techniques could be used to transform the system - rather than just as a subsidy to the present arrangements."

Again there was a pause - it was as if people were again caught off guard by my talk of transformation and doing things in a different way. I was asking for action, and that surprised them. Bryan Thwaites meantime had had time to consider his argument. He built carefully on what I had said, and drew on his experience in setting up the schools' Maths Project years before. He cleared his throat several times, and spoke at some length until Chris Wysock Wright got impatient, and interrupted. "All I want to say is that the industrialists I work with are very concerned about what they see as the products of the school system. Why is it that, after years and years of formal schooling, so many youngsters leave school feeling that the world owes them a living? They're too often inflexible, incapable of making decisions themselves, and don't know how to collaborate. Many of them can't put up a decent argument."

His passion was as palpable as that of Sidney Melman. There was no way that the authority could ignore them. Yet this, very obviously, was not the place to work out the details; there were far too many unstated assumptions around the room, and too many things people felt were best unsaid.

"I suggest, with your approval, chairman," said the chief, helpfully trying to find a way through, "that - if you agree, Iris - we record our formal willingness to go ahead with this project as broadly agreed, and leave it to the two officers, my assistant and John Abbott, to sort out the details. Then they could report back to us individually. Obviously we want to find a basis to proceed, and we'll need a paper by early May - that is in about three weeks time - to go to the education committee."

Sidney accepted the proposal and the meeting closed.

"What the hell was going on there?" exclaimed Chris utterly exasperated, and not being used to the politicians' wish never to commit themselves to anything. "Doesn't this leave you in a pretty invidious position? Aren't they now treating you as an outsider?"

*          *          *

"So, you'll go for it, won't you, darling?" Anne asked me, an hour or so later. "I honestly think you should."

My career had already dragged my family through the false starts of Bullock, then Open Terminal, then TVEI. I looked from our three happy, gloriously spontaneous young sons, to my young wife's trusting eyes, "Yes, we'll go for it. Now - let's take the kites and fly them on Deacon's Hill. It's going to be a breezy afternoon and I go back to school tomorrow. Maybe it's my last term."

"What does Daddy mean, Mummy?" asked a confused seven year-old Peter.

"What does he mean...his last term?"

"I'll tell you later. It's going to be exciting." The family had cast the die.

*          *          *

The ground had been laid out. But this was to be a struggle, not a collaborative activity. We would be doing things in spite of the authority, not with it. The authority was too unsure of its position to know how to work whole-heartedly with any partner. It was to be terrain that we were to fight over for a long time. But to fight, not over issues of importance such as what was good for children, but over which part of the turf belonged to whom. I was still young and did not fully understand the sub-agendas. I would be hurt.

Late one afternoon a phone call came through from County Hall. It was the chief's assistant. "The committee has met," he said. "The good news is that we have welcomed the project, which may go ahead over the next five years on condition that there are absolutely no extra costs of any kind to the authority. All extra expenditure is to be borne directly by the trust; we are prepared to act as your bankers, but you will be charged a nominal five per cent service charge upon each transaction. The bad news is that the authority will not agree to second you at their expense for the two years to set this up. You will have to resign formally from the authority's employment as of the end of this term, and become fully the responsibility of Education 2000. If you want to return to the authority later you may do so at the end of the second or fifth year, but we will guarantee you a salary only equivalent to that of a newly qualified teacher straight from university, not of a head teacher. There is one other thing," he added "the committee has also written in that while it understands that you will act initially as both the director of the trust and that of the project, this arrangement must last only for a year. After that you, personally, must sever all your relationship with the Hertfordshire project and concentrate exclusively on the trust. Sorry the news is not better."

"We'll take the trust's money on our terms, which will include kicking you out," I thought I could hear them saying. Is this what the chief meant by negotiating through the officers? I phoned Sidney, but unfortunately he was not at home. I tried Christopher who thankfully was in his office and listened to what had happened. Instead of the expletives that I had expected, he was reassuringly calm. "Don't fret, Sunshine. I personally guarantee your salary. The trustees would never treat you like that. If there are sides to take, I hope you feel you're on the right one." I had hoped to form a coalition that would work together to help give all children a better chance of succeeding in the future, but as it turned out I was thrust into a political cock pit. In hindsight, it was clear that to take the schools back from bureaucrats and reorient them into the community where they belonged would require a fight and the outcome would be highly uncertain. This was about ownership and who had the best interest of children at heart. These issues, I would later discover, cross national borders; my battle was a foretaste of battles to be fought out in many other countries. "Somebody must fear you a lot," had been Chris' parting comment on the phone.

\*       \*       \*

My last task at Alleyne's was to address the school at assembly on the final morning of term. Some 600 of the older boys, many wearing school uniforms for the last time, and all of them anxious to get on with their holidays, were gathered before me. It was a task I had done so many times before, that I thought I would be oblivious to the emotion. I was not. I struggled to find some appropriate words. Bob Geldof had, a few days before, staged the amazingly successful Band Aid concert for the world's starving millions. He was a man from an ordinary background, just like many of the boys in front of me. He had gone on to do something quite extraordinary. I wanted those young people to know that they, too, could do extraordinary things. The day before a rabbi from Manchester had written a letter to *The Times*, I quoted from it. "It is obvious that young people both need and want something to believe in that is greater and beyond themselves. Their cynicism is well founded. Why have religious and political leaders so miserably failed to offer the youth of this country something worthwhile to live for? Religious leaders have been preoccupied with church membership...while political leaders vie with each other to offer greater bribes in the quest for power. There is probably more latent idealism among young people now than ever before. But who is there to raise their sights and to show them a vision of goodness and holiness?"

The rabbi concluded by quoting the book of *Isaiah*, "For without a vision, the people perish."

Those people who knew me well would have known that I was speaking for myself. Education 2000 had to help generate such a vision. Moving my personal belongings out of my sixteenth century study was traumatic. I did it one evening late in the summer holidays, when I knew no one would be around. There was a blank space over the fireplace when I took down the Turkoman rug, which I had bought in the Shahrud bazaar a dozen years before. I closed the door for the last time with a lump in my throat. Nostalgia, yes; but anger too. Slowly I was coming to realise just how limited had been our vision in those early years. I could have done so much more if I had not been so unsure about trusting my own intuition. Too often I had stopped short of what I sensed ought to happen. Too often a voice of deep regimented tradition warned me away from being intuitive. "Be logical," my formal training had said. "Be prepared to justify every action with quantifiable data."

I was different now. I was stepping out into a new world with precious few fixed points; I was no longer a head master nor the employee of local government. Even my salary was ultimately dependent on the goodwill of a man I had known for less than six months. It was a job I had to make for myself, because there was a vision that needed to be created. I had a simple hope that my successors in that study should look out and see generations of more positive, creative and independent young people walking down that driveway into a brighter future than that which currently seemed to prevail. I got into the car and drove away, with no one to actually say goodbye to, yet I was deeply reassured that the pace of family life at home would give a special practical reality to my dreaming.

*            *            *

As director of Education 2000, I moved from being responsible for 60 or so teachers, 20 or more support staff and 900 pupils, to a half-time secretary, Tina Taylor, who was paid for by Letchworth Corporation. Two months later I was joined by a young graduate secondee for two years from British Aerospace, and began an open-ended consultancy with Ray Dalton, formerly a principal lecturer at Homerton College, Cambridge. I had known Ray for seven or eight years. A Hampshire man, with a reassuring John Arlott cricket commentator's kind of voice, Ray knows more about the whys and wherefores of British education than anyone I have ever met. Always punctual, he shames me in his utter determination never to appear rude or off-hand. Older than me by 10 years, he had always seemed able to make do with half the sleep I found necessary. He is, therefore, well read - well read, that is, both in terms of quality but even more in terms of teasing out just what it is that an author is trying to say. His archetypal English looks and bearing disguise an excitingly radical man, a man always looking for the new and the novel, and subjecting each to rigorous scrutiny. Politics bore him, and educationalists trying to be politicians annoy him beyond all measure; they ought, he thinks, to know better. He has shaped me quite enormously from long before all this started, and his hand was to guide me for years to come. We were to become a powerful, if small, team. Mighty oaks, I had to prove, from tiny acorns grow.

An early appointment was a fund-raiser whose previous contracts had been with well-known charities. He was strong on strategy, but less strong on packaging what he soon started to describe as "an infuriatingly abstract concept, something everybody senses is right, but which is no more substantial than a bucket of Scotch mist." He understood the need for computers. The need for a town-wide mission statement, slowly building up over a couple of years, was largely beyond him. The need to use a considerable portion of our future funds to build up a model for continuous teacher professional development worried him. "Surely that's what schools ought to be doing in any case? Isn't that what government should have been funding for years?"

The time I spent briefing the fund-raiser was time well spent for me as well as it prepared me for answering a myriad of awkward questions. The rationale for fund-raising was to be a critical issue. "What I'm saying," I repeated many times, "is that we have a system of schooling that is largely dependent on teachers rehashing every year what they taught the year before and the year before that. What they teach largely goes back to what they learnt at college or university. It's all pretty static. At its worst it's more like instruction than teaching. The idea of every teacher having to become a learner as well is very new. It's directly linked with the speed of societal change in general. What many teachers, especially those in the secondary schools, learnt in college is now out of date."

"There is a second, more profound aspect to all this. The Princeton example I'm always quoting opens up the idea that learning has to be a continuous life-long process that is owned by young people themselves. You can never stop. Now, if we want pupils to take control of their own learning, the people they're most likely to model themselves on are their teachers. So the key to our idea is building a new model of schooling where teachers are also continuous learners and where their excitement for learning permeates everything else that they do."

"Yes, I follow all that," the fund raiser replied, "That's persuasive. It would represent a massive change. But, surely, when you say you want to increase the staffing of the schools by 10 per cent, for at least two years, the implications of all this on government would be enormous. It would put a straight 10 per cent on their costs. How do you answer that criticism?"

"Now this is where we, and everyone else associated with the project, have got to be crystal clear in our thinking. It would be nice if government were to find such money - but it certainly won't, not in the present economic climate. Equally it would be totally preposterous to think that every school in the country could find private sponsors to increase their staffing by that amount. Neither is possible. Or for that matter necessary. The argument goes like this. Schools operate their present timetables using the present technologies of pencil and paper. Essays are written out slowly and are hardly ever redrafted. Introduce word processors and people start to write quicker, and eventually more accurately. As pupils do this so, slowly at first but then with increasing speed, the role of the teacher changes from an instructor to a facilitator. Go into a present classroom. Equip yourself with a stop-watch. Time how much of the lesson the teacher spends specifically on task serving the needs of all pupils."

"I see the way this argument is going," said the fund raiser, "You need the money on a test and development basis to see just how long it will take to move from the old-fashioned way of doing this, to this new way. That's a neat argument."

"It's even neater when you think it through," I replied. "Providing we can find all the necessary technology, and all the necessary professional development support- and right now we don't know how long that will take - then we would expect the schools eventually to reshape their budgets so that, out of ordinary revenue, they could find the 10 per cent from their own funds."

"How exactly?" he queried.

"By using the teachers in a different way. Slightly larger classes maybe. But most likely by breaking away from such an exclusive dependence on classroom-based instruction. It will be more about getting teachers to find different ways of getting the students to take responsibility for their own progress. And that ties up with why we think industry should welcome this. What we are saying is radical is because we are talking about the development of young people who will actually become part of the productive process, rather than dependent recipients of instruction. We're talking about progressively moving the responsibility for learning from the teachers to the children."

"Yes, I'm sure that would be enormously beneficial. How long do you think all that would take?"

"I'm not sure yet, but I have to set a figure otherwise people won't concentrate on using the money to test out new opportunities. At the moment I'm giving it a maximum of five years, providing that in the middle years - years two and three - we have enough money to run the programs with 10 per cent more teachers, then we would spend the last two years incorporating all these developments in ways that would mean that we would be self-sustaining thereafter. There is one other consideration. We have to install the necessary technology and resources to support all the changed learning strategies. That's the problematic bit. That could take longer than we think."

"And the importance of this as a national project?" asked the fund-raiser.

"That, I think, is the easiest bit. Once we get this up and running  - and remember, we'd be the first people ever to do this - then I think we would be overwhelmed with visitors. Everyone would want to see it and, once they saw it working, they'd be emboldened to try innovations themselves. At the moment everyone's timorous because no one's ever done this before.

"That, of course, ought to make it much easier to get sponsorship from national organisations to invest in what otherwise looks like a local project. In one sense it is just that - a local project. Put another way, however, it's the first of what will, I hope, become several local laboratories testing out a new national initiative. So, in backing this, a company would be backing something that could, very directly, affect everyone."

The fund-raiser grinned broadly. "You know, I think I like that argument very much indeed."

"You do?" I asked tentatively. "Well, remember it like this. If we once got such a scheme started and then working properly, it would be the pupils who would be tired at the end of term, not the teachers."

He laughed, long and loud. "That's quite, quite excellent. Surely you'll succeed in raising large sums for something you can describe like that."

It was my turn to be cautious. "I hope so. These are going to be large sums of money - two and a half million pounds in Letchworth alone, even if it can be done in as little as five years. What would help matters along is if we could get a strong endorsement from government in advance, as that would show that they were watching us very carefully. That would encourage sponsors to believe that their funds were an investment in change. The sponsors are going to be important to us, not just for the money they may bring. I want to interest our sponsors so much - in the person of their chairman or chief executive - that they start to become our biggest advocates. As they start to understand what we're doing, and feel they're part of the process, then they could become some of our most powerful friends. That's what I want to achieve."

\*         \*         \*

Before going to London the following day to talk with Bryan and Chris, I went back over the recent meetings I'd had with the head teachers. Essentially, we were trying to do two things simultaneously. First, we wanted to create a town-wide responsibility for young people. What exactly would that mean? It was a new concept, certainly for Letchworth and largely for the country as a whole which, for a hundred or more years, had thought it adequate to provide schools for the intellectual needs of young people, and left the rest of the youngsters' experience very much to chance. We wanted to improve on that. After all, as I was always reminding people, only 20 per cent of the child's waking hours between the ages of 5 and 18, were actually spent in a classroom. We wanted to turn Letchworth into what Sidney Melman called "a child-friendly town".

Our reasons were not just altruistic. Already it was becoming obvious that rapid advances in information communication technologies would soon enable young people to access from home whatever it was they had been studying in school. An alert, responsive community would be a prerequisite for the future. Parents had to be involved in their children's learning experience in ways in which, in the recent past, only a few had been. Homework was set to become at least as significant as school work.

Secondly, as I had explained to the fund-raiser, we wanted to build a new approach to teacher development, based on a far greater awareness of how children actually learned. Including how they learnt informally, outside of the school, and how the influence of friendly, well-disposed and thoughtful adults - as old Mr McFadgen had been to me all those years before - were so important. That was going to be the hardest, and in the long run the most significant, part of our programme.

Ray Dalton had phoned me the night before. "If this is going to work, then it's essential that we give all the teachers, all 250 of them, time to think this through for themselves. They have to come to these conclusions out of their own thinking, not as a result of being told to do so by some outside authority, and that now includes you. Whatever you do, don't rush them. That would spoil everything. Already people are nervous that this is just another top down initiative, or that it's a way of getting technology in around the side. Whatever you do, John, don't go on the radio or television again making promises about things which, unless the teachers want them, they could well reject."

Ray had been solemn. This was 1985, a year or so before the salary disputes were to disrupt every school in the country. "Teacher morale is very low. They feel everyone is pushing them around and if they think they are being used against their better judgement then they'll reject Education 2000 out of hand. Give them a breathing space, and don't compromise them." That worried me. I understood the teachers' position, and knew how much more they could give if they believed in what we were doing, but I also knew that I must be able to reassure Trustees that their money and support would be put to good use. I would have a difficult time in balancing various people's priorities and perceptions.

*           *           *

Bryan was greatly upset. His last meeting with Keith Joseph had not gone well, despite what Bryan had thought was their earlier friendship. Eighteen months after the publication of the *Westfield Report*, the Department of Education was showing signs of becoming unnerved by the recommendations and possibly felt upstaged by the report's invitation that groups report directly to the prime minister. Support that Bryan had anticipated was not to be forthcoming and it seemed that Keith Joseph was in no mood to offer any form of partnership funding. All he would do was provide money for a three-year evaluation of whatever we might set up. That, though valuable, did not represent enhanced start-up money. And it was start-up funds that were critically needed.

"Are you any clearer about the amount of money you'll need?" Christopher asked me.

"Between two and a half to three million pounds is my best estimate at the moment," I said, trying not to get onto the issue of leaving space for Letchworth teachers to come to terms with their own possible good fortune.

"OK. Let's think about the dinner I'm hosting at my London club in a month's time. What I want to do is to get some of my best business contacts together - people who could later become further trustees - and I want you to talk to them. Tell them why this is so important, but for goodness sake keep it simple. They don't want to be blinded with schoolmasters' talk. They just want a simple set of ideas they can remember."

What was becoming obvious was the far higher emphasis being placed on social skills - enterprise, self-confidence, creativity - by the industrialists, than I think the schools had ever realised. That was interesting, and of profound importance. Now I had to learn how to draw all these ideas together. In my presentation I had to embody a set of ideas that everyone had to understand and accept - be they academic or businessman. There could be no worthwhile development unless everyone understood what this was all about.

Some 20 of us sat down to a dinner of gracious opulence at Wysock Wright's club. Most guests were from the city - bankers and insurance people - with two or three industrialists including our new chairman, Boz Ferranti. I was cautioned not to speak for more than ten minutes, and then open it up for questions. I spoke of my experience as a head master and I made much play of the Princeton experience, and of the Swedish Work Orientation Project. The fund-raising consultant explained what each of them had to do with their contacts. This was lively discussion, much of it well informed. "I'm still not quite clear in my own mind just what it is that you'll be doing" said the quietly spoken Earl of Limerick, deputy chairman of Kleinwort Benson bank.

"I'm glad you said that," interjected the chief, who had come from Hertfordshire to show solidarity with the trustees. "You see I think that when non-educationalists get involved with these kinds of issues we need to be very careful." I froze, wondering who might take offence.

"I agree with that, of course," said Pat Limerick, seeking the common ground. "We have to be careful, but I think John is being unnecessarily coy. It seems to me that what he's talking about goes far further than other conversations about educational reform which I've been party to. Am I right? You see it as being more than vocational skills in school, don't you? You're talking, aren't you, about a whole new way in which we'll be thinking as this technological revolution proceeds? This surely will change the way we do things in the future. If we could inject such thinking, such an attitude, into young people now...well, that would give the country an unstoppable lead."

"Yes, it certainly goes far further than just the technology," I replied. "It will reshape society, and communities, and the way we do business. Schooling can't be seen in isolation, any more than can employment be seen in isolation from ordinary everyday affairs. People at large will have to change in their attitudes towards young people - just to change the schools will not be enough."

People started to talk amongst themselves and the port went around several times.

Eventually Christopher moved to close the dinner. "Before you go, could you please fill in this list, showing who your best contacts are for us to approach for support, and then we'll start on the task of raising the three million pounds."

It was a full ten years after this discussion that I read a report from an American foundation observing "no curricular overhaul, no instructional technology, no change in school organisation, no toughening of standards, no rethinking of teacher training or compensation will succeed if students do not come to school interested in and committed to learning...We need to look not at what goes on inside the classroom, but at students' lives outside the school walls." Yet, nobody was closer to doing anything with this understanding in 1996 than we were in 1985.

Anyway, that meeting back in 1985 was all splendidly eighteenth century and gung-ho...and nearly a total disaster. For over the following weeks, as Christopher and several others invited some of their best contacts to lunch, or to dinner, and tried to explain what all this was about, they failed abysmally. They couldn't tie the pieces together. As the fund-raiser had said, this was indeed a complicated set of ideas to describe, and did not represent an easy sales pitch. Bryan was unnerved. He wanted a persuasive piece of paper listing four or five points that he could describe, with another half a dozen correct answers to expected questions. "Something easily understandable that will say exactly what it is you intend to do, how you're going to do it, and a set of criteria by which you will be happy to be judged later on."

His criticisms sounded most plausible. But I knew he was wrong. So did Pat Limerick for, as he said when leaving the dinner, "We're all going to have to become much more knowledgeable. These issues raise far-reaching questions." This was indeed to become a project of exploration. We were trying to do something that had not been done before. I was forced onto the defensive by Bryan's request. I had to explain to non-educationalists why the schools, and the community, needed plenty of time to take those outline ideas and make them their own, without making it all sound complicated and I had to show that this called for sensitivity.

I had to explain why a top-down model would surely fail. In hindsight I made a major error in not taking more time in explaining to trustees and others the finer points of each section of the argument. However, it was not the last time that sheer pressure of work led me to cut a critical corner. Boz Ferranti had just written to suggest limiting our programme to the provision, as fast as possible, of 500 computers, and then standing back to see what would happen. Chris thankfully was able to understand the fallacy of such an argument more easily than Bryan. "People don't just change because you give them new tools," he said. "They need to know why they are necessary." Not for the first time was I to find that the business mind was far more attuned to the practicalities of implementing fundamental change than ever was the academic.

"It seems to me, Sunshine, as if you will have to make the presentations yourself. You're the one who can tell the story, and answer the difficult questions. I can't and I don't think Bryan can either." Bryan looked furious, but said nothing. "Tell you what, me and my mates will give you all the introductions you could ever possibly handle. We'll even come with you if you like. But if this is going to fly, we'll have to field our best speaker. That's you."

My heart sank. I thought of the delicate discussion with the heads, and their staffs; I thought of the careful documentation that had to form the basis of our development plan. I thought of those other quasi-academic groups I had agreed to speak to. I still thought like an academic. I saw long days, and long evenings in London, and I thought of our three sons. This would mean even longer hours away from home than the worst hours I had ever put in at Alleyne's.

"That's just not right," said Bryan heatedly. "John's job is in Letchworth, and when he's done that there's a conference that needs to be set up to follow on from Westfield. It's totally wrong for him to spend his time fund-raising. That's not what he's supposed to be doing."

"If not John, then who else?" said Chris in a somewhat pugnacious manner. "We all want this to succeed don't we?" Bryan was silent. He had no answer, but he was not agreeing. I had a dangerous split developing between my co-chairmen, and that could easily spread to the other trustees. I found myself progressively siding with the entrepreneur, not the academic.

*          *          *

Ray Dalton was again troubled. "Do you think they're backing away from their support?"

"No. At least I'm sure Christopher isn't. Nor do I think that most of the others would dare let go of this. That's not their nature. I'm not so sure about Bryan, but if this is going to be a fight, he'll want to keep well to the side." Although Ray had retired from Cambridge the year before, and was enjoying the slower pace of life, he knew that I was beginning to face a crisis. The one person who could work with the heads was he. He had practical applications of the theory already worked out in his mind...in fact he had had them worked out, it seemed, for several years. When he said, "You could leave the heads to me," I hardly noticed it. In fact I thought he had said it several minutes before. I pulled myself together. "You would?" I gasped, "you would hold it together until I can deliver the money through the trustees?"

"If that's the only way to get this done, then that's what I'll do. So, let's just get on with it."

*          *          *

Ray started working out the details. Each of the six schools wanted two meetings in that first year with all of their staff, and a further meeting with each governing body. Some schools wanted separate meetings with their parents' associations. The corporation wanted to sponsor several meetings with different community groups, while other organisations like the Quakers, the Methodist church, the Liberal party, the Rotarians and the employers' group, were quick to offer their own invitations. At least once a fortnight I would need to sit down with the heads at their planning group meetings. Nothing less than a day a week - 20 per cent of my time - had to be reserved for all this. That was pushing it hard. Beyond that the heads and Ray could manage on their own until we started to raise the funds which would, amongst other things, enable us to get more staff.

Slowly a common purpose emerged from the head teachers as to what it was they thought we could and should do.

> Using all of the community's resources, formal and informal, in school and out of school, to build a town rich in learning opportunities for all. A programme of four parts; Community activity as the stimulus; information technology as the means; curricular development as the result, and meeting the needs of young people as the outcome, all dependent on developing a form of continuous, professional development for all teachers, which would help them build strategies to emphasise learning, not just teaching. We want to create a genuine Learning Community.

Within four months of starting, the head teachers delivered this message to the town. That, in retrospect, was a major mistake, for the town - despite the heads protesting to the contrary - assumed that this was a school project. Something they were being invited to participate within, but not something they were expected to own. Even years later we were to feel the repercussions of this.

*          *          *

The head teachers prepared for the project by making their Fridays free of routine school responsibilities. That in itself was a remarkable commitment to anybody who understands the working of schools. With Ray, and occasionally with me, the six of them took turns to host their colleagues in their own schools and, with disarming candour, described their weaknesses, as well as their strengths. As one said: "I'm now thinking more like an old-fashioned City Father concerned about all the children of this town, than I am as a head teacher looking to further the interests of my own school." Such an attitude set the pace from an early stage. This was the schools' very own project and I had better be very careful, the head teachers' message was, in letting the trustees make claims that Letchworth had not already made for itself.

Schools, teachers, parents, and indeed the pupils as well, were fed up with the authority's training programmes which habitually took teachers out of class for a day, or for several days, and sometimes for several weeks. Their classes were then assigned to substitute teachers and we had to come up with far better arrangements. This was a major challenge. Ultimately the trust wanted to provide every teacher with the opportunity to spend up to ten per cent of their time working on ways of implementing these ideas. For a teacher normally teaching 35 periods in a week, this meant a reduction of three and a half periods. These periods, of course, still had to be taught, so the Trust anticipated using up to half the money it intended to raise to pay for extra teachers, not on a substitute basis, but as fully professional staff in their own right, appointed for the duration of the project. For a school with 50 teachers this meant five extra staff had to be appointed, and all this had to be accommodated in the timetable several months before the new school year started. To those who understood such matters this was more revolutionary, and potentially of far more long-term significance to education in the UK as a whole, than the introduction of the technology or the involvement of the community. At its simplest it was saying that good teachers have to be good learners as well. That was radical - in years past university teachers had made the case that it was through being good researchers that they also became good tutors. Now we were insisting that school teachers too were dependent on their own continuous intellectual development to be good teachers.

\* \* \*

Christmas was a glorious week of being with the family, and away from the office. It was the first Christmas in 15 years in which I was neither in charge of the school carol service, nor responsible for organising a parents' association Christmas party or dance, and it was the first end-of-term for 20 years that I was not having to write end of term reports. It was an amazing feeling of relief. I did not, however, escape completely. "You're just the kind of person to dress up as Father Christmas," said David's nursery school teacher. "Come to our class Christmas party and give the presents away." It was fun but my beard kept on slipping, and other children could not refrain from stage whispered comments of "that's David's Daddy". David, poor boy, could not help but feel desperately embarrassed.

*        *        *

My Letchworth office was little more than an hour away from meetings in the City (banking and insurance) or the West End (retailing, and the clubs at which many chief executives liked to entertain). Christopher's contacts almost always got me to the chief executives and they seemed genuinely interested in what I had to say. They were courteous and almost always followed up with many questions. On the whole, their views were enlightened, and much concerned with the future. Hardly any of them, however, had first-hand experience of education outside the private sector. These were individuals like Hector Laing of years gone by and generally knew they were out of touch and were appreciative of the opportunity to talk. I got used to three points that almost invariably were raised during such discussions. Firstly, they accepted my need to raise money. "We'll give you what money we can, though I fear it won't be as much as you'd like, and it will take some time to go through our internal company processes." What followed then was that most wanted to visit Letchworth and frequently bring some of their staff with them. Thirdly, and this was when I knew I was succeeding, they would often offer to make contact with a number of their own friends whom they thought I ought to meet. A movement was starting.

Soon my diary started to resemble a roll call of the Stock Exchange: Sedgewick's; Kleinwort Benson; Spicer Peglar; Price Waterhouse; Lazzards; Commercial Union; The Pearl; British Airways; British Aerospace; Coats Viyella; TSB; Courtaulds; Arthur Anderson; Tozer, Kemsley and Milbourne; Warburgs; Morgan Crucible; TI; Redland; Swiss Re; DeLoittes; Wimpey; GKN; GEC; Korn Ferry; McAlpine; Provident Mutual; RTZ; Coopers Lybrand; STC; Cazenove; Capel Cure Myers. My head was frequently swimming, and I found it hard to sleep. I was worried, too. Only two or three of them provided cash straight away, and this in relatively small sums. I had to justify the expenditure of vast amounts of energy and time, and I needed some more immediate results. The lead-time for releasing large donations was depressingly long; three to six months at the least I was often told. I once jumped into a taxi, but could not tell the driver where to go without first pulling out my diary. I was embarrassed. The taxi-driver laughed. "You businessmen are all alike. You work your butts off to make fancy salaries, and crack up at the same time."

Me, a businessman on a fancy salary. Is that what I looked like? Was I trying too hard to assume a new identity? Was I losing touch with my roots?

"You've got me wrong," I told him. "I'm not a businessman at all. I'm a one-time comprehensive school head master trying to stir the conscience of business to take the education of ordinary children more seriously. To work out better ways of preparing them for the world of work and for leisure. Drawing in the new technology. All that sort of thing." Enthusiastically he talked about his own erratic experience of school. When he pulled up outside the office for my next meeting, I passed over the fare, but he waved it to one side. "This one's on me," he said. "You're doing a great job. If ever I pick you up again that'll be for free as well. I've got two little daughters, so I just hope you're going to be successful in time."

After six weeks of intensive activity I came to an afternoon in which I was to address the staff of the girls independent boarding school, St Francis. There had been several questions about what was going to happen next. Good questions. Then a question came up that was more difficult to answer. A question that I needed in part to evade for fear of revealing how precarious was our relationship with the authority. I started to speak; I confused my words, and lost sight of the argument. I had to sit down, my mind having totally given up. I needed a rest. The doctor told me to go walk about for three days and get plenty of fresh air. "Play with the boys," he said, "and totally forget about work."

I was worried that my veneer had cracked but actually it was a good thing. It was better to accept this was absolutely hard work, than pretend that it wasn't. Others needed to share some of the responsibility, and now they started to do so. "Tell you what," said one of the head teachers to another, "why don't I go and talk to your staff about all this, and you then come to my school and talk to my staff about it." It worked well and this one small act - small, that is, in terms of its passing nature - signified an emerging sense of common purpose.

Tom Griffin, founder chairman of GT Management which was the first company in the UK to deal in Japanese unit trusts, joined Chris Wysock Wright and Pat Limerick as one of my three greatest business allies. We took to each other quickly. An apparent establishment man, his merry twinkle, his gloriously correct manners and gentle teasing questions made him a delight to be with from our very first meeting. He combined the best of the old and new most easily and had been educated at Eton, as had Pat Limerick and Johnny Pryor of earlier years. Yet, after several visits to Letchworth, he concluded, "You know, Eton was good for me in my generation, but I think what you've got going for youngsters in Letchworth is far better for the next generations."

# 9

# Becoming a National Issue

The trustees, or at least Christopher, knew that we could raise the necessary funds but that it would be infinitely easier if government, either locally in Hertfordshire or nationally at Westminster, would offer some form of partnership. The trustees had been offended when, in accepting the project, the authority had made its involvement conditional on no money being provided by themselves. In business terms the authority had surrendered the right to any influence, and by pleading poverty yet spending money on other priorities, they were dismissive of the trustees' and sponsors' goodwill. These things were not forgotten.

The more successful I was in the presentations I made to chief executives, the more those chief executives wanted to know why the authority was leaving it to the trust, and its friends (them) to take all the financial risk. Being able to give no satisfactory answer, they turned to their own friends at Westminster for an explanation. Subsequently, I was invited to meet the schools' minister, Chris Patten, (later the last governor of Hong Kong) at the House of Commons. He was accompanied by Virginia Bottomley and Ian Stewart, the Member for North Hertfordshire. Shortly after that I was invited to the Department of Trade to meet Geoffrey Pattie, minister for information technology. The Department of Trade later contributed £50,000 to the project but the schools' minister gave only verbal encouragement. "You should be supported by Hertfordshire," Chris Patten kept on saying, "We've already released funds through our latest grant program for this to happen. It's Hertfordshire's decision not to support you, not ours." To be recognised by, and to receive some funds from Westminster (even though they were not from the Department of Education), and particularly at a time when central government was accusing local government of not knowing how to spend its own money, did not endear me to the Hertfordshire officers.

Yet even then in 1988 I still did not fully understand this. Naïvely I thought the authority was as much part of the framework of government as Westminster itself and in asking support from central government I thought I was helping to make the case for more resources to be allocated to local government. That was the case the chief had exhorted head teachers to make with their own Members of Parliament for many years. Yet Donald Fisher was not prepared to trust us to do this on our own initiative. By keeping all his cards close to his chest (in this I believe he was no different to other CEOs elsewhere in the country) the energies of the Letchworth project would too easily be dissipated as local and central government battled for control of the schools.

The way the project was developing, it was, initially unconsciously, making the case for a new unit of change. It was fast becoming obvious that the old, rather amorphous authorities were too slow and too impersonal to be able to respond to the kinds of change we were advocating. Conversely the individual school, simply because it contained children of a given age, was too small and too self-contained to deal with learning opportunities that could not be limited just to what happened in a single school. We were arguing for systems of learning based on self-identifying communities, possibly places of the size of Letchworth. This, I was coming to believe, would be the new unit of change and it was this which intimidated the powers that be.

Throughout the summer of 1986 we worked on. The heads and the staff of the Letchworth secondary schools became increasingly convinced that it was they who had invented Education 2000, and that the Hertfordshire project was their unique opportunity to demonstrate on behalf of teachers everywhere, that this was the kind of education the community should expect in the future. Local ownership was beginning to pay dividends. More and more visitors came to Letchworth and slowly we made financial headway. In early May two of these visitors, Brian Corby of the Prudential, and Robin Broadley of Barings, promised £50,000 and £20,000 respectively, to be available immediately. By the end of May we were confident of funding a £350,000 project in 1986/7, and anticipated this rising to £580,000 for the following year. This would be enough to increase staffing by 4 per cent immediately, and by 8 per cent from September 1987. Excitement ran high and while this was not as much as we had originally hoped for, it brought life to the project and a sporting chance to show enough of what we could start to do to give confidence to raise the remainder.

There was one very bad moment at the trustees' meeting in July. Christopher was away on business, and Bryan took the chair. He asked me if the anticipated cash flow of the new donations exactly covered the projected dates for payment assumed in the budget for the next year. In a few instances these did not, without further monies which I knew to be in the pipeline, coming through or alternatively managing a small loan. The academic in him was terrified. He ordered me to cancel the contracts for the new staff (people in fact who had already been appointed and around whom whole school timetables had been constructed). I said that was impossible. He said it had to be done. Neither I, nor the head teachers, could do this without losing the project completely and for three days I did nothing, and awaited Christopher's return. I explained the situation over the phone to him as soon as he got back. "You did right to do nothing," he said. "If there's any short-fall, I'll personally underwrite it. Don't panic, just get on with it."

We breathed again and I offered many a silent prayer of gratitude for risk-takers. Shortly afterwards Anne, the boys and I went off for what must have been the best deserved of all holidays. I was, however, so much on edge that I told the office not to contact me unless it was a dire emergency. I did not learn, therefore, of the arrival of cheques the next day totalling a £120,000 until I arrived back a fortnight later. We were now in business. By October, nine months after fund-raising had started, we had raised a total of very nearly £700,000 in cash and services in lieu; it was a lot of money, but not enough.

*          *          *

Community is one of the most slippery words used by social reformers. It is perhaps why the term community hardly got any mention in the 1988 Education Reform Act, yet formalised community activity - the attempt to reach the parts of the town schools don't reach - is central for Education 2000. Its importance had been made clear back at the Westfield Conference, when the delegates agreed that "the community must be fully involved; provide leadership, ideas and finance; provide security and effect the development of relationships. Industry and commerce must participate in the 'Secret Garden of the Curriculum' and thus sow the seeds of communal activity."

Such thinking had been central to the conclusions of my feasibility study in the previous year. "Put education locally into high profile so that educational reform appears to emerge from local consciousness." It was absolutely fundamental to our thinking for Letchworth. It is the children who have found an abiding interest in the world around them who come to school anxious to use the formal structures quite literally to further their own interests. Such intrinsic motivation provides greater staying power when life gets tough, than any form of extrinsic rewards. If we believe in something because it matters deeply to us - in a way because it has become part of us - then we keep going at all costs. Indeed recent research bears this out in a striking way, as does the history of martyrs and dissidents. When something goes wrong, the immediate reaction of those who are working to achieve some reward set up by someone else is to blame the system, not themselves. Those who are doing it simply because it is their personal challenge, immediately internalise the failure - it must be something they had done wrong. They must self-adjust. They come back to the problem time and time again, until they find a solution.

Most teachers know this about themselves, yet most of us fall too quickly back into old thinking when it comes to schools. Schools, it is assumed, have to motivate pupils by setting up rewards, or their obverse - punishments.

"How can we get the pupils to take the curriculum seriously without arguing that God is on our side to justify hard work and the gaining of our own rightful rewards?" those angry teachers had said to me three years before. Governments fall into the same trap when they legislate for ever more testing and evaluation, not so much to find out where a pupil's weaknesses are and so adjust their future learning programmes, but to assess who has already mastered specific levels of prescribed knowledge. Who has passed and who has failed.

Schools in which children work hard because what they are doing matters to them, are schools surrounded by a community which - in any one of a myriad ways (like old McFadgen or the Bakhtiari chieftain) - takes time out to help young people work things out for themselves. Such communities are humane, caring and deeply challenging. They are splendid places in which to live.

Despite our early attempts to include non-educationalists at all levels of the project's administration, most people joined the project without understanding why I was so committed to the concept of community. Most teachers were, by definition, products of good schools of years gone by. The prevailing assumption, which they had not thought necessary to challenge, was that it was their teachers in their own youth who had been more helpful to them than their parents or anyone else. Good parenting, of the kind exemplified by Irish farmers or the influence of the craft masters, was fast slipping from English public consciousness. "Surely," well-meaning teachers would say, "what we have to do is to make clear how parents can better understand what we're doing, so that they're more supportive of the school?"

The increasing marginalisation of parents and the family in the raising of children contradicts the lessons we are now learning from evolutionary sciences. Throughout human history the family has been the foundation of group structure. Among hunter-gatherers labour is divided between men, the hunters, and women, the gatherers. The two sexes thus form a cooperative unit. However, cohesion exists not only within the core family (husband, wife, children) but also among members of the extended family (grandparents, siblings, cousins, uncles, aunts). The extended family is important not just for mutual help but also for cultural cohesion and transmission to the next generation.

It seemed to me, then and now, that teachers did themselves - and even more their pupils - a disservice, if they played down the critical importance of the parents. For too long society has been content to assign to the schools more and more of what had earlier been seen as the direct personal responsibility of parents and the general nurturing to be found implicitly within strong communities. However good the schools might be, they could not, and should not, raise children on their own. Schools remain institutions, with institutional rules, procedures and norms. However flexible, they cannot respond individually to each child's need. Nor do they have to, if the community with its numerous niches of separate opportunities, is aware of its critical role in helping young people shape their personal vision and their own intrinsic goals. This is the critical issue - the creation of child-friendly communities.

I had to make that argument very carefully. Good people could easily become offended. Teachers knew a lot about schools, they knew how to become good academics, but most knew relatively little about the world of give-and-take in the market-place, places where to survive you have to be quick on the uptake and know how to live with ambiguity and lack of precision.

The project set out to strengthen teachers' appreciation of the community. Firstly, we would use some of the additional staffing to make it possible for 35 teachers a year to spend up to three weeks shadowing workers somewhere in the town - this might be a managing director, a middle-ranking employee, or another professional. "Find out what you can about three things," teachers were told, "what does that organisation expect of its young employees in the first two years after leaving school. What forms of training and development programmes do they have for their staff. What changes do they anticipate having to make in the next five years in response to the new technologies?" In other words, go and look at other people from a fresh perspective, and ask of them questions you should be asking yourself. It turned out to be an extremely successful strategy.

*     *     *

Brian Spokes was a tall, powerfully built man, imbued with a sense of responsibility for young people. He had started teaching physical education in a secondary modern school more than 30 years before, and had progressed to become a senior teacher. At first he was reluctant to go to a local firm for a couple of weeks, but he sensed that such experience would be good for younger members of staff and that they would be more willing to do this if he had first done so himself. He made a special point of seeking me out on his return. "You know, John, that was an extraordinary experience for me. It's a good firm that works hard at improving its products. The employees are very much part of the team. They enjoy themselves. But, you know," and here his voice became quieter and almost apologetic, "the kinds of children I've always seen as the awkward squad, the ones who are usually a right pain-in-the-neck and who I've been disciplining all these years to try and get them to fit into our system, these are just the ones that thrive in that kind of work. Now, that worries me. I must have undermined so many children's self-esteem over the years by not valuing the very skills that would help them survive when they left school. I wish this had happened to me 30 years ago."

Nearly all the teachers found the experience stimulating and one teacher found the work she was studying so interesting that a couple of years later she left teaching to go into marketing. This, of course, was not the intention but unintended consequences are a good challenge to any system. Occasionally, teachers would say that while they had enjoyed the experience, "they could see no relevance to what children had to study in school". The two worlds, they thought, were very different, and should remain that way. Others took a different view. While the skills needed in one sphere were different to those needed in the other, was it not possible that they should be planned so as to complement one another? Direct links between teachers and the world of work outside their schools were more instrumental in changing teachers' attitudes towards the real skills pupils needed, than any grandiose, top-down, national scheme. What we had went deep into people's thinking. But it took time to build up and could not be hurried. At its most basic this was about making new kinds of friends.

A second strategy we adopted was to organise breakfast meetings, made up of equal numbers of teachers and people from particular occupational groups such as the retail trade, light manufacturing, nursing, civil servants, heavy engineering, religious leaders, trade unionists and so on. We talked for an hour, normally in groups of no more than 20 in factory canteens, in offices, in boardrooms, and sometimes even in classrooms. We tried to ensure a different group of teachers each time, so that every conversation started from scratch. It was a kind of warm up exercise, designed partly to get teachers used to talking freely and partly to inject amongst the workers of the town a deeper appreciation of what schooling could be all about in the future. Again it was about making new kinds of friends.

One of these breakfasts was hosted by the owner of a medium-sized sheet metal company. Most of his guests came from a similar background and over breakfast a few teachers enthused over the potential of new technology to help solve problems. One of them spoke about word processing, two about the use of CAD programmes in the design process. I could see that a man with a business employing four or five staff, was getting very agitated. Eventually he exploded: "I don't want kids coming to me with all these fancy skills. That's not their job, that's mine. I just want them to come knowing how to read, write, and do as they're told. I'm the one in charge. Don't give them any fancy skills. I'm fed up with all this kind of talk."

There was a painful silence and I prepared to make a diplomatic response when a man from the end of the table, who coloured his statements with adjectives not normally recorded on paper, said in effect: "You're wrong, Jock, quite wrong. The schools have got it right this time. Far righter than we have. If you don't change, and start to see it in this way, you're going to be out of business in a couple of years. The Japs will have taken you over. It could happen to any one of us, and it will be our fault. We've all got to change. Thank you, teachers, for making this so clear."

The atmosphere cleared. Everyone started to talk at once and I wished we had had a video recording of that statement. It was far better than any publicity material I could have written and the story spread through the town's grapevine. "The schools have taken the lead. We've all got to change. Join in everyone."

We settled into a routine of one such breakfast every two weeks during term-time - 17 or 18 in a year. For the individual teacher it was no great sweat, and inviting the industrialists, or nurse, or shopkeeper that you had sat with, to accompany you for an afternoon in school was not difficult. But to me, who went to every breakfast to make a short opening explanation, this became part of a punishing schedule. Yet its results were profound. More and more people thought it was right and proper to have informed debate about the future of learning. Letchworth was starting to talk, and take ownership of its thoughts.

*     *     *

By far and away the most time consuming part of our initial work with the community were the study groups which were established as the third part of the strategy. We hoped eventually to have a town-wide mission statement for learning, something similar to Princeton, and so, as the first step, the project offered to set up study groups, each made up of 10 or 12 teachers, and the same number of people from separate interest groups. Such a statement would then belong to the town, not simply to the teachers. This was rather like the breakfast meetings, but in partnership with organisations such as the Chamber of Trade, the Rotarians, the Employers' Federation, the Council of Voluntary Service and the Council of Churches. The intention was that each group would meet monthly and attempt to answer three broad questions. What does your organisation think should be the aims of secondary education? What can you do to help the teachers achieve this? Then came the important third question: What can you do with your resources to meet that same objective - without necessarily having recourse to the schools?

It is true that the value of a mission statement is largely in the making, rather than in the final product. "If you can't understand my position," said a young and somewhat cavalier local shopkeeper, "then there's absolutely no point in my coming to these meetings. I know what's right," he exclaimed as he marched from the room without a backward glance. "What does the chief education officer think are the needs of the retail industry?" asked a member of the Chamber of Trade. I was grateful that the convenor of the Council of Churches followed so quickly with his point that I didn't have to admit that it was likely that the question had never crossed the chief's mind. "We'll need two years rather than one for this work," he said. "We've a lot of doctrinal baggage to deal with as well and it's helpful to us to get rid of this. From the start, quite frankly, you've challenged us to think about issues we've been ignoring for years."

After two years it was this last group that came up with some of the most fascinating observations. "We keep on coming back to a very simple, but basic question. It's this. Education for what? No one seems to have a clear answer other than that we're united in needing an answer that is far more all-embracing than simply those work skills which may make us competitive in a highly materialistic, resource-hungry world." To their member churches they sent a simple message. "It is not good enough to leave the teaching of religion and spiritual values to the schools alone. They are secular institutions in a pluralistic world. The best they can do (and this best is often very good indeed) is to help young people to formulate deep, searching questions about the nature of faith. The school can't answer questions about the specifics of faith. It's not their job. It's ours. It's our task to be more prepared, more open and more understanding of young people. We need to open our doors and invite their awkward questions; we need to be more thoughtful. School is only one of the places where children learn. We seem to have forgotten that."

The statement worried church members. They knew that they had allowed themselves, for too many years, ever since the 1944 Education Act had made religious education compulsory in school, to ignore young people. I was often reminded of a Canadian woman I had met at a conference in Germany who had said to me: "I'm sure you English love your children but why don't you enjoy them more? Why don't you let them ask you difficult questions - the ones you haven't got fully worked-out answers to? These are the discussions which help build families."

By way of contrast there was the case of the successful young businessman who said: "My young son and I have a splendid relationship. But now he's going into adolescence he's beginning to ask awkward questions. He argues all the time. It's spoiling our relationship, and I don't like that. Next term I'm sending him to boarding school. Let the teachers deal with his awkwardness over the next few years. I'll pay them good money for that. Later we'll be able to re-connect when he's grown up and then I hope he and I will work the family firm together."

\*              \*              \*

I could not have coped had I not got a most supportive and satisfying home life. Anne was marvellous when I awoke at three o'clock, morning after morning, desperate to write myself memos about all the different follow-ups to earlier meetings. "No," she would say, her voice choked with sleep. "I don't want a cup of tea. You make one. Don't wake the boys." I drank my tea, I made my notes; I listened to music, yet still I was wide awake. Quietly I would walk around the house, hoping against hope that I would feel sufficiently sleepy in time to get some rest before the next day started. "Go for a short run each night before going to bed. Get your body to unwind as well as your brain," said our doctor.

Peter, coming up to the age of eight, was happy at school. He had excellent teachers, people who enjoyed the company of young people and knew how to excite them about learning. "What did you do today?" I asked him one Friday afternoon just before half-term. "Well, Daddy. We spent the last hour of this afternoon going over the targets we set ourselves on Monday morning. I love doing that." I was staggered. I looked at his open and happy face. "How well did you do?" I asked tentatively, wishing that someone had suggested such an idea to me, if not at the age of eight, then at 16 or even 24. "OK, I suppose. But Mr A says I need to be more realistic. I always think I'm going to get done more than I can." We both laughed. He sounded terribly like me.

*               *               *

Always the optimist, I thought I ought to take the three boys to London to show them something of the new world I was now living in. This was an adventure for me, the first time I had taken them to London on my own. I was fairly nervous as we got into the train, having put a carefully worded card into each of their pockets. On them was written: If you find this child wandering by himself it means that he is lost. Could you please phone my wife at once? Thank you very much.

"What would you do if you got separated from me?" I asked for the hundredth time. "Go to a policeman or somebody with a young child," the youngest two replied in unison. Peter looked serious. "I don't need a card. I know what to do."

Our first stop was the Kleinwort Benson office tower in the City. The boys were impressed. They had not been in an aeroplane at that stage, nor had they ever been in a skyscraper. "This is like being a bird," said David. "Look, there's the River Thames, and that must be the Houses of Parliament," said Peter. Pat Limerick came over and joined us. He pointed away to the north. "Look over there, you can see St. Paul's, and there's the Lloyd's building, and the BT tower, and down there, just below us, is the Monument. That's where the Great Fire of London started in 1666. It was called Pudding Lane then." Glasses of lemonade were produced and biscuits. The boys sat politely in big armchairs, their little feet unable to reach the floor.

"Gosh, Daddy, that was interesting," Peter said afterwards. "Who was he? You called him Pat. His secretary called him Lord Limerick, but on his door was a sign that said The Earl of Limerick. I don't understand. Does he have three names?" I tried my best to explain the subtleties of the English aristocracy to Peter as we took the underground towards the West End. They quickly lost interest in my explanation and we went into Oxford Street, and made our way into that Mecca of the London retail industry, Marks & Spencer. I was to be in for the experience of a lifetime. An inexperienced father was about to take his three and a half year old, five year old and seven year old sons clothes shopping! Each boy needed a new sweater, an apparently easy undertaking. We eventually found the children's clothes section and then I lost first Tom, then Peter; then Tom and David. All I could hear was their giggling as Tom showed how he could hide by standing up inside the girls' dresses hanging from the clothes rack. I saw his shoes sticking out below a navy blue dress. I hauled him out; he was in a fit of giggles!

"Do you need any help, sir?" asked a mature, and I thought in my nervous state, officious sales assistant., giving me a glance that suggested that fathers should never do this sort of thing. "Not yet," I said. "I've still got to get them organised."

"That's all right, sir, but if you need my help I'm just over there," she gesticulated towards the sales desk.

A friendly mother, with two well-behaved little girls, smiled helpfully. "If I were you I'd get the oldest one fitted out first, then he'll be in such a hurry to go on elsewhere that he'll help you with the two younger ones." An excellent idea. I was learning the tricks of the trade.

Peter was easily satisfied. David took a little longer. I looked around for Tom - he had collected six different sweaters and insisted on trying each one. My speed of learning was very slow!

I took them to the Royal Geographical Society for one of the annual children's lectures. This was given by two young intrepid explorers and was entitled *Surviving in Jungles*. At the end there was a demonstration of survival techniques: how to cook worms when no other food was available. A small primus stove was provided and put on top of the speaker's podium. To a saucepan of boiling water the speaker added a handful of wriggling worms. He stirred them for a couple of minutes and then started, with some apparent relish, to eat them one by one. He looked up. "Any volunteers to try these?" Peter instantly jumped to his feet. "Yes please," he said, rushing to the stage. David nestled up against me. "Ugh," he said. "How could Peter do that? That's disgusting." But nevertheless he looked on very carefully from the comfortable security of my lap; he was not sure whether Peter would survive. Tom jumped up and down in his seat in his excitement. He would have loved to have been up there with Peter but somehow he had not quite got the nerve.

We stopped at a McDonald's on the way back to the station. The boys were very tired. Only Peter had the energy to eat well. David ordered a milkshake. He was too impatient to suck it through a straw. He took the top off the drink so that he could drink it straight from the cup. It was still cold and very stiff, and came out slowly. He tipped the cup even further into the air, hoping that it would flow more easily. It did. Suddenly gravity overtook friction, and the whole pink mass of ice cream, strawberries and froth fell on his face. My grubby handkerchief performed its last useful function. It was time to go home.

*     *     *

A cloud gathering on the horizon, barely noticeable when it first appeared, was the proposal of Kenneth Baker, the secretary for education who had succeeded Keith Joseph, to go to industrial sponsors and solicit their support for 20 privately funded City Technology Colleges, to be established in the middle of deprived inner city areas. The idea, which was widely acclaimed at the Conservative Party conference in Autumn 1986, had two main themes. The first was to fund technology to create exemplary vocational opportunities for young people from deprived backgrounds, while the second was to be a highly obvious statement by central government that it could create schools of its own in those places where, they said, the local authorities had most obviously failed. It seemed such an ill-thought out idea and sensing that Baker's thinking had been at least partially influenced by our own early success in getting industrial support for the use of technology within education, I wrote to him, pointing out the important differences between us. The key one, as I saw it, was that the trust was about using the technology, not simply as a vocational preparation, but as a new tool to make learning more interactive. In doing this it would effectively start breaking down the walls of the schools, and make learning ever less and less tied to institutions. Consequently, I said, the technology and the opportunities that this opened up, needed the whole-hearted support and collaboration of the entire community. Successful colleges could not exist if they were to be part of a government initiative to reduce the power of the local community. This looked like the mixing up of two agendas with an outcome that would benefit neither.

I got no reply from Baker, which was hardly surprising given the enormous antipathy to the scheme also being shown both by the authorities and their key business supporters. Indeed it was the very companies whose industry-

education officers had been so unhelpful to us, that spearheaded the
opposition to the Conservative government's drive to introduce the City
Technology Colleges. None of these companies agreed to support government,
not even IBM who earlier had given us a token grant. It was a strange twist to
the story; one has surprising bedfellows from time to time.

At an Education 2000 presentation hosted by the large accountancy practice
Spicer Peglar, Alistair Burt, a member of parliament who was also Kenneth
Baker's parliamentary private secretary, was asked to comment on why
government was willing to give extensive support to the CTCs (something of
the order of £5 or more of government grant for every £1 raised by the private
sector) and not to Education 2000. Burt was embarrassed; he had already
suggested to his own authority, Bury, a typical nineteenth century industrial
town north of Manchester, that they should work with Education 2000
"because, if we don't do something like this to pull the community together,
Bury will become the next generation of inner cities". It was a fascinating
comment by a man who had been educated in the town and who was also close
enough to the political process in Westminster. He knew that if Bury and other
similar cities were to be transformed from the inside out then it would be
because of a decision to invest in the learning skills of a whole generation.
Schools and communities had to develop together.

So enraged was the chairman of Spicer Peglar by this lack of government
support that, the following week, with the full support of my trustees, he wrote
to Kenneth Baker arguing that Education 2000 should receive the same level
of government money as the City Technology Colleges. Eventually he received
a reply that said government was very interested in Education 2000, and that
was why they were committing £150,000 to its evaluation over a three year
period but that any direct financial sponsorship for this was the responsibility
of the local authority, not the central government. Incensed by what he saw as
simply political duplicity, he wrote back: "Much of your letter, Minister,
contains a significant misunderstanding. Spicer Peglar and, I imagine, all the
other sponsors of Education 2000, do not see themselves as being involved in
a local education authority project. We are, almost entirely, not Hertfordshire-
based companies, but national. If we thought this was only of local interest, or
was a subsidy to the Hertfordshire authority, I hasten to assure you that we
would not wish to be involved ... [However] we see in the Trust's work a focus
which, within a single broad strategy, is seeking to make those changes which
you, Sir, are frequently quoted as saying are so essential - and which we wish
to support. We have an ambition that, if we can provide the resources for the
project to succeed, we will all have a model of great future significance ... not
least in encouraging commerce to look with greater generosity at the role it
should be playing within secondary education. But the sums of money needed

to do this are simply too large to raise from normal private foundations or corporate donations without some form of partnerships funding with government. Something resembling the partnership funding you've offered to the CTCs is required. Should you do this, then I'm convinced that the private sector would support Education 2000 with even greater generosity than now. Then the program could really roll."

There was an acknowledgement to the letter, but no reply to the argument was ever made.

\*       \*       \*

Several months later I received an invitation to visit a large electronic company in Birmingham. Lucas Industries' representatives had visited Letchworth twice, but they had not yet made a donation, so when they phoned and asked if I could visit them in Solihull to discuss a major project they were working on I agreed without hesitation. It was a big company, and if there was any chance of a £50,000 donation, then a day's consultancy in the midst of a hectic week was a price well worth paying. On my arrival, I was amazed to find that they were about to make a financial commitment of £1,000,000, in partnership with an unspecified second sponsor, to work with government to establish what would then become the first of the government's much-vaunted City Technology Colleges.

"Quite frankly, John, we're not too sure what we ought to do with all this. Our chairman is keen on the scheme. I think he knows Kenneth Baker well, but we're afraid of some of the criticisms of the whole idea that you and others have made, so if you could give us your candid advice as to what is needed, we would at least avoid making the worst mistakes that you've suggested."

I was totally thrown. Me - the ultimate critic of CTCs - being asked to advise on how to design the first college, even before the head teacher was appointed. These were honest, hard-working businessmen, suddenly reassigned from their usual tasks to set up a major project, the full implications of which they but dimly appreciated and felt they had not the time to think about in any depth. They showed me their architect's initial plan. It looked just like an ordinary school, but with a vast number of computer terminals. "You'll need a larger library than that," I said, trying to find a tangible illustration of something practical that they could understand. "And the library will need lots of computers, both for individual study, and general information retrieval. You'll need wider corridors, with areas set aside for private study, each with a cluster of computers. You should be able to finance this by having fewer ordinary classrooms. You see, in this new world, the role of the teacher will be different, far more like that of a primary school open classroom."

They looked perplexed, even troubled. The architect from the Department of Education wanted to argue. "The standard department brief for a school of 1,000 pupils says we will need," he looked at his notes, "a specified number of classrooms and a library of a certain specified square footage. You're saying something very different. Why's that?"

"Because you're not equipping this, I hope, as an ordinary, traditional school. The technology changes all that. Also you're calling yourself a college. That should mean a change in practice, as well as in name."

"I'm getting confused," said another. "You talk about the need to look like one of the trendy primary School 'open classrooms'. I happen to know that our chairman thinks that they're largely responsible for the present chaos in education. He thinks primary schools are a disaster. Pupils don't learn to do as they're told. Too much exploration is not good for youngsters, he thinks. They need plenty of direction and discipline, at least that's what he said at a public meeting, and we were all left thinking that he was reflecting the minister's own opinions."

For a couple of hours I took them carefully through my arguments. It was hard work and I was not sure how much they understood. They assured me that I'd be invited back. "We will certainly need your advice and don't worry, John, this company will make a significant contribution towards your costs."

In fact I was never invited back, nor did we receive any donation. Cyril Taylor was appointed to head up the national CTC Trust and he was full of "hail fellow well met" when talking with the business community, and "let's keep the argument simple" when talking with educationalists. So simple, I thought, that he missed the real opportunity offered by the technology. "We want to put lots of technology into schools in poor inner-city areas," he told me, "where youngsters will learn useful vocational skills. Arguments about new forms of learning are confusing and speculative. They're too difficult to explain. That's not our job. Let's stick to what we can succeed with."

Taylor was envious of the number of commercial organisations that supported us and he thought he could ignore us and disparage our achievements. He was a friend of government; he was on the inside track. His sponsors could receive knighthoods, and did. Eventually 90 per cent of the CTC's costs would be met, one way or another, by central government grants. Ten pounds of government money for every pound raised from private sponsors. Even now, ten years later, I feel my blood pressure rise at the duplicity of it all. The £2 million I was to raise in our first three years would have, at that scale, have attracted £18 million of government sponsorship. Government, I later realised, probably did understand much of the significance of all this, but were more interested in those quick fixes that so appealed to politicians in a hurry. In any case no government responds warmly to major suggestions for policy change coming from outsiders. Over the next few years the efforts of the City Technology Colleges to promote their cause proved nearly terminal to Education 2000's own efforts to raise money.

Trying hard to ignore all these difficulties we pressed on, with some moderate success, at fund-raising. The trustees, quite rightly, wanted to interest some of the major foundations in our work. The active support of just one of them would have strengthened our reputation. It was tedious work. Each foundation had extensive clearance systems, and well-defined community strategies, peer group review processes and far too many academics on their boards. Inevitably, it now seems, such people and such committees play it safe - risk taking is not for them. Very largely we failed to fit into any of the sub-classifications they had already made of the problems as they saw them. We were neither a government initiative, nor one mounted by an authority. We were not simply about information technology, nor curricular development, nor were we specifically about inner city or suburban problems. As they started to grasp what we were about one of them said, with some exasperation, "are you actually challenging the very basic assumptions that underpin Western education?" The way the question was phrased implied that, if indeed that was what we were doing, then we had to be mad. The system, as it stood, had to be taken as a given.

In their terms it was easy for them to say "no." We just did not fit in.

But it was worse than that. We got very much an academic cold-shoulder, and a pretty straightforward cutting down to size. "You're meddling in academic affairs which you don't understand," they would say. "You've sold yourself to the voice of commerce, with its simplistic objectives," said older academics who, themselves, had never attempted to face the issues we were attempting to grapple with. It was easy to become downhearted. It was true that I had not spent very much time talking with academics. It was politicians who were leading the debate, often in partnership with business; the academic voice was strangely silent. I was, in a tiny way, trying to rectify this. I spent my precious time talking to the politicians, and for that the academics would cold shoulder me for a long time. Fund-raising was taking most of my waking thoughts (and a fair amount of my sleepless nights as well) and what little time was left over I was using to help Letchworth with the development of a new way of doing things.

Just who gave me the quotation I can no longer remember, but in my diary for 31 January, 1987 I noted a comment of Edmund Burke: "Those who carry on great public schemes must be proof against the most fatiguing delays, the most mortifying disappointments, the most shocking insults, and the most presumptuous insults of the ignorant upon their designs." If I was not careful, the strain of dealing with political double-speak and the tedium of fundraising were going to wear down my enthusiasm. The enthusiasm of people in Letchworth, on the other hand, provided the inspiration anybody could have needed.

*            *            *

During the first year of the project almost a third of the teachers were loaned computers to use at home, and there was sufficient money to release each of them for half a day a week to work in partnership with another teacher who had already built up some practical expertise. Not wanting to push the technological component too hard, each head teacher simply called for volunteers. It did not matter if the teachers were young or old, nor if they were mathematicians, linguists or scientists. What mattered was that they should have a good, meaningful experience, and help the next group of teachers to feel less fearful about change.

"I know I'm retiring in 18 months time," said a somewhat diminutive English teacher, who closely resembled Agatha Christie's Miss Marple, "but if no-one else is prepared to try, then I'd be happy to give it a go." Peter Wall, head master at Norton, looked at her carefully. She was the Keeper of the Teacher's Conscience, a lifetime supporter of perfect English composition, the most critical of grammarians, the devotee of nineteenth century literature and a woman with the most perfect handwriting who wanted to try out the new technology. She had her computer, and she had her staff training. People half her age were amazed and when I met her some months later, her eyes twinkled as she said "That computer has changed my life. I can get ideas out of my mind onto paper - or should I say screen - with a clarity I have never before thought possible. I'm so happy. Me, someone who used to think that an alarm clock was high technology."

*            *            *

"One of the country's rising economic stars you ought to meet is John Banham," Chris said at one of the trustees' meetings. "Currently he's heading up the Audit Commission and before that he was with MacKenzie. He's just been appointed director general of the Confederation of British Industry and if you could get him on-side that would position us well." The usual letter of introduction was written, and in early April I presented myself at the CBI's headquarters, midway up the Centre Point tower at the intersection of Oxford Street and Tottenham Court Road. I took to John Banham instantly. He was a big thinker who relished being surrounded by enthusiasts. It was easy to explain what we were doing and why, and what the outcomes could be for the country at large. I spoke of the extensive support we had already received from industry and commerce, and of our plans to get government to become an equal partner in what needed to be a national programme. "The strong support of the CBI would be an enormous asset," I concluded. John seemed impressed. Later he was to describe talking to me as being like "trying to take a sip of water from a high-pressure fire hydrant". But thankfully my enthusiasm had not destroyed my case.

"Would you be willing to make a speech at the annual conference of the CBI in Glasgow this November? You could follow directly after me. No one has more than a quarter of an hour, but it's certainly prime time. You could be sure of having the attention of all 1,800 delegates in the hall and you'll also have live coverage on BBC television."

Impressed beyond all measure, I gulped my words of thanks, trying hard to give the impression that I was daily used to being offered such a chance.

The news of the offer to make the speech galvanised the trustees. Here was real recognition. They approached new contacts with greater confidence and energy. "This project is still less than two years old," they would write, "and already it has become of such interest that it will figure as the first of the keynote speeches at the annual CBI conference. By backing us you will be backing an absolute winner."

To a considerable extent, such people responded well. Throughout the early summer, I maintained a hectic fund-raising schedule. Earlier in the year a remarkable day in January had produced donations totalling £90,000. If I could do that for just one day a month, I said to myself, all our problems would be over. It would never be that easy, but in June Allied Lyons pledged £50,000 and several companies started to talk in terms of donations of similar size, if I could persuade enough other organisations to do the same thing. This was encouraging. New companies were starting to get involved in our work, and some of these were real blue-chip companies such as British Gas, British Steel, DuPont, Lloyds, etc. There was no doubting any longer that we were dealing with an issue that readily seized people's imaginations.

So busy was I with fund-raising that I was fast losing touch with the project. It was developing a life of its own, which was as it should be, always providing that it was the right form of life. Carefully, but forcefully, I had to remind teachers that if the high levels of technology and staff training were to continue after the project funding ceased, it could only be if they had found alternative ways of absorbing the staff development costs into their normal budgets. There was no way this could be done without cutting out some other staff costs which were part of the historic way of doing things.

"The whole point of this program," I said, time and time again, "is to give you some flexibility for three or four years, so that you can find new ways of getting things done. If you want this to carry on beyond that then you will have to find ways of getting youngsters to work at least as hard - and certainly more effectively than at present - but with 10 per cent less teacher time. That either means increasing class sizes by ten per cent, or cutting the number of classes taught. The project is providing all this technology, not so that pupils have this for vocational purposes, but so that they can learn more effectively than they could with the old paper and pencil technology. That is what word processing is all about; with children learning to work in new ways, teachers' roles will change."

"Almost anyone could get better results if they increased a school's staffing and provided lots of technology," I kept on reminding people. "If that is all we are about then government would be right to ignore us. But we're about something far more profound. We are about using all these precious extra resources to stand the cost of change as you pioneer new ways of doing things."

                                    *            *            *

An experienced teacher wrote in that year's annual report that, "After many years of teaching ... Education 2000 has totally revitalised us. We have tried many things in years gone by to regain our confidence, but now we are doing so very much better. There is a positive attitude all around us ... this has injected something into our schools that people elsewhere have not yet got ..."

"We work with it," wrote another, recently qualified, teacher, "because it values our professional skills, and extends support to us to expand and further develop these. Frankly it makes us feel good. It says - believe in yourself and don't be afraid to question what you're doing."

Paul Fisher, a journalist, picked up on this enthusiasm when he wrote: "Letchworth is unique in the enthusiasm Education 2000 has generated amongst a teaching force grown weary of educational initiatives ... [they like it because Education 2000] is too broad, and too consensual to represent any one of the jargon-laden orthodoxies that threaten to crowd-out the very soul of teaching in today's highly political educational world."

The trustees took a deep breath that summer and committed themselves to a budget of £580,000 for what was to be the first full year of the programme. Two years of at least a 10 per cent teacher enhancement had been our ambition. With that we had thought we could find new ways of providing the kind of professional development which teachers needed to provide children with a curriculum that would develop and stretch them in appropriate ways. But, when the sums were done, £580,000 took that enhancement to eight per cent. So we decided we would take an extra year at the modified amount of eight per cent per annum, rather than the original 10 per cent. The project would just have to last longer if we were to get to the same place. This was probably to lead to our eventual downfall. We would not be able to create the impetus which was needed before political barriers, designed to reinforce the present system, would make the kinds of innovations we sought nigh on impossible. Time was now against us, as politicians pressed on with their own reforms which, based on coercion and centralisation, were diametrically opposed to what we were proposing. The Education Reform Act of 1988 was only 12 months away.

*     *     *

In trying to find political allies to support our programme I was introduced to Elspeth Howe, wife of Sir Geoffrey Howe (one-time foreign secretary), she, of whom it had been said, had sharpened the dagger which her husband eventually used to deliver the final blow to Margaret Thatcher at the Conservative Party Conference in 1989. She was a main-board director of Kingfisher, the holding company for Woolworths. Elspeth and Tim Clement-Jones, the company secretary, (who was president of the National Liberal Club) spent a day in Letchworth and we talked for a couple of hours afterwards.

Elspeth's advice was that, given Kenneth Baker had committed the Department of Education to support the City Technology Colleges - which Kingfisher, like so many other major companies, had declined to support - Education 2000 should seek to capture the interest of another department. "What about the Department of Trade and Industry? They have money for education which so far they don't know how to spend and that could do for Education 2000 what political interest is doing for the CTCs. The thing is you'll quickly have to start some other projects in places tougher than Letchworth. If this idea is as good as it appears, it could transform a deprived inner-city area every bit as much as it could a leafy suburb. What you're arguing for is a change in the way people learn. DTI might find that hard to understand, but they would quickly appreciate the way you integrate technology into all this. Technology is your trump card. It's a means to an end. Play it wisely. DTI could help you sell all this."

Tim Clement-Jones joined in. "Frankly this is where Kingfisher's interest would lie. By and large we're interested in the middle and the lower middle part of the market rather than the top-end. We're more concerned with places like Leeds and Liverpool, Coventry, Preston, Swindon or Newcastle, than we are with Letchworth. As soon as you're ready to diversify and set up some inner city projects we'll support you. We would be prepared to stand the cost of feasibility studies." Lady Howe moved fast and soon phoned to say the DTI could well be interested in providing a new scheme involving the inner-cities.

She hinted that costs of up to £500,000 might well be available for each project.

*           *           *

"You're looking pretty chirpy," said a grinning Tom Griffin, as we closed our last trustees' meeting before going off on a family holiday in Europe, "and well you should be. Things are looking up. You deserve a good rest. Don't spend too much time thinking about that CBI speech; that can wait until you get back. Relax for a few weeks. Let the boys take the strain. Go and enjoy them."

"Tom's right," Christopher added, "the autumn will be sheer hard work getting all this lined up, not just for the CBI speech, but preparing for the interest that's sure to follow. We're going to be busy!"

"You've got that far-away look in your eyes," said Anne as we sat out in the plaza adjacent to one of the main hotels in Padua several weeks later, drinking coffee and listening to a band playing as people strolled. Peter had just been to ask the pianist if he would play Anne's mother's favourite tune Stranger on the Shore, and David and Tom were licking ice creams.

"Tell me what you're thinking," Anne persisted, hoping that my thoughts might be on gentle, family-type issues, as well they should have been on that perfect holiday which was taking us slowly through the Alps and across the north Italian plain, and would tomorrow bring us to Venice. I looked at her and grinned apologetically. "I'm sorry. I was doing what I said I wouldn't do. I was thinking about the project, wondering how to handle my speech to the CBI Conference." Anne reached over and took my hand. "Try to stop thinking about it all for a bit longer. You'll do far better when we get back if you've had a good rest here. Let's go back to the hotel and get the boys to bed; we've got to get an early train to Venice in the morning, don't forget."

Venice was quite an experience. "It stinks," was Tom's first observation as we came out of the station. Wearing a polo shirt and shorts - as befitted the weather - I was prohibited from going into St Mark's Cathedral, and that made me furious. We nearly lost Peter on several occasions, as he was forever getting left behind. "Where is he?" Anne kept asking. "He's looking at the magazines with the pictures of girls with nothing on at the book stalls," said David, who did not miss a thing where his elder brother was concerned.

*           *           *

My rough notes for the CBI speech contained material for about an hour and a half of talk. I did not see how I could shorten it and desperately needed professional help. The trustees recognised this, and for the first time they started to spend some of our money on professional advice, rather than pouring everything we had into the Letchworth project. I knew it was money well spent, but the project staff were not so sure. After all, £12,000 worth of advice on printing and publicity was the equivalent of a teacher's salary for more than a year. Tension was slowly building up between me and staff working in the project. They were working on the slow, careful and thoughtful development of the ideas and did not easily understand the course I was taking. They thought I was becoming too theoretical and too involved in educational politics beyond Letchworth. Our two positions had to be reconciled.

The marketing and promotion experts gave me hell. They tore my draft CBI speech to pieces. They set me up in mock interview situations, and shot quite outrageous questions at me. They put me on a podium and made me speak into a video camera and then got me to criticise my own performance. They made me buy new glasses the better to sit on my nose, and they made me change my style in shirts and ties. I arrived in Glasgow with a speech that could be fitted exactly into 16 minutes and which could be understood at several levels. Stepping up to the podium, taking care not to trip over the numerous wires, or kick the banks of hydrangeas, I felt fine. Then I turned to face the audience, and I was startled to see just how intimidating 1,800 keen faces can be. As the TV cameras rolled towards me I was foolish enough to try and imagine Peter, David and Tom sitting in the head teacher's study at their school, eyes glued to the television screen, waiting, as they had reassured me on the phone the evening before, "for you to make a mistake." The audience settled into their seats. Brian Corby, the chairman of the Prudential, and one of our first sponsors, introduced me. He was to become president of the CBI two years later, and at the same time become chairman of my own trustees. I was in good company.

"Young people are a nation's most precious resource. On the quality of their education our future - our pensions if you like  depend."

I relaxed a little. The lights for the TV cameras were so bright I could not see the faces of the audience. "In 1927 Mercedes-Benz built fourteen-hundred cars," I recalled. "The directors were delighted and called for a Consultant's Report, showing their growth capability over 50 years. Eventually back came the report. By 1977, so great would have been the technological revolution, Mercedes would be capable of producing 40,000 cars per annum. The directors were stunned. This report was thrown out as being irresponsible. Why produce 40,000 cars per annum when it was obvious that the schools could never produce forty-thousand chauffeurs a year." The audience liked that. "You may laugh at some of these assumptions, but are you sure that we can do better?"

"Nation after industrialised nation is responding to the economic threats and opportunities posed to its culture and standards of living by the emergent forces of the global economy, by investing heavily in the intellectual development of its youth. Brain power is at a premium; flexibility based on education is the essential requirement to meet the challenge of change.

"The British experience of living with change has not been happy. Too often, for reasons of fear, complacency, blindness, arrogance - we have seen change as a threat, not an opportunity. We have dilly-dallied ... only to find that others have moved faster ... our smoke-stacks have fallen, our shipyards have become silent ... and vast numbers of our people have been alienated, disenchanted - their early false confidence shattered because they realise they have not got it within them to retrain ..."

"At long last the relevance of education to the state of the national economy has been recognised. Academic success alone is no guarantee that a young person is empowered to tackle the challenge of modern society with confidence.

"We need young people who have learned to live with change - people with confidence in their own judgement, competent within a range of intellectual, social and practical skills; with a flair, imagination, enterprise, able to work in teams, but also able to accept individual responsibility. People who can live with ambiguity. Not just an elite of such people, but rather a whole generation of them, hundreds of thousands of young people who can stand tall in the face of challenge.

"We need people who can think, communicate, co-operate and make decisions. People with the confidence to stand on their own feet. (This was as much acknowledgement as I could make to the powerful Princeton illustration in the time at my disposal.) These skills have not been the hallmark of too many of our people in the past - but they need to be for the future. These are the skills that the technological imperatives of the 21st century will demand.

"Why had this not happened before? No need to dwell on history, for most of you personally experienced the rejections inherent in an overtly academically based culture. We live with the social, industrial, commercial and cultural clashes to which it has given rise; a system that enabled a minority to reach the peaks of international research, yet maintained for far too long the other aspect of 19th century education which reinforced an employee-culture mentality ... with the lack of personal initiative and dependence this implies."

I acknowledged that, while most of my audience was English, we were meeting in Glasgow, the industrial heart of Scotland. "You Scots, I believe, are more genuine in your support for learning than we English. For long years you have demonstrated your faith in its intrinsic value. We English, I fear, are still ambivalent in our attitudes towards education - we're not sure that it is important…at best we may be keen on the education of our own children, but not unduly concerned about the education of other people's children. And that is not only morally indefensible … it makes bad economic sense."

There was a question at the heart of my argument. "Why is it, I am often asked, after years of conventional teaching do so many young people appear to have little personal initiative, seem so unwilling to accept responsibility … after all, at the age of eleven, so many of them left their Primary Schools, alert, excited and inquisitive?"

"Maybe you recognise such a child?" There was almost a hum of approval in the room. "The clue is in the word teaching. Good primary schools encourage children to want to learn, to explore relationships, to treat the world as their expanding oyster…the child becomes excited and motivated. Secondary schools have been saddled with the artificiality of single subject disciplines, each with a heavy load of content. The teacher takes control, the pupil does as he is told; it's the only way to cover the syllabus. The integrated view of knowledge is easily lost. Many pupils lose interest. They do as they are told because "teacher knows best", not because they any longer feel responsible. A vital attribute - that of responsibility - is destroyed; many never recover - learning is associated with failure, and this bugs them for all time.

"Learning is a personal activity. Teaching is something done to you by someone else. We have to bring about a revolution in the practice of education. We have to place the emphasis on building up young people's skills of learning. Above all we have to foster this growing desire to be independent, responsible, and creative."

"That is why I'm speaking to you today. We have to break down age-old barriers that suggest that education is solely the preserve of teachers, working in custodial-type institutions.

"Teacher has to sit down with businessman. Trade unionist with industrialist. Pensioner with student. Put your perceptions on the table, examine them, explore the common ground - create a vision, and then implement it. It will not be easy. But do it we must - at grass roots level in a thousand and more communities.

"There has been no shortage of discussion of these matters; it is action which is now imperative. We are a pragmatic race … theory, especially educational theory, makes us uneasy. We like examples. Education 2000 recognises that the issues are complex - they touch all aspects of education and the community. So the Trust is establishing what we can best describe as 'community laboratories' - whole townships working together to find some new solutions. Places in which literally all sections of society are involved to the hilt in creating rich places for learning."

"Fundamental change is dependent on the creation of a highly professional teaching force working to a set of objectives which the community at large endorses and supports. Whatever the theory, whatever are the political exhortations, it is what happens in every classroom that matters - six, seven, or even eight times a day, up to 200 days in the year. Teachers who use their subjects to develop those skills that know no subject boundaries - the ability to think, communicate, co-operate and make decisions. These are the empowerment skills."

I carried on and gave a detailed illustration of word processing as a way of fixing this in their minds. "This is a revolutionary technology. Its implications are far-reaching. It depends on two things. Teachers must be so comfortable with the technology that they will sit down and learn with the pupils. Teachers and learners together exploring how the technology can be used to enhance learning...studying just how people learn. In practice, that requires much professional development. The pupils, too, need totally open access to the technology. Lots and lots of hardware available throughout the schools, in the home and beyond."

In the time that remained I talked about some of the things that were happening in Letchworth, and how we believed that this was truly replicable across the country. I talked about the need for testing these ideas in different kinds of towns and cities. And then I concluded by saying, "The British people - your shareholders - are now so concerned at the need for a vision that they would support a lead given by you. Government cannot, nor should it, be left to do this alone. In a democracy, government is the voice of the people. The people need help to articulate a vision of that educative community of the future which, by its sheer excellence, will win for this country a secure, prosperous and worthwhile place in the twenty-first century."

Many people came up to me afterwards. Some said, "If you follow the logic of that, then schools and communities will each have to change. Where are the leaders that could now make all this happen?" It was my turn to look around the emptying hall. I thought that if I were able to persuade a significant number of the influential people in that conference hall, they in turn could persuade others with more power. I was being too simplistic. There were not many other people with more individual power than the people in that conference hall. That was not how the new world was working. In words I was to use ten years later: "There aren't any great people out there any more, there's only us." The tragedy of the 1980s was that academics had spent all their time talking amongst themselves, leaving the field wide open for politicians with little real knowledge of what ought to be at the centre of educational reform. Soon Sheila Lawlor of the Centre for Policy Studies, the influential Conservative think-tank, appeared to have more influence than all the professors of education combined.

# 10
# Opting Out or Opting In?

After the Glasgow conference I had a new status. People felt they ought to meet me. I had staked out a position, a theory, which people wanted to know more about. I felt more like a promoter, and less like a beggar; I was inviting people to join us, not just getting them to part with their money.

Quickest off the mark of these individuals had been British Aerospace. "We'd like you to visit our Preston Plant," they said. "We have a large concentration of staff there, and an active school/industry liaison team. I'm sure we could integrate some of your ideas straight away." But I was nervous about the suggestion of "cherry picking some of your ideas" and well I should have been. It was a problem that was to come up time and again in different places. People who tried to implement any one of the separate bits of what I was describing just would not get the change that I was advocating. This had to be much more than cosmetic. This had to challenge the foundation of existing practice.

I was given VIP treatment in Preston, almost as if I were a visiting oil sheikh from the Gulf with money to buy a squadron of Harrier fighter jets. It was obvious they thought I had something they needed, even if they didn't quite know what it was. I was given the grand tour, introduced to keen dynamic engineers whose careers depended on selling ever more high technology to countries who, in their own turn, were not quite sure why they needed it. I was invited to try out their latest flight simulator. The cockpit was, needless to say, incredibly realistic, even down to the smell of men accustomed to flying with high levels of adrenaline flowing through their veins. "I'll fly the take off," said my instructor over the intercom, "then I'll give you direct instructions as to what to do when we're airborne." The sound of engines was deafening. The runway hurtled towards me on the video screen in front. We shook, and then we were apparently airborne. Within seconds I appeared to be flying high over Preston. Following the instructions given, I delicately touched the controls, and the plane appeared to obey my commands. "Now be a little more adventurous and do a spiral," said the instructor.

I did, and promptly lost all control of the aircraft. The instruments screamed out a set of meaningless instructions at me. I was terrified. The countryside sped towards me with sickening speed. There was an explosion. Yet ... I was still alive. My shirt was soaked with sweat and, shaking from head to foot, I eventually climbed out of the cockpit. I gasped. "I'm sorry, I just couldn't respond quickly enough. I hope I haven't done any damage."

The instructor laughed politely. "Only to your self esteem. The older you are the longer it takes to learn these kinds of sensory-motor skills. Then you have to combine this with high level cognitive skills so that you can anticipate the psychology of the attacking airforce."

"Psychology? Who are you? What's your background?"

"Oh, I'm an applied psychologist, specialising in the training of air crews to outwit the cultural and other assumptions of an assumed enemy. That's why we've developed this simulator at a cost of several million pounds, rather than the many millions of pounds it costs to build a real aircraft. We have to be cost-efficient, you see."

Cost-efficient, I thought. Millions of pounds in simulators, many millions on a single aircraft. What order of priorities were we talking of? Just what did my country believe in? All I needed was just two or three million pounds for a single project, a maximum of £30 million for a national programme of a dozen projects. This seemed just crazy. Our national priorities had to be all screwed up. The total cost of running Alleyne's as a school for 900 pupils was less than a million pounds for an entire year. I returned to London feeling furious and I kicked myself for not having made more of an issue about the lack of investment in technology to support learning in mainstream education, when I had spoken to the CBI. Did the public actually understand that the schools were run on sets of assumptions that were not based on any firm understanding of the human brain or how human beings learn? Did they know that the total research budget for the entire Department of Education was then less than half the cost of a single jet fighter plane?

\*         \*         \*

My three sons provided a marvellous antidote to the theory making. I needed their smiles, their tears and fears, their wildly optimistic dreams and sudden despondencies, to remind me, from day to day, that this was what I was all about.

I was delighted, as only an older father can be, in their spontaneous outbursts of emotion. I revelled in the sense of being a family, and accepted when one of them thought I was being unfair. Sometimes this came in the strangest of ways. We were expecting visitors for dinner one evening, company whom I sensed (and so, obviously, did Peter) might be somewhat dull. Peter had asked me for help in the workshop with a project he was working on. I went down to the shed at the bottom of the garden, and explained what he needed to do. Then, apparently, I lingered just a little longer than Peter thought was necessary to ensure that he got it right. He paused and then looked at me carefully. "Daddy, don't you think Mummy's feeling a bit lonely without you; after all, those people will be here soon." I retreated rapidly from the workshop, like a little boy chastised.

The days leading up to Christmas were so busy that it was hard to give the family the break it needed. Four days before Christmas, Anne and the boys met me in London after I had been discussing a donation from Digital (DEC), to establish Micro-VAX computers for town-wide electronic conferencing in Letchworth. "It's powerful," said the man from Digital. "It could enable all 3,500 students in the secondary schools of Letchworth, together with their teachers, to access the central computer from their own homes. They could download any school data they wanted, and even send back their essays from home to their teachers electronically. They could have any number of moderated conferences going on at any one stage, and it would be possible for them to take place in any one of four languages, in addition to English."

"We'll be happy to donate this equipment to you," said Geoff Shingles, the managing director and the man who had sat at the table with me at the CBI conference. "This system needs piloting in a school setting. We think it has enormous potential to speed up the way people generate ideas together. We will willingly donate £500,000 worth of kit because we, like you, would want to see how young people would use this."

In writing about this incident more than ten years after it happened I am amazed how so many people misunderstand the power of technology as a tool to change the relationship of teaching to learning. In contrast, business has been radically restructured and business journals are full of articles emphasising the importance of knowledge, harnessing it, and speedily integrating it. Information technology, business people observe, is driving the process and the high rise pyramids of hierarchical corporate structures are being transformed into the low-rise of the flatter organization - less bureaucracy, more teamwork, and greater dispersal of responsibility. Businesses now organize knowledge workers into self-managed units that are held accountable for performance and are given wide freedom to choose their co-workers, hours, methods and all other aspects of their work. This, while most school systems create still more rigid structures, less room for innovation, and more centralised decision-making. No business today would survive with the same sort of attitudes as are prevalent in schools.

After my meeting with the man from DEC I took the boys to the Royal Geographical Society Christmas lecture. The hall was full of school children, the majority of whom wore the uniforms of exclusive private London preparatory schools. Sons and daughters were accompanied by parents who, 25 or 30 years before, had done the same thing with their parents and their grandparents. This was part of the middle-class London Christmas ritual. That afternoon two young men told a story about a six-month expedition cycling to the middle of the Gobi Desert in Mongolia, the furthest point from the sea on the earth's surface. There were a number of questions afterwards, such as "how heavy were your bicycles?", "how many gears did you have?", "what were your most difficult moments?", "what language did the two of you speak?" The session was coming to a close. "Any more questions?" one of the young men asked the audience in general. Tom, all of four years of age, climbed onto his seat and shouted out at the top of his voice, "How do they make bikes?"

There was a roar of laughter. The lecturer was young and sensitive and quick off the mark. He improvised and, taking Tom's question seriously, gave a quick rudimentary explanation about bike manufacturing. But Tom's confidence had been shaken. On the train home he asked seriously, "Why did they all laugh at me? I just wanted to know about bikes."

"You were right," I said. "Always ask questions when you need to know something, and never be afraid of what people think." He looked at me, still unsure. He had not liked that laughter, though it was meant kindly. I wondered how deep an impression it had made. No one likes being laughed at - at any age.

On Christmas Eve I did three or four hours of essential office work and was about to leave when the phone rang. Who on earth was still working at this stage, only a few hours from Christmas morning? I picked up the phone, half expecting to hear Scrooge or Marley's Ghost at the other end. I could not have been more wrong. "It's Brian Corby here. I thought it would make your Christmas to know that the Prudential board of directors has just approved my proposal to give Education 2000 £100,000 a year for five years. After the New Year I would like to work with you to see if we could use this to lever similar sums of money from other companies."

Phew. This was to be a Christmas to remember. My excitement, it seemed, was every bit as great as the boys as they tore the wrapping paper off their presents. But it was too much. First one, then another, trod on one of their presents. A new toy got broken. There were tears and I got cross. "We're spoiling them," I said to Anne impatiently. "They've got too many things." She looked at me reprovingly. "Don't let your grumpiness spoil their fun," she said. "You're over-tired yourself; the boys will calm down if you calm down."

After Christmas dinner we told the boys of our summer holiday plans. "I've met some people in America who would like to spend the summer in our house here in England. They've said that we can have their house just outside Washington - Washington is the capital of America like London is the capital of England. If we save enough money between now and then, we're all going to fly to America together in August."

"You mean we're going to fly in one of those big jets, right across the Atlantic?" queried Peter.

"I hope it does go right across," I said, trying to be humorous, "or else we'll have a wet landing."

That was the wrong thing to say. "Are you sure it'll be safe?" said David, always the cautious one. "I'm not sure I want to fly."

"I do," said Tom, jumping up and down in his enthusiasm. "Tell me what they say when you get into the plane." It was a fitting end to a tough year, with great plans for the future. It was almost a bribe to both Anne and the boys. I sensed that the next year was going to be even busier than anything that had occurred before.

\*       \*       \*

A few days later, I renewed my acquaintance with Hector Laing, the chairman of United Biscuits who had visited Alleyne's years before and asked "Why don't you tell my lot what's going on." He was not the only businessman unable to reconcile the good of shareholders with the well-being of the employees. He had dined one night with David Shepherd, the Bishop of Liverpool and former English cricket captain, and heard the Bishop's assessment of what the closure of the United Biscuit factory in Liverpool would do to undermine morale in Merseyside. He'd heard the argument, and still gone ahead next day with the closure; "In the interest of rationalising our profitability world-wide."

The dinner, it was said, had hurt Hector who was battling with business decisions, where traditional national paternalism was fast falling foul of the amoral assumptions of international competition. No one knew any longer how a company reconciled the interests of its shareholders with those of its employees. Hector introduced me to Steven O'Brien, the director of Business in the Community. "A sop to salve the conscience of business for taking the heart out of our old working class communities," Laing's critics had said and there was a grain of truth in that description. But at least he and his colleagues were trying to find a new balance between economic profitability and social equity. They knew they had not yet got it right.

"Most people are frightened by change," I said, leaning against the fireplace in Hector's flat in Bayswater, "because long ago - for many of them when they were young - they lost faith in their natural ability to find out things for themselves, and so were unable to do anything about it. That's how I describe learning; taking control of your own future because you know how to find things out. That's the kind of learning we need in schools, but get infrequently. Those are the skills people can take with them throughout life. Without them people fight change, and hang onto the old for all they're worth."

"I think you ought to talk like that to Margaret Thatcher," Hector said. "She needs to hear that directly, without having the idea first interpreted by her advisors. It's easy for the radicalness of all that to be lost in translation. Tell you what, the PM stays with me and my wife for a long weekend at our house in Scotland every summer. You could come and join us for dinner on one of those days. My plane could collect you from the airfield nearest your home and fly you direct to our house in Scotland."

I blanched at the thought of explaining to Margaret Thatcher a whole new way of thinking about something as abstract as human learning, and the need for communities to come together to accept learning as something which has to unite school and community. Only recently had she remarked: "There is no such thing as society, only individuals."

"Of course," I said, trying hard to ignore my feelings. "I'd be delighted."

Hector, I think, felt somewhat let off the hook. "Good, I'll be in touch to make the arrangements. In the meantime better not talk publicly about this. It'll be an off-the-record meeting."

I knew the value of that advice. I could imagine all too well what the authority would think if they were to know that I were to have a private meeting with the prime minister.

"Did you get any money from United Biscuits?" asked one of the Letchworth heads the following morning, thinking of the bottom line to all their activities.

"Not yet," I replied.

"You mean you failed to clinch a deal?" asked another, gently taunting me.

"No, it'll just take a long time," I said, reluctant to speak frankly.

*          *          *

Willis Faber, the life assurance conglomerate, which had given £20,000 a year to Letchworth asked me to visit its headquarters in Ipswich. All the secondary Heads were invited to a lunch and each head introduced himself.

"I'm John Blatchley," said the first guest. "My school was founded by Cardinal Wolsey in 1520, when Ipswich was one of the three most important cities in England. I have to admit that, as an independent school, I've never sat down with the other head teachers of the town to discuss matters relating to all the children of the town. To our shame we've never thought to do this. That, when you think of it, is pretty extraordinary. This has to be a first occasion, and it ought to be good for everyone." Viscount Chelmsford, chairman of Willis Faber, was impressed enough to offer £50,000 a year for an unspecified period, if Ipswich were to set up a comparable project to Letchworth. "There is, however, a snag," he said. "I'm afraid we won't be able to renew our contribution to Letchworth when it runs out at the end of this year. I'm sure you'll find other sponsors for that. But we're now giving you a splendid opportunity to show to your critics that these ideas are now taking off in other places. This is something we believe could work well in an industrial area, as well as in the leafy glades of Letchworth. People are bound to back you. We'll be dependent on you, of course, for advice. Much of the time I'm sure our people will be able to visit Letchworth, but it would be helpful if you could occasionally come to Ipswich and help us."

I was excited at the new opportunity this presented, but frightened at the financial implications. And well I should have been. Letchworth needed considerable support over several years if it were to demonstrate techniques that might later be widely replicable. Taking support away from Letchworth before we were able to reach a point of being self-sustaining could be disastrous. But I knew I could exercise little control over this. The project's life blood was almost totally in the hands of our sponsors, and their decisions, I was coming to see, were increasingly being made along parochial lines. "We'll put money into our own back-yard, because that is good for company image."

The trouble was that none of these back-yards had sponsors rich enough to fund everything that was needed, on their own. The sums of money - roughly an extra 10 per cent above normal budgets for the first five years - was just more than any single company could manage. If Letchworth needed about £650,000 per annum, Ipswich would need at least £1.5 million and though £50,000 is a lot of money by conventional standards, it was hardly a starter for a project of this scale. That was why we needed government support in the form of partnership funding - a pound for a pound, or some other sort of reasonable matching rate.

Ipswich was quickly followed by St. Helens in Lancashire, the home town of Pilkington Glass, a company well-known for its paternal commitment to involvement in the community. "This is good, and it goes far further than anything we've thought of before," they said. Then, at the suggestion of the Department of Trade and Industry, a number of inner city task forces set up by government as agents of regeneration after the riots in Toxteth and Brixton, asked to become involved. DTI offered to put up £150,000 a year for three years to each city once we approved them. Endless meetings had to be set up. First it was Wolverhampton in February, then, later that month, Coventry and Preston. In March it was Bradford, Leeds, Halifax and Leicester. Bury followed in late April. Each wanted to send a team to Letchworth to try and understand what it was all about.

The project team in Letchworth was welcoming, flattered I suspected by the sudden interest, but almost submerged by the weight of visitors. Then these towns wanted further discussions on their own patch, so I, and frequently one of the Letchworth heads or one of the other teachers, made a return visit. We went to Halifax in April and May, Wolverhampton and Bradford in May, to Coventry and Leeds in June and July, and to Bury in May and June. It was like a journalist's tour of those English industrial communities trying to face the horrors I had described to the CBI: the falling smoke-stacks, the silent factories, the unemployed workers unnerved by their inability to deal with change.

Publicly I was confident, relaxed, and enormously excited by all the interest. Privately - at three or four o'clock in the morning sitting in the kitchen, drinking yet another cup of tea, as I tried to work out various strategies to help me cope, I was frankly frightened. I just couldn't handle all this. Nor did I think the trustees realised just what it was that we had started. It was hard to be both optimistic (that, I had discovered, was what salesmanship was all about) and realistic about the pressures.

Progress in Letchworth was continuous, and impressive. The enthusiasm of the teachers was palpable, and already this was having highly beneficial effects on the pupils. But the pace could not be forced. Too much external interest was a distraction. The teachers wanted to get it right in their own way, and could do so only if left to work without distractions. They were also smarting under the latest directive from the authority about retraining programs. While programs set up by the trust were planned so far in advance that no substitute teachers were needed, the authority was more cavalier in its approach. Offered a considerable sum by central government for teacher retraining, the authority would not work with Letchworth to integrate these two forms of provision. "We are not allowed to give you any help; formal or informal. That is set out in the original agreement," they quoted ad nauseam. So for three years the schools were required to operate two different systems. The larger was that set up by the Trust, but this was mainly invisible because there was no disruption. The second system was highly disruptive, dependent on temporary supply cover and unpopular with pupils and parents alike.

"We're becoming schizophrenic," said the teachers. Parents, unable to distinguish between the two systems, started to associate all retraining programs with supply cover - and did not like any of it.

*      *      *

Early in March 1988 we learned that Professor Brian Griffiths, the economist who was regarded as Margaret Thatcher's primary economic and social policy advisor, asked to visit Letchworth. He spent the better part of half a day in the schools and talked extensively with local people. He was the first official to recognise the vulnerability of our position, noting that we were stuck midway between the authority and the department, "neither of whom do I see as being genuinely interested in innovation". He took copious notes, spoke to many people, and left asking for a detailed analysis of what might be the national implications of such an idea, "as I would like to speak to the prime minister about this".

Less than a month later the education secretary Kenneth Baker came to Letchworth. It was a difficult visit to manage and the teachers' unions were in uproar over the suspension of salary negotiating rights. Twenty minutes were reserved for them to meet privately with the minister to discuss salary matters and after that we did our best to ensure that he met pupils, staff and members of the public. Little time was reserved for meetings with statutory dignitaries, much to their annoyance. Baker appeared to enjoy his visit enormously and talked quite naturally with pupils and teachers alike. He was relaxed and appeared to be a good listener and was particularly struck by how little attention the pupils paid to him. "They seem so caught up in their work that we must have seemed uninteresting," said the man who was renowned for continuously preening himself for the camera. He went off by himself (wise man) and peered into places not on the official tour, talking with people who hadn't expected to be spoken with. "I'm amazed at the spectacular progress that's been made in this project. This is much more than skin-deep," he said as he was interviewed later that afternoon in front of the television cameras.

The following day, in another speech elsewhere in the country, he said, "I have just visited a project in Letchworth for Education 2000 which has taken all the schools together and has promoted the concept of the schools working together, providing a lot of extra equipment and doing it (ie information technology) across the community. It was impressive indeed. So impressive that they have virtually dropped separate computer studies. That should be the objective for which we are striving in the course of the next five to ten years."

Driving the minister in the old family Volvo between two of the schools later that afternoon, I raised the vexed question of school autonomy versus community inter-dependence, particularly with regard to schools being able to opt-out of authority control. He put down the briefing paper that he'd been studying and asked me to explain. There was just time to make a single point.

"Well, it goes like this, and you ought to know it. The local employers are actually against any one of these schools opting-out of authority control, yet at the same time they despair of the way that they feel the authority plays around with them. So they have little enthusiasm either for your policy, or for the authority's. They think that an opt-out school would, with its extra resources and prestige, quickly be seen as the best school. It would drain the better students from the other schools. The pupils from the more prestigious schools would be likely to get the better qualifications, and would go on to better jobs, and most probably leave the town for higher paid employment elsewhere. The

town, and the local employers such as these, would then be left with the weaker
students. That's how they explain it," I said struggling hard to do justice to the
deeply held views of the employers, but trying not to make it sound too
confrontational. "You see they have come to believe in trying to establish a
self-sustaining learning community. They believe in Letchworth as a whole,
not simply in one of the schools. Their concern is for all the children."

He was silent for a moment. "An interesting observation. What do you, or
the employers, think would be better?"

We were now close to our destination and were about to turn into the school
grounds. About a minute of private conversation remained. "Offer the
challenge to whole communities - places like Letchworth with less than
50,000 people - not simply to opt out of LEA control as separate institutions,
but rather together to opt into a partnership between the schools and the
entire local community. Give them the responsibility they need within their
own town. Hold the community to account for using its resources, formal and
informal, to raise the standards of achievement. Let the buck stop on their own
doorstep."

"All this technology should give you a clue," I said looking across at him as
we halted at a road junction.. "The new unit of change will have to be
something larger than a single school, but certainly smaller than an old-
fashioned education authority. Get everybody involved. There's massive talent
floating around in most communities, totally unused. Lots of people wanting
to be what I call spontaneously useful. They don't want to be pushed around by
some vast, complex, distant bureaucracy. They want to be useful within a
small, quick-reacting community - a place where they matter, and are
appreciated, and can genuinely grow".

"That's fascinating," said a minister renowned for always looking for the
politically interesting idea. "I wish we could clone this elsewhere in the
country. But as to opting in as opposed to opting out, I think we've already gone
too far with the new legislation now going through the Commons to reverse
that and go the other way. Tell me," he said, not wanting to get out of the car,
despite the obvious committee standing outside waiting to welcome him, and
desperately wondering what we were talking about, "why is your authority so
negative?"

I thought carefully. This was a politically loaded question and my answer
might later be quoted back against me. "I think they're frightened that you're
trying to abolish their power."

"And what are you afraid of?"

"Both them and you. By that I mean that I don't think either the authority or
the department has the appropriate thinking for all these new opportunities."

"Neither do I. You're right." He opened the door and tried to leap out to greet the outstretched hands of the reception committee but, having forgotten to unfasten the seat belt, fell back into the car in an undignified heap. I feared that his confusion might cause him to forget the significance of those last few words.

Just before leaving the town, I heard him ask the chief, "If all this is such a patently good idea, why's the authority not doing it for itself?"

I strained to hear the answer. "It's all very expensive," replied the chief. "They've had great difficulty in getting their money together, and they still haven't done it yet." I was furious. Was I being judged on the quality of my fund-raising, or the quality of the idea that I was trying to implement? Faint praise is even worse than criticism. Why could the community see the value of all this, but not the officers who were actually paid to run and understand the system?

\* \* \*

Ten days later I accepted Brian Griffith's invitation to "drop in to Downing Street for a cup of tea". We talked for three-quarters of an hour and Griffith asked a number of follow-up questions that had occurred to him since his visit to Letchworth seven weeks before. "These are important issues. I want to get the full interest of both Kenneth Baker and the prime minister. You ought also to talk to Kenneth Clarke, who is obviously an up and coming man. You're worth supporting. We'll have to get a proper package put together." I left feeling elated (who wouldn't after a meeting in such surroundings,), yet I was beginning to get impatient at how long this was all taking to come together.

On the way out I nearly collided with Margaret Thatcher. Not knowing the procedures I did not quite understand what was happening. I had collected my umbrella from the hat stand and was slowly making my way across the entrance hall, looking at oil paintings of former prime ministers, when I heard a porter say, "PM 15." Ten seconds later another said, "PM 5." At that he opened the main door, I thought for me to go out. It was not. It was for the prime minister to come in, which she did at such speed as to almost knock me over.

That, in hindsight, could be seen as a metaphor. During the summer the months of 1988 we came extraordinarily close to influencing public opinion but, I suspect, we were just a few months - maybe even a year - too late. The country was fast losing patience with educationalists and Baker was pushing ahead with the Education Reform Act ("we've already gone too far with the legislation"), his own political credibility was at risk with the CTCs he promoted with enormous zeal, and Education 2000 was, as he said later, "too fundamental and common sense to make political headlines." That was the ultimate problem. Baker and Thatcher were rushing too fast to handle anything as profound as we were advocating. If we could have started in 1983 or 1984, and not been left to go it alone in 1985, the course of educational history could have been very different. We entered the arena just as the tide was beginning to ebb away.

Of course I did not see it that way at the time. I thought we were riding the crest of a wave that would soon enable us to make the breakthrough we had struggled for so long to achieve. But immediately the summer holidays were upon us. It was time for our family to go to America and for the politicians to take stock of their policies.

For several summer holidays thereafter we swapped our English home with friends in Virginia. To our children, America was a land of long summer days, plenty of ice cream, and visits to national parks and historical sites. Back in England sometime later, we were driving home from a day in the country with the children. Anne played a Garrison Keillor tape describing his fictitious schoolhouse in Minnesota. "At one end of the room there was a portrait of George Washington and at the other end one of Abraham Lincoln, beaming down at us like two long-lost friends," Keillor drawled in his best Lake Wobegone style.

"That's silly," piped up 7-year-old Tom. "They weren't alive at the same time, so how could they have been friends?"

I asked Tom how he knew that. "Well," he said, "when we went to Mount Vernon they said how sad it was that Washington didn't live into the nineteenth century - and when we went to Gettysburg the actor playing Lincoln wasn't 65 years old - so they couldn't have been friends." His logic, and the connections he had built, fascinated me. Several years later, at a dinner party in Seattle, I recounted that story. "How I wish American elementary schools taught history as well as that," mused our host, a professor of education.

"That's silly," said our by now adolescent Tom. "History lessons in school are boring. I just love everything to do with America."

Anne interjected, "What's your favourite subject?"

"It's maths, because my teacher always gets us to think about connections and patterns. That's really interesting; I can see how things come together."

Patterns and relationships, emotions, the need to make sense, intrinsic interest, formal and informal learning, history dates, and mathematical formulas - these elements in Tom's learning defy any logical structure. The process of learning is wondrously spectacular and messy, and does not easily fit within a closely defined, classroom-based curriculum - particularly for adolescents.

Try as we might to accommodate children's spontaneous questions, too often their natural enthusiasm is dulled by the needs of the system for order. Nevertheless, the capacity for self-organisation ("I want to think this out for myself") is coming to be valued more and more highly in our society, which is changing so rapidly that today's questions are answered almost overnight. Some people call such an ability, wits. In the north of England, people use an old expression, *nouse*, a level of common sense that goes beyond book learning. I was becoming convinced that this was what the brain was all about.

*     *     *

On the way home that year I attended a conference in Colorado on educational restructuring. There were several hundred delegates from a score of countries, but the majority were Americans. To start with, the pace was being set by the Scandinavians who emphasised environmental sustainability. The idea was picked up by almost every speaker who agreed that life can't be split up and studied as a series of disconnected bits, so the curriculum has to be seen in its entirety. "We can never merely do one thing," said one speaker. "All solutions have side effects," said another. James Coleman, the renowned sociologist from Chicago, argued that youth culture was now so strong that it was overtaking the school in its influence. Families were becoming ever less successful in inducting young people into adulthood. Children of one-parent families were underachieving, but so too were the children of the rich and the busy. "Society," he said, "is losing the ability to regenerate itself. Schools cannot change unless the overall social context changes."

Hans Gunther Rolf from Dortmund argued: "Children are being over-extended. Families are encouraging them to grow up too fast. The spin-off from an ever more intensive, competitive existence is that society is chasing the idea of the perfect child, not the contented child. At a time when more and more families are falling apart, the school is expected to take on a task for which it is not qualified. There is a prevailing sense of pessimism among young people. We have to help young people recover a belief in the future because new information about how people learn means that we are now able to release human potential on a scale never before anticipated. Information technology will help us," he said, "but it's only a tool. It's what we're going to do with communication technology that really matters." This was exactly what I had been arguing for in England, but back home the agenda seemed so different. For the first time I was beginning to understand just how out of touch English policy makers were with what children could actually do.

I soon got vivid illustration of this from the British government's representative. Anne Jones is a personable, enthusiastic, busy, ex-head teacher, who had been recruited by the Manpower Services Commission to drive the expansion of the TVEI initiative. As a head she had been highly effective in managing the affairs of a thrusting lower-middle-class secondary school in the London suburbs near Heathrow. As a representative of government, she waxed lyrical about the increased proportion of vocational education that would now be contained within a compulsory national curriculum. She spoke warmly of the intentions of the City Technology Trust to wrest inner city schools away from local political control, and make them direct agents of central government. Anne Jones, even by my standards, was new to the international arena. She seemed oblivious of the scorn of the Scandinavian delegates who historically placed such emphasis on the education of the broad child, and of the even more obvious disdain of the Americans with their strong fear of central direction.

"Have you English taken leave of your senses?" said Birger Berthensson, principal of the Trondheim Teacher Training College in Norway. "Unless people have the broadest of broad education, they'll never understand the essential unity that is at the heart of human existence."

"Beware of state interference," warned the American Susan Fuhrman. "It leads to an immediate illusion of busyness, and far too much deference is then extended to specialists from somewhere else. External specialists too often cause people to lose faith in their own ability to find creative solutions, and rush off instead to follow the latest trends. Increased pressures of this kind destroy motivation. Concentrate your attention on understanding how learning actually takes place; the learning, that is, of teachers as well as students. Teachers have to become reflective practitioners, if children are to learn confidence in themselves."

I scribbled in my notebook and looking back now my handwriting appears even worse than usual. "Reflective practitioner = teachers who can get outside themselves, and analyse the effectiveness of what they're doing -> become teachers who are always using as a feed-back system to shape future ideas. Only if teachers are learners will they be good role models for their pupils." I had underlined that sentence heavily. I had then scribbled a further note later that night. "This is the change. Now teachers can't just get away with passing on last year's notes, they have got to be seen as professionals whose ideas are always growing and changing - how exciting." Of course I should have added a further point; "How intimidating to those who believe that education can be delivered by way of top-down directions."

Deborah Meier, an elementary school principal from one of the toughest areas in New York, closed the conference. "Remember," she said, "we have designed schools as if we were determined to drive those who work within them, teachers and students, to distraction . A school day is like a badly organised conference - discontinuous, far too much talk (much of which is unclear), hard seats, bad visual aids, bad accommodation ... all the wrong people ... little time to think, and re-order your thoughts. We may well laugh, but of course children go to school for much the same reason that adults go to conferences – to socialise with their friends. Until we start taking ourselves less seriously, but more sensibly, we just won't understand each other's learning needs. Remember Marshall McLuhan's words carefully: 'Those who fail to understand the close interconnection between education and entertainment, fail to understand the significance of either.'"

\*         \*         \*

I tried – and failed – to interest the head teachers in Letchworth but they were preoccupied with the newly emerging national curriculum. "Government is starting to tell us what to do in every subject, and setting this out in ways which look as if teaching will soon be a matter of merely ticking the right boxes on the right forms," they said. "Don't waste your time, John, on theory we're too busy to consider. Just get on with the job of raising the money." But I could no longer do that. There was a real danger that the schools were now being propelled into a way of teaching that would reinforce many of the old techniques which Education 2000 had been set up to change. Already I was sensing that people were failing to recognise just what a powerful learning tool these technologies were. Instead they were being treated as vocational skills. Instead of researching learning, government was insisting on enhancing teaching. My thinking had jumped ahead of the trust's own programs and I was beginning to recognise a tension that was to grow over the next few years.

Brian Corby, the chief executive of the Prudential, who had recently become the trust's chairman, did not take long to see the root cause of our problem. His advice was diametrically opposed to that of the heads. "You should not be wasting your time raising money. Your role has to be strategic. Leave it to the trustees to appoint the best person we can find, both to raise money, and to manage the business affairs of the trust. After all, this is fast becoming a fair-sized operation, and the trust must be poised to grow still more rapidly when we get, as I expect we will, the green light from government."

Then I received a phone call from Hector Laing. His holiday arrangements had been changed by the prime minister's need to go overseas, and so the proposed dinner had to be delayed. My relief was tinged with disappointment – relief at knowing I would not have to take on Margaret Thatcher and disappointed at the lost opportunity which might have given the trust the financial breakthrough needed to demonstrate the practicality of these ideas in ways which politicians could have understood. If I could have captured her interest at this stage, the story from here on might have been quite different.

\*         \*         \*

Many evenings after work I would return home and spend an hour or so in the workshop, using the by-now well seasoned oak given to me by my late father-in-law from the glebe lands in Culworth. I was making a Welsh dresser and a refectory table and Peter was old enough to be helpful, holding wood in place, passing me appropriate tools and learning of a carpenter's frustration when the internal vagaries of a piece of wood make joinery an imprecise art. "Watch what I'm doing," I said one evening when his attention wandered. "Try to understand what I'm thinking. Then you'll be able to anticipate what's needed next." That was exactly what my father had said to me years before, when I kept losing interest in holding the trailing lamp in the right place as he installed the new electric light system in his church in Southsea. For all I knew, his father had said it to him, and probably his father before that. It was a fine, reassuring feeling and I remember happily smiling to myself.

I bought an electric fret saw and each of the boys, including Tom, cut up endless pieces of plywood. Tom made fantasy figures; David a splendid replica of a Greek temple. His form teacher had earlier thrilled him about all things classical. He drew Greek key patterns everywhere, and taught himself the Greek alphabet from one of my old school books. Peter built a replica of a Swiss chalet, and wired up each of the rooms with little electric lights.

"Dad," said David one afternoon, "when you and Mum had those friends in for dinner last night you didn't know Tom and I were on the stairs listening to you, did you? It was really interesting." Disconcerted at not being able to remember all that we had talked about I was momentarily worried at the thought of an indiscreet comment that any one of us might have made in their hearing. I quickly looked at David. His face suggested an interesting problem, not the fun of uncovering a scandal. I smiled and relaxed, and he continued. "You see, I couldn't work out what you were all talking about. One of you started to say something and then someone else butted in and that changed what the other person was saying. Then someone else said something and by that time none of it seemed to make any sense. You just seemed to talking for the fun of talking."

"David's right," said Tom. "It was like no one ever finished a sentence. Why do people have conversations that don't get anywhere?"

Disconcerted at this analysis, I looked around for an easy explanation that would simplify the relationship between the art of talking, and the reality of community building and social bonding. "Do you remember that Louis Armstrong tape we were playing in the car earlier? The one where he's singing 'I see friends shaking hands, sayin' how do you d'you do: they're really saying, I love you.' Sometimes that's what conversation is all about; it's a way of just being nice to one another."

"Yes," added Anne. "It's what people call small talk. Women seem to be better at it than men. Men think they have to say something serious, and women seem to find it easier just to chat."

"Girls are like that too," said Peter with all the wisdom of his 12 years of age. "They're different to us. In fact, Mum, I wish I'd got a sister then I'd be able to understand what girls think. They confuse me." What wisdom!

On another occasion David and I had been walking together. He had just had his eleventh birthday and was preparing to transfer to secondary school in the autumn. He had been silent for a while and I sensed he was thinking something out so I said nothing and waited. Eventually he said, "I've been thinking what it will be like at secondary school. Is it true that most of the time you have to work on your own and aren't allowed to talk to each other? Because, if it is, I'm not sure I'm going to enjoy it much. I'd rather work in teams and share ideas. That's how I've always done it. I can work by myself, but it doesn't seem so real somehow."

We can all learn a great deal from children if we listen carefully. Those walks with my own children have meant so much to me, particularly when in more recent years I have had far less to do with the classroom than ever I did as a young teacher. In those earlier days, too, it was the questions that children asked me which, I sensed, put me far more on the spot that ever did the questions I asked them. It is much harder to ask a good question, I've often thought, than it is to give a good answer. It's even harder to question an apparently good answer. To get the question right you have to think yourself into the issue. That's why in my speeches I invariably make the point that learning is a consequence of thinking. So vigorous were the questions in my first year or so of teaching, and so many were the pupils perched on the edge of my desk long after the bell at the end of school had sounded, that playfully I used to tell myself that if I ever came to write my autobiography, it would have to be called *Please, Sir, Why?*

On a family walk in Derbyshire we were returning late in the afternoon beside a fast flowing river. The boys were excited. Tom ran on ahead, and in his hurry to climb a stile at the side of the river slipped on the top step and fell head first into the swollen waters. I was about a dozen yards behind him, and downstream. Anne, who afterwards was convinced that she saw the few seconds in slow motion, remains convinced that so swift were my reactions that I had jumped into the water even before Tom hit its surface. I rescued him easily, even collecting his glasses as they tumbled over the rocks. Anne was near to tears, I was shivering and Tom was confused and frightened. "Daddy, you didn't take your rucksack off!" exclaimed David. " Now it's all wet!"

At life and death moments such as this, emotional responses - gut reactions - are infinitely quicker than our powers of logic. I did not even think about the rucksack, or my security and certainly not my comfort. Although I was not to know the full reason for a year or so yet, as I reflected on this subsequently I knew that this was an excellent demonstration of how the amygdala - that little almond shaped section of the limbic system within the brain that regulates our aggressions, emotions and sex drive - intentionally by-passes all the carefully constructed logical functions within the brain that enable us to perform a whole array of activities efficiently from day-to-day. But those processes take time - the well trained academic weighs the evidence, and becomes indecisive. The amygdala, when activated by high emotion cuts delivery time, as it were, by vital milliseconds. Herein is an important clue to the workings of the human brain - and to the nature of human learning. In very many ways, direct and indirect, emotion is more significant than logic in driving attention, shaping action, and certainly in shaping memory. Education systems that deny this go against a key process which drives the brain; no wonder children get bored in an emotionally neutered classroom.

This insight into the importance of emotions is particularly crucial with regard to adolescents. We now know from fMRI studies that age-related physiological changes in the brains of adolescents help explain the emotionally turbulent teenage years. We can now actually see that adolescent brains are more prone to react with gut instinct when they process emotions but, as they mature into early adulthood, their instinctive responses are tempered with rational, reasoned reaction.

                        *              *              *

Teachers didn't want to sit down and talk with young people about the nature of learning; it was too threatening to many of their own assumptions. So it was left to Ray Dalton, several members of the Rotarians and myself, to meet with 15 of these young people one afternoon a week during that autumn term. We tried to be as unobtrusive as possible. It proved to be quite a fascinating discussion. They were often direct, but also honest and self-critical. They were not vindictive, but largely they were far from satisfied.

What these students disliked most was the assumption by teachers that they had got nothing to say that might shape the project. "Teachers continually regard us as being in need of treatment," said one. Another constructed her own analogy; "When I go to the doctor, I want to be told what's wrong with me. Not just give me medicine and have a note on my file. If there's something wrong with me I'd like to know exactly what it is, and what the medicine might do, because I might have a better cure than the doctor!"

"Teachers, even good teachers, frequently talk down to us. That's annoying. They're afraid of our possible criticisms and so they won't ask what we think!"

They were disarmingly constructive. They talked not just about school, but about their parents, and their families, and of the community around them. "What we need to improve the quality of our learning, more than anything else, is more contact with adults other than parents and teachers. We know what our parents think, and we're suspicious of teachers because they're paid to think like that. What do real adults think? Soon we'll be part of the adult world. In practice we know little about life after school. We want to join in more with what adults do."

"That's ridiculous," said one irate teacher. "I'm both a teacher and a parent, and a member of the community - I know as much about this as anybody does. I don't need a group of youngsters to tell me what to do."

\*　　　　　\*　　　　　\*

Shortly after Christmas I was phoned by Ernest Hall, an entrepreneur and promoter of the arts, from Dean Clough in Halifax. He was, I realised quickly, both amused and somewhat annoyed. "I've just been approached by Kenneth Baker. He obviously thinks I'm rich enough to sponsor a CTC. His deal was most generous. If I put up £1 million he and the Department would find the rest of the money. I said I was more in favour of the Education 2000 approach which would involve the whole community and he quickly said he liked that approach too, and what about getting a joint project between a CTC, Education 2000 and the Halifax Council. I explained that anything to do with a CTC was anathema to the council because of his often-stated opinion that CTCs would wrest control away from local government. I told him, John, that while we don't like local councils as they are at the moment we are far more in favour of your idea of rebuilding the community around learning, than ever we are about one of our schools being directly controlled by the government."

It was a useful tip off. Baker was getting desperate, I thought, as few industrial sponsors wished to take up his offer of funding CTCs. A day or so later I was informed by a mole in the department that it might now be possible to set up a meeting consisting of three or four permanent secretaries, Brian Griffiths from the Policy Unit and several other rising members of parliament together with Kenneth Baker. "He's looking for a way forward," I was told, "that would make the CTC initiative more acceptable. A partnership with Education 2000 might achieve that."

By now the trust desperately needed the support of government to buttress our fund-raising program. Major funding, not of a pound for pound, but of £8 or even £10 for £1 were optimistically mentioned. "That would be great," I told Brian Corby, "but there's a fundamental difference between our two organisations. We're about using the technology to revolutionise how learning takes place - to strengthen the home and the community through cooperation, whereas it seems the CTCs are about further redesign of schools, and setting individual schools against the local community."

"Leave it to me," said a confident Brian, "I can talk to both Baker and the permanent secretary at a CBI dinner next week."

"Be careful," I warned, "his officials will be well-briefed. They'll press technical questions on you."

Brian's confidence on this occasion was his downfall. Not only were there technical questions left hanging in the air, it was also pretty obvious that Baker could not make a link between our two different operations. But I, too, had made a technical mistake. I should not have left the negotiations to Brian. Slowly I was learning the difference between those issues that are best sorted out over dinner, and those that have to be hammered out around a conference table. Brian preferred the former style, while I knew that sometimes it was only the latter that would work.

I had one further chance of my own. A month later David Peake, then Chairman of Kleinwort Benson, and the man who had been instrumental in getting us one of our first grants in 1986, invited Baker to dinner with him. I was stuck between a rock and a hard place. I needed the money from the bank, urgently, in the short term. I also needed the support of the department and of Baker. Dinner was a quietly restrained, dignified affair in comfortable Georgian surroundings. The wines were excellent, as was the food. I, however, stuck to water for fear of muddling my argument. "If you don't mind going second, secretary of state, I think I'll ask John Abbott to speak first - alphabetical order and all that."

I kept my argument simple. "In a world of constant change, young people had to learn, from the earliest stages, how to take ever greater responsibility for their own learning. The skills of learning have to be made more explicit - everyone needed the highest possible ability in thinking, collaborating, communicating, and making decisions." I warmed to my task. Baker was making careful notes. "The new technologies of information and communication are trivialised if we simply see them as vocational skills. They're tools which will help all of us do many things we previously found hard, time-consuming and boring. The difference, I expect, between the secretary of state and myself, is that Education 2000 believes that this can transform the whole community, and significantly change the role of the school and the way learning actually takes place. Instead of locking up lots of technology in a school, or a college, we want to distribute it widely across the community. That is where so much powerful learning actually takes place."

Kenneth Baker then followed and would not allow himself to be drawn on the most profound question of all - just how do young people learn, and what was the contribution of technology towards that? We were both asked what it would cost. Baker talked of the £100 million, the majority of which would come from central government, needed to fund 14 City Technology Colleges. "At that scale," I argued, "Education 2000 could work in 50 towns the size of Letchworth. That's nearly a population of two million people. But it's more than that. If our plans are left to develop fully then our projects will be eventually self-sustaining. That, surely, makes it a good deal?"

The evening drew to a close. "I think we ought to meet privately, Mr Abbott. There's a lot that you and I should discuss," the minister said. As it happened it was the last time we were to meet, as a cabinet reshuffle would lead shortly to his becoming chairman of the Conservative Party. He had other fish to fry, and I guess was mightily relieved to be no longer responsible for the funding and setting up of the CTC movement. Yet, in retrospect, his promotion was the trust's loss. It was he who had invented the CTCs and it was he who struggled to promote them to industrial sponsors. More than any of his successors, he owned the idea, and if there was to be any accommodation with them in ways which might significantly modify them along the lines of Education 2000 thinking, it would have been Baker who would have understood this and could have fine-tuned accordingly. After all, he was a politician to the tip of his fingers. To subsequent ministers the CTCs were to become one of the givens and argument with them was to be largely fruitless. They couldn't understand my position because they had never, truly, worked out their own.

*     *     *

Of course I didn't know then what politics were to hold for me, and so I had welcomed Baker's offer of talks with open arms. The next few months were to be the biggest test of my resolution since joining the trust. Publicly it was clear the trust had captured the interest of ministers, and possibly of government in general, but not to the point of a public commitment. Without serious government support it was a yearly struggle to make certain we would have enough funds for the projects. We were dancing, as it were, around each other; the department for education, the city technology colleges, our sponsors, the local authorities. The mounting interest in the mechanism for schools to opt-out of authority control, and the exhaustion felt in all places from the Education Reform Act, exacerbated the situation. Like any suitor seeking a marriage with a good prospect, the trust had to look good and speak nicely, while never being certain if our suitor would finally make a serious commitment. I felt as if my facade were paper thin.

It was already April - two, or at the most three, months remained before fixing the budget for the coming year, and it didn't appear we'd receive any serious sort of government sponsorship. Brian Corby, as chairman, was preoccupied with extensive business re-organisation at the Prudential and wanted an easy compromise that would satisfy all of us for some time.

The first lesson of successful fund-raising, I knew, was not to appear to be in a hurry, yet on this occasion I had to hurry or the whole programme would grind to a halt. Presenting the best face I could, I worked behind the scenes to call up and talk to all our current sponsors, and ask them either for extra money, or a cash advance. Chiefly I had to show that we seemed to be getting closer to government, and admit openly that, without an offer of partnership funding we would never raise the full sums we needed from private sources. People respected my candour, but I knew I was in danger of mortgaging our future unless government soon came up with an offer.

It paid off to a limited extent. Old donors were helpful, and I was able to encourage the trustees that some major new private funders were likely to become involved, but most likely not until the autumn.

*         *         *

I then had to warn the Letchworth project that the funds for September would not be available at the scale anticipated and that nearly all the extra staff they had become so dependent upon in the first two years, would not even be able to have their contracts renewed. The schools were furious, and naturally associated my interest in developing the new projects and becoming distanced from fund-raising, as the main problem. That, inevitably, annoyed me. I was more than a fund-raiser. The trust needed more than a single project. However I could never express - even to the head teachers whom I knew so well - any lack of confidence in the trustees themselves. As the weeks passed, the heads saw that my suffering was as acute as theirs, and gradually I came to feel more comfortable in their company. My internal difficulties were to last for a further six months, during which time I could see the disastrous implications of having a chairman who, though totally committed to the ideas of the trust, was himself so over-committed as to leave me with a chaotic, and potentially lethal, management structure.

*         *         *

Many times business executives, or even executive officers of charitable foundations would say, "I want to support you very much, but I just can't write a short memo explaining such a massive change of mind-set for the benefit of my board. They would just not believe what I was saying. You're effectively rewriting the Western system of education. If you want money from us to do this, just you write the case ... in no more than one and a half pages of typescript." I came close to despair. Our Western model of education trains us to be so objective, to so reduce complicated issues to sub-components, and always to compare, contrast and compartmentalise, that educated people just can't grasp the big, interconnected issues. Many times educated people just can't see it. This is a real problem. Such people do not like being told that they have become too clever to see something that less educated people can grasp easily. I was later to learn that there may well be a neurological reason for this. The Salk Institute in San Diego issued a Constructivist Manifesto in early 1998 which argued that in terms of the brain "specialization may bring efficiency, but it comes at the expense of flexibility". If this proves to be true, that would mean that as education has created increasing numbers of specialists so we have narrowed the actual lens through which most people can view the world, problems and opportunities. We may have so limited our field of vision, that we have become blind to the total picture.

\*     \*     \*

This was the case the first time members of Her Majesty's Inspectorate (HMI) made an official visit to Letchworth. They said they did not want to meet with the project staff, or anyone outside the schools. "We know what you're trying to do. Our job is to see what's changed in the classrooms." At the end of three days they confessed to being baffled, and eventually came to see me. "Yes," they said, "Certainly there are some good teachers, with good lessons; we like what we see of the use of word processors in class, but we're obviously missing something. Much of the work being done by these pupils is being done outside the school, not as ordinary homework but in teams of youngsters helping each other. We don't know how to evaluate this; that's beyond our experience. Our job is to inspect what happens directly in a classroom and adjacent to this. We're not sure, either, how to evaluate your teacher development programmes; they're not systematically set up in ways we understand, yet the teachers are obviously much impressed." I smiled but refrained from quoting Einstein's famous line: "Not everything that counts can be counted; not everything that can be counted, counts."

One visitor was more perceptive. Paul Hamlyn, one of the country's most successful publishers, said, "I haven't been back to St Christopher's since the evening just before my 15th birthday, when my father took me away from the school before I was scheduled to be removed the next morning. I was unhappy in school - people were always trying to get me to do things in ways that didn't interest me. So I became bored. I quite understand why the teachers wanted to get rid of me. Instead of classroom lessons, my father, a refugee from Eastern Europe, put me to work learning the rudiments of the publishing trade. I've never looked back since because, you see, I always like seeing the total picture. I'm an inclusive thinker. I liked what I saw in the classrooms today ... that wouldn't have bored me, but I'm not sure it would have given me the skills that I use now. Nevertheless, I'll back you in anything you want to do in getting youngsters to know how to do things for themselves - particularly to understand how they can be more alert, positive and creative."

Paul Hamlyn was able to see more clearly than many a visiting educational expert. "It's terribly frustrating," said one official evaluator. "It's like trying to measure a bucketful of Scottish mist. One moment it's obviously there, then the next moment it's gone. Trouble is, like fog on the mountainside when you're lost, it's incredibly real but has no measurable substance."

"It's worse than that," another exclaimed. "I can't tell what's been achieved by Education 2000 and what might have been there in any case."

The teachers nearly tore their hair out. They were incredibly frustrated. "Can't these people see that this is exactly what should be happening? These ideas are transforming every action that we take. We don't teach separate Education 2000 lessons. These ideas percolate through everything. But," and here the teacher became progressively more reticent, "we don't know how much longer we can go on doing this. The regulations starting to come out from the Department of Education in London to support the new national curriculum look as if they'll drive education in exactly the opposite way to what Education 2000 - and we - are working towards. That would be a disaster. We think we could be running out of time."

\*             \*             \*

The following summer I took with me on holiday to Scandinavia a book, *Frames of Mind*, by Howard Gardner that had been so strongly recommended at the Colorado conference. It immediately seized my imagination. For nearly five years I had been so busy doing things (that's what the English think is work) that I'd not given myself space for serious study (often thought of as relaxation).

For years I had argued against the simplistic notion of intelligence as being reducible to a single numerical quotient on the basis of a battery of paper and pencil tests. I had seen the devastation this had caused amongst my own friends at school, when children had been given - publicly - a number and told that was where they were on the intelligence range. These were the numbers that traumatised people for life. They were the numbers that sent one child to one kind of school, another to something very different.

I had my own experience of being a competent woodcarver, and a de-skilled student of Latin to give me a valuable perspective on what Gardner was saying.

I knew - in a way that in my early years I could not have articulated - that I had a number of separate innate ways of doing things. Some of these I was good at - like solving practical problems, woodcarving, public speaking, and seeing connections - whilst others such as isolated private study, some forms of socialising and writing under pressure where I was nothing like as good as a number of other people I knew. To average all this out to a single quotient did not give a meaningful picture of me, or of my abilities.

"Over the course of evolution, human beings have come to possess a number of special-purpose information processing devices," wrote Gardner, which he then went on to describe. Gardner showed how he had identified certain essential traits that characterised an intelligence, and then how he had been able to identify seven distinct forms of intelligence: Linguistic (the ability to formulate thoughts in words); Logical/Mathematical; Spatial Intelligence (being the way we relate ourselves in space); Musical; Bodily-Kinaesthetic (being the ability to do things using one's body); Interpersonal Intelligence (being the ability to work with and understand other people); and finally, Intrapersonal Intelligence (being the ability to look deep within one's self and assess one's own thinking).

By the time I finished *Frames of Mind* - I was sitting beneath the Sibelius Monument in Helsinki - Gardner had set my mind racing along two parallel tracks. The first I had been but dimly aware of - that of intellectual predispositions towards doing things in certain preferred ways that our numerous ancestors had found helpful to their own survival. I was to learn more about this over the next ten years as the fields of evolutionary psychology and biology began coming into their own and started to add valuable insights into the biological nature of these inherited predispositions. I was a product of the 1960s. In as far as any of these topics had been discussed at university, they had been approached from a behaviouristic perspective. Each of us started life, according to this theory, with a blank slate of a mind. We were essentially shaped by our own life experience. We had inherited nothing from the past. *Frames of Mind* opened a whole new way, to me, of thinking about just how complex could be the combination of previous dispositions with which each of us have, uniquely, started our lives.

I was thrilled. I looked again at my sons and saw them as embryonic young men, encapsulating within their minds a unique range of frameworks for understanding their environments in at least these seven different ways, all of which our common ancestors had found useful in making sense of the world around them.

In making sense of their world, children often put us on the spot. Weeks after returning from Sweden on a wet, dull Saturday afternoon, we went to Cambridge, spending the last half hour before going home in Heffer's

Children's Bookshop. Peter came up to me with a book, the Usborne *Facts of Life, New Fully Illustrated Edition*. "Dad, will you buy this for me, it looks really interesting."

Anne nudged me. "Don't you dare, just you talk to him about it instead!" So inevitably I bought the book but on the strict understanding that he would not leave it around for his younger brothers to look at.

That night he took the book to bed and obviously read it through carefully. Some time later Anne went up to his room and brought the book down for us to look at together. We learnt a lot! But obviously not quite enough. Several days later he was in an uncharacteristically truculent and awkward mood. "Whatever's the matter with you?" I exclaimed.

"Don't you understand, Dad, my facts of life book tells me that when I go into puberty I'll have moods like this ... and it's up to my parents to understand me."

Teacher, teach thyself.

*          *          *

It was the writings of Peter Drucker that then became most significant to me. I had started to read his book *Innovation and Entrepreneurship*, almost as a cure for insomnia. It was in the early hours of the morning, in the hectic months of the summer of 1989, that I had the opportunity to read it closely. It was, of course, so exciting that it banished away all ideas of sleep. On one such morning I began to read: "The entrepreneur always searches for change, responds to it, and exploits it as an advantage." I knew that to be true for myself. That was what I had sensed for years. That was why I had seen such opportunities within word processing to change the way classroom practice was organised. But I honestly had not thought of myself as an entrepreneur; I was a school teacher determined to improve children's opportunities. There was something brash about the concept of entrepreneur that jarred with my conventional background. But that was just what I was becoming, it seemed to me, an educational entrepreneur. Were there others, I wondered to myself, who were looking at change in education as an advantage, not something to be tamed or moulded or fought against?

I read on with increasing interest. Here was someone who seemed to know the path I was walking, and whose footsteps could help shape mine. Strange, I thought, Peter Drucker is not an educationalist; his book was not even on the education shelves in the bookstore, but in the business management section. My excitement mounted several early mornings later, as I came towards the last chapter. "In an entrepreneurial society, individuals face a tremendous challenge, a challenge they need to exploit as an opportunity: the need for continuous learning and re-learning. An entrepreneurial society challenges habits and assumptions of schooling and learning. In traditional society ... learning came to an end with adolescence... In an entrepreneurial society individuals will have to learn new things well after they have become adults. The implications of this are that individuals will increasingly have to take responsibility for their own continuous learning and re-learning, for their own self-development, and their own careers".

I put the book down. It was already past four o'clock in the morning. Peter Drucker, a man I had never met, a man older than my own mother, living in far away California, was formalising what I had learned from my father, from old Mr McFadgen, from Donald O'Sullivan - and from many others who never ever thought of themselves as being educators. Successful, purposeful people, who knew how to stand on their own two feet, and who helped children to do the same. What I had been saying needed to happen in the Projects was more important than even I had seen if the existing system was to change from the bottom up. I was not sure that many people realised this, despite the language they used. If our Projects were to succeed, they would have to challenge the status quo and I knew that conventional school types were not good at doing this. Schools and teachers would have to change quite fundamentally, so would the community. Talking about such issues was easy - academics did it month after month in endless conferences, but actually doing something about it was immensely harder. I did not think people in the projects understood this as yet, at least not at the profound level that Peter Drucker was proposing, or that had been suggested in that discussion I had had years before with Brother Patrick in County Tipperary about the doctrine of subsidiarity.

A few months later Drucker published *The New Realities* in which he analysed the meaning of the Knowledge Society. In a section entitled From Teaching to Learning Drucker wrote, "We now know how people learn. We now know that learning and teaching are not two sides of the same coin. They are different." What can be taught has to be taught, he went on to say, and will not be learned otherwise, but what can be learned must be learned ... different people learn differently. Indeed learning is as personal as fingerprints - no two people learn exactly alike. Each has a different speed, a different rhythm, a different attention span. If an alien speed, rhythm or attention span is imposed on the learner, there is little or no learning; there is only fatigue and resistance.

I scribbled in my diary. "Fascinating; Drucker is saying, from his own experience in business - which seems close to my own way of thinking - almost exactly what Gardner is saying from the basis of neurology and applied psychology. One from the base of observed industrial processes over seventy or more years, the other from clinical testing at Harvard over a dozen years." I remembered wondering if the two men had ever talked together. I checked the bibliographies each gave. It appeared they hadn't; at least they didn't acknowledge a connection. "That's strange," I thought to myself that night, "because knowing what the two of them say I'm now much stronger, and far more confident about what I'm doing than ever I was before. If other people had this knowledge, and were able to draw such ideas together, how much more informed would be our thinking," I pondered. Then I went back to bed and slept soundly.

                    *              *              *

In January David Hancock, the permanent secretary at the Department of Education, with whom I had spent much time and who seemed broadly supportive of our ideas, retired. I would have to start again with his successor, John Caines, as the new permanent secretary. "He's an intelligent Wykamist," I was told by several people, "a very successful civil servant." "I know him reasonably well," Pat Limerick explained to me one evening, "we used to work together at ODA (Overseas Development Agency)."

Some six weeks after his appointment Pat arranged for us to have a sandwich lunch with Caines so that I could start to cover the issues I had often spoken about with his predecessor. Caines was civilised, courteous, and polite, but I quickly realised that he had no way of relating to what I was saying. It was outside his own experience. Even more important, it was outside his way of thinking about things. Whereas I was eclectic in my thought processes, he was essentially objective, reductionist and highly analytical. I suspect he believed in the perfectibility of the system about as much as I didn't.

"Before we started talking this afternoon I had wondered if it might have been better to move your project to that part of the department dealing with school/industry links, but now I realise you're better left in the section dealing with information technology," he said as he sought to summarise our discussion. I started to remonstrate, "Surely we belong to neither? If we belong anywhere it should be in the section of the Department dealing with the nature of learning, and the relationship of learning to human development?"

"There is no need for such a sub-section within the department," he replied magisterially, "learning is what happens when people are well taught."

Further remonstration was useless. We did not fit into any existing pigeonhole within the department's way of thinking. We were, I was fast coming to understand, challenging the whole system. I felt physically weak and intellectually inadequate for the task. I thought of the enthusiasm of the ordinary individuals in Letchworth, and of others in the aspiring projects. I would fail them if I could not explain all this better to those who designed and implemented the framework within which we were all supposed to work. The new permanent secretary was certainly not a natural ally to our work, yet in his response he had shown me more vividly than anyone else the inflexibility of departmental thinking. I ought to have known then just how inert was the system I was up against.

\*　　　\*　　　\*

The new minister of education was John MacGregor, previously minister for Agriculture and Fisheries. Some four months after his appointment, Brian Corby and I had an hour long meeting with him and his advisors. They were well briefed and their questions were predictable focusing on matter-of-fact type considerations such as, "How many computers are needed?" "How much time did teachers need to learn how to use a computer in a classroom?" "What arrangements had to be made to enable ordinary classes to continue when individual teachers were involved in some form of work shadowing in industry?"

"What is it that is unique to Education 2000 that we can see and measure separately from everything else?" asked one of the classically trained advisors.

"You can't," I said, "and we would be failing if that were the case."

"What do you mean? That's hard for us to appreciate," retorted another of the advisors.

"It's pretty straightforward. The school system is made up of many separate bits and pieces - programmes, courses, primary and secondary schools, colleges, etc. - which have fitted together in the past to make some form of recognisable structure. Now that structure is no longer as appropriate as it once was and needs to be redesigned. The old bits need to be fitted together in a different way to perform a new function. At this stage, as we try to fit disjointed pieces more firmly together, what we need is some good cement. Think of Education 2000 as being like a barrow-load of cement; of itself it has no strength, but when used to combine blocks of different shapes in a new way, it can bind them into something strong and purposeful. Regard that analogy with the cement as being more to do with the new philosophy - the staff training, the approach to learning - than the provision of extra resources such as the new computers. Simply put, Education 2000 is an idea which gives powerful substance to a new way of building things."

I stopped and looked around the room. Had I completely lost my audience? Thankfully MacGregor took the point, the analogy was easily recognised by a man who represented a rural constituency in Norfolk, but the advisors were largely confused, and I think slightly annoyed. Ministerial meetings were to clarify policy, and agree details - not to talk metaphysics.

My strategy worked, at least to a limited extent. During the next year we were to get a government grant towards our central costs ... a grant of all of £40,000 a year out of an agreed budget of 15 times that size. I would have to adjust what I said in future, and in saying that we were getting some limited support from government, hope that no one would ask just how limited this was. Forty thousand pounds per annum did not stack up to a demonstration of real interest when set alongside the many millions of government money that went into the CTCs.

Not for the first, or the last, time, was I to envy people whose jobs were to blast the old wall to pieces, good bits and all, and in the name of progress argue for funds to start building from scratch.

# 11
# I Can is More Important Than IQ

One of the people who had been at the CBI had been Sir Douglas Haig. Douglas had been personal adviser on financial affairs to Margaret Thatcher in the years just before, and just after, she became leader of the Conservative party. He was a man of firm opinions, but optimistic in his view of mankind who, as the Thatcher political dogma worked itself out, found himself further and further from the centre of power. But he was still well connected and when he heard what I was advocating, offered to help us focus the attention of policy-makers on such ideas.

"You have to ensure that the prime minister and her advisers understand the full implications of what you're saying. Your idea is actually more radical, in its truest sense, than present Conservative policy. You're talking about a system of education that would create enterprising people; people who don't need a system to tell them what to do. Unless government is careful in its zeal to reform it will over-legislate, and become far too prescriptive. What you're talking about would create different communities, communities that would want to take control of their own futures, because their futures matter to them, not because government tells them to do so. That is the essence of what I think basic Conservatism in the future should be all about, but it's devilishly difficult to implement, and hardly fits the dogma of any political party."

"Let me help you broaden the appeal of what you're saying," said Douglas over lunch one afternoon shortly afterwards at the Athenaeum, the ultimate seat of the British academic and ecclesiastical establishments. "I could draw together a good cross-section of influential people for a long week-end, and you could invite them to take over your agenda and make the whole concept far more broadly based. Then it would be more likely that government would listen."

Douglas proposed an impressive list of people whom he was prepared to invite to Templeton College Oxford, which he had helped to found some years before. I prepared my case carefully. John Banham, the director general of the CBI, was there; so was the head master of Harrow; the professor of education from Cambridge came; as did several corporate CEOs, and a chief education officer. The director of the Economic Social Research Council was represented, and a number of second-tier civil servants from a number of major departments also attended. We had invited Bill Clinton, then governor of Arkansas and chairman of the Education Commission of the States, but he had written back at some length saying he could only make it if we changed the date.

I was flattered by the interest, and tried to appear confident throughout the proceedings, but that was hard. These people were all over the place in their thinking. They were strong on talking, but did not seem to hear those ideas that could lead to a revision of some of their own assumptions. They were preoccupied with trying to show how such ideas could be accommodated within current legislation. It was almost as if, whenever a new thought was produced, each academic was somehow on trial to prove that their department, their organisation, their school, had already fitted this in to their existing programmes. There was no sign of a new broad overall vision. My experience should have prepared me to realise that academics easily allow themselves to become stuck within existing frameworks; their training reinforces their innate conservatism, reinforced by tenure, institutional prestige and the concerns of immediate detail. It was all very English. Polite, well written, and non-contentious, and frighteningly complacent.

Just after that meeting I sent the following memo to Brian Corby; it expressed my feelings exactly. "The trust, or somebody, has just got to be able to start thinking seriously about the issue of from teaching to learning. Currently I don't see where the intellectual leadership for this will come from. It's certainly not amongst the educationalists in our projects, nor within the trust's council, and I haven't yet picked it up amongst any of the educationalists that I've talked to in the country at large. Unless we - Education 2000 - get this right, then the country as a whole will build it's entire education reform movement on the wrong foundations, and we will continue to lurch from partial solution to another. Just look at what is happening in the official Education Reform programme. Look at the incredible emphasis that is now being put on examinations in single subject disciplines, and the unquestioned assumption that children who know a lot of material in separate subjects will, in some mysterious way, develop transferable skills that will help them deal with uncertainty and ambiguity when moving into areas of knowledge of which they have no first-hand experience. Creativity is not developed like this. I sense disaster. I actually feel very lonely".

*        *        *

A week later I drove to Brighouse in West Yorkshire to argue on behalf of the Calderdale project for a grant of £150,000 a year towards the cost of training teachers to develop electronic conferences on the new computer equipment donated to Education 2000 by Digital. If I were successful the money could be granted by the newly established government funded Training and Enterprise Council. It turned out to be a memorable drive as I was able to listen to the news reports which, minute by minute, recorded the demise of Margaret Thatcher's last hours as prime minister; of her visit to Buckingham Palace to offer her resignation, and of John Major's visit some hours later to accept the Queen's offer to form a government.

Like so many others I was anxious to know what effect these leadership changes would have on education, and on ourselves. They would not be good. In effect the deal within the Conservative party appeared to represent a trade-off between the moderates and the right wing of the party. As John Major was to become prime minister, so education and its secretary were to move farther to the political right. John McGregor was replaced by Kenneth Clarke, previously at the department of health, where he had nearly finished pushing through a major reform of the administration of the National Health System. Accountability, and cost effectiveness were to him basic concepts. It was rumoured that he was not happy at having to move departments.

My first encounter with the new government took place a few weeks after Major took office. As I was busy preparing the papers for the second Templeton Conference, now a week away, the phone rang. It was John Banham. Although we are virtually the same age, I still felt a touch of anxiety when talking with John, as he seemed to move so naturally in a world in which I was still not at ease. "This is great news, John," he enthused down the phone. "I know John Major well and Kenneth Clarke even more so. I can personally go and talk to both of them as soon as we have our recommendations from Templeton. This is important, really important. What we say will be taken notice of at the highest level ... things will start moving now."

\*         \*         \*

We settled down to work at Templeton with enthusiasm. This would be time well spent we told each other. At long last, I thought, we might have the opportunity to make an impact. As with so many other groups around the country a change of prime minister, and a significant cabinet reshuffle, was an opportunity that we had to exploit with great care.

Douglas Haig asked me to open with a speech to set the pace for the recommendations that would eventually be made. I again made the critical point:

"My own experience, over a dozen years as a head master, centres on my dismay at the impact of secondary education on children who come out of good Plowden-type experiential learning primary schools. In my experience far too many bright-eyed, enthusiastic 11 year-olds, fired up to continue their learning, find their enthusiasm dulled by five or more years of the secondary system. Bright eyes give way to opaque, and involvement in what they are doing - and the responsibility that goes with that - is being replaced by a sense of confusion as to what learning is all about.

Schooling simply gets in the way. Personal responsibility shifts to a dependence upon the teacher to tell young people what the teacher thought they needed to do. Frequently an embryonic love affair with learning is replaced within five years by an alienation from learning. The concept of producing generations of lifelong learners seems pretty insubstantial in most places. I fear that the directive and prescriptive nature of the national curriculum is making this worse, not better.

"In the pecking order that the English love to establish, tertiary education is held in higher regard than secondary, and secondary higher than primary ... with nursery education being seen as an extended form of baby minding. Surely this is all the wrong way around?

If we are talking about the creation of generations of young people who have learned how to manage their own learning, then presumably the task of the schools is to so structure this activity that progressively they *wean* the student away from dependence on the teacher? If so, then surely there are enormous implications for staffing levels and learning resources? Should not the junior years of primary school be staffed more generously, with staffing levels actually falling off in the upper years of secondary education? In my notes of the time I see that I heavily underscored the word "wean." It was the first time that I used the expression "weaning" in public to set out a new purpose for education emerging from a better understanding of the evolutionary sciences. It was November 30, 1990.

The day before the conference had started I had myself prepared a two-page summary of what I believed was the necessary statement that needed to be made. It was direct and simple. There was just one point, and it was the lead paragraph.

"The seminar at Templeton College endorsed a proposal that a select number of communities (places which have a strong sense of internal cohesion and strong local leadership) should be encouraged to explore these issues in depth, and to challenge the normal structures through which education has conventionally been delivered. Developments tested in a number of communities would then be made available for national replication."

Such test communities would need to tease out three management issues:

1. Shifting the focus of the teacher's role from that of instructor to that of manager of learning, poses significant managerial issues to every teacher. Managing schools where

every teacher will undertake such responsibilities, and where increasingly the resources opened to the pupils are more broadly based than those traditionally under the control of schools, calls for managerial skills of a higher order than hitherto. Equally, the concept of all the schools working together to respond to the community's aims and aspirations, challenges the schools to manage their resources collectively as well as individually. Eventually the program has to be able to manage the alternative development of resources and effectively distribute these.

2. The introduction of new information and communication technologies, on such a scale that all pupils would have access to them, would require skilled and careful management. Essentially all teachers would have to be helped to a position in which they find the technology so helpful to themselves that they wish to find ways of passing these opportunities on to their pupils. Such a high level of confidence takes much time to build, and is dependent upon team building, and support strategies that are almost unknown in previous models of school management. Extensive staff development programs are required to create ever richer learning environments.

3. The opportunities created through the use of information technology and other learning resources, together with the development of opportunities for learning in the community, will pose far reaching questions as to how the prescribed structure of the curriculum can best be developed coherently across all the subjects. While subject disciplines will remain a suitable classification for content, and specific subject skills for at least the near future, the focus will have to shift towards the better development of learning techniques, intellectual and social, which will be necessary to go across all conventional subjects and beyond. Traditional structures in the organisation of schools, such as the timetable, will inevitably undergo major changes, if they are to serve the needs of the developing, learning-centred culture.

In the closing stages of the discussions I circulated this paper and suggested that this might be a helpful summary. People were tired and I had blundered because they suspected that I was trying to hijack the meeting. If this was what I wanted to say then why had we all bothered to meet in the first place? It might have been a clearly worked out statement, but it was not the statement reached by the seminar. Eventually it was agreed that John Banham's paper should go directly to Kenneth Clarke, and the shorter paper written by the professional writer should go to the prime minister. We were moving into big-time political considerations. I could use my paper, it was suggested, at a later stage when we got into formal meetings.

*             *             *

In the days that followed discussion as to what needed to happen became ever more clouded by political considerations. Brian Corby, never one to ignore the excitement of high level meetings with ministers and prime ministers, felt that - as he was the ultimate boss of both John Banham and myself - it should be he who met Kenneth Clarke and hopefully the prime minister, even though he had not been at the seminar. He should, he said, be accompanied by John Banham as "it is his contact in the first place and there are CBI issues that also have to be represented." As the conference had been convened by Douglas Haig he, of course, would have to be involved as well.

I could hardly believe what was happening. A meeting with Kenneth Clarke at the department of education was set up for early in January. "If there are more than three of us it will be difficult for the minister to cope," Brian eventually said. "John, you've briefed us so well that it won't be necessary for you to come. You're the ultimate developer and manager of the ideas, and inevitably the administrator of the whole program. Your moment will come in a big way when we've secured the opening you need."

I was horror-struck. So was the department when they learned who would be putting our case to the minister. So was the Inspectorate. "Let me have a copy of your short paper," said a cryptic voice from Elizabeth House over the phone, "and I'll see if I can get that incorporated into the minister's brief. But we are worried, for your sake. This is the trust's big opportunity. No one can speak to these issues with anything like the understanding you bring. Whatever you do, use all your power to get yourself into that meeting. These people could lose you your best opportunity." Brian was not only my chairman, he was also the trust's largest benefactor. He was a man whom I respected for the warmth of his personality and his unwavering support for me. But in this instance I just could not move him. The stakes for everyone were too high. Brian was going to go his own way, and I was going to have to pick up the pieces afterwards.

*         *         *

Peter, now aged 11, finished at his primary school that summer. We had been fortunate in the quality of direction that his school received from its headmistress, Di Pickover, a woman personally and professionally committed to all those strategies that Plowden had advocated 25 years earlier. She continuously emphasised the child's developing skills, and insisted that children should take ever more responsibility for monitoring their own progress. She had an amazing empathy with children, and could bring out in even the most truculent and unhappy child abilities that no one else could see. Her fault, however, was that she consistently underestimated how much explanation of her style and her educational policy she ought to extend to parents at a time when government was pushing for a very different approach to learning. Tragically this was to make her position untenable a few years later. But under her, Peter thrived in a school staffed largely by teachers with similar ideas and convictions.

The accepted wisdom in Hitchin - good middle class town that it is - was that children thought likely to succeed at secondary school would automatically transfer either to the old boys' or to the old girls' grammar schools which is exactly how the town still thought of them even though both had been reorganised into comprehensive schools at the same time as Stevenage nearly 20 years before. They retained uniforms and all the other trappings of the earlier selective schools. Those people with less ambition, and possibly daunted by the perceived pressures of academic life, went to the one-time secondary modern school built in the more working class part of the town. It was like Stevenage all over again but several years later. Neither Anne nor I would have any truck with this. We wanted Peter to gain from what had started to happen in Letchworth, and so he - and a few others who were transferring that year as well - caught the bus each morning and went up the hill to Letchworth to attend Fearnhill School, one of the four state schools in the project. Though most of the sponsorship from Education 2000 which had galvanised teacher development programs had ceased the year before, the impact that this had made on Fearnhill had been enormous.

Peter, having been used to a computer at home since he was eight, stepped into all the opportunities that could be afforded by a school which was integrating technology into its curriculum in ways which stretched the pupils' imagination. Having recently installed a modem at home he was one of the first 11 year-olds to start accessing the school data system from home, and became an avid contributor to a variety of electronic conferences through the Ebenezer system. Electronic messaging became common place to him and his friends, who wrote reviews on books they read and deposited these electronically into the school library retrieval system.

"It's a fine system," said the librarian. "Look at this. I can immediately see which and how many books Peter has taken out of the library in his first year - 89, not quite a record." Had I taken out 89 books in all the years I had been in school? I doubted it.

"It's much more than numbers, though," the librarian continued, "take a look at this." She pulled up a title of one of the books Peter had read. "Here's the two-paragraph review he wrote. Look at this now. I can see how many of the other children have read that review; it's 110. Now, look. Not all of them agreed. Read that. There's the comment of someone who thinks he's been too generous in his assessment of the main character."

The librarian was excited at what all this could mean in building up children's reading skills. "The most important aspect of all this is the way the computer has increased the number of non-fiction books taken out of the school libraries. Not just ours, but in the other five schools in the town as well. The number of book withdrawals has gone up by some 300 per cent in the past two years. It's a case of opportunity creating a new demand. We now have over 100 computers in this school, and every one of them can access the lists of all the books in the library. A child coming to the end, say of a French lesson, and with a few minutes left before going home, goes into the system, sees that there is still a book available on Napoleon which might help in her history homework. So, with a careful eye on her watch, she hurries down to the library as soon as school ends to get the book out before rushing to catch the school bus. Before this she just wouldn't even have bothered."

Over the next few terms I watched Peter develop his own variation on the electronic conferencing system. He and a friend achieved what at the time seemed the ultimate form of collaboration - the use of the conference system to create an on-line project report. Peter phoned William, who lived a few miles away in the country. The two of them set the parameters by agreeing to go into the same space on the computer system at the same time. As Peter started to type in his thoughts so William saw them come up simultaneously on his own computer screen; then William started to add his own ideas, and then they started to move their ideas around. Then they flashed questions to each other on the screen. Later that evening both had a printed copy of their joint conversation. They were just twelve. This was when the Internet was solely used by academics. Peter's was the first generation to be computer literate and Peter, not being able to rely on me for any explanation of things technological, was self-taught. He was so good eventually that David, and later Tom, came to be over-dependent on him to sort out their problems. One night there was much shouting in the study and a furious Peter came out to the kitchen. "It's not fair. Whenever David gets stuck on the computer he asks me for help. If I give him all the answers he'll never work it out for himself. That's how I had to learn. That's what he needs to do now. If I give him the answers each time he'll never learn." Many a professor of education could not have explained it more clearly.

                              *              *              *

In the New Year I tried to get some clarity into the thinking that would be presented at the meeting with Kenneth Clarke. None of my three colleagues - the director of the CBI, the chief executive of the Prudential and the one-time financial advisor to Margaret Thatcher - liked being told what to think, and certainly not what it was that they should say. John Banham was touchy both with me, and indirectly with Brian who he suspected was making the role of president too executive. Douglas Haig, a mild mannered but consummate string-puller, was unsure whether Brian's understanding of the issues was strong enough to be in such an important position; after all he had not even been at the seminar. As far as I was concerned, I was conscious that none of them had ever been a school teacher, nor had their lives intimately inter-connected with young people on an intensive basis. To me their conversations seemed utterly unreal; theoretical, bureaucratic and distant from the day-to-day concerns of teachers and young people. The opportunity, if only we could capture it, was enormous - just what the trust had been working towards for the past four years. Now, however there was the real possibility that well-meaning people might mess it all up. My problem seemed to be growing by the hour.

The three of them met with the minister and his advisors for just over an hour on the 28 January. Brian had promised to phone that evening. "It was something of a non-event," Brian said picking his words carefully and I thought with some embarrassment, "you'll need to talk to the minister's advisors yourself to emphasise in detail what's needed. We've opened the door for you." He sounded embarrassed and had little more to say. My heart sank. I heard nothing from either John or Douglas.

"The minister was not sure what the three men were asking for," I was told politely the next afternoon by a departmental official, "and the minister was certainly confused as to what was the relationship of Education 2000 to the Templeton Group and to the CBI."

I was vastly disappointed, but little surprised. If grown men could not get this properly clarified amongst themselves, what were the chances of ever getting the department to appreciate that new forms of learning would challenge so many of the conventional assumptions that underpin current institutional arrangements for schooling?

There was just one glimmer of hope that I could recover the ground that had been lost in the meeting. I had heard two days previously that my paper, the one I had prepared in advance of the Templeton Seminar, had actually got through to the new head of the policy unit in Downing Street. Maybe, just maybe, someone there would pick it up and see its significance.

"Let's hope so," said people in the various projects. "It's not that we want government to dominate in any of the programs. The exact opposite. But the amount of money that we'll need to carry out all these ideas, and to develop them to such a stage that we can make the transformation self-sustaining, is so great that without strong endorsement from government, sponsors will never, ever, take this seriously enough."

\*    \*    \*

That February, while waiting impatiently to hear from Downing Street, I flew to Orlando, Florida to give a lecture to a conference of American secondary school principals. Two long flights, and some down time at the conference gave me an opportunity to catch up on further reading. I had, some weeks before, been encouraging head teachers in Hertfordshire to think about the concept of multiple intelligences, but had been dismayed to find so little interest in exploring the implications. I had in my mind David's comment about life in secondary school: "I can work on my own, Daddy, but it doesn't seem as natural as working in a group." And I had linked this with a fascinating piece of writing of several years before - *The Age of the Smart Machine* by Shosha Zuboff in which she had written: "Learning is not something which requires time out from productive activity; learning is the heart of productive activity."

Is it possible, I was starting to say to myself, that each of us now, in the late twentieth century, is equipped with a brain that was shaped by practices that our numerous ancestors had found useful? Perhaps these, in turn, shaped our own predispositions to do things in particular ways, far more than I had ever realised? If this were true, might it not also suggest that, if we tried to do things in ways that ran counter to our natural inclinations, we would be forever frustrated? How much were we shaped by our evolutionary past?

I thought back to *Frames of Mind*. It seems that over the course of evolution, human beings have come to possess a number of special purpose information processing devices. Just how these work we certainly don't yet know, but the fact that they give us a "biological predisposition" to be more effective in working in some ways rather than in others, now seemed indisputable to me.

In Cambridge, I picked out two very different books to read on the plane. One was a reprint of a book that I had read at university while doing research 25 years before; it was by the historian Peter Laslett, *The World We Had Lost*. In this, Laslett explained that before the industrial revolution, nearly everyone lived, worked and learned in units of no more than 12 or 13 people - the baker's shop, the farm, the ship, the haulage business. However when the requirements of economic life or technology required a working group different in size and constitution to the working family there was a significant discontinuity. People found this hard to manage. There seemed to be something significant for humans at the scale of 11, 12 or 13 people. A psychologist once told me that no one is ever likely to grieve for more than 12 people in a lifetime. It was as if that was the ceiling beyond which our hearts don't break anymore. We have 11 people in a cricket or a soccer team. Twelve people in a jury. There were 12 apostles. There are 15 people on a rugby team, and 11 on a soccer team.

Are we, I wondered, preconditioned to work most effectively in groups of a size which seem to have served our ancestors well? Even amongst the most primitive tribes in the Brazilian jungle, if the group gets beyond 12 or 14 fighting men (with women, children and dependent relatives that means a group of 50 or 60 people), it either divides of its own peaceful volition, or it splits through bloody rivalry. So why do we, in our "enlightened" post-industrial age, put children of five or six into classes of 30, 35 or even more? Wasn't this a discontinuity on a massive scale?

It was in this mood that I first started to read *The Fifth Discipline*. Peter Senge's opening paragraph excited me. It was almost as if I were involved in uncovering an increasing number of clues in a detective story. I read: "From an early age we are taught to break apart problems, to fragment the world. This apparently makes complex tasks and subjects more manageable, but we pay a hidden, enormous price. We can no longer see the consequences of our actions; we lose our intrinsic sense of connection to a larger whole." I thought of that awful meeting I had had with the permanent secretary several months previously. He could only function through thinking in terms of putting people into prescribed pigeonholes. He had no framework for handling ideas that went across the general picture. If you were not of a size to go into a pigeonhole you were either cut into pieces, or ignored.

I read on with mounting interest, trying not to ignore the stewardesses' persistent attempts to make sure I enjoyed the lavish lunch. "Real learning gets to the heart of what it means to be human. Through learning we recreate ourselves. Through learning we become able to do something we were never able to do before. Through learning we perceive the world and our relationship to it. Through learning we extend our capacity to create, it is part of the generative process of life. There is within each of us a deep hunger for this type of learning." Senge quoted Bill O'Brien of Hanover Insurance, "[The hunger for this type of learning] is as fundamental to the human being as the sex drive."

I was only 14 pages into the book, but already the significance of Senge's thinking hit me. Powerful thoughts were coming at me from every direction. What I had sensed many years before, and what I had tried to express so weakly in my feasibility study of 1984, were coming through from many other sources, but in language that I was not familiar with. Yet, I saw that it all fitted together, and while I had by no means all the pieces in place - indeed I hadn't even turned many of them the right way up yet - it was beautifully illustrative of what I had been trying to say at the Templeton Seminar. With such material as this we could construct a far more compelling case than just building our argument on what evidence we could collect from the expensive projects that we were struggling so hard to support.

With time to spare that evening in New York, I headed for one of the world's best and largest bookstores, Barnes and Noble on Fifth Avenue at 18th Street. Timorously I made my way into the section on neurobiology. Here were titles so abstract that I nearly gave up my quest. Fortunately I persevered, because it was there that I found Sir John Eccles' book, *The Brain and Creativity*. He was a Nobel prize winner and lived a few hundred yards from the bookstore I normally visited in Cambridge, England but it was my lot to read his work for the first time late at night in a New York Hotel.

Initially, it was the picture of the bone with the inscription of the moons phases etched on it some 30,000 years ago that first caught my imagination. Then I started to read; I had to skip certain sections as being beyond my technical understanding, but I kept on reading well into the night with all traces of jet-lag completely vanished. For the first time I started to understand the significance of CAT scans and functional MRI. Nowhere had I read anything like this. At no time had I come across an educationalist who, in looking to understand the nature of learning and what makes us human, had ever sought to understand the brain at the level of its functional complexity. As I read more, and thought of the other things that I had recently read, it started to become blindingly obvious that if we did not understand the true nature of how humans learnt, no wonder we have dysfunctional schools.

\*              \*              \*

Shortly after returning from Florida I met John Mills, the education specialist at the Policy Unit in Downing Street. He could not have been more affable, supportive and encouraging. "The issues you raise are too important for us to ignore, given John Major's specific interest in education." He went on to comment that all the reforms currently proceeding at government level needed to be infused with a far greater sense of mission and excitement. "The prime minister is looking for initiatives and schemes which might help demonstrate just that," he said. He was remarkably frank, and it was easy to talk of the difficulties of being stuck between the interests of the education authority on one side and of central government on the other. He offered specific help. "The department must be helped to recognise the potential of all that you're talking about. I understand you're to meet shortly with Kenneth Clarke. I'll suggest to the prime minister that he prepare the way with Ken Clarke by whetting his appetite for what an idea such as this could achieve."

Mills then made a most unusual request. Could I prepare a speech for the prime minister to deliver that would say all the things that Education 2000 was advocating? It was a fantastic opportunity. What would be the effect on the nation if John Major were to be seen making all this his own personal crusade? I looked at Mills carefully. Yes, he was being serious; this was for real. "Let me have the speech within the next ten days, as the prime minister wants to lead on issues that will involve the whole community and the significance of new technologies." These are issues, John Mills went on to say, which the prime minister could invite other significant people to take up with him. "It's my job," Mills had concluded, "to put up schemes in ways which the prime minister can make them happen. So, help me with a possible speech ... and let's see if we can make this happen." The crowds outside Downing Street may have wondered just why I was grinning all over my face as I left and went out into Whitehall.

\*        \*        \*

I had no time for self-indulgence as that evening I left for Leuven in Belgium where I was to participate with a number of cognitive scientists at a NATO advanced seminar. As luck would have it I was able to make my presentation on the first day and then slipped away to my funny little room on the third floor of the typical late nineteenth century small town European hotel in which I was billeted. It was indeed small, and the woodwork much over painted. The wash basin taps were of Edwardian design. The basin itself was cracked and chipped, and - of course - there was no waste plug. The windows with heavy exterior shutters, were large and faced on to the grey granite walls of the town prison just across the street. There was no space for a table or a chair so I sat, my back up against a heavily carved bed head and tried to think like a prime minister. I excused myself from several of the other presentations, and got up early each morning to write further. I tried to merge a description of the way we had done things in the projects with the heady language I had heard in Florida and with the solid reading I had done over the past year. I wanted to find words for John Major to use that would catch contemporary imagination and given the country something to aim for. "Wake up everybody," I wanted the prime minister to say, "learning is far too important just to be left to the schools to do in isolation. We all have to be involved. Streets that are unsafe for children to play on are as much a measure of failed educational policy, as are classrooms with burnt out teachers."

After hours of scribbling, and the steady accumulation of torn up pieces of paper   some of which blew out of the window and fluttered across to the prison yard opposite - I had a speech. I tried it on my colleagues on the last night, putting a prime ministerial authority behind the words. Part of it went like this:

"I have a dream ... to turn Britain into a Land of Learners.

"Flexibility is the key to a nation's prosperity. Our citizens need to be confident of their ability to learn new skills, and explore new situations. This calls for fundamental changes in the way in which we as individuals view education, in the role which we expect schools to play, and in the relationship between teachers and the taught.

"These changes have already started. Good schools - and we have many more than the media will normally acknowledge - encourage children to want to learn, to explore relationships, to become inquisitive, to treat the world as their expanding oyster. They become excited and motivated. Learning is their thing. They become hungry for more. At a young age they feel a sense of personal responsibility for their own learning. They are set for success early in life. More than that, they are the nation's best investment in the future.

"Too many children, however, never achieve that sense of ownership; for them education is something done to them. School is a place where they go to be taught. They are passive, and uninvolved. The teacher operates a system that the child but dimly comprehends. Conformity rather than inquisitiveness; dependency rather than responsibility, are the outcomes. The child is uncertain and fearful of change; the status quo is to be defended at all costs.

"The Learning Society of which I speak cannot be created by government diktat alone. As individuals we have to rediscover in ourselves a belief in learning, and recognise that, collectively and individually, it is learning which enables us to evolve, and so avoid the fate of the dodo.

"Like the proverbial horse, no outsider could force it to drink against its will, so too learning has to be encouraged from within. Some of you probably found this easy; many of us however certainly did not. Many have assumed that this is not for them and turned their backs on ever considering learning again, and too much of that becomes a national disaster.

"Learning depends on motivation. ("I know it's going to help me; I want it ... so I'll stick at it"). Learning and self-esteem are interconnected. Out of this partnership comes confidence, and confidence can become an unstoppable acquisition. Our young people go to school to learn how to structure, handle and reflect upon information. Knowledge and ideas in isolation are of little value.

"Young people need much encouragement to practice these skills in a variety of real settings if they are to become proficient. Progressively, as the child grows in years and intellect, they need to be weaned from their dependence on the school, on the teacher, and move out into the community. This concept of weaning seems to me to be important if we are to ensure that, by the age of 18 (or hopefully 16) every child is to walk away from school feeling ready for a lifetime of learning managed by himself.

"It is curious, when you look at our schools, to note that the largest class sizes are in the early years of Primary education, and the smallest are in the final years of the sixth form. Should it not be the other way round?

"Despite valiant attempts by educationalists, bureaucrats - yes, and politicians - it has proved impossible over more than a century to create schools that can do all these things in isolation from the rest of the country. The harsh lesson, which we have taken far too long to learn, is that quality education is as dependent upon the support of individuals within the community, as it is upon what can happen in the schools. Frankly, unless young people are surrounded by adults - parents and other adults - who value learning and strive to apply this, then the messages of school are rapidly lost. Happy is the child whose parents are also learners.

"Think about life in our homes. Technological and economic change have won back many of the hours which earlier generations had to spend in the factory. We have, gradually, reallocated this time. The average family now spends as much time watching television each week as children spend in school lessons, and that has to be amazing. Surely that is not what active young minds and bodies need?

"If a child has difficulty in reading, should we further increase the staffing in our schools, or should we help the parent to help the child? If a child is confused (and which child never is - it is an essential part of growing up) to whom do they turn? As the conventional family broadens into additional partnerships it is still the informal, non-institutional contact with adults other than teachers that is so essential to children.

"These are complex issues that go beyond the power of government and politicians alone to change. They concern the value judgements of individuals, and the collective determination of communities to create a quality of life for the benefit of all. Education, and the quality of our national life, have to become ever more interconnected. Government can lead in setting the agenda, it can even facilitate the discussion ... but it is millions upon millions of so-called "ordinary people" that have to fill in the details. Communities have to come together to use their resources more effectively. We have to devise powerful ways to support parents, particularly in disadvantaged areas, to give their children a better start in life.

"While British schools have been at the forefront internationally in the use of new information and communication technologies, there is still much that has to be done before the full potential of these is realised. If we are to place - as I believe we should - a greater emphasis on encouraging children to become more active learners, then they will need greater access to an expanded range of learning resources - books, computers, audio-visual equipment and the experience of a range of adults to mention but four things. This has considerable implications for the role of teachers, as well as for pupils.

"It is not simply a matter of changing the way teachers work, or the way pupils learn. It probably requires changing the way schools are organised, the way communities take responsibility for supporting learners both young and old alike, and the worth society places on education including what it will pay for it. These changes need to take place progressively and simultaneously; each needs to support the other. Each needs careful nurture if it is to be effective."

*        *        *

I rehearsed the speech to my colleagues in Leuven after dinner on the last night. They had, by that time, already consumed considerable amounts of beer. However, they were incredulous. "You mean you think it's actually possible for a prime minister to really say something like that?" queried one of the cognitive scientists. "If somebody like a prime minister were to give such a powerful lead, that would turn education systems upside down ... in any land. Do you think there's a real chance such a speech could ever be made?"

I let the Policy Unit have the speech the day after I returned from Belgium and wondered what would happen next. Brian Corby and I met with the education secretary Kenneth Clarke on 6 June. The meeting started late, but Clarke was sufficiently well briefed to let our meeting overrun. We talked for nearly an hour. Immediately Brian, more experienced in such procedural affairs than I, expressed his surprise to the minister that there was no member of the department present, only his own personal political advisors. "Surely, Brian, it was you that asked for this meeting with me alone and not with the department," the self-assured minister replied with a smile.

"I wasn't aware of that," said Brian.

"Well, here we are, officials or no officials, so let's just get on with it. These sound like interesting ideas which I must say I am predisposed to take seriously. We have a growing proportion of individual schools going their own way. Maybe competition will go too far for its own good. I'm interested in arrangements for collaboration which raise standards and don't cost more. We've probably brought all this on ourselves by creating an opt-out mechanism based on individual schools, and not communities. Sometime we'll have to rein all this in." Clarke was a good talker, but he also listened carefully - more, I guessed, to the things that he wanted to hear rather than just to get a better understanding of a situation which he but dimly understood. His driving mechanism was his love of politics, and his deep conservative free-market convictions. He didn't appear to have a natural empathy with the needs of young people.

Yet Clarke saw in what I was saying an opportunity that could well help him as well as us. If we succeeded, so might he. "Yes," he said, "I'm certainly prepared to write an endorsement for your next fund-raising prospectus. Then I would like to visit one of your projects. Probably at the beginning of September, and follow that up by meeting a cross-section of people from your various other programs who could show me how all this could then be rolled out on a much bigger scale across the country." Clarke's political ambitions were great. He wanted successful programs that were on a grand scale.

As we left Clarke said, "All this sounds a good idea. The difficulty will be to get a crusade going that involves everybody, when traditionally the English want to see confrontation." It was an interesting comment from a man who seemed to many to characterise confrontational politics.

*        *        *

"A good meeting," said Brian in the car on the way back to the Prudential, "but it was strange that John Caines, the permanent secretary, wasn't there. I wonder if there's a rift developing. I wonder if the rumour's true that the interest of the Policy Unit is coming to be resented. Some civil servants, as well as ministers, see the Policy Unit as a non-elected inner cabal. We'd better be careful. In the meantime let's get on with following up the details which Clarke requested. Fix a date for his visit to Letchworth, alert all the other projects, and let's get that draft prospectus to him quickly so that he'll write his forward before the summer recess."

I was excited as I told Anne about the meeting when I got home that evening. I was reassured that Clarke meant business when the following morning his diary secretary called to reserve certain dates for the September meetings. I was, in retrospect, too excited to be prudent. I did not follow-up to see if any serious harm had been done to our relationship with the department officers, though like Brian I was at a loss to know why they had not been at the last meeting. I was, at the back of my mind, fearful of becoming involved in a struggle between the Policy Unit and the department. That, I said firmly to myself, was not my affair.

Several days later I was lunching with Pat Limerick and talking through a number of issues. "I've been thinking about that meeting you had with Ken Clarke," said Pat. "I sense Brian could be right. There may well be a tension developing between Caines and the Policy Unit. I think you ought to contact Caines directly, defuse the situation by letting him know it was nothing to do with us that he was left out of the ministerial meeting. If there isn't a problem then it doesn't matter, but if there is a difficulty growing it puts us in the clear."

It was a most logical suggestion and I agreed to do so, but my heart wasn't in it. I was not as wise as Pat; even more, I was still intimidated by Caines' position. The nervous school boy of all those years ago did not like stepping out of line, and Caines as permanent secretary had cut me down to size when he had completely failed to understand my explanation of Education 2000. The fact that he had classified me as being about information technology still rankled with me. For my part, John Caines was unapproachable.

So the phone call I should have made slipped down my list of priorities. I easily justified this to myself, if I even thought about it, as I had already cleared the next three days in my diary to finalise the text of a new prospectus on which the trust would base its fund-raising. I needed to agree to the wording of this for the project leaders by the end of the week so that they could then pass this to Clarke for him to write the foreword. The phone call never got made.

I finished the prospectus, and managed to get it to the project directors in advance of our two-day conference in Birmingham at the end of June. It was the best conference we had ever had. Everyone was pleased with the progress they had made over recent months, and the thought that the minister would endorse the prospectus gave hope that, at long last, our difficult days might be over. Maybe we were coming out into more gentle pastures where not all of our time would be consumed by problems of fund-raising. We talked at length about how the projects would present their ideas to the minister in September. "This is exciting," said Janet Lawley, the exuberant headmistress of Bury Girls Grammar School, one of the independent schools involved in the trust and a prime figure in the Bury project. "I sense that things are moving in our direction at long last. There's so much we could do, if we could be seen as having government acknowledge publicly that this is important. Then the sponsors would feel that we're worth taking notice of."

I drove home that night feeling contented. Anne and I sat down to dinner, and I started to explain the reasons for my enthusiasm. The phone rang and Peter went off to answer it. "It's for you, Daddy. I think he said his name was Pat Limerick. Didn't we go to his office in London?"

As I went to pick up the phone I had a premonition of what all this could be about. I had still not contacted John Caines. "I'm sorry, John," said Pat. "I have bad news for you. I met with John Caines earlier this evening at a reception in the City. I'm afraid he's furious. He had just heard of your meeting with Kenneth Clarke. He thinks you're trying to cut him out, and are using your contacts with Downing Street to undermine his authority. I'm not sure there's anything you can do right now. I've tried to calm him down, but I fear you'll find that, from now on, things will not go so well in your dealings with the department as you had anticipated. I'm sorry, I really am, but forewarned is forearmed as they say. I'll talk to Brian over the weekend, and then perhaps next week we'll see if there's anything else that can be done."

*     *     *

The next three weeks were awful. Again I had foolishly allowed myself to be intimidated. Instead of accepting this as nothing other than an overgrown schoolboy version of a playground standoff which could have been best handled by my going direct to the permanent secretary (always assuming that he would have seen me, which he might not), I willingly accepted Brian Corby's offer to go himself and talk directly to John Caines on our behalf. Sitting in Brian's splendid office at the Prudential my reservations that I could never make the case on the trust's behalf as well as I should, were coloured by what I perceived to be my own lack of personal status. At a silly level (but nevertheless real to me) I would arrive at the department by way of the London Underground, while Brian would arrive in his chauffeur-driven Bentley and get VIP treatment from the moment he entered the building. It's silly, but that is exactly how I felt.

I had been deeply hurt by the permanent secretary's reaction to my earlier presentation, and I was acutely aware of how badly we had all handled the follow-up to the Templeton seminar. My own conscience was clear; in no way did I think I had been devious in my own dealings with the department, but I was still extremely embarrassed by the Corby-Banham-Haig meeting. I was also getting tired out by all the unnecessary political activity and I was losing my capacity to laugh. I needed a holiday, and I just wanted no more to do with this. Soon the family and I would be cycling across Scotland. Resignedly I left Brian to go and talk to John Caines. The meeting achieved little. The department's attitude towards the trust would not, it seemed, improve.

# 12
# Playing the Game

The chance to present my ideas to a wider audience of influential educationalists came from an unexpected quarter. It was the request to be the keynote speaker to the annual conference of the Girls' School Association, the organisation which represents the heads of the girls' independent schools of England. My earlier fears that the Girls' School Association was a female form of the Headmasters' Conference - solid, respectable, but essentially predictable people for all their outward good cheer - dissipated when Anne and I arrived one late October evening at the hotel in Bristol where the conference was assembling. It was a splendidly organised event, purposeful, calm and nicely elegant. I was well prepared and, I thought, relaxed until, minutes before going on the stage, a head mistress of a well known girls' school quietly reminded me that, when speaking in public, I should be careful never to split my infinitives.

The speaker the previous evening had been Baroness Blatch, the government minister in the Lords responsible for education. She had offended her audience, as was explained to me, by treating independent schools as if they were an extension of government policy. My audience wanted something more interesting than this and this was my opportunity to lift discussions of these issues into the elite private sector. It was in their schools that the children of the wealthy were educated. If I needed acceptance in an English culture, these people, and the folk they represented, had to take me seriously. If I did my job well, at that stage in the day, they could concentrate for a session of an hour and a half. If I worked them hard the next speaker might find his job quite difficult. That was not my problem. Lord Walton, a scientist and chairman of the National Commission on Education could make his case whatever way he wanted.

Elizabeth Diggory, the president and later to become the head of St Paul's Girls' School in London, had given me the best possible spot for my talk. Nine o'clock in the morning is when adults are at their most alert and I started my speech by telling them of a telephone conversation I had had with Professor Ted Sizer, one-time dean of education at Harvard. "There's a tumult within the education systems of the Western democracies," he had said. "Dramatic economic and technological change has undermined, and is continuing to undermine, social structures. Pre-eminent amongst these structures is education. In seeking solutions there's a daily battle developing for the souls of future generations. It's based on differing understandings of how learning takes place. On one side is the assertion that greater government control can establish such a perfect system that, operating this centrally, the system can be made to deliver highly effectively.

"On the other side there is increasingly a view that learning emerges from a sense of personal inquiry; that it works best when it is seen in its full social setting; that confidence in learning is an integral part of self-esteem and enterprise; that schools and communities have to learn to combine and respect each other as being essential components in the creation of a new learning community (which is itself a new form of society).

"Within the United States this is almost reaching the proportion of a Civil War. Many people are intellectually attracted to the latter view, but find their professional future, and their professional activity, dictate that they should advocate the former. It seems to me that this same battle is now raging in the United Kingdom," I said. "The tensions are as great here. The arguments are as confused. Positions become polarised. There is an understandable rush to find immediate solutions."

"It is my job today," I said, "to add some vision to this agenda. Discussion about education has to be more than about administrative arrangements. 'Administration without vision,' I read recently, 'is like rearranging the chairs on the deck of the Titanic.' As citizens of one tiny island we're all in this together; it's up to us to ensure that this is no Titanic.

"You in the independent sector are an intrinsic but special part of that system. You may feel that you are spectators rather than players, yet you will be much influenced by the outcome of the struggle between your colleagues in the state schools and a government that is becoming ever more prescriptive and centralist. As critical observers of the game your support off the pitch could well shape the final result. You helped to choose the players. Sometimes you can bypass the system and go straight to the head girl, or boy, in a way which is denied to the players whose professionalism is too often dismissed as vested self-interest."

There was a ripple of good-hearted laughter. They liked the analogy. This was going to be a good morning. I turned back to my text.

"We know that as a consequence of long evolution, the brain has modes of operation that are natural, effortless and effective in utilising the tremendous power of this amazing instrument. Coerced to operate in other ways, the brain functions reluctantly, slowly and with abundant error. Frank Smith, in *Insult to Intelligence*, said, 'reluctance to learn can not be attributed to the brain. Learning is the brain's primary function, its constant concern, and we become restless and frustrated if there is no learning to be done. We are all capable of huge and unsuspected learning accomplishments without effort.' Do you remember the comment of Saint Augustine? 'I learnt most, not from those who taught me, but from those who talked with me.'

"The full implications of this are daunting. Not only do they require a reappraisal of how learning takes place (it is *not* the opposite of teaching), it requires a reconsideration of the place that young people have in society, and a reconsideration of the role and importance of the entire community - itself an elusive concept which needs redefining. Learning is a social activity; it has to be seen in its full context."

Then I put up a slide which sought to contrast the differences between successful academic and commercial working practices. It needs, reader, to be studied carefully. Take time out now and think it through for yourself.

Conventional academic success has involved:
1. largely solitary study
2. genuinely uninterrupted work
3. concentration on a single subject
4. much written work
5. a high analytical ability

While commercial success involves:
1. working with others
2. constant distractions
3. different levels across different disciplines
4. mainly verbal skills
5. problem solving and decision-making

In my lecture I covered the bottom section, and slightly laboured and caricatured the skills accepted as best practice in school. I then covered the section on schools and slightly glamorised the skills of the world of commerce. I pressed my point home. "In reality, it's these latter skills which everyone of you has to practice everyday, isn't it?"

They nodded vigorously, and a head mistress called out, "I've got a junior section in my school and what John Abbott is saying is absolutely right. I was talking about this with a businessman, who is also one of our fathers, and he said that if children were too good at working in the academic model, they might not be much use later in business. They would find the different working practices too hard to take. That slide would explain why. It's simple and clear, and I'd like a copy of it."

There was a murmur of approval. I moved to put up the next slide.

"Stop," exclaimed another head mistress, jumping to her feet. "You're missing the main point with that slide. Don't you see it?"

I shook my head, confused as to the point she was trying to make. She looked at me witheringly. "That's because you're a man. Don't you realise that the top set of skills represent a male perspective, the lower represent female skills and predispositions." The room was quickly filled with the chatter of an informed audience. "Isn't this why young women are finding it easier to get jobs in the modern fast moving knowledge economy than men trained in the earlier set of skills?" asked another headmistress. The loud chatter of "yes, yes, yes" proved that she had made a point well accepted by the audience.

The audience was anxious for more. In the remaining half an hour I concentrated particularly on the evolution of predispositions and natural learning strategies.

"Research is emphasising the evolved nature of the brain in response to its environment over countless generations. This evolution is every bit as dramatic and refined as the obvious physical aspects of shape, skin, configuration, limbs, etc. Work on the nature of language development from Chomsky onwards suggests the strong possibility that each brain is born with the strong predispositions to learn language in a particular, natural, way - regardless of the actual language group the child is born into. The brain is no clean slate as regards language development, rather the analogy is closer to an old fashioned gramophone record needing a layer of wax removed from its surface before revealing its pre-formed structure.

"How many generations it takes for such predispositions to form, or to be obliterated, we don't as yet know. Personally I find it more than of passing interest to hear that gurus of management theory tell us that we should run our schools (or anything else) with no more than a dozen people reporting to us; that we should build up teams able to take virtually full responsibility for their tasks; and that we should be generous in our praise, always investing in the person as the most significant resource. Interesting because if you study society in pre-industrial time you will find that the vast majority of English people lived, worked and learnt in units of no more than 13 people in the centuries before the industrial revolution.

"Are we not seeing, in each new generation, an expectation - a mode if you like - that has not yet been obliterated by six or seven generations of an industrial culture which cruelly shattered those natural structures which, over generations, so largely shaped the brain?

"If that interests you, then consider this. How quickly can predispositions form, or how quickly are they lost?" Jean Healy, writing in *Endangered Minds* in 1992, stated: "Today's students have shorter attention spans, are less able to reason analytically, to express ideas verbally. These changes may, in fact, represent a cusp of change in human intelligence. A progression into more immediate, visual and 3D forms of thought. Our growing crisis in academic learning reflects societal neglect of the neural imperatives of childhood.

"The brain is doing many things at one time - processing thoughts, emotions, imagination, and these predispositions all operate simultaneously. The brain operates most effectively when it's dealing with "natural" situations, that is, when it's dealing with multiple, complex and concrete experiences in which it is interested, and which it thinks it can draw benefit from. It processes parts and wholes simultaneously. It works with both generalisations and specifics at the same time. It's both trying to subdivide and compartmentalise ideas, whilst always looking for possible relationships and discontinuities.

"To create uncluttered or contrived learning environments where the brain has no room for peripheral perception is to frustrate its most natural form of functioning." Later I went on to talk about informal learning. Recent research at Jordan Hill in Glasgow into the nature of homework showed that, for most young children, the most appropriate location for homework was not a desk in an isolated bedroom, but a corner of a kitchen table with some light music, and mother or father going quietly about their business. Surprised? - surely not!"

After a further half an hour I came to my conclusion. "None of us is yet able to do justice to these ideas. Yet I am convinced that to understand the insights which are emerging from this disparate range of subjects has to be the challenge of out times. Once we understand this we can do things much better."

I concluded with a passage from Howard Gardner written the previous year in *The Unschooled Mind.* "We run the risk of investing incalculable resources in institutions that do not operate well, and that may never approach the effectiveness that their supporters and, for that matter, their detractors would desire. It is my own belief that until now we have not fully appreciated just how difficult it is for schools to succeed. We have not been cognisant of the ways in which the basic inclinations of human learning turn out to be ill-matched to the agenda of the modern secular school."

\*       \*       \*

The following day I met with Brian Corby. I tried to summarise the reactions to my speech in terms of the significance the ideas had had for the audience. "These ideas transcend normal party political agendas, and challenge our departmental way of thinking. They are not easy for anyone to handle. They need a long time scale, and this calls for a blend of the theoretical with the practical. My biggest difficulty is getting past the various filters that allow the prime minister, or secretary of state to think only about those things which their advisors have predetermined are politically manageable. This calls for a national crusade to stimulate a new way of doing things."

Brian who was enjoying his emerging national role within the CBI with the access this gave him to ministers, drew me back into our financial situation and the need to fund the projects. Brian - the actuary - always understood money. There was another problem with his thinking that was to inhibit my personal progress for the next couple of years - something that I don't think he even saw as a problem, but which subtly affected my every action. Theory, Brian was convinced, would never change anyone's assumptions, however well expressed. "Show me, and I'll believe" was both his credo and the credo he was assured all senior politicians and their advisors lived by. "Will these head mistresses find money for us to finance the work in our projects?" he said in a voice of sweet reasonableness.

While the Girls' School Association wrote to me afterwards to say that they had "printed more copies of your speech than any other speech at any earlier conference because our members want to share these ideas with staff in their own schools," the trust itself did absolutely nothing with the speech. It was simply filed away in my office. No one in the projects wanted to read this. Like all sections of the maintained education system they had fallen into believing that there was no longer any room for personal initiative; they had to do what Government directed. It was the independent schools, specifically the girls' schools, which felt that they were still in a position to carry out radical transformation of their arrangements - if they could see how to do this.

My energy for broader campaigning had to take second place to the daily needs of the nine hungry and largely dependent projects and, in third place - so far down the list that it was not to be considered for five more years - was the writing of this book.

Brian had recently met John Patten, the new minister of education, at a reception hosted by the CBI. As host Brian had invited the minister to meet us. Patten could not easily refuse and a date was fixed. "We must get our argument right for this meeting with Patten in three weeks time," Brian said to me one afternoon. "He's a strange person, but he was once an Oxford don so you ought to be able to get him to understand what we're about."

\*          \*          \*

I left Brian's office and wandered back through Russell Square, past London University and Dillon's bookshop, in a reflective mood. In my head, and almost in my briefcase and in the office filing cabinets, I seemed to be carrying a set of ideas, and an explanation of how they related, which was of the greatest importance. Yet I was feeling pretty weak, and my energy strictly bound by the physical constraints of what could be fitted into a single day. I was constrained even more by something far less tangible. It was all to do with the status that comes when people know who you are. Status helps you over the little irregular bumps that normally punctuate life. With an ability to ride the bumps, it is moderately easy to remain equitable. Brian could easily do that. With a recent knighthood and with a headquarters staff of a thousand or more, and with many more in his scattered corporate empire, he could never appreciate that, when we hit a bump, it took all my personal energy to pull us up to the other side. I did not have the energy necessary either to exploit the enthusiasm of the independent school heads, or to do the endless lobbying with the United Nations - both the UNDP program in New York, and UNESCO in Paris .Yet I needed to do both these things in order to move the international proposal made at Annapolis up to a point where somebody with relevant authority could actually act upon it.

So deep in my thoughts was I that I hardly noticed the city gentleman with his bowler hat and rolled umbrella walking rapidly past me. He came to a pedestrian crossing some 50 yards in front of me where a young mother with a small child in a pushchair was waiting for the green light. Glancing up the street and seeing no traffic coming, he stepped off the curb and started across the road. "Stop," shouted the young mother. The man stopped, and stepped back onto the pavement. "Why?" he inquired, somewhat confused.

"Because I'm trying to teach my young daughter how to cross the road. I've told her you must always wait for the green light. Then she saw you step out on the red. How can I get her to understand if she sees someone like you doing the opposite?"

With great composure the man bent down to the child. "Your mother's absolutely right. I shouldn't have tried to cross the road like that. Don't you ever do a thing like that."

The light turned to green and all of us crossed the road. I was thrilled. This was what a learning community was all about. But it put me on my guard. It could easily have been me being reprimanded by that young mother. At all times each and every one of us has to live what we believe. We never know who may be watching.

\*　　　　\*　　　　\*

I had read many press comments about John Patten, but being the optimist I was I had hoped that I would find him reasonable and constructive. The secretary of state's new office was moderately spacious, and fitted in some style between oddly shaped walls, windows and a dipping ceiling. Patten rose to greet us, brushing his hair from his eyes in a studied gesture; with the same movement of his hand he then checked his tie. He was anxious to talk, flattering Brian so effusively that, for once, Brian himself was stuck for words.

Sitting opposite him, I could not but help noticing the nude sketches on the wall behind him. These, it seemed, were all part of the ploy. He turned to me. "Do you like my etchings? They're by Augustus John. Aren't they fine? Do you know that the Foreign Office is telling me to take these down whenever Muslims come into the room. Damn cheek. The minister of a Middle Eastern country was here last week so I turned them round. I bet he spent all his time wondering why."

I was shocked. With such an attitude I could never ever take him seriously. Eventually he gave me a few minutes to say what we were all about, but I did not think he was listening. His eyes flickered from Brian to me and he broke into my explanation to make justifications for his own policy. "The Grant Maintained Schools are leaping ahead – now they're free from local authority control they have only to answer to me. They're good schools – do you approve of them, Sir Brian?" Before Brian could even formulate an answer Patten continued. "Even my chauffeur has children attending a Voluntary Aided School where every parent has to agree, in advance of the child going to that school, to attend every parent's evening. That's what good education is going to be all about, isn't that so, Sir Brian?

"Now, Mr Abbott, what's all this you go on about international research? What is there that we don't already know?" It was incredibly hard to think of an appropriate response that would do justice to the ideas, yet mean something to him. I limited my explanation to about three minutes, which seemed to be the outside of his attention span and then I offered to send him a résumé of both Robert Reich's *The Work of Nations*, and Howard Gardner's *The Unschooled Mind*. He never stopped long enough in making his inconsequential comments even to acknowledge the offer.

Obviously becoming agitated that the meeting had gone on longer than planned, he broke in and said, hurriedly, "Yes, you have my support. No, I have no money to spare, but give me a paper of two or three sides setting out your proposal and I'll get my people to have a look at it." And with that we were shown out. I had never seen Brian so annoyed. That helped me just a little to realise that I was not the only one who saw this situation as being so totally impossible. That England, once the epitome of delegated responsibility and local accountability, had regressed to the point where individual quirks and idiosyncrasies of such a minister had to be taken seriously. It seemed a travesty of democracy.

*         *         *

Later that evening my professional annoyance at the outcome of this meeting was replaced with a different, more immediate, family worry.

Each of our sons was continuing to grow in their own particular ways, regardless of the pressures and frustrations that their father was experiencing. While Peter was outgoing and developing confidence in playing the saxophone in the North Hertfordshire Youth Orchestra, David was becoming more sensitive to the tensions to be found in modern society. One evening I found him in tears in his bedroom. I put an arm on his shoulder and asked what was the matter? Between his sobs he blurted out, "If I'm not successful when I grow up, and my job doesn't work out, will you and mum let me come back home and live with you?"

I was distressed. It was not a topic we had ever spoken about. But it was obviously a lively topic of discussion on the school playground where several of the children David knew had fathers who had lost their jobs, and one of whom was having to sell his home.

Such comments draw children and parents close together, and in future I resolved to talk more openly about such matters of general concern.

\*       \*       \*

Al Shanker, the president of America's top teaching union, wrote to me to alert me to a book he had just read in manuscript form, and which was to be published that same month. It was John Bruer's *Schools for Thought*: a science of learning in the classroom. It was to prove to be a thoughtful, scholarly book which merited Al Shanker's comment. As it happened, my copy of Bruer's book reached me from an American bookstore an hour or so before I flew to Copenhagen to meet with a group of Danish head teachers for a two-day seminar. The schedule was relaxed, even including a dinner in the Tivoli gardens, and I had a good opportunity to read a sizeable proportion of the book in one session. "Current methods of schooling are relatively successful in imparting facts and rote skills," Bruer argued, "but they are far less successful in developing higher order skills." The argument was identical to Gardner's. "Youngsters can memorise large bodies of information for limited periods, but don't understand this at a profound enough level to be able to give it real meaning." Such learning is cognitively superficial and does not develop a way of thinking that is in any sense transferable. And it is transferability that is essential if individuals are to develop genuinely flexible skills, be creative and solve novel problems. Transferability means applying old knowledge in a setting sufficiently novel that it also requires learning new knowledge.

"If formal schooling is to have a commercial value over and above developing basic skills, it will be because we have learned how to develop such higher order skills intentionally, not accidentally, for the many rather than solely for the elite."

This was a fascinating and powerful argument, and I needed to go further and show that as a minority of a child's time is spent in a classroom then we had to be far more aware of the significance of informal non-school based learning. Even Bruer, and many other cognitive scientists appeared to be hung up on a virtually exclusive emphasis on formal instructorial processes, and had failed to acknowledge the significance of learning on the job so well expressed in cognitive apprenticeship. Link this with studies into the relative significance of intrinsic and extrinsic motivation and many people's own personal experience will quickly show the milestone significance of critical informal learning situations in their own lives which have triggered that stubborn determination which is such a feature of intrinsic motivation. In my case it was woodcarving.

In some detail Bruer explained how skills of transferability emerge when there is a careful blend of both subject-specific expertise, with a conscious effort to understand your own learning patterns, strengths, and styles. He argued that, "You can't learn a few general purpose learning tools. Nor do you develop transferable skills just because you are a specialist. It is when these two ways of learning come together that education systems will make a cognitive leap."

This was central to the argument I was putting together. Here, again was part of the theoretical underpinning that I needed if I was to make the connection between formal and informal learning absolutely clear. Here was the theoretical base for my claim that youngsters had to become "reflective practitioners." It was not just enough for teachers to think about their own learning. It was essential that teachers build up these skills in their pupils as well. It was a further clarification of the Cognitive Apprenticeship Model of learning. *Making Thinking Visible* was a brilliant explanation of a natural process.

As chance would have it there was a further note from Shanker awaiting my return from Denmark. "There's another good book coming out on the development of transferable skills. It's called *Surpassing Ourselves* and it's a study of expertise by two Canadians from Toronto, Carl Bereiter and Marlene Scardamalia. When you've read it let me know what you think." *Surpassing Ourselves* is concerned with understanding how metacognitive skills that go beyond what comes naturally can be developed. They explored the difference between specialists and experts. The argument goes like this: specialists, by working within the well defined parameters of the specialism, know their subject from top to bottom. They know all the rules, all the tests, and all the possible combinations and formulae. Their authority rests on the depths of their knowledge and the understanding of the rules, and is uncluttered by the need to access extraneous influences. Such people exude confidence - in some this comes through as arrogance. No one can better them. Discussion with such people is often difficult. Just where their specialisms fit in a bigger picture does not trouble such people, for that is essentially unquantifiable, imprecise and highly uncertain; there are no rules for that kind of thing so such questions are best left unanswered.

A caricature perhaps, but in essential aspects often true. So the world has come to be fearful of specialists for, in some hard to define way, we sense that they are just not real. Their single mindedness gets all of us into trouble. They think the world apart and that makes us personally schizophrenic.

Experts, argued Bereiter and Scardamalia, possess certain additional qualities that make them special people. Experts start off as specialists. They know an awful lot about their own subjects. You can't fault them on detail, anymore than you can fault a specialist, but they have one vital attribute - they are able to get outside themselves and their subjects and look at their specialisms from a distance. They are essentially quizzical. They ask themselves uncomfortable questions about their specialisations significance and its possible relevance. They are intentionally playful; they ask awkward and tantalising questions.

In a sense they know so much about their subject that it makes them inquisitive about many other things. They are quick to grasp the overall situation, rather than just dealing with single parts. Big issues fascinate them. Howard Gardner defines them as people who think about a concept by drawing on insights from several forms of intelligence. I think of them as I think of craftsmen of old - proud in their skills, humble in their attitudes, essentially inquisitive, and as concerned for the quality of what is not seen as much as that which is seen. People able to have both their feet on the ground and their heads in the sky.

Bereiter and Scardamalia explain all this in their own direct way. "Experts tackle problems that increase their expertise, whereas specialists tend to tackle problems for which they do not have to extend themselves (by going beyond the rules and formulae they accept). Experts indulge in progressive problem solving, that is, they continually reformulate problems at ever higher levels and thereby uncover more of the nature of the issue. They become totally immersed in their work and increase the complexity of the activity by developing new skills and taking on new challenges."

Here was the vital significance of this argument; experts with such high level "open thinking" have to be vastly important people in a culture such as ours which is changing so rapidly that it is hard to see where it is headed. Unlike the specialist's supreme confidence within a specialism (not much use when the boundaries of that specialism are falling apart) the expert is essentially humble and questioning, more aware of what he does not yet know rather than what is already known. They know the rules, but they also know how to reformulate these, and when to break them to fit new circumstances. They are persistent, industrious and curious and are always searching for perfection.

There are not many such people around and rarely can schools create them alone. Characters such as Donald O'Sullivan the diplomat turned lecturer, Brian Tuohy the hardware store owner, Philip Ireton the proponent of the welfare state, Iraj Bahraman the governor general of Hamedan, or Johnny Pryor the down-to-earth idealist born with a silver spoon in his mouth. Such people thrive on the edge of chaos and order and provide an energising force in a society. That is why I wrote this book.

The creation of conditions in which expertise can develop bridges the two extremities of learning theory - the practice of open experiential learning, and the rigours of subject specific disciplines. It is in the study of expertise that we find the clue we need to both creativity and transferability of knowledge. While specialisation has become a feature of modern society, it is not, however, particularly natural to the human brain which has evolved over the millennia to be a multifaceted, multi-tasked organism that is predisposed to think about any piece of data or idea, from many perspectives. The glory of human learning is that it is a highly effective, but essential complex, messy, non-linear process. The brain can, literally, do almost anything if the stimulation and the feedback systems are good, and the environment challenging and open. A National Curriculum, or outcome-based education, that is highly prescriptive quickly saps the creative energy of enterprising people, and quickly removes the space for imagination.

To paraphrase Bereiter and Scardamalia, an expert society will not be a heaven in which all problems have disappeared, but a realistic utopia in which problem solving will be a highly valued part of life. Progressive problem-solvers stay healthier, live longer, and experience the intense mental pleasure known as flow. They repeatedly go beyond their well learned procedures, avoid getting stuck in ruts, and challenge themselves by reformulating problems in an evermore complex and challenging way. They are able to transform apparently insoluble predicaments into soluble problems to the benefit of everyone. Yet, many of our present institutions, especially the schools - be they in any country - penalise expertise rather than cultivate it, for such skills need the more open invigorating breath of informal learning.

*             *             *

With such ideas buzzing around I despaired at ever finding anyone with whom to share my excitement. Then I thought of Sir Geoffrey Holland who, some months before, had taken over as permanent secretary from John Caines.

Geoffrey was held in high regard by many as being a person who got things done. He was regarded as an establishment man but with a well-tuned ear to new, unconventional ideas. Knowing also that he had recently acted as an advisor to the Church of England Synod on employment matters I thought he might resonate with that array of my concerns which jumped from the spiritual to the technological. He ought, I rationalised, to be able to get his mind around all this. Geoffrey offered me a breakfast meeting and his candour took me off my guard. I had expected to pour my woes out to him; I had hardly expected to find that he, too, was nearly at the end of his tether. "The Department is totally unable to respond to new ideas, to formulate a vision, to give a lead, or be entrepreneurial. People from outside just can't get a response. [I knew that.] It's the worst of the civil service mentality; always polite and affable; always looking to dot the Is and cross the Ts, but never questioning the direction in which it's moving." He went on to say that he did not think the department had ever understood what Education 2000 was about, and it was when he had heard one of my speeches that he felt he got a grasp on the significance of the ideas I was chasing. These ideas were not, unfortunately, what present politicians were looking for. Inwardly I groaned.

He commended the trust for its tenacity, and said he well understood how awful it must be bashing one's head continuously against a departmental brick wall. But he had no constructive advice to give. He seemed completely drained. As I left he asked if I could loan him "the three books you think I ought to read over the summer." I suggested Gardner, Bruer and Bereiter and Scardamalia.

Later that afternoon, as I sat in my office in Letchworth arranging with my secretary to send Geoffrey Holland the three books, I thought back to that meeting three years previously with John Caines, Geoffrey's predecessor. "There is no need for such a sub-section within the department to deal with how learning takes place," he had retorted to my plea not to leave Education 2000 as being the concern of the IT section of his department, "learning is what happens when people are well taught."

Geoffrey was paying the price for many years of departmental blindness and inertia. The world around was changing, yet the department had no way of understanding this and adjusting accordingly. At the most fundamental level the department had no way of learning for itself. It seemed to be left to Geoffrey to do that as part of his summer holiday reading.

We sent the books off, but heard nothing. Three months later, in an attempt to stimulate some reaction, I wrote and asked if he'd finished with the books. There was no answer. Later the books came back, without any comment. Was I being stupid in raising such an issue or was this just right "off limits"?

\*          \*          \*

Some weeks later I had a phone call from an undersecretary at the department, Brian Norberry, who had once visited Letchworth. Norberry suggested that, as the paper I had prepared at the minister's request had touched on a whole variety of topics, there was no one official in the department who was qualified to respond. He therefore proposed convening a meeting of 12 or 15 section heads, each of whom had an interest in part of what I wished to talk about. We could meet for two or three hours one afternoon in July and I could then explain my ideas and concerns to them. Was this to be an opportunity, or another waste of time?

Everybody in the trust wanted to advise me on how I should proceed. Foolishly I listened too closely to those one-time civil servants who I still thought were my best guides as to how to talk departmental speak. They were impressed at the size of the team being gathered to meet with me, but were nervous on my behalf. "Whatever you do, don't talk too much about research," they said. "Don't go into the details you did with the Girls' School Association and, whatever you do, don't overplay your US connections - that would make them xenophobic. And don't be too critical of present government; remember, it's the job of the civil servant to be loyal to their political masters' policies." It did not leave me much room to manoeuvre.

I tried to keep my own counsel and prepared myself well for the presentation. Sir Christopher Ball, Chairman of the RSA Committee on Learning came with me. "He's here as my friend," I explained rather lamely as we all shook hands. It was almost as if I was an errant headmaster with my professional adviser sitting along side me, under judgement by my governing body for a professional misdemeanour.

The room we met in was small, stuffy and dominated by a large table. At my request an overhead projector had been provided which sat uncomfortably midway down the table in the only possible position to project onto the screen which filled one corner of the room. It was impossible both to see the screen, and to sit comfortably. Several people came in late. There was little pre-presentation chat. People, even within the department it seemed, did not know each other well. What to me was an extraordinarily important meeting - the culmination of years of thinking and lobbying - was all too apparently of little significance to the department.

"I must thank you all for sparing the time to come this afternoon," said Brian Norberry in his introductory words (as if they were doing me a favour in not going about their normal business). "You've all read John's paper. This is an unusual meeting. I doubt if we've ever met as a group before." I have talked with John several times about these issues, but I have to confess that I am still not clear in my own mind about what all this actually means." He gave me a weak smile. "Put me down, John, as being agnostic rather than atheist." He spoke in the polished prose, with the occasional academic quip, that marks the man or woman on the civil service fast track.

I'm sure he meant to be friendly, but he was not giving anything away. He certainly was not encouraging anyone to take my side. I was on my own. So, it seemed, was each of them. They all sat heavy. It was almost impossible to get a feel for the group - except, of course, that they were not a group. Each one listened carefully for what the implications would be for their work if the minister decided to follow-up on what I was proposing.

My slides were good. I kept anecdotes to a minimum, and concentrated on the concepts that had underpinned all my recent speeches, including that to the Girls' School Association. Midway through I tried to get them to smile. I showed them the slide which contrasted the working practices of academics with those of the normal workplace. I got a slight glimmer of interest. I mentioned the comment about male and female working practices, and a few eyes sparkled but only for a moment. Emotional responses are precluded from the repertoire of good civil servants. I tried hard to draw them into matters of meta-cognition, and of transferable skills. I spoke of the way information technology challenged conventional arrangements for teaching.

I looked hard at Philip Lewis, the senior official responsible for IT in schools. He was standing in one corner looking slightly bored - he had heard this before. Then it hit me. Yes, of course he had heard this before. He had even said it himself. But neither he nor anyone else had gone that much further and taken a responsible leadership role on this, and challenged other people to think about how this profoundly changed the nature of their roles and responsibilities. Philip's career had started in the Prison Service. He had progressed quickly within the department of education and knew more about the details of information technology, and IT policy, than anyone else. But on his own admission he did not have much of an interest in learning theory. Nor had he ever been a teacher. His judgements were always specific to his own area of specialisation. The big picture was not his concern. Knowing what Philip knew, I speculated, how could he do nothing within the department? Looking at how he and his colleagues were standing there it suddenly became blindingly obvious. He did not want to, nor was he expected to, upset the delicate balance of relationships within the department. Departmental smooth running - collegiality - was more important to all these people than a changed system. And there was the answer to all my frustrations of the past years; the department, and the authority, was there to defend the system from change.

I finished speaking and Brian Norberry then invited questions. A silence. It was broken by a woman who obviously felt compelled to be honest. "Please don't be surprised if none of us is anxious to ask any questions. You see, what you've said would mean that some of us here would be losers, and some winners. Obviously we don't want to antagonise our colleagues by suggesting we know in advance which way this will go."

Grateful for her honesty I nevertheless gritted my teeth as I made my reply. "You, or someone, will have to make a decision on this sometime soon. You either carry on doing the same things, or do something different. Whatever you decide will have massive implications one way or the other for children."

The atmosphere lightened fractionally, and there were a couple of safe, non-contentious comments. Then the chairman closed the meeting.

"I don't think you'll get much encouragement from them," Christopher said as we sat for a few minutes in one of the anterooms. "They're sifting all this through in terms of what they think will interest the minister."

For a couple of days I fumed. I could not think coherently, and I was afraid to put pen to paper. Nothing seemed to make sense any longer, and I wondered whether I could muster any further energy to push still more for this idea to be taken seriously. Then I wrote a carefully worded letter to everyone present at the meeting, summarising all the points that I had made, or wanted to make. I heard nothing. There was no response and John Major never did use my speech. Learning was not on the agenda. Once again I felt on my own, not helped by what I sensed was a growing feeling amongst some of my trustees that maybe, just maybe, I did not know what I was talking about. After all, they must have been saying to themselves, surely the Department of Education can't be completely wrong? Maybe it's John who's out of step.

# 13
# Becoming an Internationalist

And, of course, I *was* out of step with those who were forcing schools into the parade ground mentality of tightly controlled government directives. What I was learning meant I couldn't march to the drum beat sounded by the likes of a *Times Educational Supplement* headline which declared "Primary effects last to GCSE". The leading teachers' newspaper in the UK heralded research showing "the quality of a primary school has a significant impact on pupil achievement and attitudes." It went on to quote Peter Mortimore, the director of the London Institute, "These findings are very exciting for primary schools. Despite five years of secondary schooling, the primary influence can still be traced." This was 1993! Were educationalists crazy? Even on a slow news day, surely this was not news? It was what every observer capable of looking beyond the separate boxes of primary and secondary education had known for years. Certainly it was what parents knew. It was what Ignatius Loyola had known four centuries back when he had claimed, "Give me a child until he is seven, and he is mine for life." It was what I had observed on becoming head master twenty years before. Certainly the Spartans knew it, as did the Soviets and the Nazis. Where was our sense of proportion, and historical perspective? Had we not the confidence to accept this until it was proven by some type of long-term statistical analysis? No wonder it was so hard to move the educational establishment if its every move had to be justified by numbers, not intuitive wisdom?

The arguments had got stuck. What had grown out of the Education 2000 experience was the need for government to create the conditions for a shift that would release the creative energies of people to find new ways of doing things. However, government policy was going ever further in the opposite direction. Politicians, having unleashed an unprecedented number of new initiatives, promised a five year period of stability designed to make England's present education system more and more efficient by tightening the regulations, and increasing the draconian nature of assessment of the current traditional practice. In government's often quoted desire to increase productivity, all aspects of financial control had to demonstrate efficiency. This was the language of the accountants; efficiency was the driving concept, not effectiveness. Returns had to be immediate. Outcomes had to be prescribed in advance. Parents were encouraged to use the league tables of examination results to compare the performance of schools and, if necessary, to move their children from one school to another. Schools became increasingly preoccupied with spending money, only where it would show immediate returns on publicly acknowledged criteria - in other words on examination results. Earlier extracurricular activities - the things people remember with affection long after they have left school because they were events which mattered to them - were being pushed even further to the side.

In contrast, all over the world people were beginning to stress effectiveness rather than simply efficiency. Effectiveness takes a long-term view of the developing child and sees expenditure more as investment than social cost. It looks more broadly at all those factors that impact on the development of the child's intellect and skills. It provided the framework for me to start the argument for a model of learning based on the weaning principle, and an accompanying reversal of the current distribution of resources, and an acknowledgement of the importance of informal learning.

Politically this argument won no friends in Britain, which was strange given the Conservative government's rhetoric about creating an entrepreneurial society. In all my discussions with ministers I believed this was truly what they wished to achieve but, by failing to understand that enterprise, creativity and original thought grew from the experience of a full, varied life style that needs far, far more than just good experiences in a classroom, they failed abysmally in their objective. The trouble was that, to a politician, to emphasise change in schools was to appeal immediately to the electorate. To talk about all the other changes necessary to create an environment rich in learning opportunities was to challenge the electorate itself to change - and that the politicians were fearful of doing.

Personally, I was aware of being pulled apart by two forces. Formally there was Education 2000's declared policy of building up the projects so that, over a period of years, they could act as demonstrations of the theory as first set out six years before. "Give people something they can see and be impressed by, and go away saying 'I like that very much. I don't need to understand the theory, but that's just what I think we need to do.'" However an alternative strategy was forming in my mind. Something far less expensive and less problematic than running our own projects. It was, I thought, comparatively simple. If the trust could make a systematic search of the literature emerging from research programs world-wide, together with a study of successful implementation strategies for each of the key aspects of what we saw as whole systems change, then surely we could construct a synthesis which could be used to make a compelling case for the changes the trust sought? This would not take as long to do, nor would it need anything like as much money as our current heavy investment in the projects.

The trouble was, hardly anyone else understood my dilemma. "Read the books in the evening, when your work is done," was the advice of colleagues. "Research should have a relatively low profile in the affairs of the trust," said a feasibility study commissioned by the trustees, "we're essentially a doing organisation. Good theory will emerge from our actions." I had to bite my lip. People don't like being told too often that it is only you who can see things clearly.

Cultivating a sense of being the outsider was a self-indulgence that didn't fit with being a project leader. However, it is unwise to ignore the signs of stress in oneself and my doctor readily concurred with me that I could no longer carry such an enormous strain. It would be sensible to clear my diary of all matters of pressing daily urgency, I told the trustees in late January. That way I could focus on the implications of a new way of thinking about learning, based on the research which I saw waiting to be gathered and digested from the world at large. They agreed that I should spend the next four months, leading up to the May election, doing just that, and leave the day to day affairs of the trust to others. The sabbatical was the metaphorical equivalent of taking off a rucksack at the end of a long day's trek, stretching exhausted muscles, and delighting in the realisation that one can still stand upright. My elation was dented, but only for a short while, by the reaction of people in several of the projects. "How will we hold on," they said, "until you come back?" I was cross. I had worked hard, I thought, to give them the confidence and the ability to stand on their own feet. That was how I felt at the time and, with my diary freed up, I began a period of international travel which eventually culminated 3 years later in a move to Washington and the 21st Century Learning Initiative. This chapter abandons the story's chronology in favour of a thematic approach intended to being together some of the insights I was privileged to hear and read.

It was the tears running down the face of Aklilu Habte, an Ethiopian, speaking at the Annapolis, Maryland, conference of the International and Comparative Educational Society that helped me most as I tried focusing on the future. His first teacher had been a village headman under the village baobab tree. At the age of 12 he had been identified as a youngster of potential by the emperor's advisors and taken to Addis Ababa to train as a Coptic priest. He measured up to his early promise and, before the revolution that displaced Emperor Haile Selassie, he had become chancellor of the university of Addis Ababa. He fled the country and later became a special advisor to UNESCO on numerous missions concerned with that part of Africa.

"Have you people ever stopped to think what the over-emphasis on Western education has done to my country, and countries like it?" he asked. "You came to Africa and told us that our traditional way of learning was out-of-date. You said that our way of formulating knowledge was inappropriate." You emphasised the dominance of narrowly defined intellectual skills. We listened too carefully to your advice. So we told parents that they needed to care for their children only when they were very young, but that proper learning would now be organised by professionals in schools. The old men were saddened as no one wanted to learn their wisdom, and the old women mourned for the grandchildren who would never come and talk with them. We emphasised higher education, and our students did well, many of them very well. So well that they were over-qualified and there were no challenging jobs for them in Ethiopia. They started to leave for lucrative careers here in America, in Europe, and in Australia. Many of them left our country for good, denying it the leadership it desperately needed. Society became increasingly unstable. We had, as it were, too many people trained to be clerks and few wise enough to be leaders, nor did we have responsible enough workers for the good of the country.

"So these men, like me, had to flee. My country became ever more unhappy. Far too many of those who remained have been de-skilled by this alien system of knowledge and learning. I look around me in Washington where I now live, and I see many young people who through the nature of their personalities, just do not fit into this restricted western view of learning. It is not what their inherited predispositions cry out for. So you Americans fail them. Once rejected, they become a threat to your lifestyle, and a rebuke to your ignorance to how it is that, through learning, we achieve our full humanity."

I was much moved by Aklilu's analysis of western epistemology. Learners everywhere so often seemed disconnected to reality - they saw bits, not wholes and had an unbelievable confidence in the effectiveness of the system. It was clear to me that what Aklilu was lamenting was the loss of the natural learning arrangements that had existed between the generations in Ethiopia and which had melded work, living and learning together into a meaningful existence. It was the breakdown of apprenticeship caused by the injection of the western model of education that had severed the age-old connection between the generations. This same thing happened in England in the nineteenth century when workers moved into the factories of the industrial revolution. Government had then needed to provide an alternative to the control of parents and grandparents whose employment was now in large factories rather than in the home, the small shop, the farm or the artisan workshop. From that point on the learning of children was increasingly the domain of professionals.

It was not just the Western world that was screwed up by the false assumptions about learning. The way we had exported these to the rest of the world had had quite devastating consequences. Later in the conference a research paper from Rwanda showed that parental support was the greatest single variable in children's performance in schools. "It is," said the spokesman, "a very European model built up by missionaries. Note this; 92 per cent of all children wear school uniforms in the semi-tropical rainforest - that seems bizarre. Yet only 55 per cent have exercise books and only 13 per cent have a maths book. Children struggle over great distances to get to schools, and often arrive exhausted, despite the fact that 79 per cent of all homes have a radio. Yet there are no radio programs of an educational nature for children. Learning is seen as essentially the affair of the school." The speaker went on to say, "It is very similar to the situation in Ethiopia. New forms of learning which emphasise the school and the university have significantly weakened the role of the community, and our sense of mutual interdependence. It is bad for our country."

Listening to all these presentations were more than 600 delegates from a large variety of countries. One speaker noted that there were now more students in the universities of Asia than there were in all the universities in all the OECD countries. Looking around the conference this was beginning to become obvious. There were people here from the Pacific Rim, from India and Pakistan, from Europe (14 from the newly established Commonwealth of Independent States), and from North and South America. There were only four Britons besides myself. We British, it seemed, were too busy queuing up for invitations to join national curriculum working parties.

That night, back in my room, I pulled out the papers that I was preparing for the next trustees' meeting back in England. One was a report dealing with the English national curriculum, written by Mary Marsh, head teacher of Holland Park School in London, and a member of the trust's council. "The process of change that the national curriculum has followed has been fragmented and directive ... the concept of the national curriculum is good in principle, but its development and implementation in practice exposed flaws in the original concept. The detail is too prescriptive and centrally controlled, and it leaves no room for creativity and flexibility. The strengths of good primary practice aren't being learnt at secondary level - differentiation within a class, working as a team, or in groups, confident independent learning and individualised assessments. All the recent amendments and directives put through by Parliament are quite contrary to this.

"It is extraordinary that schools are being required to revert to rigid terminal assessment dominated by simple written tests when the wider learning world, including further and higher education, and certainly many employers, increasingly value a competence-based accreditation of achievement. There are enormous dangers nationally if this is wrong, because schools are legally required to follow its prescript. Hence the teachers' passionate desire to change parts of this before it is ever put into place. What is most alarming is that so few people are actually involved in making these decisions. And those who do have very little current experience of what actually works in schools. Sadly the views of anyone in education are no longer trusted and so their comments, which are echoed by many others, are simply rejected without consideration. The nation took to the streets in the defence of the miners several years ago. If everyone really understood what was going on would they now do the same for the learning of young people in England?"

I sat back in my chair and swallowed hard. Why was it so hard for people to understand what this was all about? Arrogant as it sounds I realised it is not people's ignorance you need to fear, it's what they know that isn't true anymore that causes the problems. That was the root of the problem. The neurobiological base of all that was well explained by Howard Gardner.

I first met Howard at a conference in Virginia. We talked easily and I spoke of the time when my academic career had been saved by my success as a woodcarver. "A good example of apprenticeship," retorted Gardner. "That is what I will be talking about in a few minutes time, when I'll explain my research in my new book, *The Unschooled Mind*. Such forms of learning are innate to the human species, yet we've largely forgotten their efficacy." Gardner is in no a way charismatic presenter, and looks and talks very much like a university lecturer. He writes on the screen, often blocking with his own body the very illustration that he is trying to share. Yet he is so obviously the master of his material, and so clearly both original and careful in his thought, that he holds his audience spellbound.

"Pre-school children develop models, beliefs, and incipient theories from their earliest encounters with the physical and spatial worlds in which they live. They learn a vast amount of knowledge, skills and capabilities quite naturally. They seem endlessly to pursue new learning and to develop intuitive understandings of how to interact with their experience. Such conceptions as evolve in children's minds at this early stage are often flawed, inadequate or plainly wrong. By the age of five or six they have quite robust and serviceable sets of theories about mind, about matter, about life, and about self. These theories persist throughout their lives.

"I'll give you an illustration. How many of you have problems working out the old conundrum of which is the heavier, a pound of lead or a pound of feathers?" An amused murmur went around the room. "Even graduate physicists when asked a question like this out of context frequently get it wrong. Even when a school is successful, it typically fails to achieve its most important purpose - namely the development of understanding. We have failed to appreciate that in nearly every student there is a five-year old unschooled mind struggling to get out."

I liked that expression "an unschooled mind struggling to get out". I was struggling so hard to get all that down in my notes, that I missed part of what followed. But what I heard set my mind racing. " ... until now we have not fully appreciated just how difficult it is for schools to succeed in their chosen, appointed tasks. We have not been cognisant of the way in which the basic inclinations of human learning turn out to be ill-matched to the agenda of the modern secular school."

There were many questions: "Would you say, Professor Gardner, that most students don't really understand most of what they're being taught?" asked an earnest young man with a deep Southern accent.

"I'm afraid they don't," Gardner replied, "all the evidence I can find suggests that that is the case. Most schools have fallen into a pattern of giving kids exercises and drills that result in them getting answers on tests that look like understanding. It's what I call correct answer compromise; students read a text, they take a test, and everyone agrees that if they say a certain thing it will be counted as understanding. But the evidence from 20 or 30 years of research is really pretty compelling; students simply don't understand in the most basic sense of the term. They simply lack the capacity to take knowledge learned in one setting and apply it appropriately in another." I scribbled vigorously in my notes. This was critical. To deal with high levels of uncertainty in a rapidly changing world requires transferable skills, I noted. Transferable skills are the ones that really matter - skills that give us the confidence to change deeply held and treasured assumptions. How does this happen - that is the key question. I looked up from my notes as Gardner took another question.

"So what is the implication for what, and how much, I should teach in my classroom when I get back to high school next week?" asked the archetypal teacher.

Gardner looked pensive. "One obvious implication, one that very few people have begun to take seriously, is that we have to do a lot fewer things in school. The greatest enemy of understanding is coverage. As long as you're determined to cover everything, you actually ensure that most kids are not going to understand. You've got to take enough time to get kids deeply involved in something so that they can think about it in lots of different ways and apply it - not just at school, but at home, on the street and so on."

If only, I thought to myself, I could have persuaded the permanent secretary in London to have listened to that presentation, and to have done so with an open mind. Another influence on my thinking was an article recommended to me by Al Shanker who was president of the American Federation of Teachers. It was by Seely Brown and was about apprenticeship.

Brown's words had a familiar ring and reinforced my own experiences of learning. Apprenticeship, he wrote, is a method of organising teaching and learning by which important information is passed from one generation to another. Since the beginning of human history we have taught our children how to speak, how to grow crops and look after sheep, build a house or a cabinet, or to manage a household by showing them the skills and helping the next generation to model their behaviour on ours. By this model, learning and doing are inextricably connected and so too is the significance of each sub task seen in the context of the finished product - youngsters saw the essential connections between the tedium of sharpening a chisel and the beauty of the final carving.

The article went on to describe the four components that comprise the cognitive processes of apprenticeship. The first is Modelling; that is, the master showing the young learner how to do a task, and why it is significant. The second is Scaffolding; the provision of essential support for the young learner while learning all aspects of the new task (scaffolding supports a wall until the cement is quite dry). The third is Coaching; this, together with continuous discussion between master and apprentice, and between apprentice and apprentice is an essential part of learning. Such verbal exchanges go far beyond specific procedures, as may be found in a book, to include a whole range of intuitive understandings and folk wisdom whose significance was often hidden to the outsider, yet was an intrinsic part of craftsmanship. (Mr. Roast had exemplified that to me 25 years before.) The fourth and final component was of the greatest significance. Seely Brown called it Fading. Fading is the technical description for the reduction of external support - the taking away of the scaffolding - as the young learner becomes ever more proficient and therefore able to do things increasingly on his own. This culminated in the production of the masterpiece, the ultimate demonstration by the apprentice of his mastery of all the necessary skills so that Jack was as good as his master.

In apprenticeship, learners can see all the sub-processes being worked through - they are strictly visible and explicit. "In schooling, the processes of thinking are often invisible to both the student and the teacher. Cognitive apprenticeship," Seely Brown went on to say, "is a model of organising learning that works to make thinking visible. Although modern schools had been relatively successful in organising and conveying large bodies of factual and conceptual knowledge, standard pedagogic practice renders key aspects of expertise invisible to students," wrote Seely Brown. "Too little attention is paid to the reasoning and the strategies that the experts employ when they acquire knowledge or they put such knowledge to work to solve complex and real life tasks. Conceptual and problem solving knowledge acquired in school remains largely inert. In traditional apprenticeship the expert shows the apprentice how to do a task, watches as the apprentice practices portions of the task, and then turns over more and more responsibility until the apprentice is proficient enough to accomplish the task independently. That is the basic notion of apprenticeship". In other words, I concluded, it is about intellectual "weaning" - giving you sufficient skills to do things for yourself.

The article helped me tie together many thoughts and was highly influential in shaping what I would say in the future, particularly to explain "making thinking visible." The brains of our ancestors had slowly evolved in ways which could handle just such forms of learning, and that helped explain our predisposition to work in collaborative, problem-solving teams. It explained why we are so interested in talking about what we are doing, and how the successful worker is the one who can best gather ideas from other people. This was what I was soon to understand as a learning system that went with the grain of the brain. Now I had a theoretical framework that could be used to challenge teachers to go beyond the normal jargon which suggested that they should be "reflective practitioners" by helping them realise that this was only the beginning of the task. In the future teachers would have to go much, much further and ensure that pupils had to become reflective practitioners. That is what learners had been centuries before. It is what modern systems of learning had largely ignored. Here was the root of a world wide problem.

Back home, I was used to being ignored. At the grassroots level this was understandable because British teachers were preoccupied by national curriculum prescriptions. I was more riled by snubs from policy makers and had to learn that the likes of a cancelled meeting with Kenneth Clarke and the pointless encounter with John Patten were par for the course. The less interested government seemed to be, however, the more in demand I was as a public speaker and one of my invitations was to chair an annual international roundtable at Somerville College, Oxford. Among the 60 or so delegates were 20 American academics and education ministers from the Philippines, Belarus, Norway, the Congo, South Africa, Estonia, Sudan, Portugal, Sweden, Jamaica and Ethiopia.

In previous years, I was told, either the British secretary of state or his permanent secretary, had welcomed the delegates after dinner but neither was available. Where was there any semblance of reality in all this? I, the officially rejected, being asked to stand in for officialdom.

It turned out to be a delightful evening, a curious mixture of Oxford formality plus the warmth and exuberance of the Americans, and the wisdom of people from every continent. Sir Richard Southward, the vice chancellor, presided at dinner and formally welcomed the delegates. I drank moderately, fearful in case the fine wine should go to my head, but quickly found that, as I rose to speak, I was surrounded by an audience that was both attentive and quite ready to have its thinking stimulated. In the 20 minutes at my disposal I challenged them to think about learning rather than schooling. "Travelling the world as you all do, no doubt you have been faced by the similarity of the issues which constantly crop up in each others countries. Crisis in schools is as real in New York as it is in London or Sydney. Is it really just a coincidence, that all that is wrong is that teachers have gone soft? Gone soft, in all countries, in the same way? The coincidence is far too great. At a period of uncertainty it is much easier to blame teachers than to look at the deeper issues that inevitably underline this lack of confidence in a system which appears to have had its day, and which no amount of tinkering appears to significantly change. Is it not possible that the whole system is now out of step, both with the demands of modern society and with the brain's normal learning strategies? Aren't most of us so overawed by the scale of the problems that we continue to confuse learning with schooling? Learning and schooling are not synonymous."

Two weeks later Anne and I and the three boys were in Australia where I was to address the annual conference of the Australian Secondary Head Teachers. The day before my lecture, Tony Hill, the head master of the prestigious Melbourne Grammar School, made a powerful speech that I would have been delighted to have made myself.

"Teaching is equated with telling; knowledge is equated with facts; and learning is measured by our students' ability to recall. Our methods are inefficient with students waiting their turn to participate in groups that are too large for genuine interaction. For many students classes are boring, rigid and interrupt rather than encourage learning. Classes are either too large or too small. We persist with lock-step promotion of our students in all subjects, rather than in taking account of their individual development. Common sense tells us that each individual grows and learns at a different rate. Our class structures, teaching methods, curriculum and timetable take no account of this obvious fact. Whilst we spend large amounts of money on new technology, we rarely use it creatively to assist in learning. We do not really help our students learn how to think."

"Essentially our students are not sufficiently challenged. We under-estimate their capabilities. If anything, the work they are given is not hard enough. We confuse long hours of work with genuine intellectual challenge - the latter is often sadly lacking. We have rules and rituals that take up an enormous amount of time and energy to little purpose. We have an obsession with uniform, rather than with the elements of genuine courtesy. We persist with punishments which are barbaric and which are far too often totally ineffective in changing behaviour."

"Our schools should be places where students and teachers develop an understanding of themselves, gain an appreciation of their relationship to society, have a sense of community which goes far beyond the school walls, work extremely hard, and have a lot of fun in the 'zealous and voluntary pursuit of knowledge' - so much so that they want to continue that pursuit for the rest of their lives."

It was a fine speech, and rightly applauded. Things in Australia were, it seemed, just as they were in the UK. Aklilu Habte was right. The British model of learning "was one of the most influential of colonial exports." "Well done, Tony, good stuff," people said, as they made their way out of the rather dingy classroom which served the needs of the fringe presentations. I stayed behind, and found that only two or three others really wanted to push thinking on such issues. "Yes, it's very depressing," Tony remarked, "I didn't intend just to give a speech that got loud applause. I wanted to shake them so hard that they felt uncomfortable, felt that they would have to go out and change things at a profound level. It did not do that. Will anyone ever hear this and take notice? Will anybody help build a new agenda? We've given up any belief in ourselves being able actually to do anything about what most of us can quite clearly see is not as good as it needs to be." He turned to me. "I hope you're more successful tomorrow than I have been!"

The speech I gave was similar to that which had so moved the heads of the Girls' Schools of England the previous year. It certainly extended the thinking in Tony Hill's speech of the night before, by rooting the changes which needed to be made in a better appreciation of how humans learn. The audience seemed to sit heavy. I tried my hardest to alter the pace of their thinking by changing the inflection of my voice, by using periods of silence, and by drawing on anecdotes.

Eventually I caught Tony Hill's eye, and he slowly winked, a wink acknowledging our mutual frustration with our audience, and in his case I thought there was something deeper - it was more than frustration, it was despair. Shortly after he announced his resignation as he moved to the United States, while another member of the audience was shortly to move to England and become the head of Eton College.

There was a polite round of applause when I finished speaking, and several invitations to repeat my speech to several groups as we toured Australia over the next three weeks. My three sons sat in the front row. As people stopped to talk with me on the way out I was aware of one head teacher talking in a rather peremptory manner to David. It was not until several days later that I discovered what she had said. By that time we were in Sydney and David, following up one of his assignments from school, was squatting on the plaza in front of the Sydney Opera House, busily sketching various views of that extraordinary sail-like structure that encases the auditorium. His sketch was masterful, giving the whole structure a vitality and almost a sense of movement. "That's fantastic," I said. But David frowned. "Do you remember the headmistress who spoke to me after your lecture?" I nodded. "Well, she said it was wrong that we'd come to Australia with you in school time because we should have been in class. I don't believe her. She didn't know what she was talking about. I could never, ever have got the feeling of this place from a photograph. It's awesome. I'm sure it'll change my views about architecture forever! It was worth coming all the way to Australia just to see this."

"She didn't know what she was talking about" - that was the direct, and candid view of a 12 year-old; a terrible indictment of an older generation determined at all costs to hold on to the institutional arrangements which, for fear of upsetting the system, would have children study the extravagant flowing lines of the Sydney Opera House from a photograph, rather than in reality. And we wonder why it is so difficult to motivate youngsters! Are we really that blind?

*         *         *

Let me fast forward now to autumn 1998 and my own moment of truth that came to me in Tokyo where a conference had been called by the Asian Development Bank. The delegates - economists, nutritionists, trainers, educators and community affairs specialists - spoke about the changing needs of education around the Pacific and revealed the universality of educational problems. To me, well-versed in the fact that the English who always thought it was the Japanese who got it right, I was amazed that it was they who were the most concerned. Collapsed classrooms, where learning has to stop because of disruptive pupils, are now being reported by nearly half the elementary and junior high school teachers in Japan. "What on earth is happening?" I asked with my stereotypic assumption of neat, well-organised, and incredibly well-disciplined pupils hanging on their teachers' every word. "It's complex," I was told, "but essentially Japanese children are more attuned to the fundamental changes that are going on in society than are their teachers, and even more so than the Ministry of Education." Tetsuya Shikushi, a Japanese commentator told me that Japanese students were looking for more open, honest exchanges with their teachers who could stimulate their imagination. "The natural response is for people to want to give the schools more regulations and more rules, but the real need is for more freedom."

"Schools have no room for innovation, and they have been very slow to respond to growing individualism," observed another.

An official from the Singapore Ministry of Education commented, "You westerners have been overly impressed by the performance of our pupils on international tests. Surely you realise that if you take all the students who will take these tests and, for four days a week for many weeks in advance of writing the test you give them practice papers, then of course they will get high scores. But that proves very little. We, apparently like the Japanese, know that we have to do something better than this. If we are not to be seen as an intellectual gulag then we must cut our national curriculum by at least 30 per cent to create space for individuality, creativity and spontaneous interest."

"We have lost our sense of direction," said an Indian professor of philosophy. "Twenty years ago the declared aim of my university was the creation of honourable people. Now our chancellor decorates his mantelpiece with photographs of himself standing beside his new Rolls Royce." Some people were thoughtfully silent, some laughed, but many quickly lost patience with the professor. "We are here to talk about education for economic growth," said one of the organisers, "not to talk about values." There was a stunned silence, and the delegates broke for tea.

"How old are you?" asked one of the Australians joining a group sipping their coffee and pondering the inevitable question, education for what? To my amazement most of them were in fact younger than I, and were obviously relieved that soon they would take retirement and leave the answer of this critical question to others.

Later that evening I took the opportunity of going out by myself and quietly walking through a Buddhist temple. It was peaceful, and only a few young people were around. I began to feel my age - 60 next birthday. Feel, not in the sense of feeling decrepit, but in the reality that I could not expect to be as active in the future, as I had in the past. I felt an enormous imperative to finish the writing of this book for a wider audience to see their own impatience reflected in mine and, most importantly, to encourage a conviction that something can be done.

*     *     *

I return now to the chronology and the departure of Brian Corby, the Education 2000 chairman who had been tireless in helping find ever more contacts to approach for fund-raising. He was preparing to retire as chief executive of the Prudential early in 1994, and was anxious to unload his other responsibilities and when I contemplated running the trust without him I became immediately nervous. Then, just before Christmas, I met up with David Peake, the recently retired chairman of Kleinwort Benson who had hosted the dinner at which Kenneth Baker and I had set out our alternative cases for bank sponsorship years before. While Brian had always been pleased to paint the big picture as our chairman - and gained for me access to the great and the good - David was far more interested in the detail, and the quality of the trust's thinking. He was shortly to make an ideal chairman.

That summer, the government invited responses to the draft proposals for the national curriculum. As a trust we made a careful response, trying hard to persuade officials to think more carefully about the learning process, and not simply to base the curriculum on the study of separate disciplines. "It has been the priority given historically to the study of individual disciplines over and above the study of how to equip young people, quite explicitly, with the skills of learning, which has largely created the present crisis in schools," the trust had written. "To continue a reform process that assumes, firstly, that the current subject disciplines are the appropriate framework for learning how to learn, and, secondly, that the skills needed to be creative and productive in the twenty-first century automatically - by some process presumably of osmosis - grow out of these disciplines, is, we are convinced, ill-founded."

"Just what exactly do you mean by that?" asked Ron Dearing, when he and I were invited to talk about the significance of what we had written over tea one afternoon. Here was an opportunity to explain directly to the man who had been called in some time before by government to resolve the stalemate that had developed over the national curriculum. The one-time chairman of the Post Office, he had quickly been characterised as Postman Ron by the educational press, but John Patten had been unusually shrewd in appointing Ron Dearing for here was an accomplished negotiator, conciliator and a good listener. That Dearing had been appointed at all was a measure of the breakdown between those intellectuals concerned with educational policy, and the politicians. For months they had argued detail, and got further into an impasse. Ron Dearing made no claims to being an educationalist; tragically that was not what government thought it needed. It was his skills as a conciliator that were needed, for government was after a compromise, not an intellectual breakthrough.

Dearing was well used to people asking to meet him to press a special case, and he had many strategies to prevent him compromising himself. Yet, as I looked at him again, I saw a man who was obviously a good judge of character and an adroit manager of people. Here was a good man, but also a man who must have had his fill of trying to unravel the knots tied by academics. I hoped, as he looked at me, he saw in me an honest man as well, trying hard to deal with the frustration of putting important ideas into simple words. If I was right, he needed what I had to say if he were to find any way of breaking out of the restricted, unimaginative thinking which so hedged in the national curriculum.

We got on well. He quickly acknowledged my point that not everything could happen in school. He identified with the idea of reversing staffing ratios between the primary and the secondary schools, and immediately commented that expenditures on books and other learning resources had to increase.

Then I sought to show him those things could be related if we really came to terms with the new understandings about human learning. We had to show youngsters how they could, quite systematically, learn how to manage their own learning. "Learning," I said, "is a learnable skill."

"Tell me," he asked, "at what stage do children really show the capability to begin to understand their own learning? Is it 14 or do we have to wait until 16?"

The question amazed me. I had to be careful not to let my eyebrows jump too far. Carefully I talked about my own experience of working with children in primary school, including my own children. Then I talked about the school in the Bronx, and the teachers who had been trained at the London Institute in the 1960s. And I talked about the need for young people passing into puberty to start taking responsibilities for themselves. He understood that.

To my delight one of his advisors, the woman with special responsibility for Key Stage 4, entered the conversation by saying, "I know this is not really my area, Sir Ron, but as a mother of a ten year-old boy in primary school I'm really impressed with how he copes with his own learning. In fact, I sense he's developing the very skills and attitudes that John's talking about, and my fear is that secondary schools just won't be able to handle this."

There was silence. "Surely that's not the case, is it? That would be a disaster." exclaimed Sir Ron. The rest of us looked at each other. This was scary. These were the people heading up the work of the national curriculum. The voice of a mother challenging the status quo was too difficult for them to deal with and there was another long pause. This posed questions that went beyond Sir Ron's brief - these were things politicians did not want questioned.

Sir Ron tried to change the topic. "Tell me about your interest in international research," he asked. I sketched out the salient points and said how much I thought the UK could gain from being a partner in this. He picked up his ears at this, as if it were a completely new idea. At any rate it was an idea that could be put into action relatively easily- a program, self-contained and readily assessable, could then be set up.

Soon it was time to wind up the meeting. I gave him a couple of papers about the proposed international program, and why it was important. He shook my hand with genuine warmth. I liked him and wanted to help him. I was terrified at the responsibility heaped on his shoulders, largely because academics, policy makers, and administrators had not been able to resolve these issues by themselves. I heard no more from him, and a few days later learnt he had been ordered to take an extended rest. As well as being responsible for the national curriculum he was also the chairman of the company that had been successful in its bid to administer the National Lottery. Was there a connection?

 

＊      ＊      ＊

The summer half term was fast approaching. With three rapidly growing sons of ten, 12 and 15 what do you do with the opportunity of four days together which does not involve spending too much money? A bike ride seemed the answer, with the promise of a good meal each evening. The first day we went to the Essex/Suffolk border and cycled through Long Melford, Thaxstead and Cavendish. It's a fascinating part of England. In the sixteenth century it was the richest, and the most densely populated part of the country, a wealth built on the world trade. Each village, and there are many of them, has a well-built church and plenty of thatch on the wattle and daub cottages. Finchingfield is a particular gem. It's a rich area again, we noted, judging by the number of Volvos driven too fast around the narrow lanes. "It's too close to London," said Anne, "and the houses are so expensive because they've been bought up by London commuters for weekend cottages."

The second day we went further afield, to a part of Lincolnshire that I had not visited since I was a child. Running down between where the low, fertile hills of the inner Lincolnshire Wolds meet the rich loamy soils of the fens, reclaimed in the seventeenth century, are a string of villages with names dating from the days of the Viking settlements - Dowsby, Donsby, Haconby, Graby, and Thwolby. A perfect example, I told the boys, of spring-line settlements, with wealthy villages based on a rich agricultural economy of sheep and cattle rearing on the hills, and highly fertile arable farming on the reclaimed peats. "Look at the map," I had said to the boys, "you can see each of these little villages has a church. A sure sign that long ago they were wealthy. Look, each village stretches along a single road and most have what the map calls an inn, a superior kind of pub, often acting like a small hotel".

I was really looking forward to this particular ride. Nostalgia was at work again. Here the boys would see old England, a rural idyll that must surely have benefited from the agricultural profitability. "Just remember, darling, you're no longer a teacher," Anne reminded me. I was in danger of trying to give the children too many informal lessons.

We cycled first through the low hills of the Wolds. The fields were tidy and neat. The large farmhouses looked so impeccably well cared for that I doubted if any farmer now lived there. Then we came out onto the Fen. The large fields stretched far into the distance, a mosaic of colour reflecting at least half a dozen major ripening crops. We cycled into one of the villages, and the next, and the next. I was horrified. What I had remembered with such delight as rich rural scenery seemed to be decaying. Communities with the stuffing knocked out them are a sad sight. Then I saw several signs indicating to which large agri-business each track of Fen belonged.

"Dad, look at that huge farm machinery in that barn," said one of the boys indicating a size of tractor I had previously associated with the Canadian prairies. Most of the farms, and farmhouses, which had previously worked this area were now clearly out of business, the farmyards covered in weeds, and the outbuildings falling down. One ex-village shop was now a video store. What had been farm labourers' cottages now provided cheap accommodation for people from Bourn, or Graton or Spaulding. Churches, whose churchyards had imposing gravestones set up by proud and relatively wealthy generations in the past, looked ill-cared for. So did the war memorials. Outlying farm houses almost invariably had large aggressive looking dogs tethered in their yards. Large signs warned "beware of the dog." We needed no further warning. When you're on a bike you feel pretty vulnerable. A large paper sign, now smudged by the rain, posted across a notice board in the middle of one village read "Save our School." The school in another village was already closed.

"I don't like this, Dad," said Tom, "let's get away from here."

"What's gone wrong, Dad?" asked Peter as we sat eating our sandwiches. "That was rich soil. It's not as poor as parts of Scotland were when we cycled through the Highlands last summer. Someone's making a lot of money if they have such huge machines. The houses in the village look lovely from a distance, but the villages aren't very lively."

"Well," I took a deep breath and started to explain, "I don't think I like it either. It's what's called factory farming and it's all part of a massive change that's sweeping agriculture world-wide. It's a feature of what the economists are saying is the marvellous new concept of agri-business. The running of farm land as if it were a factory. I guess very little, if any, of the land is still owned by the people in the village as it probably was 20 or 30 years ago. The land would now be owned by an investment trust that isn't even necessarily English. Such investors would have joined together many small farms, knocked down the fences, put in a lot of equipment and, instead of employing old-fashioned farmers who would have lived in the village, they employ instead technicians who work the big machines. They probably live in the towns so the old villages are, literally, dying on their feet, but one day soon I expect many of these houses will be bought by people living in the towns - as holiday homes; just as they were in those Essex villages."

"Where does the money go if it doesn't go into the villages?"

"Well, the profits are shared out between the shareholders. They could live anywhere, but most of them would live in the large cities, and I doubt if very many of them would have any clear idea of where their money comes from. But you see, to organise farming like this means everyone can have cheaper food."

"Well if it means doing that to the countryside I wouldn't mind paying more for my food," said Peter. "There was something frightening about those villages. Many of the people looked depressed. And the dogs were frightening."

Everything is connected to everything, I have kept telling the boys in conversation after conversation. Every activity has its consequence. Wisdom is the ability to get everything into proper focus. Technology itself is neutral, it's up to us how we use it. I hope the lessons will be with all of us for a long time. Hopefully they will grow to be the young men who, in years to come, will practice the question the ancient Navajo used to ask of each other about any proposed new way of doing things. "What effect will all this have seven generations on from now?"

We put our bikes away after three days holiday, feeling saddle-sore, stiff, yet with splendidly tanned faces and arms. In subsequent years we have talked several times about what we saw in those villages and in the farms. An illustration will suffice to show how it is that the most trivial, apparently passing, instances in early life profoundly shape the way young people's thinking later develops.

"Dad," said Tom some years later as we drove the Skyline drive through the Shenandoah National Park in Virginia, "I want to be a farmer when I grow up. Not a farmer of one of those big factory farms in the Fens, but something like Seamus' farm in Ireland - about 50 acres."

"Well, you have to be quite rich to start with," I replied.

"But wasn't your grandfather a farmer - your Dad's Dad?"

"Yes, he had three farms in Devon, each of less than 100 acres."

"Well, wasn't he rich?" replied Tom thinking he had solved the problem.

"No ... I'm afraid things were different then. When he sold those farms people weren't very interested in agriculture, and the prices were very low."

"Well," said Tom, "that's what I want to do. I'll learn everything I need to understand; I'll get all my ideas together and plan it carefully. How much money will I need to get set up?"

"Fifty acres at £3,000/acre is £150,000. Add the cost of the buildings and equipment and the animals and you would need probably another £200,000. Then you'd need what's called an operating float of about £100,000. So I guess you'd need at the minimum £500,000, plus a small house and trucks - call it £650,000."

Tom's face lengthened. "Where would I get all that money from? Does that mean that I'll have to spend all my life doing a job I don't want to do just to save enough money so that, when I'm old, I can buy a farm and do something my great-grandfather used to do?"

"I think I'm going to be a politician when I grow up," Peter concluded. "It must be really interesting to try and sort out problems like this. It needs everyone to get together to sort it all out." His brothers looked at him in amazement, and with a growing sense of admiration. Anne looked disconcerted and I knew why - the reputation of politicians in England and

America seemed to be at an all time low, and the thought of her son getting caught up in this terrified her. Deep down I have to admit I was thrilled. Peter was trying to make sense of the world and was not daunted by the scale of the problems. Immediately, however, Peter had a difficult problem. For five or six years he had been using a computer at home to word process his essays. He was good at doing this and worked fast. Then his teacher warned him that he ought to give up using the computer for the next six months so as to concentrate on getting his text right the first time for the GCSE exams he would be taking the following summer. Peter was furious. "Doesn't anyone realise I type three times faster than I can write? And anyway, I don't think in a straight line, so why should I write in a straight line? If technology can't be used in exams then no one will ever take any notice of it, will they?"

I smiled to myself. "Peter's taking after you more than you realise," said Anne later that evening.

# 14
# The Newsworthy Brain

The Society of Education Officers is neither a trades union, nor a professional lobby group. It is a society of like-minded people of high intent, education officers from the youngest, ambitious professional assistant arranging school bus schedules, right through to the most senior of chief education officers who, in the time of the Inner-London Education Authority, included people controlling budgets of hundreds of millions of pounds. In 1985, the year I started Education 2000, Donald Fisher was the president of the SEO, and I doubt if he would ever have anticipated that within less than a decade I would be invited to address the society at its winter conference. However, it was not just that my position had changed for, starting in the mid-1970s, when Britain's precarious economic position led to the intervention of the International Monetary Fund, stringent reductions on internal services including education, and the escalating centralist tendencies of a Conservative government, had meant that the society members had felt under increasing threat. Indeed, in the early 1990s even the existence of a local education authority was at risk with the establishment of the School Funding Agency.

For all the large budgets that they controlled, the chief education officers, and the Society of which they were part, remained more like a collection of mature schoolteachers, rather than businessmen or administrators. That I was invited to address them at their winter conference was, given the relationship that had existed in Hertfordshire years before, quite remarkable. Working my, by now, usual tight schedule a snowstorm in Chicago almost prevented me from getting to Harrogate from a conference that I had addressed in Wisconsin 36 hours previously. Flights out of O'Hare were diverted and I ended up in Zurich when I had expected to be in Manchester. A quick shift of plans enabled Anne to meet me in London with the car, together with our three sons, and we made it to the conference with half an hour to spare.

The reception they gave us as a family was warm and courteous. Conversation flowed easily. Nevertheless I knew deep down that they still thought like teachers. By that, I mean they thought of learning in terms of schools. And, as most of their teaching experience was in secondary schools, when they thought of schools it was with the needs and aspirations of secondary teachers in mind that they approached problems. Few primary teachers ever made it through to chief education officer, possibly because they realised that they got more satisfaction teaching pupils, than ever they would working through the syllabus of their subjects year after year in secondary schools. Children are always different; subject teaching can too easily become formalised and repetitive.

Their biggest limitation, however, is that most of them were classic success stories of the education system. They had done well at school - mainly in the grammar schools, not the independent schools. Many got scholarships to university. After finishing their degrees either they hadn't want to stay at the university as dons, or they hadn't been invited to do so. Yet they had obviously not been tempted to leave the world of academia, and so became schoolteachers. They were not natural risk-takers. Many of them left the classroom for administration after a few years of subject teaching which had not taxed their imagination very much. A few got through to headships early and after five or six years had decided, in their early forties, that administration was better than a further 20 years of running a school. Their value systems, therefore, were those of the school and the academic. They wrote splendid papers, but they agonised over painful decisions. Procrastination often became their natural retreat. More deep thinking than many politicians, more humane and concerned for detail, they were no real match for politicians-in-a-hurry, who played, at the end of the twentieth century, by the ruthless rules of survival.

Two hundred members of the Society sat before me, good, caring men and women delighted to be away from their offices, and the endless special pleading from locally elected counsellors, and the machinations of their chairmen of committees to whom each was answerable. Some had their notebooks and pencils at the ready, but most sat back comfortably expecting me to speak well, tell a few good stories, but not to challenge the way they thought. They were tired of being challenged head on.

I had to take them stealthily into my thinking. I told a story to break the ice - the one about Mercedes Benz. They enjoyed that, and laughed. Then I got to business.

"I have been invited here to share a vision with you. It is an exciting vision, but not a comfortable one. It means taking control of innovation, and shaping it - rather than being shaped by it. More certainties however have to collapse before that vision can be achieved. We have to work in deep water. We will all be out of our depth - no one will be tall enough to keep even one foot on the bottom. Gillian Shephard (secretary of state for education) says that there will be a five-year period of consolidation. I must tell you that there won't be. This is a false dream. Change sets its own remorseless agenda. If we want to shape this we have to ride the wave; being a breakwater wears you out."

Several laughed somewhat hollowly at that. "Many aspects of this vision have already been identified; most involve sacrificing sacred cows and challenging institutional inertia. If we are timid and play it safe, we won't get there. You will never leap a canyon in two short jumps, says an old Indian proverb."

I invited the audience to think again about the world in which youngsters were moving. "Markets, once jealously guarded and protected, are becoming increasingly open and global. As competition intensifies, our lives become increasingly shaped by economic and social trends that transcend national boundaries. It's easy to feel powerless.

"Until recently the model of a successful business or social organisation was one where decisions were taken at the top and then transmitted downwards to those who were expecting to obey orders. Today the situation is totally different. We all have personal experience of this. Organisations have opened up; networks of smaller units, each with a high degree of autonomy, are becoming ever more important. The individuals who work in these re-shaped work places need the confidence and the ability to think for themselves. The ability to learn and go on learning matters as never before.

"The highly industrialised countries of the West have moved into the Knowledge Society. Workers have now to be learners as well if they are constantly to develop their own capabilities. Sometimes they have to compromise their own specialisations to support the overall aim of the organisation. Knowledge workers are dependent on other people, yet they also need to be independent. Organisations come into being for specific purposes – and when that purpose is completed the individuals separate and then re-group. As Bob Allen, the CEO of AT&T, recently remarked, 'in the future there won't be jobs, instead there will be a series of projects.'

"Workers will each need to continuously learn new skills on their own. They can expect to find professionals drawn from many backgrounds and linked through electronic networks as close colleagues. Each must keep abreast with the leading edge of change because that is where the comparative advantage now lies.

"In addition to the basic skills of numeracy, literacy, calculation and communication – let's call these the old competencies, those without which people can't start to function in the knowledge society – we now need a whole series of new competencies. We need the ability to conceptualise problems and solutions using at least four basic skills; abstraction (the manipulation of thoughts and patterns); systems thinking (interrelated thinking); experimentation; and collaboration. We will all need these skills for our ever more complex social lives, as well as for work and employment.

"So what does all this mean for us?

"I would suggest that schools now have a vital role in starting a dynamic process by which pupils are given the confidence to manage their own learning, to cooperate with colleagues, and to use a range of resources and learning situations which progressively wean them from their earlier dependence on teachers and institutions. But such skills, practices, and attitudes cannot be taught solely in the classroom, nor can they be developed by teachers alone. There is now the need to recognise and exploit the fact that schooling in the future must involve both learning in school as well as learning through a variety of community experiences. Young people require a new learning environment, made up partly of formal schooling, and partly of informal learning opportunities. They need the support not only of teachers but of their peer group, and critically - adults of all kinds. 'Every child needs a whole village to complete its education', as the oft-quoted Indian proverb has it.

"The Knowledge Society is increasingly non-hierarchical. It grows out of an emerging awareness of the individuals own responsibility to find new opportunities. It has to be about what people feel about themselves. The context of education, when the public thinks about it, is perceived to be concerned with the mastering of specific disciplines, even if their own post-school experiences would suggest to them the limitations of such an argument. The influence of universities upon the secondary curriculum is now extending downwards into primary education. The key person in the Industrial Age was seen to be the specialist - the person who can analyse, rather than the person who can take a broad view.

"We despised the generalist as the jack of all trades and master of none." In the economy that is emerging it is the expert, someone even better than the generalist, that is most needed. These are the people who are able to spot new patterns, connections and embryonic ideas from a variety of sources and see how these converge to solve what were otherwise intractable problems. The development of expertise, the ability to look imaginatively across specialisms, is the key skill in the emerging economy.

"Yet there is a real paradox. While publicly proclaiming conventional scholarship, at the individual level the specialist is often dismissed as being narrow and lacking practical credibility. The education system is blamed both for failing to equip everyone with basic skills, whilst also being too restrictive in its definition of success. At a gut level there is an increasing recognition that a better education system has to mean a different system, not just more of the same.

"Too often we have set out on bold reforms with too little preparation, an unclear understanding of what we are doing, too few resources, and far too short a time scale. Even if an increasing number of people are feeling deeply unhappy about the status quo, fundamental reform remains largely unattractive."

"I have a proposal based on the assumption that, if we were to have a better understanding of how the brain worked, we could design a new model of education more compatible with the brain's natural processes. We could move resources around throughout the various sectors of the education system, and across formal schooling and informal learning. We could, I believe, eventually construct a better system at no greater cost than at the present. But we have to think differently."

"Let me give you an analogy that many people have found useful. Man's survival depends both on eating and thinking; both processes are synonymous with life itself. By studying the nature of food and the digestive system, modern science has, over the past 50 years, enabled us to become healthier and live longer. Now we can apply similar techniques to the understanding of the brain. Having improved man's health we can now improve the use that we make of our intellectual processes."

"The tools to do this are now at hand. Medical science now enables us to study the processes of the brain directly, not just by observation of external phenomena. As the Nobel Prize winning biologist Gerald Edelman (the discoverer of the human immune system) wrote, 'we can now link psychology to physiology ... we can link external processes to internal processes. The brain does not always work in the way we used to think it did. The study of learning, which started with the philosophers, has broadened to embrace anthropologists, bio-chemists, psychologists, artificial intelligence researchers, and is now having its boundaries further extended by biologists and neurologists. It is advancing so quickly that it is difficult to keep up. We have to be competent generalists to see where all this is going.'"

Suddenly the brain has become newsworthy." I asked how many members of the Society had watched Susan Greenfield's lecture three weeks before from the Royal Institute, televised by the BBC; it was less than five per cent. "You had better look out," I said, "because soon you will have children bringing legal charges against you for failing to utilise what is now known about learning in your schools and your own lessons." That shocked them. "You're right to be shocked. Have you not read of patients taking their general practitioners to court for failing to apply a new, approved drug to cure a serious disease?" When 14 year-olds know more about how the brain works and how learning takes place than do administrators or professors of education, then we really have a problem.

"Hidden inside a thick and highly protective skull, it has been almost impossible to see the brain in action when it is alive, and only recently have the tools of modern medicine - CAT scans and the like - been able to show something of how it actually operates. That little grey mass is an amazing complex of structures which, in each of us, reflects the whole of man's evolution. Within our brain, some scientists suggest, exist three separate brains – a reptilian brain around the brain stem which controls the most basic of human functions and is, as it were, a residual function sufficient for the needs of man's predecessors several million years ago; a mammalian brain which controls emotion, sexuality, memory, survival instincts, etc., and around that there is the third – the cortex – which is the most recent and amazing evolutionary achievement. This controls our thinking, seeing, hearing and creativity. It is possible, therefore, to study the workings of a primitive brain through the study of each one of us. Because when pressures become too great, and we feel under enormous threat and can't cope, we effectively downshift; we ignore our higher order skills and processes, and revert to the more basic survival techniques of the jungle which rely on the less sophisticated brains.

"The brain is designed to constantly make sense of its surroundings and reacts to the environment on the basis of selectivity. This enables it to adapt to each and every new stimulant, and to decide which are to its benefit, and which should be ignored. A mechanism therefore designed for survival and growth in any situation – not in any sense a robot waiting for a puppet master. Truly it is the essence of intelligence; inquisitive, imaginative, creative and certainly inventive.

"The brain is designed to perform many tasks at the same time – thoughts, emotions, imagination and predispostions all operate simultaneously. We know that the brain operates most effectively when it is dealing with natural and complex situations. It processes the wholes and parts simultaneously. It works with both generalisations and specifics. It is both trying to subdivide and compartmentalise ideas, whilst always looking for possible relationships and discontinuities.

"The creation of uncluttered learning environments where the brain has no room for peripheral perception frustrates its natural functioning since it automatically registers the familiar, while always searching for the novel. Learning and self-esteem are intricately interconnected; to frustrate the individual's capacity to learn is to destroy much of what it means to be human. Learning is an immensely complex business which we seek to simplify and codify at our peril. To put faith in a highly directive, prescriptive curriculum is to so go against the grain of the brain that it will inhibit creativity and enterprise, the very skills needed in the complex, diverse, Knowledge Society that we desperately need to prepare our children for.

"All this takes us beyond the school, even beyond a pyramid of schools, or even schools as a species that neatly defines planning for the effective management and delivery systems for education. We are dealing," I said, "not with schools and the agenda of education but, at the deepest and most profound level, with what it means to be human, and how we develop our humanity.

"Writing in *Schools for Thought* in 1993, John Bruer said: 'If we change our representation of intelligence, learning and teaching ... we change relationships between students and teachers, schools and the community ... and our representation of what the classroom and schools should look like. This will cost [a great deal in research into new applications] and if we want to improve our schools, and if existing methods are not working well enough, we have little choice but to make this investment. We should focus on the educational process, not the product.'

"We now have the knowledge available to construct new systems of learning that will give us more intelligent and thoughtful young people. We have been ignoring the signs of this for years. Because we are so loyal to the system we have grown up with we are reluctant to change the current schools for fear of the stress this will cause. We claim that we are doing this to protect those children whose home life is already unstable, but in reality we are now requiring the schools to do more than they could ever cope with.

"We run faster to stand still. Look at the teachers - can they take anymore? Look at the pupils - are we confident they will do better than us? We see change as a threat. We ignore the technological, social and economic developments that surround us, instead of using them to our advantage.

"A New Orleans newspaper comment on a speech I gave to American head teachers put it succinctly:

> At a time when we are trying to get young children to do things for themselves, we actually put the youngest children into the largest classes (and then let them drown), and then put the oldest into the smallest classes (and make it ever easier for them to lean on the teacher for more support). As the outside world becomes an increasingly attractive place to find things out, and to experiment with ideas, we are trying to put evermore things into the schools. Abbott said that all this had to change by a redistribution of money (including funding work to be done in the home rather than in the school) but without any extra money in total ... just better value. Sounds like the Brits have the same problem as us - maybe they are farsighted enough to do this quicker than us. If so, the US had better look out.

"Let me conclude. Currently you and I, and our colleagues, have largely lost the educational initiative. It is the politicians who call the tunes. In terms of bold, imaginative, critical thinking we have not given the country the lead it needs. Unless politicians are given ideas from those who have been there and worked things out for themselves, all they can ever do is mount political initiatives with a time scale of four years or less. The structure of the department for education is there to ensure the continuance of the present arrangements. It has no expertise of its own - perhaps no interest - in the consideration of the wider aspects of learning.

"We can't go on like this. Society should not even let us. By we in this instance I mean all professional educators. We can't go on trying to do this all on our own. We can no longer play within the same old rules. Society - thinking people at large - know this, but don't quite know what to do.

"If ever we are paying the price for our emphasis on specialists and bureaucracies it is now. In this vacuum politicians are having a field day. We may well be affronted by what they do - incensed at the shortness of their time scales - but we have failed to produce an alternative vision.

"The problem is partly intellectual and partly a matter of power.

"Intellectually we have to get our minds around a whole new way of thinking about how learning takes place. This needs an initiative bigger than any single authority can handle. This is a national issue. Britain doesn't even have to do the research on its own. Nor does any other country. What we do have to do is search the research from around the world and meld it with the best of all your experiences and then present a powerful case of circumstantial evidence as to why we need a new system of education that genuinely goes with the grain of the brain.

"And the issue of power. What is the administrative unit in which all these ideas have to be worked out? Peter Drucker, in *Post-Capitalist Society* wrote, 'so far no country has the education system which the Knowledge Society needs ... learning has to permeate the entire society. Schooling will no longer be what schools do. Increasingly it will be a joint venture in which schools are partners, rather than monopolies ... schools will be only one of the available teaching and learning institutions.'

"The unit of change is eluding us. I believe it is smaller than a conventional local education authority. It is certainly larger than a single school. It has to be something, Drucker says, 'that ordinary people can get their arms around.' We have to build a new definition of community where living, working and learning are all of one piece. Can the Society of Education Officers make such a vision a reality?"

I sat down to a reassuring round of applause. I got up, and smiled as I acknowledged their gratitude. But then I looked at their faces. They were confused, worried and during the coffee break that followed, their fears and frustrations broke forth. "All that is fascinating and challenging. You've helped us join all the pieces together, some of which we hadn't fully understood earlier. But you must understand this. We just can't respond to what you've set out. Education officers no longer have the power which we used to, and which we would most certainly need if we were to do anything with such ideas. In practice such thoughts as you've shared with us only go to increase our frustration and dismay that, by becoming agents of the centralist policies of government - many of which we don't believe in - we've become part of the problem. You can no longer look to us for solutions."

Several people came to me with their diaries already opened, trying to get my agreement to give such a speech in their own authorities. Then they went back to the lecture hall to debate still further their concerns about matters administrative.

"There's one person you need to speak to about all this," one of them confided in the bar later that night, "and that's Gillian Shepherd, the new secretary of state. Unless she gets interested in this and takes it to the prime minister, nothing will happen. How good are your contacts with her?"

This hit a raw nerve. David Peake had just written to Shepherd asking for a meeting with her to present the department with a copy of my new book, *Learning Makes Sense*. Her reply had just been received. It was polite but gave not an inch. "While I'm always willing to discuss new ideas, I understand that the trust's proposals are essentially similar to those made last year to John Patten ... [who] explained why the department could not support the proposals as then formulated. I find it hard to see that any further meeting could lead to a different outcome."

†        *        *

In a sense I concluded the Senior Education Officers speech by something which I said a few weeks later when addressing a special seminar of the American Academy for the Advancement of Science in Atlanta on the subject of learning at home in the twenty-first century. It was a group of some 250 academics, mainly from higher education. I wanted, first, to get the audience to focus on learning, and escape from the assumption that this was synonymous with schooling. I said, "the classroom can no longer be the unique gateway to learning with the teacher holding the key. Opportunities for learning exist within society and its individual communities. So institutionalised has learning become, however, that it will not be able to respond to the new opportunities of the twenty-first century with anything like the ease of the informal sector."

"Strategically we make a grave error if we assume that those higher order skills needed in a Knowledge Society can ever be developed in the classroom alone. The educational infrastructure has so over-emphasised formal learning and so marginalized informal learning and intuitive understanding that people have lost confidence in their natural ability to learn.

"Of the new technologies which are creating a new learning paradigm, the simplest and oldest is word processing. It has revolutionised the office and has enabled us to escape from thinking about writing as a strictly linear activity. We move ideas around until we are satisfied that we have finally defined our intended meaning. Educators are comfortable teaching with the assistance of information technology, but policy makers are not prepared to let the technology change the way schools do things.

"The school is being sidelined by technology as the restrictive practices of schooling are increasingly recognised and the point of action becomes the home. The technologies of television and video, everyday technologies, provide an astonishing array of resources for learning which schools and institutions have been reluctant to utilise to their maximum potential. Those children who can use CD ROM or other computer-aided facilities on demand in the home have an enormous advantage over those who are dependent on a few minutes a day of special activity within a school system.

"This presents equity issues, not merely of a financial nature, which are of enormous and growing significance. As the home becomes more the gateway to learning, so the proximity of sympathetic adults who provide quality time becomes ever more critical. Even without powerful technology, the child in the home today has access to more learning opportunities than ever before. In human terms it means that a child potentially needs support for 12 or 16 hours a day with self-evident implications for parents and those other adults whose roles will become increasingly significant and for whom training or parenting skills will be of paramount importance.

"All too often a curriculum is about facts, not about processes. As such, the power of technology, at least in formal education, is being constrained by a curriculum that is firmly fixed in the technology of an earlier age - high levels of memory skills and paper and pencil dexterity. With this thinking technology is relegated to a vocational skill. The potential to facilitate learning is largely being ignored - it is like transporting a jet engine on the back of a horse and cart. However, expertise does not exist in the pure air of understanding process in isolation from content however. We need to work in order to understand how effective learning takes place, and how people become knowledgeable and expert."

"What you're talking about are TAFYs," exclaimed Bob Beck from the University of Chicago. I looked somewhat blank, being only able to think of the children's nursery rhyme, "Taffy was a Welshman, Taffy was a thief." I looked up as he enlightened me. "Technologically Advanced FamilY. In some parts of Massachusetts and Connecticut, significant numbers of young professionals are now working largely from their own homes with a battery of electronic technology. Many of them are beginning to remove their children from school and educate them at home because of the access technology gives them to all levels of learning opportunities." A number of the audience looked concerned. "Surely," said several, "learning is far more than just having access to information?"

"Of course it is," said another, "but listen; something else is starting to happen. I've heard of some elementary schools where parents started to do this, but then the parents realised what the previous speaker has just said - learning is more than just receiving and processing information. It's essentially a social, problem-solving activity. So the parents proposed that their children attend school for two days a week for mainly social, collaborative, sporting kinds of functions, and work at home for three days a week."

Some of the audience were obviously intrigued and saw real opportunities in this. Others were becoming confused, if not outright hostile. "But listen," said the speaker from Texas, seeking to bring his argument to a close, "this is actually fascinating. Haven't good schools always emphasised the importance of homework alongside class work? Surely it's the skills of independent study on which every youngster will be dependent for success later in life. Isn't what is starting to happen a new definition of that relationship? Isn't a new model of learning emerging almost by accident? This is exciting!"

*      *      *

Ithe way to that conference in Atlanta I had bought a copy of *Sophie's World* by the Norwegian high school teacher of philosophy, Jostein Gaarder. Several of my Scandinavian friends had spoken enthusiastically of the book which describes itself, lightly, "as a novel that thinks it's a history of philosophy. When it's translated into English, as surely it must be, do read it," they urged me. "It's a best seller here, which is somewhat surprising as it was really written for high school students aged 15 or so. It's in the guise of an intriguing novel which makes even the most abstract thoughts of philosophers of all ages quite fascinating."

It was not until the return flight that I had a chance to start reading the book. It does indeed make delightful reading, weaving as it does an Alice-in-Wonderland use of language with summaries of the most advanced thinkers of all time. Here is how it begins. "Sophie Amundsen was on her way home from school. She had walked the first part of the way with Joanna. They had been discussing robots. Joanna thought the human brain was like an advanced computer. Sophie was not certain that she agreed. Surely a person was more than a piece of hardware?"

"Is life more than just a piece of hardware? Philosophers think so," wrote Jostein Garder. "They believed that man cannot live by bread alone. Of course everyone needs food. And everyone needs love and care. But there is something else - apart from that - which everyone needs, and that is to figure out who we are, and why we are here.

"Who are you? Why are you here?

"The world itself becomes a habit in no time at all. It seems in the process of growing up we lose the ability to wonder about the world. And in doing so, we lose something central - something philosophers try to restore. For somewhere inside ourselves, something tells us that life is a huge mystery. Philosophers never quite get used to the world. It continues to seem a bit unreasonable - bewildering, even enigmatic. Philosophers and small children thus have an important faculty in common. You might say that throughout his life a philosopher remains as thin-skinned as a child."

I became engrossed that night reading this wonderful book, and escaping from the minutiae of considerations about the brain, or the politics of education, or the difficulties of fund raising. A child's eyes are so clear, and so bold. They can see, and be helped to see, the grandeur of the big picture ... they know, and are not frightened to accept "that life is a huge mystery."

As it turned out it was weeks before I finished the book because I foolishly showed it to Peter when I arrived home next morning. Even though he was revising for GCSE he asked to borrow it that evening "to see what it looks like." He in his turn became so intrigued that he had read more than half of its 400 pages by the end of the week, and shortly after announced that he had loaned it to one of his friends. "I always thought philosophy could be fascinating but now I know why it is! Why can't we study really interesting things like this at school? It makes me think again about what "A" levels I should study. It would be great if I could study philosophy at the same time as the sciences. But as it won't fit in with my options they may not be able to timetable it."

*          *          *

Some while after returning from Atlanta, David Peake suggested that I ought to sit down for dinner with him and Tom Griffin and summarise where I thought I had got to before we met for our next trustees' meeting. The three of us, and David's wife, met in David's London home behind Holland Park. We talked as I wish we had done several years before. We did not speak of the problems of finding money for the projects, or of opening up another possible line of communication to the prime minister or to the department. Instead we discussed where I had to go to find the people who, from research and practical experience, could assist the trust in making an unstoppable case for the kinds of innovation I saw as essential.

"England's become a most uncongenial kind of place from which to conduct such work, hasn't it?" said Tom.

"It seems to me that Americans are far more used to this kind of big thinking than we are," said David. "Certainly you ought to be able to find one of the big American foundations to help. Some of them do have an international perspective. Maybe you ought to go and live in America for a couple of years and get such an initiative set-up. After all, everything you've been finding out in recent months seems to suggest that many other countries are in a similar position to England. Politicians want to provide a better system of education, but instead of incorporating the findings of research into more creative structures they are busy reinventing the past.

Tom Griffin continued: "It seems to me that there are many thoughtful people scattered across a number of countries who would benefit greatly from an international forum of good practice based on the best theory and practice. This couldn't easily be dismissed as a political statement and could lift the level of debate and practice across many countries - including England. In fact Education 2000 could use the existence of the Initiative to embarrass the English to take notice of the ideas."

And so it was, on a balmy early May evening in the heart of establishment Holland Park, two one-time merchant bankers decided to recommend to their fellow trustees that I go to America and conduct our campaign from an international perspective.

Anne could hardly believe the news later that evening. The boys were frankly incredulous at breakfast the following morning. And I was the most incredulous of all - I just did not think it could happen. Maybe it was my natural nervousness at work, and maybe I was overawed at the problems of moving the family to another land.

"So you ought to be," many around us were quick to say. "Isn't that a terrible risk to take with the boys' schooling? After all, Peter has a good chance of getting excellent A levels, so surely you don't want to disrupt his sixth form career?"

I started to bristle. What was so special about a sixth form that was more important than living in another country for two years? Surely, if Peter's education to date had been as good as I thought it had been, wouldn't he thrive on the challenge of coming to terms with another kind of school system?

"You'll need to be careful about David and Tom," said other well-meaning teacher friends. "After all, they're only 12 and 14. They might find it difficult to fit into the national curriculum when they come back. They may find they've been left behind." That did it. If the English national curriculum was being reduced to a specific form of treadmill that one dare not step off of for fear of being left behind, and other experiences were being discounted, I wanted even less to do with it. "Don't worry," I told the family. "We'll certainly go to America. There are still a lot of arrangements to make, and some of the detail is a bit vague, but I am going to America, and you're all coming with me." Only late in the evening when I was alone in the house, while everyone else was asleep, did I allow myself to think about all the logistics of moving a family from one continent to another

*          *          *

May 4, 1995 was the fiftieth anniversary of the Allied Armies victory in Europe. Late that evening bonfires were lit along a chain of high points each in sight of the other and together covering the entire country. These were the same places which had been selected for transmitting a message across the country had the Germans landed in 1940; the same hill tops which would have been used had Napoleon landed in 1805, or should the Spanish have landed in 1588. I took the three boys to the top of Deacon's Hill, a mile or so out of Hitchin. We looked to the north across the Bedfordshire plains to other lights flickering in the growing darkness, and to the south towards London, and to the east towards Cambridge and the Fenlands. It was a precious few moments which I had not anticipated, for in a most graphic and emotionally rich way we saw England stretching before us just as our ancestors had understood the country before them. Here below us through the fields on the side of Deacon's Hill stretched Ermine Street, trodden by ancient British travellers long before the Roman invasion, while to our left was the fast moving traffic on the M1 motorway and to our right the line of towns that marked the route of the old Great North Road. It was a precious moment that the boys would remember when they were my age for, in that moment, the events of 50 years ago became very real to me. Remembering it I hoped it would help them in their turn to appreciate what a hundred years of history would mean. If we were going off to live in another land, I wanted the boys to consolidate their sense of where we had come from.

An event the previous evening had reminded me of the significance of parenthood. Peter had come with me to a lecture in London given by Jane Goodall, the primatologist, talking about her work with chimpanzees. Something she said about chimpanzees' cultural habits struck me forcefully. "A young chimp who is orphaned may learn to physically survive by watching other chimps. That is, he or she will know how to find food and live moderately comfortably. But I know of no orphaned chimp who ever made it beyond adolescence into a full adult relationship with another chimp. Such orphans had never had the opportunity of learning from functional parents what it would mean to be a grown-up. Other chimps, who had come from functional families, were just not interested in forming relationships with them. As they approached adulthood, orphans stopped looking after themselves and quickly died. Amongst our nearest relatives in the animal kingdom, culture is an essential part of growing up. Instincts alone are not enough. This could have enormous implications for the human race, and for that growing proportion of young people who have no firsthand experience of what good parenting means."

However busy I was going to be in our new life, I realised, our family life had to come before anything else.

*       *       *

Two weeks later I set out on a massive tour across North America to speak with many of the people I wanted to be part of the team. I started in Seattle with Dee Dickinson. I then went to Eugene, Oregon, and met with Bob Sylwester, whose work on interpreting neurology for educationalists had helped me so much. Then I flew to San Francisco to talk with Marian Diamond and others at the University of California Berkeley, and later flew on to Palm Springs where I met with the Caines. The next day I drove to San Diego and met with Gerald Edelman, whose thoughts on the brain as a "biological self-adapting system" were rapidly attracting worldwide attention. To me he seemed to epitomise the Faustian bargain of modern times. "We are," he said with a curious mixture of hopeful enthusiasm and some real trepidation, "about to discover the ultimate mysteries of life." Intellectually this excited him, yet it left him with an enormous problem. "What is the Big Idea around which we will now organise civilised existence?" It was the ultimate cry of the reductionist scientist to humanity's aeons long search for meaning.

Maybe, I speculated, the human mind could no longer cope with the scale of knowledge that science was making available to us? Or was it the structures we used for handling knowledge were just too limited? In my bag I had another book. This was the latest work of the theologian Matthew Fox, *The Reinvention of Work: a New Vision of Livelihood for Our Times*. It is a most stimulating book. It is full of profound insights and terrifying questions for those thinking seriously about the future. In this Fox appeared to follow up part of what John Eccles had written in 1989 when he wrote *Evolution of the Brain: Creation of the Self*. Like Edelman, Eccles too was a prize-winning neurologist. Yet his conclusion was radically different. "I maintain that the human mystery is incredibly demeaned by scientific reductionism, with its claim in promissory materialism to account eventually for all of the spiritual world in terms of patterns of neural activity. This belief must be classed as a superstition ... we are spiritual beings with souls in a spiritual world, as well as material beings with bodies and brains existing in a material world."

Belief systems are by their nature subjective, passionate, and irrational. They can backfire. Remember the stunned reaction of my students in Turkey all those years ago when, in light of our Western Christian background, we were told not to go and dig out the people buried in the rubble from the earthquake because it was the will of Allah and therefore not to be tampered with? Predestination is as much a tenet of faith as is free will; nurture is of as much concern to an evolutionary psychologist as is nature. If we were to find a way of expressing a more effective story about how humans learn, and actually become human, we would have to develop a synthesis crossing many ideas and values. It would have to be a story based on best evidence, experience and even faith, and it would have to be told in a language that would embrace many other languages, and a multiplicity of ways of coming to know. Some of which might come from disciplines and value systems anxious to maintain their own exclusivity.

From the West Coast I returned to Chicago, made a side trip to Milwaukee, and then to Boston to talk with David Perkins and then to New York, Washington and finally to Toronto to meet Carl Bereiter and Marlene Scardamalia.

I arrived back in London with my head throbbing, my notebook full of jumbled up suggestions and, frankly, a better appreciation of the scale of what this was about. This scared me. I knew that if I let most people know of the range of my recent thoughts, they would take fright! Even my trustees. This sounded just too big, too all embracing, and for the English in particular, just far too metaphysical.

We - the trustees, the people in the projects, many teachers at large, certainly many parents - were all on a journey, probably even on the same path, but certainly not at the same point. Back in 1985 when I had started out with Education 2000, I was promoting an approach to learning that emphasised the child's need to learn how to accept ever more responsibility for their own progress. This, I argued, would give them the essential skills and confidence to deal with change. This required massive teacher development programmes; the use of new technologies and the involvement of the whole community. Many of our earlier supporters shrugged off the concept of new learning strategies, and wanted to focus solely on the computer. That was just about where the Department for Education still was. However, many teachers had gone further. They realised that computers and networks were only tools towards enhanced learning skills. They were a means to an end, and certainly not an end in itself. Some of those teachers had gone further still, and realised that such technology broke away from the physical limitations of classroom walls, and they were already exploring the significance of the community as the place for learning in the future, not just the school.

A smaller proportion (of what was already a small proportion in any case) were starting to ask profound questions about the relative relationship between formal and informal learning, and how this led to creativity and flexibility. These were the people who were most receptive to the story I wanted to tell. A story of human learning that paid proper deference to our deep-seated, inherited predispositions, and a structure of learning that genuinely extended the "grain of the brain." Finally there were others, some of whom took a long time to get to this position (while others seemed to get there almost in one quick leap) who were wanting to ask some pretty basic, profound questions. The questions they asked were broadly similar to those asked by young people. "What kind of education, for what kind of world?"

"This is the most difficult issue of all," people would say, "because unless the goals of education are genuinely meaningful and attractive to those who should stand to benefit, then it is all a bit of a sham. People need a sense of vision. They need to know that their learning will help them make sense of the world. They need to see that learning helps to make meaningful connections. Learning helps them make sense of things. Without a unified vision, without a sense of the value of what you are doing, you become listless and a half hearted learner."

This, I was convinced, was the reason why Peter and his friends had shown such interest in *Sophie's World* when I brought home my copy from Atlanta. It was the reason I was most receptive to the urgency of Gerald Edelman's comment, and why it had so disturbed my thinking. Without an appreciation of the Big Idea, education sinks too easily to a matter of administration.

\*　　　　\*　　　　\*

Meanwhile I had a schedule of lectures to give, including a conference just outside Warsaw in mid-September, set-up by the Foundation for Education for Democracy. This was a Polish foundation established after Solidarity had taken power from the Communists. Leading revolutionaries such as Wiktor Kulerski, who had been one of the primary strategists for eight years in the mobilisation of public opinion against Communism, and who had become vice-minister of education, was the president of the foundation. Wiktor is the authentic voice of Poland, old and new. The Kulerski family had played a long and honourable part in recent Polish history. As a boy he and his family had been hunted by the Gestapo who wanted him because of his father's role in the Polish government in exile in London. His father had been foreign secretary to Poland's prime minister Stanislaw Mikolajczek, and attended regular meetings of Churchill's war cabinet. Wiktor's grandfather had been one of Poland's leading publishers and had represented the Polish minority in the German Reichstag. Wiktor had been a teacher of biology, history and art for 22 years. He is a passionate believer in the creativity and potential genius of young people. He feared the ultra-conservative tendencies of the Polish teaching profession to subvert the opportunity for free thought that he and so many of his contemporaries had spent a lifetime fighting for, and which had led to the overthrow of Communism.

The conference was held in a dacha that had been, five years before, a training centre for Communist economists. The communists had looked after their own well. This was a comfortable, if remote, retreat. The Communist régime might have collapsed but the caretaker still kept large, noisy guard dogs whose fangs deterred any of us from wandering off into the forest, and deterred any local people from inquiring about what was happening within. Forty or so people, members of the Polish parliament, vice-ministers of education from several countries, members of the press, American and British diplomats, as well as senior Polish educationalists gathered for two and a half days. They also came from Romania to the south and Lithuania to the north. They were a dour, unresponsive group of people who waited to be told what to do.

Most of the conference was indeed insufferably boring, and the long, contrived public statements of the various delegates did not translate well - despite every effort of the young and dynamic woman interpreter who tried to get some spirit into her translations by carefully modulating her voice. It was hard for her to do so, the limitations of the spoken voice are real. Then I noticed a curious thing. I was sitting at the back of the hall, and away to one side. I was probably the only person there who could see into the interpreter's cubicle. Although the interpreter obviously assumed that no one was watching her, she was nevertheless vigorously using her hands to gesticulate and to give some form of substance to these dry statements. I watched her, fascinated. Slowly her words in my ear began to make much more sense as I watched her hands. "Thinking for ourselves is not what we have been trained to do," she translated from one of the speakers with a heavy touch of irony, "we have never been trained to take individual action. That is not what the last 45 years in Poland have been about. You can't expect teachers to get students to think for themselves when they themselves don't know how to think for themselves."

I smiled to myself at the irony and then I realised that the interpreter had spotted me watching her. Suddenly she smiled as well, happy that at least someone had been sufficiently aware of the significance of what had been said. Then I looked again at the audience. There seemed not to be a flicker of comprehension on any of their faces.

Never before had I realised so clearly that communication has not only to be a two-way process, it has also to recognise the visual as well as the aural. How we share ideas between ourselves has always to recognise the variety of ways in which messages are exchanged. At the core of this, there is something incredibly simple. We listen most carefully to the people we like, and who seem to speak not to our heads but to our emotions. That young woman doing the interpreting understood better what the older man was saying than he almost did himself. She was still living the paradox that he was trying to describe. She wanted to find a solution because her life was still before her; he, poor man, was in effect carrying out a post-rationalisation for his own failure. She was almost beautiful, and in a face that already had some of the scars of hard life, there was the radiance of a new generation determined to succeed.

There were three American speakers - Al Shanker, the President of the American Federation of Teachers (AFT), Adam Urbanski a vice-president of the Federation, and currently from Albany in upper New York State, and somewhat incongruously, Chester Finn, the former American under-secretary of education from the conservative Hudson Institute. There were also two Germans, an Israeli, myself and an Anglicised Pole who for 30 or more years had, as an Oxford don, come to see himself as "Intellectual Poland in exile". He and Wiktor were like chalk and cheese; both highly intelligent men, but one the pure academic, and the other the man of action (the similarity with Chris Wysock Wright and Brian Thwaites was striking).

The conference had been carefully set up to help the former Eastern Block countries come to terms with what the organisers had hoped would be the achievements of Western education (surely the latter had to be better, the naïve assumed, for how else could Western democracies have eventually overthrown communism?). Shanker and Finn engaged in a public debate as to which of them more truly represented the party of law and order - which of them would, in effect, be the harder on classroom disorder and the rigorous application of standards. Shanker, the man who had so challenged my own thinking over earlier years and who had given such a lead in calling for a radical transformation of the whole process of schooling, suddenly appeared to have reverted to a policy that seemed to deny so much of what he had earlier advocated. "Drive the schools harder," was his message, "let us get on with our job by taking the troublesome pupils away from us." Gone altogether was the argument to "think and work smarter."

At the time, this was hard to accept (the Israeli delegate who, like me, had earlier been much influenced by his arguments, was almost beside herself with annoyance) but soon we were to learn that Al was in remission from his cancer that was to kill him within two years.

"Go back into his earlier writings," I urged people, "because for several years Shanker nearly brought about the revolution that is still waiting in the wings."

Adam Urbanski brought the conference to life just once by quoting a piece of research he said he had just learnt of from California. The biggest predictor of a child's success at first degree level was, in first place, the quantity and quality of discussion in the child's home. Secondly, the amount of independent reading, regardless of the subject matter the child did for itself. Third was the clarity with which the value systems were understood and practised. Fourth was strong, positive peer group pressure - good, steady friends. In fifth place was the elementary school ... and far further on down came the secondary school.

This was an easy set of ideas to understand and ponder. Urbanski repeated it twice for people to write down.

Terry Ryan, a young American from Illinois who had organised the conference with Wiktor Kulerski, drove me back to the airport. A dynamic, hard-working, but eminently well-organised man, I had taken to him quickly as the conference started, and for several days I had seen his extraordinary ability to get people to work together, despite their initial differences. He would be leaving Warsaw in a month, and returning to the US, where so far he had not got a job. "Well," I said, "you've heard me say what kind of things I think need to happen during the speech I gave. I'll be in Washington - I hope - by the end of the year. The most I can do now is to offer you a job for six months as my PA/secretary. After that I'll just have to see how things go. What about it?"

He grinned all over his face. "Done," he said. "That would be great. It would be a real blast to work with you. Added to which I've never been to Washington."

It was my turn to sound amazed. An American - a bright man who for two years had almost been the voice of America in his segment of Poland, had never been to his capital city? "Why should I?" the good federalist patiently explained to me, "Springfield, Illinois is where most of the effective action is. It's the governor who is more significant to most Americans than the president. It's only when you're overseas that you seem to equate the president with the voice and spirit of America."

I flew on to Oslo where I was addressing a conference on distance education utilising telecommuni-cations. Here I heard and met Aharon Aviram who spoke with great passion and elegance about the work of his institute in Israel, the Centre for Futurism in Education at the Ben Gurion University of the Negev, and within an hour or so I had added him as well as Terry Ryan to the team in America.

*         *         *

Back in England I remember coming close to panic late one evening in early December as I returned to my well-worn office in Letchworth, cluttered as it was with the books, papers and memories of a dozen years. Tomorrow, I thought, I have to decide just which of these are worth crating up and entrusting to the shipping company to deliver to me in Washington in early January. Just what will I actually be doing, in this new office I've been offered in Connecticut Avenue, barely a five minute walk from the White House?

One of the last lectures I gave was at a conference in a well-established hotel by Lake Windermere in the Lake District. It was the annual conference of the secondary head teachers of Cheshire. They became much engaged in what I was saying, and fortunately someone recorded the discussion that followed.

"As you unpacked these ideas for me," said one of the head mistresses, "I saw with far greater clarity than before just what was needed. For a few minutes I was back with that enthusiasm I remembered so well when I first studied education at university. Then I thought of the reality of my school and my local community. I crashed. Between the theory and the practice there is an almost unbridgeable gulf. Society - it is not just government (in any country) - will not let us do this, even though as individuals people sense that this is right. They are frightened and confused; the scale of all this just paralyzes people. Many are living with incomplete ideas and outdated concepts, but do not know how to let go.

"We need help. Two things will have to happen simultaneously. At a professional level countless educational leaders need to understand far better how to work with these ideas, and that is scary because many of these challenge the basis of what we have done for years, and go beyond the walls of the school. At a public policy level, someone has to go even further with all the energy of a crusade. The public has to realize that the education of young people (and the continuation of life itself) is much more than an institutional activity. Every adult has a responsibility. Unless somehow both these issues are addressed, nothing much will happen."

It was an appropriate exhortation with which to send me out to the New World.

Then, absolutely out of the blue, David Peake had a personal letter from John Major, the prime minister, asking for an explanation of Education 2000's thinking, and what this might entail. Many of my papers and books were already crated up and on their way to America as I sat down in my stripped down office to write what David exhorted me to keep to six or seven sides of double-spaced text at the maximum. I drafted and redrafted. It was not that I was tired that I could not make the document sparkle; everything I wrote was correct, reasonably well thought through and was certainly concise. It was, it seemed to me in desperation, just too big an idea to express cold on paper. As with the speech I had written for him to deliver four years previously (the one which never got anywhere) I tried to write it for him. Then I realised that such an approach would not appeal to his advisors who would inevitably read it first, and only if they approved it would they let him see it. So I redrafted yet again, and then sent it off, hoping against hope that it would at least get me an invitation to return to Downing Street and discuss this with him.

*       *       *

We booked tickets to fly to Washington two days before the end of the year. Prior to this Anne and I had spent a long weekend in Reston, in northern Virginia, house-hunting in late November. We had found a modern three-storey townhouse to rent that was spacious, comfortable and beautifully located on the side of Lake Thoreau. It was within easy walking distance of both South Lakes High School and Langston Hughes Middle School. This was also within comfortable commuting distance of central Washington and my new office at the Rothschild Group.

# 15

# The 21st Century Learning Initiative

The deck outside our new bedroom window had disappeared. Rubbing my eyes I saw that snow had drifted up to the top of its railings. I tried opening the front door only to discover a veritable wall of snow. "Twenty-eight inches of snow has fallen in Northern Virginia," said the 24-hour weather channel, "and upwards of another 20 inches can be expected in the next few hours. This is the worst blizzard in 74 years." Government offices, including schools, were to remain closed for eight days and this delayed the start of the school term.

None of the boys had been unduly nervous about going to an American school, but after a while of being housebound by the snow, and not knowing anyone at that stage, this delay slightly unsettled them. A week later Peter went into the penultimate year of high school as a junior (grade 11) and registered for English, math, biology, marine biology, psychology, US/Virginia history and chemistry. By Virginian law, he had to make up on American History, and for this had to go into a first year class. He also took drama and theatre arts, and wind band. The flexibility of the credit system intrigued us. We were pleased that subjects such as theatre and orchestra which, in England, were classified as desirable but not essential and therefore treated as extra-curricular, were rated as full subjects, each meriting a lesson every two days. Having played the alto saxophone in England (outside classroom time), in Virginia Peter was quickly offered the opportunity to play a brand new baritone saxophone in the wind orchestra, bought by the school especially for him to use. David went into the first year of high school (grade 9) a term after the rest of his class had started. Having begun to study nine subjects for GCSE in England the previous September, the requirement to study seven subjects was a reduced curriculum. The facilities for art were especially good and he was to be in his element. Tom started at the adjacent middle school, named after the African-American poet Langston Hughes. This was a recently built school of interesting contemporary design and housed nearly 1,100 pupils, for the two years of grades 7 and 8 (12 and 13 year-olds). We were immediately amazed to see how physically mature were many of the other students and, although Tom was one of the tallest in the school, he still looked like a young boy and spoke in a careful and unassuming way.

\*　　　\*　　　\*

During the days of snow-bound inactivity I had an opportunity to reflect and to plan. I had come a long way, in distance, in career terms and in my thinking. The task ahead was to think strategically. My starting point was a British Engineering Council report of several years before which concluded that, for every technical innovation of the past decade, all the component parts necessary had been known for at least 20 years before someone thought of a way of recombining these to create something new. Our problem in education is the same. It is not an absence of available information that is the problem because we already know a lot about the human brain, about how learning takes place and how societies function. True, we will know more from neuro-biology and other subjects in five years time, but the main direction seems pretty clear. We have a great deal of circumstantial evidence when we call for learning strategies based on the principle of weaning children away from reliance on teachers and when we challenge the existing system as being upside down and inside out. More evidence would always be useful, but - at the level of a first approximation - we have quite enough to design better and more effective systems. "Beware of the intellectual's search for creeping academic perfection" Tom Griffin had frequently warned me. The issue is not one of information; it is not one of more research. The issue is one of resolution. There has already been too long a delay in starting to implement such new structures. We have to act with responsibility and determination. That means we have to find other people of like mind, and win the political support that will give communities the space to innovate at the level people believe in their hearts is necessary.

I run ahead of myself because these are essentially the conclusions of the 21st Century Learning Initiative's multi-disciplinary team which, on six separate occasions over the next two years was to meet in the great hall at Wingspread. A total of 60 people from 14 countries participated at one or more of these meetings. Mostly there were some 25-30 people on each occasion and usually we met for three days at a time.

The group was intentionally broad in its experience. That was how I had set it up. There were people from neurology and cognitive science; school-based innovators; policy makers; educational administrators, and others deeply interested in the potential impact of information and communication technologies. Some of these were strictly rationalists, while others in their search for interconnectivity between different forms of experience were more philosophical and even metaphysical. This inevitably bred tensions, and some misunderstandings.

I had a second concern. I was searching for a process that would create a synthesis, the painting of the broad picture in ways which would be helpful to vast numbers of people currently confused by the babble of specialists each touting their own wares. We in the West, because we don't know much about the art of synthesis, retreat into our specialisms. When we are prised out, we feel that the most we can give - grudgingly - is a slight modification of our own position; in other words, we compromise. We look for the lowest common denominator, and come out with statements so general that no one is offended, and nothing really has to change.

This is best illustrated in current publishing where an editor, having selected what appears to be a fascinating title, invites a dozen people to write their own thoughts about their own particular sub interest. You read this, hopefully looking for a common theme, and most often you are disappointed; each has written apparently oblivious of what the other might have said! You turn to the editor's introduction and again disappointment frequently follows. Too often this is full of platitudes and grateful thanks. The reader is left with much discreet information, but no clear idea of what thoughtful people could say if they were forced to think about a general conclusion to their own advanced thinking. Synthesis, we think, happens by some form of subconscious osmosis! Of course, in most cases, it just doesn't even happen.

Fifty years ago Erwin Schroedinger, himself a refugee from Austria and a physicist of great international standing, challenged academia to reconsider the nature of the interrelationship of formal disciplines in a famous paper he delivered at Trinity College Dublin in 1943, *What is Life*? He wrote, "we have inherited from our forefathers a keen longing for unified, all-embracing knowledge. The very name given to the institutions of highest learning remind us that from antiquity and throughout many centuries, the universal aspect has been the only one given full credit. But the spread, both in width, and depth, of the multifarious branches of knowledge during the last hundred odd years has confronted us with a queer dilemma. We feel clearly that we are only now beginning to acquire reliable material for welding together the sum total of all that is known into a whole; but on the other hand, it has become next to impossible for a single mind fully to command more than a specialised portion of it. I can see no other course (lest our true aim be lost forever) than that some of us should embark on a synthesis of facts and theories, albeit with a second-hand and incomplete knowledge of some of them - at the risk of making fools of ourselves..."

Here I was under no illusion. I was asking very intelligent people, each of whom was making their daily living from their authority as a specialist, to take the risk of making fools of themselves lest their true aim of improving the mental capabilities of young people, when at the most appropriate age, should "be lost forever." But as Hamlet said, "there's the rub." How could we go beyond our arts as specialists, and develop the skills of synthesis ... real synthesis that put no topic "off limits"?

Ours was a unique platform that included four ex-ministers of education. There was Luis Alberto Machado who had been the world's first ever minister for national intelligence in Venezuela in the mid-1980's. There was Aklilu Habte whose earliest schooling had been beneath the tree outside his African village (now he sat next to Charlie Bray, Aklilu having risen to being a senior advisor to UNESCO, and Charlie having been an American ambassador). There was Wiktor Kulerski from Poland, Aharon Aviram from Israel, Frank Method, senior educational advisor to USAID. There was Eduardo Barriga from Colombia, and Wadi Haddad who had risen from being the son of a village schoolteacher to become deputy president of Lebanon in his mid-thirties. There was Peter Henschel and Etienne Wenger of the Institute for Research into Learning at Palo Alto, Karlheinz Duerr a curriculum specialist from Germany, and Paul Wangemann, the educational manager at Motorola University. Bob Sylwester of the University of Oregon also attended.

There was Peter Mortimore from the London Institute of Education, Judith Robinson from the Education 2000 project in Leeds, and Ian Smith of the Scottish Consultative Committee on the Curriculum. There was Jackie Thayer Scott, president of the University College of Cape Breton in Canada, Ken Tolo who was a senior advisor to the secretary of the US Department of Education and Rod Cocking who was a program director at the US National Academy of Sciences in Washington. Dee Hock, the founder of VISA (the world's first virtual organisation); Betty Sue Flowers who is a professor of English at the University of Texas, and Parker Palmer, the Quaker philosopher each joined us at one of the meetings. In retrospect we were short of non-educationalists leaving a heavy responsibility on Tom Griffin as a one-time banker to remind us of the relationship between academic expectations and those of commerce. In Ron Brandt we had a communications expert whose pen had been well-shaped by many years as editor of ASCD's Educational Leadership, and Ted Marchese, vice-president of the American Association for Higher Education.

This chapter therefore echoes a variety of voices from a range of establishments, united in a belief that education should be release every young person's innate abilities and not to be too prescriptive in advance as to what these should be. Our problem was best defined by the senior US educational administrator. He said, "You are probably right in your intellectual analysis. I think you are certainly right morally, but what you're calling for just won't ever happen. Politics won't let it." That was what we were up against.

The status quo. Inertia. Established practice. The strength of what is known, as opposed to the unknown. Vested interest. The power of credentialism. Academic arrogance. The fear of change, and the terror of having to relearn a skill gone rusty over 20 or more years. The power of the system rather than the potential of the individual. All of these I knew were enormous issues which unnerved ordinary people and, which in the absence of any clear vision of an alternative set of arrangements, meant politicians felt under no pressure from their constituents to chart a new course. Yet, it was too easy to blame the politicians. It was the fault of all of us for not having got our act together - for not having sorted these matters out in a way that spelt a clear alternative. The politicians felt quite safe tinkering with the present arrangements and blaming the teachers for going soft, whilst those in the academic establishment do not see a threat to their established structures, and power bases. They argue solely for more money, and that diverts them away from asking more profound questions about how the system could be transformed.

Bob Sylwester is a man whose ideas are eroding that power base. "What you have to realise is that the medical profession is at least 50 years ahead of us in theory and research," he says. "We started maybe two years ago in terms of the biology of learning. The conventional wisdom used to have it that 90 per cent of what we knew about the brain was learned in the last 10 years. Because of the development of functional MRI two years ago, 90 per cent of what we will know about the brain in just three years will have been learned in the last three years. What is happening is a phenomenal influx of new information. All this is happening on our watch. We don't have to apologise for the last 50 years, but we sure as hell are going to have to apologise to our grandchildren if we drop the ball at this point."

We will stay with Bob because his lucid anticipation of a unified brain theory to inform pedagogy proved a touchstone for our thoughts. "It's important for educators to understand that this theory is emerging out of the material world of biology and Darwinian natural selection," he told us. "It will thus seek to explain cognitive behaviour through the electrochemical actions of neural networks, and not through such disembodied concepts as mind/spirit/soul/enthusiasm. It will, as it were, seek to explain from a biological perspective the "how" of existence but will leave still unanswered "why" humanity, at its finest, seeks to go beyond the apparent rules of biology in its search for ultimate meaning and the development of man's highest capabilities. The evolutionary base of the theory will obviously disturb those who reject Darwinian evolution, and this may spark educational controversies. Understanding the mechanisms of consciousness will obviously be an important discovery, but reducing the consciousness/joy/love/beauty/ metaphor to the mere actions of neurons will certainly disturb those who would view such reductionism as the loss of something indefinably human. This will create a potential social problem. If a given behaviour is determined principally by the ready availability of certain combinations of neurotransmitters, we're chemically redefining such concepts as free will and responsibility, then we've removed a lot of the romance from falling in love."

A life without purpose, without its own innate sense of value and direction was the reverse of the reasons that had set me out on this search to understand human learning better, all those years ago. While the intellectual excitement of the first biologist to construct such a theory might satisfy their personal search for meaning, it could have a devastating impact on future generations.

"Most young people operate well below their natural level of intelligence," David Perkins told the group one afternoon, "and if this could be raised by 20 per cent the results would be a very different world indeed." His was a fascinating presentation. "Intelligence can be taught," he said, calling upon his own research at Harvard. He identified three components to intelligence; the fixed neurological intelligence linked to IQ tests; the specialised knowledge and experience that individuals acquire over time; and reflective intelligence, the ability to become aware of one's mental habits, and transcend limited patterns of thinking. Although all these forms of intelligence function simultaneously, it is reflective intelligence, David said, that affords the best opportunity to amplify human intellect. This is the kind of intelligence that helps us to make wise personal decisions, solve challenging technical problems, find creative ideas, and learn complex topics in different areas. It is the kind of intelligence most needed in an increasingly competitive and complicated world.

Sitting in the bar later that evening, somebody said to David Perkins, "I've been thinking of a way to describe your three levels of intelligence. It's almost as if each one of us is born with a different kind of brain that could be likened to different kinds of cars. One could be the most magnificent modern Rolls Royce, and another could be the most clapped out old Ford. Your second level of intelligence relates, for example, to how well any of us can read and understand a map of a terrain. But surely your third level of intelligence - reflective intelligence - is the way each us uses ever more sophisticated means to plot the most appropriate route to follow. It's almost like driving instructions. It seems to me that someone with a super brain can make a terrible mess of things if they don't think about how they use it, while somebody with limited intellectual capacity but with a thoughtful approach to life can go much further. Is that how you would describe it?"

David looked pensive. "Yes," he said, "that's a pretty good analogy."

Dee Hock - founder of VISA - doesn't deal in analogies. "When my grandchildren ask my advice about education, I tell them that if they are clever, well motivated, perceptive, and if they work very hard, the school can't prevent them from being successful."

Such a harsh assessment angered several, particularly Dale Shuttleworth who had spent most of his adult life trying to transform education systems in Canada from the inside. "How is a school superintendent who has spent 15 years serving that kind of system supposed to feel when he hears you say that, even when he agrees with what you're saying?" Dale asked obviously with deep emotion.

"You're trapped," Hock said.

At this point Stephanie Pace Marshall, the executive director of the Illinois Mathematics and Science Academy, probably one of the best known of all American high schools, asked, "At what point should we, as individuals, step forward? Why is it that we all feel so trapped?"

Dale rushed in with his reply. "It's the superintendents who are the most trapped. They know that things are not right. They would resonate with many of the ideas set forth at this conference, but they are trapped because they have no choice. Their job is to fight in the trenches to try and bring forward their vision or their sense of what could happen, but they have some major obstacles. They have teacher unions, elected representatives and parents who have different visions, values and interests."

Stephanie interrupted, "I disagree profoundly. I think superintendents can bring the whole system together. It's up to them to say we're trapped, and challenge the community to work out the reason."

Maybe conditions in Canada are different to Illinois I found myself pondering. I knew that David Little back in Stevenage would have sided strongly with Dale, and I suspected that the Canadian system was already getting more locked in to a top down model. I knew also that the Norwegians were experiencing the same stresses as the Canadians and the British.

Dee Hock re-entered the discussion. "I mean trapped in a slightly different sense. Such a man has gotten good in the system. He has succeeded. He is able to manipulate the system to get a reasonable life for himself. He may not believe that he's doing as much as he is capable of, but he has succeeded within that system. I think most people who have succeeded in the system deep down are facing some level of frustration, but they don't realise how heavily they are conditioned and how much they repeat that pattern no matter how hard they try not to."

"It's the great trade-off," said Dale. "You've got a pension to protect."

*               *               *

Stephanie opened one of the later meetings by saying, "I want to know how we can create conditions that say that learning is a social endeavour, and that complexity - both of the brain and of the world in which we live - requires collaboration." She was talking about a whole new system of learning. She read us the words of an 11 year-old sophomore at the Illinois Mathematics and Science Academy who wrote: "I wish I could still draw. When I was in elementary school I used to draw decently. I loved to draw in pencil and in chalk. Art of all kinds intrigues me. I also love music, and painting, and carpentry, and metal work, and, dancing and sewing, and embroidering. I want to dance in my own ballet class, play my clarinet, and draw thousands of pictures. Really good ones. Create beautiful poems, cook and sew for my children, decorate my home, have a good marriage, be an active volunteer, go to church, be an astrophysicist, go to Mars, and understand all my questions about life. That's not too much to ask, is it?"

"The tragedy of our times," said Stephanie, "is that practitioners say that this is indeed asking too much. I am here because I believe we have it within our power, now, to say that this is not too much. We have it within our power to release human creativity on a scale not hitherto thought possible. Right now we are locked into an economic myth that permeates all our thinking. Life is seen simply as an economic race. It's black and white; the winner takes all. That's too simple. That's why I argue we need a new story."

*      *      *

Before we were able to give that issue the attention it needed, Carl Bereiter, a cognitive scientist who I much respected, had sought to dismiss the Initiative's interest in neurobiology by saying, "I am uncomfortable with the emphasis on brain research and neuroscience. There is a long history of quackery and it seems that this may be escapist. That somehow scientists are going to look into all this and find the answers to all the things we have been unable to answer seems naïve." I knew that he was joined in his criticism of the neurosciences by John Bruer, again another man whose writing I respected enormously, who argued in late 1997, "educational applications of brain science may come eventually, but as of now neuroscience has little to offer teachers in terms of informing classroom practice."

I asked Bereiter what he thought of a recent paper by John Cleveland, *Learning at the Edge of Chaos*, in which he explained learning systems theory from a business perspective. To me his analysis was brilliant, yet he came from a different background. "It describes in exciting terms a style of education that corresponds fairly closely with what we have been trying to develop in (our) classrooms," Bereiter replied. "Yet I doubt whether the author of that article and I would find much to talk about. We live in different, though complementary worlds."

This I found hard. The problem of trying to get these complementary worlds to find much to talk about gripped me, it seemed, at every corner. "Don't ask me for advice on how learning takes place," said the eminent neurologist dismissively at another conference in Virginia, "I can't deal with issues at that scale. That's not meaningful. Now if you want to talk about phonemes, and how we could, over a period of several years, develop programs to deal with particular aspects of dyslexia, then indeed we could talk and define a rigorous research program."

I invited John Bruer to join the Initiative, but he declined. "I am not convinced that the Initiative shares a commitment to using sound research ... I am struck by the overwhelming presence of what might be called 'change agents' (in your team). Given my preference for substance over process I doubt if I could contribute much, or work productively with the current cast of characters." I felt snubbed.

Carl Bereiter, who works closely with Bruer, was more understanding of our predicament, for he wrote: "(both research and high level policy statements) are needed. Ideally they should work in concert, but that is not how things have developed. The chasm between one sphere of educational activity and another is wider than it should be - wider than it would be in any comparable area of change; in medicine for instance, or economics or in telecommunications. That has been a long-standing weakness of the educational field. [The connection of research] with policy-making remains tenuous. It is clear that you sincerely want to connect science with pedagogy, but bringing that about will be a Herculean task."

It was a sober, if devastatingly accurate reflection of the situation I was trying to deal with. Turf wars seemed to be raging all around me.

"Debate is the nature of scientific discourse," noted the academic bureaucrat, Rod Cocking of the National Research Council. "You have to start with the evidence in the research and then begin drawing conclusions. When you start making recommendations then it becomes difficult. There will be a strong amount of debate!" That was an understatement. Time and again much of such debates seemed highly specific. Too often such debate sank back into trivia, and reeked of personality struggles. The situation which Schroedinger had described in 1943 had grown far worse by the late 1990s. Intelligent people were not prepared to take the risk of making fools of themselves - the unintended consequences of specialisation were to continue making synthesis very difficult.

It was some while before I came to understand just some of the reasons why this situation had so deteriorated. In America, at any rate, research programs are ultra dependent on the continuing support of sponsors, many of whom appear to get much satisfaction from cheering on their own team, and prefer to see their work standing in splendid isolation. In addition, the principle of peer group review is strongly adhered to, and this encourages the academic splitting of hairs to justify the creation of evermore sub-specialisms. There is a third reason. Once major foundations become highly attached to a program then they appear to be more concerned with its continuation, than with ideas which might replace it.

At one profound level the Initiative ran up against this at an early stage. American foundations are committed to the reform of schools and seem unwilling to look at a programme such as that advocated by the Initiative which seeks to develop a broader approach to a perennial problem. One well-endowed New York foundation, which we expected to be sympathetic to our ideas, wrote, "While all this is exciting we are concerned that the broad scope of the project will diminish any potential for making an impact on school reform in this country. We recognise your interest in and reasons for the transnational aspects of this project, but we are not convinced that outcomes of such a broad effort will have any substantial impact on the major school reform efforts currently under way here. Further, without the active and committed involvement of the national leaders in school reform – at the practitioner, academic and policy levels – and without a much sharper focus on the issues confronting our country's education systems, we question what the impact might be." So financial tensions underpin research programs in a way that makes it difficult for genuinely new ideas to intrude onto the agenda – and that agenda is essentially political. A program that cannot easily be classified as the property of the Republicans or the Democrats has few natural allies. A middle way is even more difficult to define than in the UK.

Time and again the financial resources we had anticipated would help us develop this programme failed to materialise. I could not believe just how difficult it was to explain our work to the programme officers of the big foundations. Often, it seemed, they saw their job as twisting what we had written into a totally different argument, and thus forcing us into new arguments which were not of our making. I don't mind fighting vigorously for what I believe in, but dealing with some of the foundations was like a boxing match conducted in the midst of a deep fog, with one arm tied behind one's back. I was frequently reminded of those lines from Kipling's *If*:

> If you can bear to hear the truth you have spoken
> Twisted, to make a trap for fools.

*                *                *

Early one morning at Wingspread we were treated to a presentation by Parker Palmer on epistemology entitled *Towards an Understanding of the Violence of Our Ways of Knowing*. To make his point, Parker cited a conversation that had taken place back in June 1744. A new treaty had been concluded in Virginia between the English settlers and the Indians of the Six Nations. The white men invited the Indians to send several of their sons to study at the newly established College of William and Mary in Williamsburg (the only building in America thought to have been designed by Sir Christopher Wren). The elders of the tribe duly considered this offer before replying. "We know that [your people] highly esteem the kind of learning taught in your college. We are convinced that you mean to do us good by your offer but you, who are wise, must know that different nations have different conceptions of things. Our ideas of education happen not to be the same as yours. Several of our young people accepted such an offer years ago and attended the College of the Northern Provinces [Harvard]. They were instructed in all your sciences, but when they returned to their people they were no longer good runners. They were ignorant of every means of living in the woods, fit neither for hunters nor for counsellors; they were totally good for nothing. We are obliged by your kind offer, though we decline it ... but to show our gratitude ... do send us a dozen of your young men and we will take care of their education, instruct them in all we know, and make men of them."

How many of us, I thought to myself looking around the room at Wingspread, would have loved to have been sitting in on that original conversation, and with the advantage of hindsight that 250 years of history could offer us?

"What the Indians of the Six Nations knew," Parker went on to say, "was that every way of knowing becomes a way of living. Epistemology becomes an ethic. Those Indian elders were engaged in a battle, not just for land and status, but about *whose way of knowing* would prevail in the shaping of young lives. Education is a form of soul-making, or of soul-deformation."

"I want to make a link between our Western forms of knowledge, and the violence which I believe this leads to in our way of thinking." He went on to unpack his argument. Violence does not simply mean hitting someone with a stick. It also happens when we violate the integrity of another person. There is physical violence and there is intellectual and mental violence. As Akililu Habte had said so powerfully at the conference in Annapolis some five years before, the Western way of thinking heavily emphasises objectivity, analysis, experimentation, and values instruction over active participation.

"We encourage the learned to be objective," Parker observed, "to study something as if they are not personally involved because we fear that personal involvement somehow taints the truth (the intellectual basis for moving senior civil servants in England from department to department). We have elevated the fear of being subjective to the point where we have removed all forms of emotional intuition (the thing which the Indians so valued, and which modern brain research shows to be so significant) from our 'Ways of Knowing'. Taking our cue from Newtonian physics we believe that further and further analysis can lead to the understanding of anything. The events of the past 300 years are often taken as evidence for the validity of ever more refined forms of analysis. But now we, at the turn of the 21st century, realise that to know anything in depth is not the same as to understand everything. You can take an old-fashioned clock to pieces and study all the wheels, hand springs and cogs, but at that level you won't see what makes it work. Unless you are wise, and have a mental model in your head of what should be the correct relationship of each wheel, spring and cog you will never succeed in reassembling this to give it life."

*          *          *

Peter quickly adjusted to an American high school, as he had already built up good work habits from his school in England and had well thought-through ideas of his own. He easily adapted to his new courses, and enjoyed taking up American history from scratch, yet he managed to maintain the rigour of an English A level tradition across a broader range of subjects. This quickly brought him to the favourable attention of his teachers, and helped him make an amazing array of friends. He found no difficulty in keeping on top of his academic work whilst also participating in a range of extra-curricular activities, chief of which was to be the school production of West Side Story, where, rehearsals having started before we ever reached America, he was recruited as a replacement Shark.

We were impressed with the energy that went into this production, and the scale of the resources made available through the school. They even had choreographers from the John F. Kennedy Centre for the Performing Arts to coach them ... my son, significantly more musical and agile than I had ever been, but my son nevertheless, being given training in dance by world acclaimed experts! It was a great performance. On the last night, instead of the curtain going down, the audience flocked onto the stage. Bouquets of flowers, hugs and kisses marked an overwhelming recognition of a job most splendidly done. Peter seemed to have received more kisses from girls in one night, than I had had in an entire lifetime.

American schools, we quickly discovered, seem preoccupied with grades. Anything of any significance has to be reduced to a grade, aggregated over time, averaged out and totted up. On the result of a grade you move up or down. It seems like extrinsic motivation gone mad. So is the systematic accumulation of material to go on your university entry application. "I'm doing Latin in my first year of high school," said Tom's friend Brendan, "it's boring, but Dad says it'll look good on my college application in four years time. I'll drop it at the end of the year." Teachers exhort youngsters to join the National Honour

Society and explain that this means that their voluntary activities can be credited on their university application forms.

Grades nearly drove David to distraction. He is a good worker, one of the best, and once he gets started on a topic he wants to explore it fully, even if that means not having time for the remaining questions. American high school grading systems are, it seems to us, highly inflexible and rely on "the correct answer syndrome" so well criticised by Howard Gardner. David, not in any sense because he wished to be confrontational, kept on clashing with such centrally designed evaluation systems and their over- dependence on multiple-choice questions. Writing, as he now does, some extraordinarily good poetry and creative English that is beautiful in its cadences and its pace, he has never got more than B+ for English, "because my teachers here are so fussy about grammar and stuff. Even our school in England didn't worry so much about that. It's strange in a land that says it's all about freedom, but the Americans are addicted to rules."

Tom had still been 12 when we moved to America and although even then tall for his age, he was prone to curling up on my lap late of an evening when tired. The sight was obviously pretty bizarre. "I can't see your father anymore!" said Anne one evening, trying tactfully to save me from suffocating. American food and fresh air were obviously good for Tom and he went through a growth spurt that summer and autumn. By Christmas he was already six feet tall and only fractionally shorter than David. Tom found it hard to cope with the rapid onslaught of adolescence, which compounded his sense of being different, which he had felt, rightly or wrongly, on arriving in America. From being the most outwardly cheerful and incorrigible of the three he became, in what seemed only a matter of weeks, unsure of himself and often surly.

This had its effect on David who also started to become uncharacteristically argumentative and confrontational. With David giving the lead, both of them wanted to question absolutely everything we said, and most of the suggestions we made. David, in particular, wanted to question much of what happened in school, and for a while worried us that he was deliberately harming his chances. Because of the size of American high schools it is very easy for a child to slip a few points into the great morass of the average. David knew well what he was doing, and after an evening of argument over issues which, half an hour later we could not even remember, would suddenly show his old self and his enthusiasm for whatever was the interest of the moment.

It was Tom who worried us most. Always more self-contained and less emotionally expressive than David, it was far harder to read him. He was not forthcoming about what he did in school, though we knew from his teachers that he could be charming. We noted, as they did, that whenever possible he was drifting towards the back of the class. "He's very popular," his teachers would say, "and the girls just love him" In trying to "act cool", he seemed sometimes to treat the friendly approaches of his peers too lightly. Then we found a packet of cigarettes in a drawer in his bedroom, and an admission that, yes, the smell of smoke we had noticed several times before was not just to do with the cigarettes others were smoking. Anne was naturally upset by all this, and my patience was tried hard ... but I did have a background of dealing with adolescents over many years that gave me something of a sense of perspective.

But not enough. One day I returned home to find that both David and Tom had had their hair cut very close. I hit the roof, and of course said all the wrong things, at least to their ears. I asked them what they thought "our friends would think of them, and what assumptions their teachers might now make about them." I went too far and even suggested that if they went for a job or university interview, they might be dismissed out of hand. I was being terribly English, and was desperately preoccupied with writing the Synthesis. I was over-tired. Anne was uncertain of what to say. Then Tom claimed first not to have been given his report card, then to have lost it, and when finally we got his report we saw the reason. He failed German in the last quarter, largely because he just did not do his homework.

"It was," said Peter, trying to act as family mediator, "a storm in a teacup." Yet the storm lasted intermittently for six months. By most families' experiences it was but a faint brush with the enhanced hormones and brittle emotions of adolescents. Even we knew that, however great the turmoil, we should be able to work it out. And we did. At its worst none of them ever forgot to come and say goodnight each evening, or to kiss us as they went off to school each morning. We were lucky.

David got through it quickest, and strangely enough it was a sudden liking for coffee that finally did this. It came about the same time that he decided to become a vegetarian - at least it was the second time he had made the decision, and a decision he was still holding to more than 18 months later. Slightly envious of Peter with all his highly confident friends (largely three years older than David), he and several of his friends found a coffee shop with something of the feel of Paris' Left Bank. Quickly David became the intellectual bohemian and at 16 went off to the Salvation Army thrift shop and bought himself a tweed jacket. This coincided, completely serendipitously, with my return from a visit to England with a brown woollen scarf as a present. Soon scarf, jacket, coffee and poetry all about the deeper meaning of life, became David's lifestyle. His confidence grew rapidly too, when after several months of what seemed aimless "strumming away" on an acoustic guitar he started to make real music. Just before Christmas he announced that he wanted to make his own electric guitar, from scratch; no kit, and to his own design.

I am not sure to what extent I was thrusting on him my own decision for some good physical activity but, at about the same time, I realised that I too could not be really comfortable in our ever-so-well equipped lake-side home, without setting up a workshop. So, one weekend, we built a bench and while I worked on the design for an oak chest, David laid out scaled drawings for an electric guitar.

I know little about guitar playing, and even less about the niceties of the electronics. I stood gaping as he spoke most knowledgeably with the men in the music store about the technicalities of guitar construction. When he scorned the purchase of a pre-shaped neck "because my Dad'll show me how to do this, and between us we'll put in the tension bar," I knew that I, too, was committed. We spent more money than logic said was right on buying the mahogany, maple and rosewood, and I nervously watched as David started the cutting. The neck really was difficult, and needed techniques I had never learnt before. Between us we eventually got it right. Very quietly David said one evening as we finally got the neck to fit the body at the right angle, "Dad, did I ever tell you how much I admire the things you can do?" It felt good, very good, and I knew that all the harsh words we had sometimes exchanged were always cast in a framework of love and respect.

I thought Tom ought to get stuck into a project of some kind, and gently probed to stimulate an interest of his own. It took a long time to materialise, but when it came it was well conceived, and of real significance. Just when he and David started to rekindle their interest in all things Celtic we are not sure. It certainly had much to do with the music of the Levellers, an English group taking their name from the anarchists in the English Civil War, and much to do with the blood and gore of the film Braveheart. What Tom wanted was an oak box which would fit under his bed, carved on the front with Braveheart's cry of "freedom," and on the top with the interconnected circles of the Levellers' logo. Designing it, and buying the right wood, was relatively easy. Getting some good dovetail joints made in well-seasoned oak was hard; oak cuts and shapes well under confident hands, but is terribly obtuse if the hands are indecisive, and the tool not well held. The job took several months to complete, and several joints represented a tussle of wills between us. It was like building the Batavia three years before. But it was well worth while, and I wonder what confidential documents will get locked away in it over the years!

Peter needed no external incentive to work hard during his last year. The ultimate enthusiast, he just pushed on with everything. In the autumn of 1996 he played the baritone saxophone in wind band, and the base drum for the marching band. He practised extremely hard. The wind band performed extraordinarily well at the East Coast semi-finals of the School Bands of America competition, and became one of the 17 bands from the entire United States to compete in the All-American Band Festival in Indianapolis. This was a grand affair with the bands spending nearly a week sharing their special pieces and taking part in workshops and master classes. Peter was elected Treasurer of the International Thespian Society, and also took an active part in debating and the making of student films.

As the final year wore on Anne and I, like so many other American High School parents, found ourselves also becoming preoccupied with grades. I had difficulty dealing with the idea of bonus points, of someone getting 105 percent, or of a point score of 4.25 on an authentic maximum of 4.0.

I had also to get used to a family of three highly competent computer-literate sons to whom the Internet, web sites and the daily use of e-mail was simply second nature.

"Dad," said David at breakfast one morning, "I saw a really good film last night with Andrew. It's called *If*. Do you know it? It's really good. It reminds me in some ways of *Dead Poets' Society*." I suggested that the title could well have come from Kipling's poem of that name. David looked as if he only partially remembered that. Anne went and got out an anthology and read the full poem aloud. "That's really awesome. I didn't know Kipling wrote that. I'm going to put it on my web site so that my friends can read it."

"What do you mean, on your web site?" I asked, probing for a description.

"Oh, I've got six web pages. This one's my poetry one. It's called Polite Dave's Poetry Page. Polite Dave is my nickname. There are two other Daves in my class. It's not that they're not polite, I guess it's just my accent or something. I put all my poems up on my page and get other people to add their favourite poems. Then we send each other e-mails saying what we think of them. You and Mum come and see it." It was, to quote David, a truly awesome experience. He had written some amazing poems of a kind we had never dreamt he was yet able to write. It was indeed true, as his art teacher had told us the year before, that he was developing an amazing imagination.

"Look, it's linked to my other pages, and to other music pages I've discovered. Here are some of my e-mails. And here are the other links I've already made. One of them links my page to Peter's page on philosophy. That's called Bakhante's Dock on the Lake.

I could see how first Peter, and then David and soon, no doubt, Tom, were pulling all their experiences together. *Sophie's World* had done more to shape Peter's choice of university subjects than ever had a formal textbook. Peter came in and joined us. "I've got my page built with a link into Dad's Initiative page. I'm building a lot of other links as well. The e-mail bit's the most useful thing right now. I go into my e-mails before I go to school in the morning. That means, with the time difference, I can pick up all the messages from my friends in England that they sent several hours before. I then reply while they're still in school. They reply to me when they get out of school and I'm still in class. I pick up my messages at 4 or 5 o'clock in the afternoon and reply to them as they're about to go to bed! So allowing for time changes, and the different hours of schooling in the two countries, we can get two exchanges of ideas into each day."

"And all that just for the cost of a local telephone call?" asked Anne somewhat incredulously.

"Yep. It's just the $18 a month we pay to the carrier. And all local calls are free here anyway."

"What's this?" I asked picking up some pages of photographs and richly phrased descriptions extolling the virtues of large country houses and small castles in the west of Ireland.

"Oh, that's Tom," said David, "he got through to the Irish Tourist Board site and got these e-mail addresses of people with houses to rent next summer. So he got them to send him details - look, some of their colour pictures are great! You know he's going to be asking you if we can rent one of them and then get some of our friends to come along as well to share the price. But don't let him know I've told you. He wanted to ask you himself - when he thinks you're in a good mood!"

Peter was in a hurry, and didn't dawdle, though I knew there was a lot more he could have told me about the way he used the Web. It would have to wait. Right now he had yet another rendezvous with his friends by the lake.

Then Peter had a shock. It happened like this.

He had gone ahead with his application for Cambridge that autumn. He had decided eventually to opt to read English rather than one of the sciences (the discussion he and I had been having that day nearly a year before when this story started). His application looked impressive - he had a strong recommendation from the high school, with estimates of high finishing grades and verbal and non-verbal reasoning scores that put him into the highest category normally expected for entering Princeton. He had nine grade As at GCSE, three of them with stars. Only in one subject - English Literature where he had been confidently estimated an A by his teacher - had he got a B. At the time we were all so delighted with his results that we did not think to question this; mark grabbing was undignified and we thought unnecessary.

He hoped for at least an invitation for an interview. None came. His application was turned down. In amazement, and some annoyance, I asked for an explanation; after all, I had presided over the applications of several hundred Oxbridge candidates over the years. "We could not take seriously," wrote the college admissions' tutor, "an application from a student who, intellectually, had jumped ship midway through a sixth form career by both leaving England to attend an American High School, and then changing his mind about what he wanted to study. In addition," the tutor went on,

"Cambridge has plenty of candidates with results at GCSE as good, if not better, than Peter's." The inference was, presumably, that we should have challenged that B.

Peter was disappointed, but not unduly concerned as he was enjoying life hugely in America. He had no difficulty in accepting the offer of a place at the University of Virginia, but agreed to apply for Cambridge again the next year while taking a gap year.

Strangely enough it was David and Tom who were most put out by this incident. To varying degrees both held Peter in high regard, and respected the way that he worked. David has developed as a naturally gifted young man with a strong artistic temperament. Whereas Peter thinks fast then just gets on and does a job, David is his own man - he needs to know that this is something of which he approves. He has a strongly developed sense of right and wrong, a rapidly emerging interest in poetry and literature, and a fine artistic eye. He was knocked far harder by Peter's rejection from Cambridge than Peter himself. "What's the point of all these exams if that's what happens to someone as good as Peter? It's so unfair. I won't compromise my art just to satisfy an examiner, and I won't paint just to make money. If teachers can only say we should work hard to get good results so that we can get good jobs ... that's no good for me. They can keep it!"

                    *               *               *

At the same time Tom, now 15, gave us a very special insight into the feelings of an adolescent by letting me see a copy of one of his poems, written spontaneously one Saturday afternoon, and appropriately called *Am I?* (This poem is totally unedited).

> It's all mysterious in so many ways,
> and infantile thoughts overcome my want to be mature.
> Am I mature, and are these just
> events that happen at this age?
> Does matureness include childish behaviour?
> I'm in this all the way as myself,
> and in this I hope to be alone when with
> all those things that influence me,
> but with friends that respect all this chatter.
> And bow down on their knees for
> the feelings and emotions of myself,
> if I bend my legs and do the same for them.

                    *               *               *

At the conclusion of the Wingspread conferences we turned our minds to the most intangible but most significant aspect of human learning, namely how cultural values and assumptions create the framework within which we seek to construct meaning. We had spent much time on the nature component of human learning, but what about the cultural aspects of nurture?

All forms of Western thought have been influenced over the past 300 years by three concepts taken from the natural sciences and then assumed to apply to social structures. The first of these is Newtonian physics and the supremacy of reductionism, determinism, and universal truths in the scientific enterprise. To classify knowledge in separate components was immensely attractive to the scientific mind of the Enlightenment, and enabled quite enormous strides to be made through the development of specialised disciplines. Reductionism gave enormous status to the specialist, and to the predictability of causal effects, while reducing people's ability to see things in their entirety.

By the early twentieth century the study of quantum mechanics led physicists to a better understanding of the fluid nature of matter, and the permeability of what people had come to see as self-contained, reducible, specialisms. Increasingly, science was forced to recognise the significance of context and connections in the evolution of further scientific understandings. Separate disciplines alone do not give us a full enough appreciation of life; in fact they often fail to account for the very things which actually "make things tick."

The second concept was Darwin's theory of evolution, predicated on the survival of the fittest; a theory which was instantly persuasive. An immediate overemphasis on the dominant species, and the lack of appreciation of the collaborative nature of nearly all everyday activity, led to an apparent scientific justification for the pre-eminence of competition over collaboration. The third concept was the emerging understanding from psychology that initially emphasised the behaviourist nature of incentives and rewards. The brain was seen as a blank slate waiting for external inputs to shape it, regardless of any inherited characteristics. External motivation, argued the behaviourists, drove behaviour, especially learning. What was needed was instruction - hence the emphasis on schools, and the reworking of the outdated assumptions that have been described in this book.

These scientific ways of understanding led to some brutal consequences when they were applied to the organisation of human behaviour. The American engineer Frederick Winslow Taylor took the scientific understandings of his day and studied their application to manufacturing industry. Developing a technique that would later be known as time and motion studies Taylor sought to apply machine-type processes to human labour. He proceeded to time and analyse every move that a worker made, and quickly concluded that to make manufacturing more efficient it was essential to break away from the earlier techniques of the craftsmen. He was convinced that further improvements in productivity could come about by making each worker conform to a scientifically prescribed form of work as mechanical as that of a machine.

Taylor's principle was simple: "You do it my way, by my standards, at the speed I mandate, and in so doing achieve a level of output I ordain, and I'll pay you handsomely for it, beyond anything you might have imagined." By this principle Taylor had merged reductionism (each worker does one specialised part of the manufacturing process) with the predictability of determinism (engineers would determine the best way of doing every bit of the process and then tell the workers exactly what to do) with the belief that there was always one best way to do every job. Darwin's survival of the fittest played out as successful workers slowly moved up the shop floor from one specialised job to another better paying one, and those who couldn't stand the pace fell by the wayside.

Extrinsic motivation was what kept formal schooling working. This was essentially predicated on behaviourism. Scientific management led to such levels of improved efficiency that it was quickly applied to most other fields of human endeavour, including education and government. It is of more than passing interest to note that in 1914 a machinist gained prominence by debating with Taylor that "we don't want to work as fast as we are able to. We want to work as fast as we think it is comfortable for us to work. We haven't come into existence for the purpose of seeing how great a task we can perform through a lifetime. We are trying to regulate our work so as to make it auxiliary to our lives." Scientific management reached its zenith at the Chicago World's Fair in 1933 when it proudly proclaimed as its motto, "Science finds/ Industry applies/ Man conforms." It was a complete turnabout - the day of the thinking, reflective, imaginative craftsmen was dead. In future, man would live to work, not work to live.

This was a Faustian bargain - a selling of the soul and of individual thoughtfulness for immediate material gains, but with an inevitable day of reckoning at some point in the future. Workers were forced to operate in ways that went against their evolved human modes of functioning. However, in return for their submission to the specialists, society became increasingly rich, while potentially creative people became listless and frustrated. Adam Smith understood this clearly a century earlier in the late eighteenth century when he observed that factory work for most led to what he called "stupefaction". While scientific management led to vastly increased productivity, it effectively shattered the earlier seamless web of living, working and learning, which had previously melded mental predispositions with working practices. The dependent society was the inevitable, if unintended, consequence of Taylorist principles. "I'm not responsible, it's the system."

For most of the twentieth century the idea of scientific management was so persuasive that it spread without question from the industrial sector right across all aspects of social organisations. Writing in 1910, Taylor suggested that the lessons of scientific management (there is one best way of doing things) "can be applied to all social activities: to the management of our homes, the management of our farms, the management of the business of our tradesmen, large and small; of our churches, our philanthropic institutions, our universities and our government departments." Science, technology, and capitalism were seen as intertwined, driving change from an agrarian society to a manufacturing one. The politics of the day were focused on how best to enable the majority of the population to share in the wealth and benefits of the new manufacturing order. Hence the rise in labour unions, child labour laws, compulsory education, anti-trust laws and pension systems. This is the world we have become so accustomed to living in that we rarely ask ourselves why it has to be like this. That was just what that 11 year-old at the Illinois Mathematics and Science Academy was challenging. Not until we deal with this issue, Stephanie Pace Marshall rightly argued, could we restore humanity to our way of living.

Nowhere was the link between scientific management, behaviourism, and the subdivision of knowledge into specialised disciplines more controlling than in education systems. Education is characterised by concepts such as instruction, courses, supervision, grades, modules, tasks, assignments, programs, tests, intelligence measurement, placement, specialisation, etc. It requires students to climb upwards through a sequence of levels and institutions thus facing an increasing risk of elimination as they approach the higher levels of the system. The cream rises to the top, and all others rise to the level which is objectively theirs to hold. In such a system jobs, ideally, are determined by how well and how far a person progresses.

Young people are quick to recognise that such a system fails to appreciate many different kinds of aptitudes, interests and experiences and consequently many of them simply become bored and disinterested. To compensate for the loss of intrinsic interest in the work itself, the system is buttressed with extrinsic rewards (marks, grades, prizes, scholarships) so keeping people going in things that don't interest them. "Most of the time, what keeps students going in school is not intrinsic motivation - motivation derived from the process of learning itself - but extrinsic motivation - motivation that comes from the real or perceived consequences associated with success or failure."

Basic skills, uniformity and conformity were what Taylor required, and what educationalists began to accept as the natural order of things. Taylor observed in 1900 that "the antithesis of our scheme, is asking the initiative (of the workers) ... their workmanship, their best brains and their best work ... our scheme does not ask any initiative in a man."

However things are changing rapidly; there is a new economic reality as the twenty-first century dawns which paints a totally different picture even to that of just ten years ago. The changes are dramatic; suddenly there is a premium on people who know how to use their brains in an inclusive way. Problem-solving, flexibility, creativity, adaptability, team-building, group intelligence, networked intelligence, the kinds of things advocates of Taylor tried to smash out of workers are now what give businesses their competitive advantage.

What this means in practice is that, in contrast to the system of scientific management where the initiative, brain and insight of the worker were actually seen as impediments to the smooth operation of a business or organisation, today the new approach to work emphasises people and teams of skilled workers who are continuously innovating and identifying new opportunities both within the business and in the environment in which the business operates. This means employees either add value or get their walking papers.

For nearly a century, generations of workers have been dumbed down to suit a Taylorist model of organisation. Evolution, of course, works more slowly than social change and so children born today retain the same predispositions towards working in a social collaborative way as did any of their distant ancestors. The human spirit is too indomitable to be easily tamed by scientific management. Indeed at a geo-political level the events of the 1980s in Eastern Europe may well have been as much a revolt against the dehumanisation of scientific management in the factories as they were a rejection of communism.

Contemporary society, for many, has meant coming to terms with finding new roles that are separate to the creativity that used to be associated with work. This is a desperately difficult task as it represents a real discontinuity with our evolutionary past where every adult had a role to play in the well-being of the group. It is the issue that my son Tom sought to understand when he had said, a year or so earlier, "Why can't I be a farmer like my great-grandfather without having to spend 30 or 40 years saving up enough money to buy a farm even smaller than great-grandfather's?"

The question raised as you are introduced to a stranger "What do you do?" is not so much an inquiry about your salary or your status, but more simply "who are you? - what is your role? - how should we relate to each other?" This is harshly limiting, especially given that an unemployed adult male is unique amongst the species of the world for having no role to play. There are now more than one billion adult males in the world either unemployed or so underemployed that they can't earn their own living. This is about one adult male in three - a shocking thought. In the closing stages of the twentieth century, scientists are increasingly coming to terms with the limits of a reductionist, deterministic model of the world, and the brain in particular - but social policy has been slow to recognise the critical importance of such context and connectivity in all forms of social arrangements.

Darwinian concepts of evolution and mutation involved in developing new species, show the critical significance for all forms of activity exploiting niches which are dependent on other species. In other words collaboration and mutual tolerance are as much a part of biology as is survival of the fittest. Behaviourist psychology is now seen as an overly simplistic understanding of complex processes. Yet again there is a convergence; as science clarifies its early assumptions ("it's not as simple as popular works on science used to lead people to think!"), and as we get a better understanding of the processes involved in human learning, so too are organisations coming to understand the vital differences between short-term efficiency, and longer-term effectiveness. This convergence has massive implications for the way school curricula have to be devised so as to prepare young people for the decisions they will have to make if they are to create policies in their lifetimes which are ecologically sustainable, and morally and socially equitable.

Quantifiable learning, particularly over the last 100 years, has depended upon close association with an instructor who used chalk and talk to convey information. The curriculum moved at the speed of handwriting. Learning was dependent upon verbal assimilation and memorisation, checked by tests, all at a specific time and place, and in a stepped relationship to other learning.

To make it palatable good teachers attempted to be charismatic. This, in its turn, created another unintended problem. Pupils looked for teachers who could make essentially uninteresting material interesting - they jollied people along, if necessary by telling numerous funny stories. However, if the critical balance between external good-humour, and the development in the learner of their own intrinsic interest and responsibility was not appropriate, this led inevitably to good pupil performance in the test being associated with the charisma of the teacher. The classic teaching for the test syndrome. This led, on the part of pupils, to teacher dependency and a lack of personal responsibility. It is of this which leaders of industry and commerce have been so critical. "Give me guides on the side, not sages on the stage," pleaded the chief executive of Boeing in a swingeing attack on this over dominance of teachers in pupil learning.

Just as we are undoubtedly on the brink of new understandings about learning and the brain, so too are we beginning to see how radical developments within technology could enhance the way in which young people acquire and assimilate knowledge. New information and communication technologies could expand enormously opportunities for individual and group learning. The significance of these technologies lies in their ability to be interactive and to simulate activity that would normally be impossible within a classroom. However, current school curricula remain predominantly about facts, not about processes of learning. As such, the power of these technologies within formal education is being constrained to work alongside courses fixed in the working practices of an earlier age which valued short-term memory skills, instruction and paper and pencil dexterity. With such thinking, information technologies are relegated simply to a vocational skill by most conventional educators. Their potential as a tool to enhance learning is being ignored, and trivialised.

Few policy makers, even now, recognise that young people between five and 18 spend only 20 per cent of their waking hours in a school. Learning can (and does) happen anywhere but formal education is strangely ambivalent about the role of the community and informal experiential learning. Only slowly are educators coming to talk about AOTs, an awful acronym for Adults Other than Teachers - all those people, parents and others, who intentionally or unintentionally impact on the experience of young people.

By contrast with the emasculated form of community we now experience, our ancestral environment where our cognitive presdispositions were shaped was rich in varied forms of multi-generational interactions and tasks. It was these numerous interventions that provided the motivation, inspiration and information which were encapsulated in cognitive apprenticeship. It is an arguable thesis that it was the taking of responsibility for learning away from the home and community, and placing this in institutions, that effectively undermined the proper functioning of both community and home. Another unintended consequence? The same could happen if homework is replaced by more school work. Learning is not only a collaborative activity, it is a community building activity as well. As St Augustine commented over 1,500 years ago, "I learnt most, not from those who taught me, but from those who talked with me." Modern research shows just how perceptive and exact such a statement was. The active mind learns wherever and whenever it is stimulated.

In contemporary society, interactions between adults and young people are continuously declining. The pressures of modern life, it is too quickly accepted, make it hard for adults to find time to spend with children. "I must work harder to satisfy my rising expectations," people explain as they fall prey to the influences of advertising. This has a powerfully negative impact on children to the extent that, on average, a father of a 14 year-old now spends no more than five minutes a day in solo contact with his child. And these children are the lucky ones. "Half the children in my class have no father at home," state many teachers. So the role of family nurture falls solely on the mother, who is now being forced to become the primary breadwinner. Even in copy-book nuclear families, a mother whose ancestors spent 24 hours a day in contact with her infant child is now restricted to a few hours of so-called quality time. Consequently there is less time for good people to be involved in the community, and this means children rarely experience spontaneous forms of learning that can trigger real passions for exploration and discovery. Yet, as the American author Patricia Hersch notes, "the most stunning change for adolescents today is their aloneness. The adolescents of the 1990s are more isolated and more unsupervised than other generations ... not because they come from parents who don't care, schools that don't care, or a community that doesn't value them, but rather because there hasn't been time for adults to lead them through the processes of growing up." Our closest living relatives, the chimpanzees, demonstrate the importance of early experience in moulding adult behaviour. Researchers have observed that baby chimps with affectionate, supportive and playful mothers are best able to form relaxed relationships with other members of the group throughout life. Orphaned chimps, even though physically strong, almost invariably fail to form strong emotional relationships as they pass out of puberty, and quickly die.

Parenting is a biological necessity for humans, a necessity that is, for the child who has no way of accumulating the wealth of intuitive understandings, cultural mores, and emotional maturity, unless he or she is cared for unstintingly over many years, by patient, well-meaning, and determined parents, supported by other adults in the extended family, which in turn is supported in the greater community. But look at where most parents are when children most need them. Economic arguments advanced by governments suggest that we can replace the responsibility of parenthood with childcare. While it is possible for caregivers to provide high levels of technically appropriate care the absence of a genuine emotional component (unconditional love) places limits on the range of social and empathetic skills that can develop. Stanley Greenspan, an American psychologist, suggests that we are approaching an evolutionary crossroads with more and more children in settings that are not conducive to meeting their irreducible needs. "The impact will likely be slow and insidious. People may gradually become more self-centred, and less concerned with others. Thinking may become more polarised ... impulsive behaviour, helplessness and depression may increase," writes Greenspan. Children within a strictly controlled, non-spontaneous environment, will become narrow and unimaginative in their thinking as they are cut-off, more and more, from the broader more open and uncertain world of the adult and the community at large. "For more than a decade," said an observer at Gorbachev's State of The World Forum in October 1998, "education has been about learned helplessness."

# 16

# What Kind of Education for What Kind of World? Do we want our children to grow up as battery hens or free range chickens?

Late in 1996 the 21st Century Learning Initiative started to draw these ideas together into a single synthesis which exploited the transcripts of the six conferences as well as some 500 books accumulated over the two years. The resulting document, which we called *The Strategic and Resource Implications of a New Model of Learning*, concluded with these recommendations: "It is impossible to bring children up to be intelligent in a world that does not appear intelligible to them. There is just one major policy guideline that follows. No innovation of this scale can occur unless society is broadly aware of how all the issues raised here interconnect. This is not solely about schools. It is about reconnecting children with adults in ways that develop their social, emotional, practical and intellectual skills. This involves a policy initiative broader than anything normally conceived of as the responsibility of a nationally designated ministry of education.

"As this policy and its components are worked out within numerous communities, so thinking people's attention will inevitably turn towards the creation of initiatives and curricula that will better equip young people to handle holistically the complex social, economic, technological and environmental issues that will be the essence of sustainable success in the twenty-first century. This proposal, by focusing on learning rather than schooling, provides the clue for the transformation of educational provision in ways that can be accommodated at no higher cost than at present.

What, then, are we waiting for?

\*       \*       \*

After some months the *Policy Paper* came to the attention of Dick Riley, the US secretary of education. He wanted to know more and invited Stephanie Pace Marshall and myself to visit him in his Washington office. Our conversation proved to be a prcis of a long intellectual journey. What's now repeated here is more of a monologue than actually took place but it is, I believe, the coherent story which, if properly understood, would change the world. I was fearful that in a precious 20 minutes we would make little impact on the secretary and Stephanie broke a moment of anxious silence. "What you must understand, Dick, is that from all the work we in the Initiative have done a simple conclusion emerges - our current system of education is upside down and inside out. We have inherited it from earlier times when the assumptions on which it was based were reasonably congruent with national needs. Now we know that many of those assumptions were largely incorrect, and are antithetic to the kind of society modern technology and the economy are creating. It's a simple situation, and John can tell you the argument clearer than anyone ..."

I tried to make my voice sound confident. "Let me explain what Stephanie means and why we think that research on learning is becoming so important. We have had many years of school reform. People are getting tired of it, and it does not seem to be getting us far. We need a new way of looking at things.

"My starting point is that I don't believe that learning and schooling are necessarily synonymous. I guess that that is the experience of just about anyone who has ever stopped to think about their own learning. Some of the most important lessons I've ever learned occurred far away from a classroom, and they certainly weren't planned." Riley nodded. "That's true," he said. "Not only do I know that for myself, but many of the successful people I know actually did badly in school, and many of those who at school I thought were going to be brilliant later in life seem to have just disappeared. Yet I could not have got to where I am now without the help I got from school. Are you and your colleagues any closer to explaining this?"

"Yes, we are. But first it calls for some real out-of-the-box thinking. We have to escape from the pupil/teacher/school paradigm, and look at what we now know about how humans function, and especially how we learn. The neuro-biological and evolutionary sciences are providing us with a wealth of data about the human brain, about the mind, and about consciousness. The story starts many millions of years ago. It's on the brain's ability to take in a message, analyse it and develop an appropriate response, that we humans depend for our survival. Those individuals that can't develop appropriate responses perish and their genes disappear. Gradually, over all these millions of years our brains have developed techniques with which to understand our environment and so respond in ever more effective fashions. One of these you must have had quoted to you frequently - Howard Gardner's work on multiple intelligences.

"Essentially these different forms of intelligence enable us to look at any situation from a number of different perspectives. We see something in terms of its shape, its colour, its contrast; in terms of its relationship to other objects, or to other people. We have different ways of describing this to each other - in words, in visual images, in musical terms, and so on. Not everyone is equally proficient in each of these mediums - some people have inherited a greater ability to be introspective, while others have a greater ability to be sociable and collaborative. The endless combining, and recombining, of these genes over the generations gives each human a unique set of predispositions. While each of us shares some similarities with our brothers and sisters we are in no sense clones. The recipe always comes out slightly differently, as it does with our own children.

"Now this, Mr Secretary, is where the story gets us closer to young people in today's schools. From archaeology and cultural anthropology we are discovering a vast amount about the environment in which man has lived for the greater part of the past few millions years. By studying the internal measurements of skulls archaeologists are able to estimate the size of the brain, and then build up an estimate of the speed at which the brain has grown. They're then able to plot the kinds of artefacts found in association with skulls of particular sizes, and so slowly sketch out how brain and technology have fed each other's development in the past. It seems that for 95 per cent or more of the past million or so years our ancestors lived in small, relatively self-contained extended family units migrating almost daily in their search for food across the open savannah, and only within the past 10,000 years have we started to settle down.

"Those that survived best out on the savannah were those whose predispositions enabled them to respond rapidly and effectively to the ever changing threats and opportunities of such a lifestyle. One predisposition we know much about is that of language. Without the ability to communicate effectively and easily between themselves children would have been highly vulnerable in such environments, so would young children who could not empathise with other children, or with adults. Isolates did not survive long when the tribe moved away.

"Recent books written on brain-based learning describe the perfect learning environment as being an open, problem-based, task-orientated project where people of different skills combine to satisfy a common objective which has relevance to their immediate well-being. Knowledge is constructed, such books argue, through a continuous process of interaction with real-time problems where the value of new information is constantly being assessed to improve people's life chances. Problem solving; collaboration; multi-tasking, and emotionally rich environments where the challenge is pitched just a little beyond one's present level of competence.

"While infrequently described as such, these are the latent predispositions which every child is born with - these are the survival skills developed by so many of our ancestors out on the savannah, and now passed on to us. These represent our preferred way of doing things. It is thought likely that there has been little change in these predispositions for at least 30,000 years. You can take man out of the Stone Age, but you can't take the Stone Age out of man.

"What we are now coming to understand better is that, within the brain of every new born child, all the successful adaptation strategies that have been useful at any stage during our ancestors experience, are recreated afresh in each and every new generation. Just what the mechanics are to transmit such predispositions we do not as yet properly understand, but we do know that the way we use our brains in the earliest years of life do, in subsequent years, literally shape the neural structures of the brain. While the brain is generally economic, it is also loath to remove a successful predisposition in case, hundreds of generations on from now, this might again have a survival value. For instance each of us can still distinguish between 4,000 smells, for what good that does us.

"This is where all this gets close to our problems with schools and, if truth be known, with society at large. The biology of who we are has been bumping up against the whole change in our way of life that started, roughly 200 years ago, in the early stages of the industrial revolution. Up until then the survival of each individual was dependent on their ability to use most if not all of these predispositions. In practice an active daily life so drew upon these predispositions that people developed their intelligence through everything they did. Survival required thoughtfulness, adaptability, collaboration and streetwise skills, all of which contributed to a sense of the individual's well being. While the technologies of the early nineteenth century were already significantly different to those of the seventeenth century the way people actually lived had hardly changed for 1,000 years.

"The machines we created in the nineteenth century required people to operate them in highly routine, systematic ways. In return for increased production we effectively dumbed people down; the last thing a factory owner wanted was for an employee to show any form of initiative. Of course the payoff was that goods became cheaper and more plentiful, but the essential links between living, working and learning were shattered. Only part of the brain would henceforth be needed. The nineteenth century required far less of an individual's intellectual powers to survive than any previous century. Instead of using their brains inclusively to take in everything around them, they needed only formal, routine and focussed skills.

"Only very recently have we come to understand this. Such learning theory that existed in the nineteenth and early twentieth centuries was generally behaviourist - people needed rewards to do tasks. Our brains were seen as blank sheets awaiting instruction; and intelligence was dimly thought of as being completely innate and inherited. So, as country after country developed an education system (initially as much to keep children off the streets as to give them useful skills) so this rapidly came to reflect the industrial factory model. When universities were asked to advise on the curriculum they did so by suggesting a highly reductionist model of learning. To such early educational experts the study of learning was a strictly academic affair. They measured what happened in classrooms when people performed abstract tasks, but they hardly ever deigned to study the calculating ability of an apprentice working on the job such as Benjamin Franklin, or a street trader on the Whitechapel Road.

"Yes," interjected Stephanie, "The link between the factory model of education and the factory itself was often parodied in America by suggesting that all a youngster of 16 had to do was to slouch out of the back door of the school and straight through the factory gates across the street and start drawing a wage for doing some mind-stifling task."

I continued: "Deep down many people became deeply frustrated because life was no longer fulfilling. The daily challenge of making sense of their environment had been replaced by a dull recognition of waiting to be told what to do. Despite six, eight or ten generations of such limited demands being placed on our sense-making skills our genetic inheritance has not yet been modified one jot. Children are still born with latent predispositions, as it were, equipping them to take on the whole world. During the past two centuries, formal schooling has struggled to provide appropriate simulation of real life situations. It met inevitably with only limited success. For those who have been able to succeed in abstract terms, there are as many for whom schooling has been a disaster because they are more practically orientated. Industrial society has no place for children in the world of adult affairs. Here children are seen to be in the way. So we have progressively turned childhood into an ever more extended virtual holiday; in reality we have trivialised adolescence, by denying them the opportunity of learning from their own experiences, and making them good processors of information provided by other people."

"Can you explain that a little better?" Dick Riley intervened. I was ready to give an explanation and pulled a piece of paper from my notebook. On it I drew two lines crossing each other and divided the horizontal line into the first two decades of a person's life and the vertical line reflecting the scale from dependency at the bottom to independence at the top. Everything that we understand about our intellectual development suggests that below the age of seven or eight, particularly below the age of three, we are heavily dependent on external encouragement and stimulation to develop the brain in ways in which survival skills develop. If children do not get such stimulation at that age, learning such skills later on is just far more difficult. While adults may be ambivalent about their roles as parents, to a child good parenting is utterly essential if their intellects are to develop. Now, if I understand all this correctly, the natural tendency of young people when they move into puberty is to reverse this dependency. (They were the hunters of 10,000 years ago - they were active especially at night time and slept only when day was near.) They want to be in control; not because they want to be bloody minded, but because all the hormonal changes going on within them are pressing them to show that they can now use what they learnt earlier to become fully functional, independent people.

"So you have a line of intellectual weaning that moves, or should move, steadily towards independence as children get older - always providing, that is, that the right skills have been developed below the age of seven or eight. If they haven't, then adolescents are desperately ill-equipped to deal with their own internal inherited predispositions. Result? Chaos.

"Now I want to put two other lines on that graph which reflect the school system which has grown up over the past century. The first represents generally the amount of money each country allocates for education according to the child's age. Note that expenditure increases with age, while little of that expenditure is for the under-fives. As most of the money spent on education is for teachers' salaries we should now add a line showing class size. See how this goes in exactly the opposite direction to the natural progression towards weaning." I paused to let the implication of these lines sink in. "So of course you call it upside down," said Riley. "We have the largest classes when children are young but, looking at this, the period when predispositions are at their most fertile, we leave their education largely to chance."

"Look at the other end," said Stephanie. "Look how ever-decreasing class sizes clash with the adolescent's increasing wish to be independent at about the age of 14 or 15. No wonder we have problems; no wonder so many young people feel bitter."

"That's fascinating. But you also say that it's inside out. Explain that to me."

"It goes like this; over the past century, as the by-products of the Faustian bargain have progressively played themselves out and the community has become less tangible and families have fallen apart, the pressure has been on schools to do more and more of what the home and community had done for youngsters. Into the 20 per cent of their waking hours that children spend in classrooms we have tried to squeeze more and more. Teachers have been faced with totally impossible problems. Classes have become ever more formalised, and pressurised but, for vast chunks of time - the greater part of the day - we leave children largely alone to their own devices in ways which never happened before in our evolutionary past. A 16 year-old American out of school seeks to fill in his or her time by partying with whoever or whatever grabs their immediate attention, whereas his or her great, great-grandparents would have been fully involved earning the family living or raising the next generation."

Dick Riley wanted to discuss this, as it was a matter obviously close to his heart, but I was determined to move the argument on as I didn't want to become side-tracked before getting to my main point.

"Over the past 20 or so years the nature of employment has changed beyond all recognition. The big factories have closed as rapidly as the smokestacks have fallen. No longer can the 16 year-old slouch across the road from the school-gate to the factory yard. Suddenly the cry is for young people who know how to learn; who are well motivated, inquisitive, adaptable; who are good at working in teams as well as by themselves; who are socially aware and good citizens. There is something quite fascinating going on here. That list of skills of course is not new. It's what everyone practised in one form or another before the industrial revolution. These are the skills which I believe the research is saying are latent predispositions in each one of us. These are the skills humans are all about. These are the things we have a preference for doing, providing - and this is absolutely fundamental to the way evolution works - there is a challenging enough environment for each of them to be developed when the moment is most right. A challenging and supportive environment is every bit as necessary in the time young people spend outside school, as it is within the classroom.

"This takes me to the core of my argument, Mr Secretary. You see, in a historical perspective, I believe that with the wholesale adoption of the industrial schooling model of the past 100 years, we have gone off down a siding; we have left the main line of human development. By going down this siding, we have enjoyed its material benefits, but it has ignored and destroyed the skills that we now need. I don't believe we can get to where we now need to get to by carrying on down this siding. I think in fact that we've hit the buffers. We've got to go back to the main line of the development of the human brain as was largely being practised in the more inclusive world of the late eighteenth century. In a real sense we have to reconnect with who we actually are - that's why this argument is about much more than just schooling. It's about us as adults, as people. To survive economically and socially we have to devise new ways of linking living, working and learning, but we have to do this in a twenty-first century way. Utterly central to this is the fact that, in the future, the individual will matter much more. I'm not a de-schooler, but I do believe that the changes to formal education have now to be as profound as the changes in employment. We still go to work, but the factory looks very different and within it each individual is far more responsible than in years gone by. I believe in the future children will still go to school, but the school will look different, the hours will not be the same, and the role of the learners and the teachers will be different."

We had already overrun our time by nearly an hour, but I quickly pulled a further piece of paper from my bag. I redrew the horizontal line representing a child's age, and then used the vertical line to propose a new way of allocating resources to young people's education.

"Let's assume a constant expenditure between the ages of five and 18 as a starter, and look at the pre-fives and post-18s later. Averaging out such expenditure in the UK·that might be about £2,500, in the US about $6,000. Make the starting assumption that we would develop a set of arrangements that mirror, as far as possible, the biological process involved in weaning. But we have to go far beyond this ... we have to go beyond just what comes naturally. So we need to develop a pedagogy that emphasises the young child's mastery of a range of skills, and that child's growing ability to plot how he or she uses these as they move into ever more advanced work. The child as a thoughtful, reflective practitioner who by the age of 18 is largely able to take responsibility for directing their own work and realising that they'll be doing this for a lifetime. As early as possible we must aim to get the child to be a worker. We, and they, have had enough of their simply being recipients; integrate this as quickly as possible into the life of the community with real tasks for young people to do, and real responsibilities for them to shoulder.

"As a starting point provide classes for five year-olds of no more than 10 or 12. Provide training for teachers that helps them construct learning programs that combine - in the child's mind as well as their own - an understanding of both content and process in ways which make children's thinking visible to themselves. This will significantly change the role of the teacher making it essential for them to model the techniques of good learning that children will need to copy. This means that teachers need continuous on-going professional development, probably at the level of at least 10 per cent of the school budget."

I marked off ten percent on the bottom of my new graph for such costs. "Now think in terms of the use of the new technologies, especially as they can provide a level of interaction in learning that classrooms often cannot. While I'm convinced that good teachers will remain essential I'm no longer convinced that the teacher technology of chalk and talk is applicable for all kinds of learning. It's not. So let's be realistic about this and increase investment in the technologies of learning from less than 10 per cent at the age of five to 20 percent at the end of secondary schooling. Now look at something else. That 80 per cent of the time children spend outside the classroom. In America, as in Britain, there is an ever increasing number of early retired people who are fit and strong and have many professional skills. At the moment we waste them. Immediately such people don't want to become teachers, but they would be interested in sharing their expertise with young people informally. These are just the people that adolescents need to be able to relate to - almost surrogate grandparents. We should recruit this army of people but they will need training and support. We advocate spending 10 per cent of the school budget on doing just this, with the expectation that it would pay off dividends of three or four times the level of that invested.

I then drew two further lines on my graph, one slicing off 10 per cent of expenditure for community training costs, and then of the greater significance adding a steadily rising line on the graph showing what the benefit of that involvement would be as children grew older.

"Quickly tell me what impact all that would have on class sizes, and on the fascinating issue of the under-fives and over-18s," Riley asked.

"Starting with classes of 10 or 12, but limiting overall expenditure to no more than at the present, that would suggest classes of 40 or more at the age of 18. But that need not be the case. If we do our job properly when children are getting such intensive support in the earliest years then it would actually be better for them if, probably before the age of 16, little more than half their classes would be formally taught. For most of the time it would be more helpful to them if they worked on their own, and accessed the rich learning resources that such schools would then be able to provide. Too much teaching makes young people too dependent on the teacher."

Stephanie interjected again. "Remember that statement made by the Canadian. If this were to happen, it would be the pupils who would be tired at the end of term, not the teacher."

The secretary for education smiled broadly, not something I imagine he often did. By now his secretary had given up dropping gentle hints about time, and was standing over him and flapping a diary sheet.

"These are such fundamental issues," said Dick Riley, "that I need to know and understand them far better. If you could call a meeting of secretaries of education from particular countries so that we could discuss the possible logistic and strategic implications of all this, I would certainly come, and I would encourage the others to do the same."

\*      \*      \*

We stepped out of the Department of Education onto Independence Avenue and hailed a taxi. We were elated but stuck to business and Stephanie reminded me how I'd quoted to Riley the title of my recent speech to the English head teachers at their annual conference: "Do we want our children to grow up as battery hens or free range chickens? I think that's a clever way of focussing people's attention on an absolutely critical issue. I fear for the future. The education of youngsters wise enough, energetic enough, and good humoured enough to deal with all these changes needs real free range chickens - battery hens flunk it the moment the cages, their comfort zones, are breached. What the world of the future is going to need are confident, proud - strutting chickens that explore every nook and cranny of the farmyard and are afraid of nothing."

With the knowledge that we are now gaining about the learning process, it is certainly possible to improve present schools, but not I believe by much. As has been said many times, there is more to young people's learning than simply schools. That is why I set out to write this book, and to write it in this particular way. Although I've made my living as a teacher, and have a deep professional interest in all aspects of children's development, I'm convinced that the most important part of that development is what happens informally in the home, in the community, and with their friends. It is here, where children really feel that they are living, that they start a lifelong process of making sense of issues that they find fascinating. It is children who come to school excited by what is happening around them, and wanting to know how to do this better, who capitalise on school; not the other way round. It is this I think our society is in danger of ignoring. By ignoring this we're losing sight of what it means to be human.

To be a good father has mattered to me more than being a good head teacher (though I believe that it was with the enhanced interest that fatherhood gave me that propelled me into asking fundamental questions about schools). Because of this I could never think of school in the abstract as a system. It was to me always a collection of individuals - real faces, with real questions and real problems, and real hopes, not simply numbers to be efficiently processed through a curriculum. That is why I could not tolerate what schools, and this was back in 1985, were doing to pupils.

This book is as much about real children as it is about the search of the research. That is why I started the story with my conversation with Peter by the side of the lake in Virginia, and why it will end with his views in the postscript on the challenges facing his generation. An autobiography obviously spans many years, and people change quickly. Oliver Flanagan eventually found real satisfaction when he trained to be a stone mason and not simply a college trained pig farmer, and he is now employed by the Irish Board of Works restoring old castles. Gareth Jones recently retired from the RAF, and went to Buckingham Palace to receive his OBE. Howard Davis continues his rise and was recently one of the two official rapporteurs at the annual meeting of world business and political leaders at Davos. Amongst the audience of 15 year-olds I once lectured to at Stowe School when recruiting boys for the Schools' Hebridean Society expeditions in the early 1960s, were Richard Branson who went on to become the founder of Virgin, and his friend Mike Fischer, founder of Research Machines, Britain's largest manufacturer of school computers.

Some years ago, Mike repeated back to me almost exactly the story of the wolves coming out of the caves in the mountains, just before the Turkish earthquake, as I had told it 25 years earlier.

In the spring of 1996 I was invited for the third time to Downing Street to discuss the Education 2000 proposals. "Surely," Dominic Morris, the prime minister's advisor said, "so many of our educational problems have their origins in the progressive child-centred learning policies of the late 1960s?" I carefully laid out my case, and spoke about recent research into the nature of the brain, and what this suggested for effective learning programmes. "I can't really fault your argument," said Morris, "but it's all based on having a supply of good teachers. We don't think we have these so we have decided instead to go for a system that is so well designed, so efficient, that it is virtually teacher proof." For nearly an hour we argued, but conservative party thinking was not for turning. As the door of Number 10 closed behind me it was like the death knell of Education 2000. The conviction of the trust that the British system of education could be transformed had been rejected by the more politically acceptable strategy of playing down idealism and vision in favour of pragmatic cynicism. The cold grey light of Whitehall that afternoon seemed very harsh.

I gained a great deal out of the public school I attended, but I never wished my own sons to go to a boarding school as I did not want them to grow up removed from the influence of home and community. It has shocked me over recent years to realise just how many parents still seek to fob their children onto school institutions because they don't want to be troubled by their teenage moods and awkward questions. And of course private education in England has been, and perhaps is ever more, a status symbol - a statement of having "arrived" and now being able to provide for your own children in a way not possible for other people. So, probably more than in any other country, England has come to see learning as the thing teachers are paid to do for other people's children. The comment of that Bakhtiari chieftain in the mountains of Iran is chilling, "How can young people learn the wisdom of their parents if they don't work alongside them?" Chilling too when you get that much closer to the research and recognise the critical importance of apprenticeship-type learning situations in feeding the extensive and diverse interconnected neural networks of the brain.

\*           \*           \*

I had always felt uneasy that we English do little, if anything, to mark the end of 11 or 13 years of schooling, unless a pupil is one of the fortunate few to win a public prize. We just say a generalised formal goodbye at the end of the notices at the last assembly of the term, mention a few of the successful pupils, and everybody shuffles off. The Americans, on the other hand, love celebrations. Over the years the expression "to graduate" has come to mean the successful completion of 12 years spent in elementary, middle and high school. Everyone who has completed the course becomes a graduate and families honour their sons and daughters by holding big family parties in the days leading up to graduation. Everyone dresses up. Parental pride is palpable, and in a land characterised by immigrants, graduation still symbolises the rite of passage to new nationhood.

Peter had been busy in the workshop for several weeks building a replica of the oak chest that I had made earlier in the year. "I need the exercise as well as you," he said early one evening as he planed a particularly hard piece of American red oak. With a shade temperature still in the lower 90s, he carried on working while I sheltered in the air-conditioned comfort of the house. I took him some cans of soda and asked him what the rush was.

"Well, I've decided to give the chest as a thank-you present to Mr Franklin for all the help he's given me in music. He'd like that so I've still got a lot of work to do in only a few days!"

It was past midnight and into the early hours of graduation day that he finally carved its new owner's initials on the lid, and fixed the hinges and the brass drawer handle. The oil was still damp when his friend Christian arrived with his car to help Peter take the chest into the music department.

We heard second hand of what happened when he gave the chest to Tim Franklin, a most popular and outward-going man, held in high regard by the students who greatly appreciated his musical professionalism and who warmed to his spontaneity. He was, as he told us an hour or so later, "Simply speechless. Bowled over; I just couldn't prevent myself from crying. And do you know what Peter said when I asked him how he had ever learnt to do anything as complicated as that? He said he had learnt it from his Dad; and that you had learnt such things from your Dad; and he had learnt it from his Dad ... I'll treasure that chest like nothing else I've ever been given."

It was not until we were given our programs that we learnt that Peter was one of only nine out of some 400 students to be graduating with honours. That, I realised, was the significance of his 4.15 grade point average. Already other parents were coming up to congratulate us, and we hadn't even had a chance of congratulating him ourselves.

The orchestra struck up *The Land of the Free*. The 400 students of the class of 1997, wearing royal blue gowns and mortar boards, filed into the hall to loud applause. No stiffly formal WASP function this, none of the solemnity of school chapel, nor the almost unnoticeable goodbyes at the end of an Alleyne's career in Stevenage. Everyone stood as the colour party marched in with the national flag. The principal went to the podium. Everyone cheered. "We are here to honour the class of 1997, and then it will be my privilege to declare them graduated." There was even more cheering. "First, I will invite each of the nine honours' graduates to join me, and I will tell you a little bit about what makes each special. Firstly, Peter Abbott ..." Neither Anne nor I could look at each other without our eyes watering. After all 400 students had crossed the stage and been presented with their certificates, the principal again stepped to the podium. "I declare the class of 1997 graduated," he declared. There was a roar of approval, and 400 mortarboards soared to the ceiling. There could have been no one unmoved by the experience. It must have been a wonderful way to have ended one's school days. I wished we could have done it like that in Alleyne's.

Several days later Anne wrote a simple letter to the English press. The *Independent* published it almost immediately.

"On a warm June evening my husband and I watched our eldest son graduate from an American high school, one of nine to graduate with honours out of nearly 400 students. We are an English family, living for two years in the prosperous Washington suburbs of Northern Virginia.

"We have a great deal to thank the high school for, and are lucky enough to do so in person. But we are conscious, too, of our son's fourteen and a half years of learning back in England. Those years have to figure large in our thanks. The achievements for which our son was honoured were a reflection of all that is good in the English state school system.

"This is one mother's thank you for a stimulating and caring play school, a primary school positively visionary in its approach and a secondary school daring enough at that time to keep at bay the restrictive shackles of a national curriculum.

"We have no regrets that our eldest son completed his school days in America. He wouldn't have missed such a rich experience for the world. And he knows, as we do, that it was his English years that shaped him into the man who was honoured the other day."

\*         \*         \*

For many years, whenever the subject of going to university first came up, I had encouraged each of the boys to think in terms of a gap year between school and university. Peter had made this his own idea a while back and so, when his friends from South Lakes High School scattered to universities across the continent for their four years of wide general education, and his friends in England began their three year degree courses in single subject disciplines, Peter started a four month period as an intern in Congress. (No, he was not with Monica Lewinsky - she was in the White House, Peter was at the Capitol)

Sometimes he and I would travel into DC together on the Metro. On occasions this had its bizarre moments. Early one morning I was cross-checking the first draft of the chapter which included a description of Peter's birth. Looking up and seeing him sitting next to me, laptop computer on his lap, scanning the editorial column of the *Washington Post*, I gasped; was it really possible that such a tiny scrap could have grown into such a man in such a short time!

In January Peter went to the House of Commons to spend the remaining six months of the year as an unpaid research assistant. He had only been there a few days when a letter from Magdalene College, Cambridge arrived offering him a place for that autumn to read English. Anne and I were happy that, at last, the problem of an apparently incompatible form of assessment either side of the Atlantic seemed to have worked itself out. We talked long on the phone that day to Peter in London - the conversation which had started on the dock below our house that afternoon 18 months before - and to start with Peter was not at all sure that he would accept the Cambridge offer. The rejection he had received 12 months earlier had temporarily thrown him and the attractions of UVA (University of Virginia) in Charlottesville were strong in the mind of a young man who, for the first time in his life, was living 3,500 miles away from his family and his friends.

I was to be in England ten days later to address a conference of head teachers, and had arranged to collect Peter from London so that he could come with me. He climbed into the car and grinned. "It's not an easy decision at all," he said, "Cambridge is an excellent university but so is UVA." My heart started to falter. Was Peter really about to turn Cambridge down? "If by accepting Cambridge any of my friends were to assume that I'm thinking that things English are automatically superior to things American then I would certainly be inclined to go to UVA. I dislike the social connotations that so many people think are the reasons for going to Cambridge, even though I admire the opportunities which would be open to me."

I shifted the conversation, leaving him to carry on thinking the issue through as we drove north. Later that evening, after I had spoken to the heads, we were sitting having dinner at tables of 10 people. Peter was sitting opposite me, talking with a woman head teacher. "Which university are you going to go to?" I heard her ask Peter. He looked up, grinning as he caught my eye and turning to her said quietly, but without any indecision, "Cambridge".

# Postscript

*What is the view of those whose task it will soon be to make the world a better place in which to live?*

*Readers will have first met Peter the day he was born. He is now 19 years old and preparing, at the time of writing this, to enter university. He, like many of his contemporaries, sees the world through a different lens to that of my generation. Rarely, however, do young people of his age get a chance to voice these ideas, to share their views and opinions with the greater world.*

*Here is his take on the world, his views and his opinions, in his own words, unedited either by his father or the editor.*

We had just left the movie theatre after watching *Saving Private Ryan* and were discussing the movie and its content. An English friend, my two brothers and I were arguing that the film neglected to show the presence of any of the other Allied powers, hence damaging its historical credibility. An American friend disagreed, saying the movie was merely the story of a group of soldiers and their mission, not a documentary on how World War II was fought. Whilst agreeing with the principle, I continued to argue that Hollywood must, in showing historical films, assume some responsibility for portraying the truth from all its angles.

At this point the group went its separate ways, leaving me and a few of my closest friends. It was a warm, Virginian evening and we wanted to keep talking. We decided that we would go to The Place, a small hill which overlooks Reston and provides, on a clear night, as good a view as we have come to expect. As one friend recently described it, the only way to see for miles in suburban Northern Virginia is to close your eyes and look within.

We fell to discussing a certain scene in the movie, the one in which, after capturing an enemy radar station, Tom Hanks and his detachment find a German soldier still alive and accuse him of killing one of their number. By this time the German has surrendered and the American soldiers begin to argue as to whether or not they should execute their captive. Eventually, Hanks' character turns him loose but the scene made us think: does the presence of war preclude the practice of peacetime morality?

We discussed this idea for some time, moving on into a consideration of the death penalty and, sometime later, into the existence of God. These discussions were not unusual and it was on frequent occasions that I would find myself with one or more friends discussing, either in my bedroom, out by the lake, or at The Place, issues of such import. Whilst many others were bemoaning the lack of entertainment in our quiet DC suburb, we were finding that our minds could soar in contemplation of such complex ideas.

In an attempt to create something a little out of the norm, I tried to simulate these discussions in cyberspace on a forum-based website of my own construction. It worked very well for a couple of months and, as a result, I now have a considerable amount of fascinating dialogue on issues ranging from gun control to human rights violations and from genetic cloning to the US Constitution. Recently, however, the number of contributions has begun to dwindle and, at present, the site lies dormant, waiting for me to kick-start it back to life. There are probably many reasons for the site's decline, but I strongly believe the key reason is that the majority of young people are simply not attuned to discussing substantial and meaningful ideas. One friend, after visiting the site for the first time, came to me and asked, "Why don't you just have a site like everyone else? Couldn't you have a typical teenager's page with pictures of your friends and information about your life?" Young people don't like to be forced to think, they prefer entertainment handed to them on a plate and, unfortunately, this is what they are getting.

But these big questions *have* to be asked, and especially by young people. My generation is uniquely poised to assume stewardship of our planet. Like no other turning-point in history, the dawn of the 21st century presents such immense challenges and opportunities that failure to live up to them could have potentially catastrophic consequences. If we do not start thinking, do not start beginning to be critical of the world around us and do not start to be genuinely discerning of popular culture then our world, and the world of our children, will surely reap the effects.

But why are young people not thinking, why are we not as actively involved in taking responsibility for our thoughts and our actions? Why do we not perceive ourselves as being ready to assume responsibility for our planet and our neighbours? We recognise what needs to be done, yet we shrink from doing it. We complain too much, yet fail to offer solutions. Why is this? Perhaps it is because the problems can often seem so vast and intractable that we feel powerless to effect any significant change.

The current situation does not, on first examination, look good. Faith in our political systems is the lowest on record, the current media climate is dishonourable and destructive, established institutions are failing to meet the challenges of a radically different era and the distinct moral foundations of the past are being discarded by a doubtful and aimless society. Dee Hock, founder and CEO emeritus of VISA describes us as being "in the midst of a global epidemic of institutional failure." Add to this the disgrace of Third World poverty, the dangers of global terrorism and the threat of looming environmental crises and we have a debt that our generation will *have* to repay or, like a millstone, place it around our children's necks.

What example do we have to look up to? Our leaders have lost the ability to focus on the big picture, to focus on the *real* problems that beset our communities. They have, through lack of courage and insight, chosen to shirk the responsibilities that have been bestowed upon them. The offices of our leaders and governments are spiritually, morally and intellectually bankrupt. Their political agendas are pathetic in their myopic approach to problem solving and contemptible in their partisan bickering. Where are the great ideas, the powerful crusades and the dedication to setting the world right, no matter what the political or personal cost?

As their president came under fire for his extra-marital affairs, the American public was caught up in a whirlwind of sordid details and a costly and nationally embarrassing investigation while millions around the world lay dying from starvation, ethnic strife and preventable disease. In Britain, ill-considered plans for a Millennium Dome continue to net hundreds of thousands of pounds while across the globe communities break down, fifteen year olds hang themselves and families are destroyed. Constructive dialogue and meaningful change is hampered and obscured by a plethora of interest groups, wealthy individuals and dogmatic ideologues who polarise issues to fit their own, private and often anachronistic beliefs.

Other areas have their problems too. In the academic and professional arena energy is wasted as valuable research is diluted and destroyed in its attempt to cross disciplinary boundaries, artificial barriers put into place to make it easier for more and more academics to specialise in an even narrower field of study than their predecessors. Artists don't talk to biologists, physicists don't talk to politicians. This is not how it should be.

In his book *Consilience*, the Harvard biologist EO Wilson argues that the fragmentation of knowledge into specialisms has killed the idea of unity and wholeness, leaving students awash in a "slurry of minor disciplines and specialised courses." He goes on to contend that "The greatest enterprise of the mind has always been and always will be the attempted linkage of the sciences and humanities. The ongoing fragmentation of knowledge and resulting chaos in philosophy are not reflections of the real world but artifacts of scholarship." We have accumulated so much fragmented knowledge that we have trouble understanding it all and arriving at common conclusions. We need those who can see across these false academic boundaries and arrive at a unity of ideas and a collective wisdom.

Thus my generation is, right now, inadequately equipped to deal with the colossal range of ethical, political, social and economic issues which face us. We do not have the materials with which to build a definite, unified and hopeful vision for the future and we cannot get any closer to being so unless we begin to think for ourselves, begin taking stock of the situation before us and begin to take responsibility for what is fast becoming *our* world.

So how did we get into this position? Let us retrace our steps. In 1637, Rene Descartes published his *Discourse on Method*, in 1687 Sir Isaac Newton published his *Principia*, in 1859 Charles Darwin published *On the Origin of Species* and in 1881, Frederick Winslow Taylor pioneered his time in motion studies in Philadelphia. These seemingly unconnected events have inextricably woven their legacy into our current social climate.

These thinkers have had a profound effect on the history of modern civilisation and all postulate a reductionist and temporal view of mankind. Much of Western science is predicated on such principles and many of our social institutions are founded on similar ideas. It is a view of the world that tells us that we are but mere cogs in a machine of stupendous proportions, tiny parts which have no concept of the whole, no belief of greatness beyond ourselves. It is mechanistic and without soul, wholly rational in its unrelenting hunger.

If we as a race are so emotional, and basic biology tells us that we are, why then are so many of our institutions barren, mechanical places; places like our offices and schools which we attend at best half-heartedly? The disconnect goes back a long way, back even before Descartes, Newton and Darwin.

The concept of human emotion and spiritual need has always been the domain of religion and, though religious thought gave birth to modern scientific inquiry, the two methods began to part company in the 16th century. Copernicus began the revolution in 1543 with his radical concept of the earth's position in space. The split was furthered when many of the great minds of the Enlightenment rejected the notion of God, contending it an "unnecessary hypothesis." Religion has been equally suspect of science, wary that its inquiries stray too much into what the church believes is sacred territory: ask Copernicus or Galileo whether they thought the church was open-minded and tolerant! The two moved further and further apart and mankind has suffered much from that split for we are, and have been since the dawn of time, a deeply emotional and spiritual people. Our humanity desires spiritual nourishment for, without it, we could not live: we are human precisely because we are not rational automatons.

Now, at the turn of the century, man is still searching for spirituality but in places far removed from the cathedrals and churches of yesteryear. We are seeing a deep-rooted change in the public's perception of organised religion. Over the past century at least, established religions have failed their adherents and succeeded in disenchanting potential converts. Their dogmatic approach to belief, their inability to confront and embrace new discovery and their refusal to enter into dialogue with unbelievers has resulted in atrophy and disillusionment. We now see New Age beliefs, pagan religions, holistic living patterns and other such philosophies rapidly gaining in popularity as people go elsewhere to fulfil that part of their being which desires so strongly to believe.

But many do not believe, and if they do believe it is often in something insubstantial, something which fails to truly nourish their being. This absence of belief, the idea that many, if not all, of our endeavours are futile, has manifested itself in a generation, my generation, that is lost. We are a "tribe apart" for whom the future is not bright with promise, but cloudy with doubt and scepticism. We have lost a sense of meaning, a sense of purpose outside of our own lives. But that is not what man is about. As the Austrian psychiatrist Viktor Frankel puts it: "Man's search for meaning is the primary motivation in his life." Another great thinker, Albert Einstein, put it thus: "What is the meaning of human life, or, for that matter, of the life of any creature? To know an answer to this question means to be religious. You ask: Does it make any sense, then, to pose this question? I answer: The man who regards his own life and that of his fellow creatures as meaningless is not merely unhappy but hardly fit for life."

Collectively, our parents' generation is much to blame. They have failed to teach us to be inquisitive, have failed to teach us that sense of awe and wonder about the world around us, that one sense of God which can be common to all and transcend individual beliefs. Oasis say it in *Listen Up*, "I don't believe in magic, life is automatic." Where is the mysticism, the sense of awe and adventure, the wonderful feeling that you are intensely alive in a world where almost anything is possible? School shootings, teen pregnancies, loss of social cohesion and drug addiction are all symptoms of this disease, this inability to wonder, to dream and to have the emotional capacity to leave physical constrictions behind. Mankind has sought knowledge at the expense of wisdom and gained progress at the expense of its humanity. Previous generations entered into a Faustian bargain and it is our generation that is suffering the consequences.

We are very different from our parents. Like no other generation before us, we have had to spend hours alone. The number of single-parent families has dramatically increased, forcing the remaining parent to work longer hours to support their children. More and more often, children are left at home without any contact at all with either their father or mother. Recent studies have shown that adolescents now spend only 4.8 per cent of their time with their parents and only 2 per cent with other adults.

In her book *A Tribe Apart*, a study of adolescent life in my home-town of Reston, Patricia Hersch asks the question: "How can kids imitate and learn from adults if they never talk to them? How can they form the connections to trust adult wisdom if there is inadequate contact?" Children simply cannot grow into maturity without the presence of parents and other adults to support and guide them. Unfortunately, when the children then turn to drugs, alcohol, sex or violence to fill those lonely hours, the parents take the easy route and blame the school, the community, video games or frequently their child's friends. It is always simple to redirect the blame, but always excruciatingly hard to shoulder it yourself and to seek a change for the better.

Our parents' generation has also failed to teach us to think independently, to think for ourselves. As a result, many of my contemporaries seem incapable of making any form of judgement. We live in a culture which fosters ambivalence and apathy. Popular culture indoctrinates in us the idea that we must never judge because, in our modern society all things are acceptable. We must tolerate everything and learn never to question the validity of another's actions, no matter how much we disagree privately. Eventually we stop even disagreeing and all dissolves into a relativistic quagmire of indifference and boredom. This is not what we want. We cannot build nations, communities and thoughtful people around non-existent foundations. What we desperately need are young people with keen minds, eager to seek out the base and boundaries of their own opinions and beliefs. The world needs its future leaders and thinkers to be highly reflective, to be constantly critical of their own lives and the lives of others. We do not need arrogance and self-righteousness and we do not need conflict and fanaticism but we do need humility, responsibility and a readiness to make informed judgements. We need to be discerning, to know what we accept, what we don't and why.

But we can't place all the blame elsewhere. While it is vitally important that we know why we are the way we are, it is just as important to refuse to be labelled as finger-pointers and criticisers. It is easy to blame others for our predicaments and wallow in our problems but far harder to say "Okay. They put us here but it is we who must find a way out." We need to analyse our situation, recognise the path we took to get there and find ways forward to make the situation better.

So what can be done? Well, in science at least, Einstein has already begun the revolution. When he published his groundbreaking theory of relativity in 1916, he began to challenge Newton's carefully ordered universe. All of a sudden there seemed to be rules that weren't really rules and exceptions to what seemed to be carved-in-stone reality. Now we have fractal, quantum, chaos and complexity theories which have seen some of the greatest minds alive investigating areas which seem to reveal a little more of "the mind of God", areas of science which seem to require more faith than fact, more of the super-natural than the natural. The Cambridge physicist and Anglican priest John Polkinghorne believes that "the rational beauty of the cosmos indeed reflects the mind that holds it in being."

Scientific language is also changing. As scientists encounter stranger and stranger phenomena, they are finding that traditional scientific concepts are simply not good enough and are turning to metaphor and poetry for accurate descriptions. It is apparent, and encouraging, that science seems to be taking a little more notice of the spiritual. Happily, the reverse is also true. The church is listening to science like never before. In 1992, Pope John Paul II apologised for his church's condemnation of Galileo. In 1996 he even went so far as to endorse evolution as part of God's master plan. This is approaching the kind of open dialogue that we need. After all, as Einstein himself put it: "Science without religion is lame. Religion without science is blind." These changes are not taking place just in the laboratories and cathedrals, but in the bookstores and on the news-stands. In July of 1998, *Newsweek* published an issue entitled "Science Finds God." Such progress will hopefully lead to a change of heart, a shift from wholly reductionist, temporal philosophies to a recognition of the spiritual and sacred aspects of our lives. Perhaps then this emerging mindset will filter down through to other institutions, perhaps eventually even to the personal level where we will learn to recover some of our lost wisdom and understanding.

However, even with all these changes we still need people to effect them. We cannot hope to make true progress until the entire socio-political sphere catches on to these ideas and catches up with them. Traditional practices do not work any more: the issues are simply too complex to be reduced to polarities. We need a marriage of traditional conservative and liberal thought, a union of left-wing tolerance and social conscience with the political right's concept of individual responsibility. Gone is the need for tree-hugging and unconditional approval of everything and everybody. Gone also is the pietistic and moral self-righteousness which characterises much of the current conservative movement. My generation needs young people to be courageous and thoughtful enough to see beyond the polarised views of our parents' generation. We need to bring together aspects from all political viewpoints and form a new way of thinking, a new political and social paradigm fit to face the challenges of the third millennium.

There are many, many more issues which face our societies and we need leaders who can deal with these problems, not just leaders in the political sense but members of our communities who, through their vision and example, can set the pace for future change. It is not always the big events which alter our nations' legacies, but the everyday ones which compose the course of people's lives. Each one of us holds more power than we know, more power than most of us ever have the chance of exercising, By refusing to move seats in 1955, Rosa Parks single-handedly ignited a civil rights movement that would consume the United States. During World War II, 1,300 Jews were saved from certain death in the gas chambers by Oskar Schindler, a relatively unknown German businessman. Do not fall into the trap of thinking that these things can only be done by extraordinary people in extraordinary times; they can be done now, by ordinary people in these seemingly ordinary times. Action at a local, community level often has the effect of moving upwards and outwards and, in Parks' and Schindler's cases, occasionally instituting momentous change.

At the political level, we need leaders who can simultaneously learn from and see beyond our chequered history, who can act with empathy, understanding and wisdom yet display strong moral conviction and firm, decisive leadership in times of rapid and oftentimes overwhelming change.

We need leaders in all fields, men and women adequately informed to recognise advances in all disciplines and with the insight to be able to unite them in a common purpose and apply them to a common goal. We need physicists, musicians, priests, biologists, artists and young people who are capable of effecting change at all levels. We need more effective governments, cuts in bureaucracy, sympathy with other nations, a more informed populace, greater voter turnout, environmental awareness, and increased social responsibility.

It's a long list, but in reality the list is even longer. Cynics will cry *"Naïve!" "Impossible!" "Dreamer!" "Why not add 'World Peace!'"* and *"It will never get done."* It certainly won't get done if it's never considered. After all, it is the cynics, not the dreamers, who cause the problems. It is they, in the immortal words of Oscar Wilde, who know the cost of everything and the value of nothing. The world, and our children, need those who have the courage to dream and those with the courage to fight for those dreams.

And there is much to be hopeful for. Many of my contemporaries are chafing at the bit to be allowed a say in how the future will be told. We have our opinions, our thoughts and our ideas that we so desperately want to make known. And they are not naïve, ignorant ideas but cohesive, meaningful and deeply passionate ones that we hold very close to our hearts. Given the tools and the opportunities we can capitalise on these possibilities and make something happen.

What is needed now is a change of heart, a shift towards being hopeful and away from being doubtful, towards being constructive and away from being destructive. We will effect change, we will improve living conditions across the globe and we will show everyone that we can overcome their scepticism and cynical beliefs. The human spirit is limitless in its scope and awesome in its power to change life for the better. History has shown this to be true and history will show it again.

We may have been termed Generation X by the media but, as one visitor to my web-site recently put it, that X can be taken, as it is in algebra, to mean a set of unbounded and infinite possibilities. I have confidence that my generation, once stimulated, energised and empowered will build a world of hope and confidence, not through naïvety or ignorance but through a hard-working pragmatic approach and a dedication to the belief that we can.

# Bibliography

This bibliography is divided into six sections, the first five of which correspond to the major themes to be found in the 21st Century Education Initiative's Policy Paper; the biology of learning; the science of learning; the organisation of knowledge; information technology; and informal spontaneous learning. The last section deals with matters of philosophy, history and social affairs.

## I The Biological Nature of Learning
### The Evolutionary Sciences, the Brain Sciences, and Molecular Biology

Michael Gazzaniga, *Mind Matters* (1987)
Renate Nummela Caine and Geoffrey Caine, *Making Connections* (1991)
John Eccles, *Evolution of the Brain: Creation of Self* (1991)
Gerald Edelman, *Bright Air, Brilliant Fire* (1992)
Michael Gazzaniga, *Nature's Mind* (1992)
Christopher Wills, *The Runaway Brain: The Evolution of Human Uniqueness* (1993)
Steven Pinker, *The Language Instinct* (1994)
Michael Gazzaniga (ed ), *The Cognitive Neurosciences* (1995)
Robert Sylwester, *A Celebration of Neurons: an educator's guide to the human brain* (1995)
William Calvin, *How Brains Think, Evolving Intelligence, Then and Now* (1996)
Robert Kotulak, *Inside the Brain: revolutionary discoveries about how the mind works* (1996)
Matthew Ridley, *The Origins of Virtue* (1996)
Joel Davis, *Mapping the Mind: The secrets of the human brain and how it works* (1997)
Terrence Deacon, *The Symbolic Species: The co-evolution of language and the brain* (1997)
las Dehaene, *The Number Sense: How the Mind Creates Mathematics* (1997)
Ernst Mayr, *This is Biology: The Science of the Living World* (1997)

Robin Karr-Morse and Meredith S Wiley, *Ghosts from the Nursery: Tracing the Roots of Violence* (1997)

The Office of the President, *The White House Conference on Early Childhood Development and Learning: What new research on the brain tells us about our youngest children* (1997)

Steven Pinker, *How the Mind Works* (1997)

Henry Plotkin, *Evolution in Mind: An Introduction to Evolutionary Psychology* (1997)

Terence Sejnowski and Steven Quartz, "The Neural Basis of Cognitive Development: The Constructivist Manifesto" Behavioral and Brain Sciences (1997)

Lawrence Wright, *Twins and What They Tell Us about Who We Are* (1997)

Marian Diamond, Ph D , and Janet Hopson, *Magic Trees of the Mind: How to Nurture Your Child's Intelligence, Creativity, and Healthy Emotions from Birth Through Adolescence* (1998)

Michael Gazzaniga, *The Mind's Past* (1998)

Dean Hamer & Peter Copeland, *Living with our Genes: Why they matter more than you think* (1998)

Judith Rich Harris, *The Nurture Assumption* (1998)

Donald Hoffman, *Visual Intelligence: how we create what we see* (1998)

McLean Hospital Press Release, *Physical Changes in Adolescent Brains May Account for Turbulent Teen Years* (June 1998)

Nigel Nicholson, "How Hardwired is Human Behavior?" The Harvard Business Review (July 1998)

Ian Tatersall, *Becoming Human: Evolution and Human Uniqueness* (1998)

Christopher Wills, *Children of Prometheus: The Accelerating Pace of Human Evolution* (1998)

Bryan Appleyard, *Brave New Worlds: Genetics and the Human Experience* (1999)

Ann and Richard Barnet, *The Youngest Minds, Parenting and Genes in the Development of Intellect and Emotion* (1999)

Robert H Blank, Brain Policy: *How the new neuroscience will change our lives and our politics* (1999)

David B Cohen, *Stranger in the Nest: Do Parents Really Shape Their Child's Personality, Intelligence, or Character?* (1999)

Lee Dugatkin, *Cheating Monkeys and Citizen Bees* (1999)

Ian Robertson, *Mind Sculpture: Your Brain's Untapped Potential* (1999)

Frank Wilson, *The Hand: How its Use Shapes the Brain, Language and Human Culture* (1999)

# II The Science of Learning
Cognitive Science, Developmental Psychology, and Anthropology

Lev Vygotsky, *Thought and Language* (1962)

Sir Alan Bullock, *The Bullock Report: A language for life* (1975)

Howard Gardner, *Frames of Mind* (1983)

Mihaly Csikszentmihalyi and Reed Larson, *Being Adolescent* (1984)

Robert Sternberg, *Beyond IQ: a triarchic theory of human intelligence* (1985)

Lauren Resnick, "Learning In School and Out" Educational Researcher (December 1987)

Shoshana Zuboff, *In the Age of the Smart Machine* (1988)

Mihaly Csikszentmihalyi, *Flow: The Psychology of Optimal Experience* (1990)

Sylvia Farnham-Diggory, *Schooling: The Developing Child* (1990)

Peter Senge, *The Fifth Discipline* (1990)

Robert Sternberg, *Wisdom: Its Nature, Origin and Development* (1990)

Allan Collins, John Seely Brown, and Ann Holum, *Cognitive Apprenticeship: Making Thinking Visible* (1991)

Howard Gardner, *The Unschooled Mind: How Children Think and How Schools Should Teach* (1991)

Jean Healey, *Endangered Minds* (1992)

David Perkins, *Smart Schools: From Training Memories to Educating Minds* (1992)

Carl Bereiter and Marlene Scardamalia, *Surpassing Ourselves: An Inquiry Into the Nature and Implications of Expertise* (1993)

John Bruer, Schools for Thought: *A science of learning in the Classroom* (1993)

John Bruer, "The Mind's Journey from Novice to Expert" The American Educator (Summer 1993)

Howard Gardner, *Multiple Intelligences: the theory in practice* (1993)

Alfie Kohn, *Punished by Rewards* (1993)

David Perkins, "Teaching for Understanding" The American Educator (Fall 1993)

John Cleveland, "Learning at the Edge of Chaos" Chaos Network Newsletter (August 1994)

Antonio Damasio, *Descartes' Error: Emotion, Reason and the Human Brain* (1994)

Edward L Deci, *Why We Do What We Do: Understanding Self-Motivation* (1995)

Daniel Goleman, *Emotional Intelligence: Why it can matter more than IQ* (1995)

David Perkins, *Outsmarting IQ: The Emerging Science of Learnable Intelligence* (1995)

Roger Schank and John Cleave, "Natural Learning, Natural Teaching: Changing Human Memory" *The Mind, the Brain and Complex Adaptive Systems* (1995)

Stephen Jay Gould, *The Mismeasure of Man* (1996)

Joseph LeDoux, *The Emotional Brain: The Mysterious Underpinnings of Emotional Life* (1996)

Steven Mithen, *The Prehistory of the Mind: The cognitive origins of art, religion and science* (1996)

Leslie Brothers, *Friday's Footprint: How Human Society Shapes the Human Mind* (1997)

Howard Gardner, *Extraordinary Minds* (1997)

"Exploring Intelligence" <u>Scientific American</u> (Winter 1998/99)

National Research Council, *How People Learn: Brain, Mind, Experience and School* (1999)

# III Culture and Nurture: How Our Ideas Shape Our Thinking
## The New Sciences, Economics, and the Social Sciences

Adam Smith, *The Wealth of Nations* (1776)

Charles Handy, *Understanding Organizations* (1976)

David Hargreaves, *The Challenge for the Comprehensive School: Culture, Curriculum and Community* (1982)

Charles Handy, *The Future of Work* (1984)

Peter Drucker, *Innovation and Entrepreneurship* (1985)

Peter Drucker, *The New Realities* (1989)

Charles Handy, *The Age of Unreason* (1989)

Peter Drucker, *Managing the Non-Profit Organization* (1990)

Robert Reich, *The Work of Nations* (1991)

Mitchell Waldrop, *Complexity: The Emerging Science at the Edge of Order and Chaos* (1992)

Peter Drucker, *Post-Capitalist Society* (1993)

James Howard Kunstler, *The Geography of Nowhere* (1993)

Hugh Mackay, *Reinventing Australia* (1993)

Robert Putnam, *Making Democracy Work* (1993)

Charles Handy, *The Empty Raincoat* (1994)

Peter Coveney and Roger Highfield, *Frontiers of Complexity: The Search for Order in a Chaotic World* (1995)

Peter Drucker, *Managing in Time of Great Change* (1995)

Charles Handy, *Waiting for the Mountain to Move* (1995)

Dee Hock, "The Chaordic Organization" World Business Academy Perspective (1995)

Jerome Bruner, *The Culture of Education* (1996)

Fritjof Capra, *The Web of Life: A New Scientific Understanding of Living Systems* (1996)

Stephanie Pace Marshall, *Leaders, Learners and the Hero's Journey* (March 1996)

Michael J Sandel, *Democracy's Discontent: America in Search of a Public Philosophy* (1996)

Jared Diamond, *Guns, Germs and Steel: The Fates of Human Societies* (1997)

Kieran Egan, *The Educated Mind: How Cognitive Tools Shape our Understanding* (1997)

Charles Handy, *The Hungry Spirit: Beyond Capitalism - A Quest for Purpose in the Modern World* (1997)

Robert Kanigel, *The One Best Way: Frederick Winslow Taylor and the Enigma of Efficiency* (1997)

Geoff Mulgan, *Connexity: Responsibility, Freedom, Business and Power in the New Century* (1997)

John H Holland, *Emergence: From Chaos to Order* (1998)

David Landes, *The Wealth and Poverty of Nations* (1998)

Geoff Mulgan, *Politics in an Antipolitical Age* (1998)

Parker J Palmer, *The Courage to Teach: Exploring the Inner Landscape of a Teacher's Life* (1998)

Virginia Postrel, *The Future and its Enemies* (1998)

Leonard Shlain, *The Alphabet Versus the Goddess* (1998)

Meredith F Small, *Our Babies, Ourselves: How Biology and Culture Shape the Way We Parent* (1998)

George Soros, *The Crisis of Global Capitalism* (1998)

Daniel Yergin & Joseph Stanislaw, *The Commanding Heights* (1998)

Edward O Wilson, *Consilience: The Unity of Knowledge* (1998)

Sally Goerner, *Web World and the Turning of Times* (1999)

William Leach, *Country of Exiles: The Destruction of Place in American Life* (1999)

Jonathan Weiner, *Time, Love, Memory: A Great Biologist and His Quest for the Origins of Behavior* (1999)

Robert Coles, *The Secular Mind* (1999)

# IV The Technologies of Information and Communication

Seymour Papert, *Mind-Storms: Children, Computers, and Powerful Ideas* (1980)
Nicholas Negroponte, *Being Digital* (1995)
Clifford Stoll, *The Silicon Snake Oil* (1995)
Don Tapscott, *The Digital Economy: Promise and Peril in the Age of Networked Intelligence* (1995)
Seymour Papert, *The Connected Family: bridging the digital generation gap* (1996)
Michael Dertouzos, *What Will Be: How the New World of Information Will Change Our Lives* (1997)
Paul Gilster, *Digital Literacy* (1997)
The President's Committee of Advisors on Science and Technology *Report to the President on the Use of technology to Strengthen K-12 Education* (1997)
"Technology Counts" Education Week (October 1, 1998)
Jane Healy, *Failure to Connect: How Computers Affect Our Children's Minds - for Better and Worse* (1998)
Robert Keohane and Joseph Nye, "Power and Interdependence in the Information Age" Foreign Affairs (September/October 1998)
Don Tapscott, *Growing up Digital: The Rise of the Net Generation* (1998)

# V Spontaneous, Informal Learning:
## The Significance of the Home and the Community
### Sociology, History and Political Science

James Coleman, *Equality of Educational Opportunity* (1966)
W J Rorabaugh, *The Craft Apprentice: from Franklin to the Machine Age in America* (1986)
Arthur Kornhaber, *Grandparent Power!: How to Strengthen the Vital Connection Among Grandparents, Parents and Children* (1994)
Penelop Leach, *Children First: What Our Society Must do for Our Children Today* (1994)
Amitai Etzioni, *New Communitarian Thinking: Persons, Virtues, Institutions, and Communities* (1995)
Rhona Mahony, *Kidding Ourselves: Breadwinning, Babies and Bargaining Power* (1995)
Irving B Harris, *Children in Jeopardy: Can we break the cycle of poverty?* (1996)

Mary Pipher, *The Shelter of Each Other: Rebuilding Our Families* (1996)

Laurence Steinberg, *Beyond the Classroom: Why school reform has failed and what parents need to do* (1996)

Susan Allport, *A Natural History of Parenting* (1997)

David F Labaree, *How to Succeed in School Without Really Learning: The Credentials Race in American Education* (1997)

David Blankenhorn, *Fatherless America* (1998)

Stanley Greenspan, "Why Encouraging Daycare is Unwise" The American Enterprise (Summer 1998)

Patricia Hersch, *A Tribe Apart: A Journey into the Heart of American Adolescence* (1998)

Sylvia Ann Hewlett and Cornel West, *The War against Parents: What We Can Do for America's Beleaguered Moms and Dads* (1998)

Kieren McKeown, *Changing Fathers? Fatherhood and Family Life in Modern Ireland* (1998)

OECD, *Educational Policy Analysis* (1998)

The Mental Health Foundation (UK), *The Big Picture: Promoting Children's and Young People's Mental Health* (1998)

"A Survey of Recent Articles: The Battle Over Child Care" The Wilson Quarterly (Summer 1998)

Margaret Norrie McCain & J Fraser Mustard (Canada), *Early Years Study: Reversing the Real Brain Drain* (April 1999)

Bob Rae, *The Three Questions* (1999)

# VI  Philosophic, Historical and Social Underpinnings

Samuel Smiles, *Self-Help* (1859)

Erwin Schrödinger, *What is Life?* (1944)

John Robinson, *Honest to God* (1963)

Jacob Bronowski, *The Origins of Knowledge and Imagination* (1978)

Christopher Alexander, *The Timeless Way of Building* (1979)

The Methodist Church Home Mission, *Shaping Tomorrow* (1981)

Martin Weiner, *English Culture and the Decline of the Industrial Spirit 1850-1980* (1981)

Education 2000, *A Consultative Document on Hypotheses for Education AD 2000* (1983)

Peter Laslett, *The World We Have Lost* (1983)

National Commission on Excellence in Education, *A Nation at Risk* (1983)

Neil Postman, *Amusing Ourselves to Death* (1985)

Paul Fisher, *Educational Change with Consent: Education 2000* (1988)

Peter Drucker, *The New Realities* (1989)

EF Schumacher, *Small is Beautiful: Economics as if People Mattered* (1989)

Dee Dickinson, *Creating the Future* (1991)

Jostein Gaarder, *Sophie's World* (1993)

Peter Singer, *How Are We To Live?: Ethics in an Age of Self-Interest* (1993)

John Abbott, *Learning Makes Sense* (1994)

Matthew Fox, *The Reinvention of Work: A new vision of livelihood for our time* (1994)

David Orr, *Earth in Mind: On Education, Environment and the Human Prospect* (1994)

Danah Zohar & Ian Marshall, *The Quantum Society* (1994)

George Johnson, *Fire in the Mind: Science, Faith and the Search for Order* (1995)

Christopher Lasch, *The Revolt of the Elites and the Betrayal of Democracy* (1995)

Jonathan Sacks, *Faith in the Future* (1995)

Neil Postman, *The End of Education: Redefining the Value of School* (1996)

John Habgood, *Faith and Uncertainty* (1997)

John Polkinghorne, *Belief in God in an Age of Science* (1998)

Stephen Jay Gould, *Rock of Ages: Science and Religion in the Fullness of Life* (1999)

© The 21st Century Learning Initiative, 1999

Further information, including many reviews, can be found at:
**www.21learn.org**